THE
HISTORY OF
ADVERTISING
40
MAJOR BOOKS
IN FACSIMILE

Edited by
HENRY ASSAEL
C. SAMUEL CRAIG
New York University

A
GARLAND
SERIES

THE DEVELOPMENT OF
MEDIA MODELS
IN ADVERTISING

An Anthology of Classic Articles

EDITED BY
C. SAMUEL CRAIG
AVIJIT GHOSH

GARLAND PUBLISHING, INC.
NEW YORK & LONDON
1986

For a complete list of the titles in this series
see the final pages of this volume.

Library of Congress Cataloging-in-Publication Data

Main entry under title:
The Development of media models in advertising.
   (The History of advertising)
   1. Advertising media planning—Mathematical models—
Addresses, essays, lectures.   I. Craig, C. Samuel.
II. Ghosh, Avijit.   III. Series.
HF5826.5.D48   1985   659.13'0724   84-46068
ISBN 0-8240-6762-2 (alk. paper)

Design by Donna Montalbano

The volumes in this series are printed on
acid-free, 250-year-life paper.

Printed in the United States of America

Contents

Linear Programming Models

"Linear Programming in Media Selection," Ralph L. Day (*Journal of Advertising Research*, June, 1962)

"Allocating Advertising Dollars by Linear Programing," James F. Engel and Martin R. Warshaw (*Journal of Advertising Research*, September, 1964)

"Media Selection by Linear Programming," Douglas B. Brown and Martin R. Warshaw (*Journal of Marketing Research*, February, 1965)

"Linear Programing and Space-Time Considerations in Media Selection," Stanley F. Stasch (*Journal of Advertising Research*, December, 1965)

"An Exploration of Linear Programming in Media Selection," Frank M. Bass and Ronald T. Lonsdale (*Journal of Marketing Research*, May, 1966)

"Linear Programming and Media Selection: A Comment," Stanley F. Stasch (*Journal of Marketing Research*, May, 1967)

Other Programming Approaches

"A Goal Programming Model for Media Planning," A. Charnes, W. W. Cooper, J. K. DeVoe, D. B. Learner, and W. Reinecke (*Management Science*, April, 1968)

"Note on an Application of a Goal Programming Model for Media Planning," A. Charnes, W. W. Cooper, D. B. Learner and E. F. Snow (*Management Science*, April, 1968)

"A Media Selection Model and Its Optimization by Dynamic Programming," John D. C. Little and Leonard M. Lodish (*Sloan Management Review*, Vol. 8, 1966)

Incremental Search Procedures

"Toward an Explicit Model for Media Selection," Philip Kotler (*Journal of Advertising Research*, March, 1964)

"A Practical Procedure for Media Selection," Douglas B. Brown (*Journal of Marketing Research*, August, 1967)

"A Practical Procedure for Media Selection: Comments," Robert J. Schreiber (*Journal of Marketing Research*, May, 1968)

"The True Probability of Exposure," Seymour Banks (*Journal of Marketing Research*, May, 1968)

"Reply to Schreiber and Banks," Douglas B. Brown (*Journal of Marketing Research*, May, 1968)

"A Probabilistic Approach to Industrial Media Selection," David A. Aaker (*Journal of Advertising Research*, September, 1968)

Simulation Models

"A Computer Simulation Model for Selecting Advertising Schedules," Dennis H. Gensch (*Journal of Marketing Research*, May, 1969)

"A Media Planning Calculus," John D. C. Little and Leonard M. Lodish (*Operations Research*, January–February, 1969)

"ADMOD: An Advertising Decision Model," David A. Aaker (*Journal of Marketing Research*, February, 1975)

Measuring Audience Duplication

"How to Estimate Unduplicated Audiences," J.-M. Agostini (*Journal of Advertising Research*, March, 1961)

"Measuring the Net Cumulative Coverage of a Print Campaign," Richard A. Metheringham (*Journal of Advertising Research*, December, 1964)

"Net Audiences of U.S. and Canadian Magazines: Seven Tests of Agostini's Formula," John Bower (*Journal of Advertising Research*, March, 1963)

"Net Audiences of British Newspapers: A Comparison of the Agostini and Sainsbury Methods," J. M. Caffyn and M. Sagovsky (*Journal of Advertising Research*, March, 1963)

"Net Audiences of German Magazines: A New Formula," Walther Kuhn (*Journal of Advertising Research*, March, 1963)

"Net Audiences of French Business Papers: Agostini's Formula Applied to Special Markets," Marcel Marc (*Journal of Advertising Research*, March, 1963)

"Measuring the Cumulative Net Coverage of any Combination of Media," Pierre Hofmans (*Journal of Marketing Research*, August, 1966)

"Predicting Audience Exposure to Spot TV Advertising Schedules," Robert S. Headen, Jay E. Klompmaker, and Jesse E. Teel, Jr. (*Journal of Marketing Research*, February, 1977)

"A Nonstationary Model of Binary Choice Applied to Media Exposure," Darius J. Sabavala and Donald G. Morrison (*Management Science*, June, 1981)

"An Empirical Test of the Performance of Four Exposure Distribution Models," John D. Leckenby and Shizue Kishi (*Journal of Advertising Research*, April–May, 1982)

Introduction

The Development of Media Models in Advertising

Selecting the most "cost efficient" media vehicles for communicating an advertising message is a multifaceted problem that has attracted considerable attention from researchers and practitioners on both sides of the Atlantic. This anthology brings together a sample of important research pieces on media planning. These articles trace the historical development of mathematical media models as well as define the current state of practice and thinking. We hope that this will provide readers with an appreciation of the past, clarify the present state-of-the-art, and generate questions for further exploration.

The anthology covers a time span of about twenty-five years starting in 1960. In the 60's the availability of computers led to the development of a number of mathematical media planning models. While many of these early models have not stood the test of time, they provided the impetus for the development of the field. The publication in 1961 of Agostini's article and in 1964 of Metheringham's article on estimating unduplicated audience makes 1960 an important watershed.

We have tried to represent in this volume the diversity of methods and issues that have characterized this area since that time. Our aim has been to select research pieces that have made significant contributions to the field by presenting new ideas and paving the way for future researchers. Selecting the particular pieces to be included in the volume was not, however, an easy task. While we would like to have included a number of other pieces, space considerations forced us to restrict our selection. The thirty-three articles included here provide a succinct commentary on the development of media models in advertising. In making our selection we have attempted to balance the coverage of the different themes and include both American and European experiences.

The volume is organized in seven sections. The first section, which includes articles by Dennis Gensch and Simon Broadbent, surveys the early mathematical media planning models used by British and American agencies. The articles provide excellent historical perspectives to the development of this field. In addition, they discuss experiences with a number of the early approaches developed in Britain and the United States.

The second section of the volume is devoted to three articles published between 1960 and 1963 in *Operational Research Quarterly* by Alec Lee. The three papers together present a comprehensive framework to view the various facets of the media scheduling problem and develop a series of mathematical approaches for finding desirable media schedules. The first of these three articles, coauthored with A. J. Burkart, discusses the problems of securing "maximum impact" and "maximum coverage" for a campaign and develops procedures for obtaining mathematical solutions to these problems. The second article in this section develops and further refines these themes for static campaigns. The third paper considers dynamic campaigns involving the spacing of advertising in time.

The next three sections of the volume are devoted to examples of a specific mathematical optimizing approaches applied to the media selection problem. First are six articles on the use of linear programming models for media selection. Linear programming is a useful mathematical tool for the allocation of limited resources among competing uses. With the availability of computerized procedures for solving linear programming problems in the early 1960's, its use for media scheduling problems were very natural.

While linear programming approaches were greeted with much enthusiasm initially, as Gensch notes in an early article in this volume the rather restrictive assumptions of this method severely limited its usefulness. The dissatisfaction with linear programming approaches led to the development of alternative approaches. The articles by

Charnes, Cooper, and their coauthors and that by Little and Lodish attempt to overcome some of the limitations by using goal programming and dynamic programming models. While these methods do not necessarily overcome all the problems of linear programming, they deal more explicitly with such problems as differential targets for different audience segments, use of frequency distributions instead of just average frequency values, and scheduling of insertions. Three papers in this genre are included in the fourth section.

The fifth section contains six papers illustrating the use of heuristic incremental search procedures. The basis of the incremental approach is first to include in the solution the vehicle providing the greatest impact. The list of other available alternatives are then ranked according to the level of their incremental impact, and the vehicle with the highest rank added to the list of chosen vehicles. This procedure is continued until the budget is exhausted or a schedule with the desired level of impact is obtained. Iterative procedures are simple to implement and allow the user to consider a variety of factors evaluating the desirability of vehicles. However, a word of caution is necessary. Due to its incremental nature the procedure may not end with the "globally optimal" solution. (For an example of this see the article by Broadbent in Section I).

A major problem with the mathematical programming approaches is the need to simplify what is inherently a complex problem to fit the assumptions of the models. Consequently, a number of authors have proposed simulation approaches that provide a richer description of the complexities of real world problems. Three such simulation models have been included in the sixth section of this volume. The first of these is the AD-ME-SIM model of Dennis Gensch developed in conjunction with the J. Walter Thompson advertising agency. The model incorporates the media planner's evaluation of media vehicles and types of advertising in order to evaluate proposed media schedules. The Media Planning Calculus of Little and Lodish incorporates a marketing response model that considers both viewing habits and advertising decay. The authors present an on-line computerized system, MEDIAC, that uses a heuristic procedure for selecting the optimal schedule. The ADMOD model proposed by David Aaker, the third paper in this section, considers not only media scheduling but also budget and copy decisions.

An integral and crucial part of any media selection model is the estimation of between and within vehicle duplication of audience.

The efficacy of any schedule depends on the accuracy of these predictions. The final section of the volume is dedicated to articles on estimating audience duplication. The section starts with Agostini's and Metheringham's seminal pieces and empirical tests of these methods of estimating unduplicated audience from a number of different countries. The last three articles present a number of more recent models and comparison of their predictive performance.

In compiling the volume a special note of thanks is due to the authors and the associations who so graciously granted their permission for us to reprint the articles. In particular the American Marketing Association and the Advertising Research Foundation deserve special mention.

C. Samuel Craig
Avijit Ghosh

Acknowledgements

The following articles, reprinted from the *Journal of Advertising Research* are copyright by the Advertising Research Foundation:

"Linear Programming in Media Selection," © 1962,

"Allocating Advertising Dollars by Linear Programing," © 1964,

"Linear Programing and Space-Time Considerations in Media Selection," © 1965,

"Toward an Explicit Model for Media Selection," © 1964,

"A Probabilistic Approach to Industrial Media Selection," © 1968,

"How to Estimate Unduplicated Audiences," © 1961,

"Measuring the Net Cumulative Coverage of a Print Campaign," © 1964,

"Net Audiences of U.S. and Canadian Magazines: Seven Tests of Agostini's Formula," © 1963,

"Net Audiences of British Newspapers: A Comparison of the Agostini and Sainsbury Methods," © 1963,

"Net Audiences of German Magazines: A New Formula," © 1963,

"Net Audiences of French Business Papers: Agostini's Formula Applied to Special Markets," © 1963,

"An Empirical Test of the Performance of Four Exposure Distribution Models," © 1982.

The following, reprinted from *Operational Research Quarterly*, are published with the permission of Pergamon Press, Ltd.:

"Different Approaches to Advertising Media Selection," © 1970,

"Some Optimization Problems in Advertising Media Planning," © 1960,

"Decision Rules for Media Scheduling: Static Campaigns," © 1962,

"Decision Rules for Media Scheduling: Dynamic Campaigns," © 1963.

Articles from the *Journal of Marketing Research* are reprinted with the permission of the American Marketing Association:

"Media Selection by Media Programming," © 1965,

MEDIA PLANNING AND COMPUTERS BY 1970:

A Review of the Use of Mathematical Models in Media Planning*

SIMON BROADBENT
The London Press Exchange

1. *Presenting the Data*

1.1. *Description of the Problem*

The media scheduling problem is complicated. It can involve all five main media: press, television, outdoor, cinema and radio. Within each medium there is a wide choice of vehicles. The way these vehicles reach people has been extensively researched.

This is not the place to list media research data. It will be enough to indicate that in this country for the press we have the National Readership Survey, the Evening Newspaper Advertising Bureau Surveys and a great deal of research on individual publications. On television we receive reports from the panels of Television Audience Measurement Ltd, and recently the individual viewing data from these panels have become available. There are other sources of information about press and television exposure; for example, the Attwood Consumer Panel measures the readership and viewing of housewives and the AGB Panels for the major television companies measure television exposure. The other media are less thoroughly investigated but the IPA Poster Surveys give us information about outdoor advertising and the cinema and radio industries provide data about their media.

Most of this media research goes only as far as "secondary coverage", as the Market Research Society (1963) calls issue reading or being in the room with the set on and tuned to ITV. The media planner is more concerned with advertisement exposure or "open eyes confronted by the advertisement", as the ARF (1961) puts it. We are not without evidence on this point. Attention value studies on television, page traffic and advertisement noting studies are all in this area.

Some planners have stated that they are also influenced by more subjective considerations. The media weighting methods employed by S. H. Benson, The London Press Exchange and Ogilvy and Mather in their media models are examples.

The people advertising is designed to reach may be simply defined —for example, all housewives—or they may be described in a far more detailed way. When research data on product usage is available it has been argued (Phillips and Webb, 1965) that only an analysis of

* Based on the winning paper entered for the Thomson Silver Medal and Award, 1965, and reprinted here by permission of the Thomson Organization Limited.

such data into a large number of cells is adequate. Thus as well as media weights we may have target weights.

Other requirements of the campaign introduce further complications. For example, the time-period available and the strategy that may be laid down about timing introduce another dimension. The balance of cover against frequency has to be determined. The cost structure of the various vehicles is a prime consideration. The availability of the various times and spaces which might be bought also has to be taken into account.

By now our original description of this as a complicated problem will probably be seen as an understatement. Some discipline in the form of a check-list or other procedure is required just to make the problem manageable. It is this reduction and presentation of the data which form the problem discussed in this section.

Before we give examples or discuss media planning any further we should mention one additional and unnecessary complexity which unfortunately affects this paper. This is the language difficulty. The same words have been used by different people to describe different concepts and different words to describe the same concept. When we outline here specific methods, we have tried to use the same terms as their authors. When discussing media planning generally, we have tried to use standard terms or where there may be confusion we have followed LPE practice since Broadbent (1965b) contains a set of definitions.

1.2. Examples

(a) *National Readership Survey.* Our first example of the use of a computer for presenting media data is so simple that it may be overlooked. The National Readership Survey tables basically analyse the readership of the publications by certain demographic groups: sex, age, social grade and so on. Previously this analysis was done on card sorters and most analyses of this type are still so done. Since 1960 the NRS has been analysed on a computer. Two advantages are gained: higher speed and more accurate weighting. For the October 1964–June 1965 tables the computer printouts were reproduced directly to take advantage of the higher speed.

(b) *TV Audience Composition.* Our next example is again a job which can be done, but more slowly, on punched card machinery: the tables of audience composition produced by Television Audience Measurement. These take the individual viewing data and give a demographic analysis for each quarter-hour.

(c) *TV VIP's.* We take this example from the LPE media model (Broadbent, 1965b); S. H. Benson (Phillips, 1965) has announced a similar approach. Here the concept just mentioned—the audience composition during a quarter-hour—is taken a little further. Instead of a table being produced showing the full and detailed breakdown of the audience, the marketing weights or values of the individuals exposed are taken into account and a single weighted viewership figure, relevant to a particular campaign, is calculated for each time-segment.

The computer is used to carry out several additional processes which simplify the task of the media planner. The weighted viewership is multiplied by the media weight relevant to that time and divided by cost. Finally, the figures for valued impressions per pound for each time-segment and day are ranked in order of magnitude, i.e. the computer sorts the VIP values. The final effect is that the media planner is presented with a simple table which makes his task much simpler. A great deal of information has been reduced to obtain the end result.

1.3. Likely Developments

(a) *Target Population*. Our last example points the way towards a whole family of applications for each medium. Instead of the media planner consulting tables of readership or viewership while carrying in his mind a definition of the target population for his advertising, he will be able to specify this target explicitly. That is, he will *not* say to himself "The product we are advertising is mainly for housewives and is bought more by young housewives, but other women are also important, so let us look at readership figures by age within sex."* Rather, if multiplicative weighting is used (which is easier than full cross-analysis and may be perfectly adequate), he will write down a table as follows:

Sex		Age	
Housewives	1·00	16–34	1·00
Other women	0·50	35–54	0·25
Men	0·00	55 plus	0·00

He will then obtain from the computer the readership of publications or the viewership for times and regions *weighted* in the way he has specified. He will not have to carry out such a weighting approximately in his head.

(b) *Score–Cost Ratio*. There is no need to stop at weighted readership or viewership. Nearly all the media models in existence weight these measures in similar ways to that already mentioned. Perhaps the first example was BBDO's rated exposure units. Bensons use the word "score" to denote the weighted readership multiplied by the media weight.

It is also obvious that the ratio of this score to the cost of an insertion indicates the value of a single insertion, and again most models use this ratio in one form or another although different names are given to it. LPE as already mentioned uses "valued impressions per pound"; Bensons use "score–cost ratio"; Mathers use "cost per thousand value units"; Mediaplan uses the inverse quotient "cost/norm" and so on.

We therefore envisage the media planner specifying not only the target population, but listing also the sizes or lengths of spot he is interested in and allotting each advertisement size in each vehicle a

---

* This example looks confusing until we remember that the market researcher recognizes three sexes: men, housewives, other women.

media weight. Inside or outside the computer the cost of the insertion is provided and the score–cost ratio worked out. The ratios may be ranked in order as in the LPE method as this gives the planner a rapid indication of the most suitable buys.

(c) *Query Service.* The service suggested is just one example of the power of the computer to present the data meaningfully. It offers a single type of calculation by a standard programme; a simple input will ensure that the relevant analysis is output. If we allow more flexible inputs, the media data stored in the computer can be used to answer more general queries.

We are very nearly at the stage where the computer can be treated like a room full of clerks with desk calculating machines and card sorters. Most queries which can be addressed to these clerks can be asked of the computer. The only difficulty is communication with the machine.

(d) *Reading Frequency.* Some of the media data likely to become available over the next five years will be more complicated than at present. We choose as an example questions on regularity of reading or reading frequency. Such data will also complicate—but not impossibly so—the query service envisaged above.

The calculation of various indices may be necessary, for example, the main analysis of the reading frequency questions for a publication may give, on a demographic breakdown, the proportions of the population claiming to read six, five, four, three, two, one, less than one and no issues per week of a daily publication. Call these proportions x_6, x_5, x_4, x_3, x_2, x_1, x_e and x_0. From this data four summary figures could easily be provided by the computer.

Claimed readership of an average issue

$$x_6 + \frac{5x_5}{6} + \frac{4x_4}{6} + \frac{3x_3}{6} + \frac{2x_2}{6} + \frac{x_1 + x_e}{6}.$$

If the frequency question performs in the same way as the standard readership question this figure will be the same as NRS readership. Otherwise an underclaim or—more likely—an overclaim compared with NRS readership will be revealed. If validating data are available by which informants' readership claims can be reduced (for example by tests of "proved" reading within each frequency group) then adjusting factors can be included in this and the subsequent measures.

Read regularly: $x_6 + x_5$.

This is an arbitrary definition of regular readers but one which is commonly used, i.e. informants who read three-quarters of the issues or more.

Ultimate cover: $x_6 + x_5 + x_4 + x_3 + x_2 + x_1 + x_e$.

This is the proportion who will have read at least one of a large number of issues. It is the figure to which effective cover ultimately rises; in practice it is usually nearly attained after half a dozen issues and is therefore a practical figure for most schedules.

Regularity index: ultimate cover/claimed readership.

The regularity index is 1 if all readers read all issues. It will be more than 1 in the same proportion as the cover of a large number of issues exceeds that of a single issue. The index therefore assists media planners to select publications which are read repeatedly by the same people (a low value of the index) or those which have a higher effective cover over a number of issues than their readership indicates (a high value of the index). A low value of the index is an advantage to a publication in a schedule where frequency is required; a high value is an advantage where cover is required.

Without thorough analysis, such as a computer can provide, it is clear that frequency data may be difficult to understand and use. The data also affect the assessment or analysis of press schedules, as pointed out in §3.3.

2. Constructing Schedules

2.1. Description of the Problem

Production planning, the control of factory and warehouse stocks, the organization of transport networks and many similar management problems have been considerably assisted by operational research. It is not too inaccurate to say that some of these problems have been "solved" by a computer. Many people have therefore attempted to "solve" the media planner's problem. They have used the computer to produce schedules which some claim are "optimum" schedules, while others state more moderately that they are improvements on existing schedules.

This is a much more difficult area than the presentation of data covered in the previous section. The main reason it is more difficult is that the criterion by which a schedule can be called "improved" involves more than media elements alone. The advertising schedule is only part of the advertiser's total marketing mix. His real objectives are not media objectives—they involve considerations of advertising effectiveness and profitability. Some kind of response function is needed to transform media evaluations into marketing evaluations. It is hard to state what response functions should be used and to construct the effectiveness measure which the planner is trying to maximize. Certainly no standard solution is possible—the objectives of different campaigns are different. Not only may they be aimed at different target populations, not only may different media weights be attached to the advertising vehicles, but the evaluation of coverage against frequency may be different.

Some essential parts of this full problem are insufficiently formulated. For example, very little is known about the competitive effects of advertising, the rate at which response builds up in time as a result of successive exposures and decays thereafter, or about the link between intermediate measures (such as issue reading, advertisement noting and even attitude changes) and increased sales which are the ultimate objective.

The second reason why the problem is formidable is the complexity already noted. Mathematical methods of optimizing in a complex situation are powerful only when certain restrictions are obeyed. The imposition of these restrictions on the media problem may emasculate it. When the problem is left in its full complexity, these restrictions may be broken and the standard methods of solution become inapplicable. The constructor of a media model therefore faces a dilemma. He can solve a problem which may not be the right one. It is unlikely he can be sure he has found the true optimum in the real problem: the number of possible combinations of advertising vehicles and number of insertions is far too large for a complete check ever to be carried out.

It is therefore considered unlikely that there will be one generally accepted method of constructing schedules by computer during the next five years. This is not to say that the methods already published and those which are under development are wasted. We should be very well satisfied by *improvements* in media schedules. We expect a variety of methods of solution depending on the assumptions made in each case, the data employed and the ingenuity of the constructors of media models.

2.2. *Formula or Individual Approaches*

We shall not list here or in §3.2—let alone try to summarize adequately—all the methods published so far or those known to be under development. A review of the models published up to 1963 has been given in Broadbent (1964). The situation is not fundamentally different in early 1966 although several new English, French and American models have appeared. A wide-ranging discussion on the most recent English models has been published in Broadbent, Chilton and Phillips (1965).

We do attempt to mention the most typical and instructive of the media models. In them we see a clear dichotomy. On the one hand, the models can take a mathematical or formula approach, in which the media data are reduced to a comparatively few parameters and various simplifying assumptions are made in representing how vehicles actually reach people. We call this the "Formula Approach" and we list some examples of formula models first (§2.3). Alternatively, some models use the data about individuals in their full complexity (whether in their original form or artificially combined or constructed); we call this the "Individual Approach" and we list some individual models in §2.4.

Each approach has its advantages and disadvantages. The formula approach scores in that the full power of mathematics can be used. It is possible to be certain (subject to the assumptions made) that the optimum schedule has been obtained. Secondly, the data used can come from quite separate sources, which are easily combined.

Against these advantages, it is not usually known how drastic the assumptions have been nor how sensitive is the solution to these assumptions. Conceivably the problem solved is no longer the relevant problem. Further, it is sometimes hard to see how competition or time can be introduced into this formulation of the problem, i.e. further development of these models may be difficult.

The individual approach can claim that it makes fewer simplifying assumptions. Its representation of the real world is generally more accurate. Individual models can theoretically be extended, e.g. against competition or into time, without serious difficulty when suitable data are available. However, this approach suffers by being restricted to only one heuristic method of obtaining a solution; stepwise construction or modification. This method may be used in ingenious ways, as we shall see, but it is not certain to find the true optimum.

The existence of these two approaches forms the dilemma already noted. It is possible that the formula approach—or rather some particular version of it—has not sacrificed anything of importance. We can only find out whether this is so by assessing the optimum it provides in a wider model where its restrictive assumptions are not made. We can then see whether the "optimum" can be seriously improved—or not. Similarly the fear stated above that the stepwise approach may not provide a true optimum can only be allayed by seeing whether the process converges on a similar schedule from several starting points, and not merely from the origin.

It is hoped that the next five years will provide sufficient experience, and shared experience at that, to enable this difficulty to be resolved. At present it is impossible to say whether one approach or the other is superior. There will be no *theoretical* solution—the answer depends on *practical* examples.

Before we describe some actual models, we consider briefly the method of stepwise construction. This is also called hill-climbing and the gradient method. It is a method employed in several branches of mathematics where exact solutions do not exist and it appeals strongly to intuition. The schedule is constructed in steps, at each step the insertion or insertions being bought which give the greatest increase in effectiveness for the money spent; the result of earlier buys is taken into account. The models differ in their statement of effectiveness, which determines the value of each possible next buy, as well as in the complexity of the media and other data considered.

The obvious analogy for this method is with a man who tries to reach the highest peak in a mountain range by taking each of his steps in the direction with the locally steepest upward slope. This vivid representation also reveals the flaw possible in the approach: what if there is a valley between the highest peak and where the man now stands? The straightforward method will not be far-sighted enough to send the man down into the valley because of the greater height he will ultimately reach. In other words, this method may produce only a local optimum.

A simple example of this difficulty is given in Broadbent (1965a). Suppose we have three units of money to spend and two vehicles to choose from. We may spend all three units in one of the vehicles, or two in one vehicle and one in the other. We show in the diagram below the effectiveness (supposed known) of each combination of one, two and three units of expenditure. The stepwise method starts at the bottom left-hand corner and decides at each step whether to go up (one more unit in vehicle A) or to the right (one more in B) depending on which effectiveness figure is higher. Clearly the stepwise method follows the route 0–5–7–9, i.e. it spends all three units in Vehicle A. It cannot find the actual optimum in this case, which is to spend all three units in Vehicle B.

	Units of expenditure					
	3		9		*Effectiveness*	
Vehicle A	2		7	8		
	1		5	6	8	
	0		0	4	7	10
			0	1	2	3 *Units of expenditure*
				Vehicle B		

Of course the existence of such a counter-example does not prove that such traps exist in real life, let alone that media planners have fallen into them. We need, as already argued, more data about the actual effectiveness surfaces encountered in order to decide whether the danger is serious. It can be argued persuasively that this method in any case produces better schedules than those now used, even if they are not necessarily the best. Further, commonsense suggests that for many media situations and response functions the effectiveness surface will be sufficiently well-behaved to make the dangers remote.

Stepwise modification has also been mentioned above. This differs slightly from stepwise construction. Instead of starting from the origin (i.e. no insertions having been bought) and only *adding* insertions at each step, stepwise modification starts at some feasible point on the effectiveness surface (i.e. some plausible schedule having been produced by manual or other means) and as well as *adding* some insertions, others are *deleted* so that the amount spent remains approximately constant. Modification is a more thorough examination of the response surface in the neighbourhood of the initial schedule. If two or more different starting schedules lead by stepwise modification to approximately the same final schedule we are more confident we have reached a genuine overall optimum.

A final variant of these approaches starts with an initial schedule which does not exhaust the budget, consisting of vehicles which the planner is fairly certain will be on the final schedule (mandatory insertions). This is used as a starting point from which further expenditure is made.

2.3. Examples of Formula Models

(a) *BEA*. Several papers from British European Airways culminated in Taylor's simplification (Taylor, 1963) of the press scheduling problem to the state where no computer was used. Only a nomogram was necessary. The assumptions made were obviously strong; for example, that the duplication between all publications was normal (i.e. at random) and only one family of response functions was allowed. Taylor's paper is a powerful example of the mathematical approach carried to an extreme while still retaining a recognizable and defensive model. However, the limitations are probably too severe for most media planners to accept.

(b) *BBDO*. The best known formula approach is that of Batten, Barton, Durstine and Osborne in the U.S. (Wilson and Maneloveg, 1962). This states the effectiveness of a schedule as the sum of the weighted OTS it produces. This is maximized subject to some reduction for later advertisements in the same vehicle and to restraints, some of which are imposed by physical limitations (e.g. 12 issues of a monthly in one year) and some by judgment (e.g. at least half the budget on TV). Maximization is then a problem in linear programming to which the simplex algorithm provides an exact and unique solution.

This approach is historically of great importance. It was notable for its explicit use of media and target weights, leading to rated exposure units; these weightings have been followed by most later approaches. It was aggressively publicized by the agency which had two unfortunate consequences. First, some other agencies reacted by condemning all computer optimization as unrealistic, a position they may well now regret; second, some agencies wrapped their own developments in a security blanket, fearful lest they should seem to overclaim but thus stifling discussion.

The weakness of this approach lies in its formulation of effectiveness, which depends on a linear response function. It assumes that each advertising impression on an individual is equally valuable to the advertiser, whether this person has received none or 50 previous impressions. This is usually unrealistic; it is like saying that three girls aged 20 are equivalent to a woman of 60. The approach is sometimes condemned by saying that the media problem is non-linear, implying that a linear programming solution is inappropriate. Such criticism applies properly to this formulation of effectiveness, not to the simplex algorithm. Other formulations to effectiveness may be more reasonable while still yielding to this algorithm; a new approach is under development by BBDO.

(c) *Ogilvy and Mather*. The solution offered by International Computers and Tabulators to the press scheduling problem and applied principally by Ogilvy and Mather (Taylor, 1964) depends on a method of cyclical approximation. The objectives the schedule has to approach are set up as profiles of the OTS it produces. A trial solution is in effect tested. Aspects in which it is weak (for example, too few impressions on housewives in Scotland) are corrected by changes made to produce a second trial solution. This in turn is tested and so on. Effectiveness is here defined as a combination of the extent to which the criterion profiles are met and of a balancing of frequency against cover—this is the effect of the parameter U in the model. The latter can be varied and usually four different values are used. These result in four different solutions; the first has a short list of vehicles, many insertions, high frequency and low cover. The others progressively increase the list, reduce the number of insertions in each and the frequency achieved and extend the cover. The planner's final choice between these four is made intuitively.

As in many formula approaches, this method does not distinguish the number of impressions one individual receives; further, it is not easy to see how the choice between the four or more suggested solutions can be made.

(d) *ICI Fibres* (*Mark 2*). The first model (Carpenter and Rawes, 1963) published by British Nylon Spinners (which has since merged with ICI Fibres Division to form ICI Fibres Limited) was an assessment model and so is referred to in §4. The second was recently described (Rawes, 1965). It is a press-only model; issue reading is reduced by an ad-noting figure. The simplifications made to ensure it is practical are to assume that the readerships of publications are independent and that the response to successive advertisement-notings follows the geometric progression used by BEA (Taylor, 1963). Media weights are not employed, and target weighting is on an all-or-nothing basis. With these restrictions, a stepwise construction method guarantees that the optimum is found. It is claimed that substantial improvements have been produced. For an advertiser one of the major advantages of a model of this type, which can print out effectiveness figures for a range of appropriations, is that it helps to decide how much to spend, as well as where to spend it. The gain or loss in effectiveness resulting from increases or cuts in the allocation can be weighed more rationally against the costs or savings involved.

2.4. *Examples of Individual Models*

(a) *HAMM.* The earliest example of the individual approach was the high assay media model of Young and Rubicam in the U.S. (Moran, 1962). Full details of this model have not been published but it appears to be the most ambitious of all media models. It includes timing in the schedules produced, i.e. it outputs not only whether to buy pages in *Life* and how many, but also when. It can take as its objective the result of the schedule in terms of brand share, i.e. it uses figures for advertising effectiveness which few practitioners claim to know.

(b) *S. H. Benson.* The method offered by English Electric–Leo–

Marconi, developed with S. H. Benson, has been published in detail
(Phillips, 1965; Phillips and Webb, 1965). It was applied first to press
only, using the National Readership Survey as its data source but has
since been extended to TV. A response function is not at present
explicitly stated, but the effect of earlier buys during construction is
taken into account by a handicapping function. The model is said not
to describe the effects of advertising; the intention is to group the
distribution of numbers of issues read as closely as possible to avoid the
wastage of some individuals seeing many more issues than others.

This intention and handicapping function are equivalent to a type of
response—in fact some statement of response and effectiveness must
always be made in a media model. It is instructive to look at the
system in this way. Suppose that the Nth insertion is about to be
bought. The handicapping function states that an individual who has
been covered by none of the publications on the schedule retains his
full weight of unity. An individual who reads a total of r issues from
the publications already on the schedule is given the weight $(N-r)/N$;
thus an individual who reads all the issues bought so far has zero weight.

This is equivalent to saying that the additional response of an individual to reading one more issue depends on the number of issues already
read: it is $(N-r)/N$ for an individual who has read r issues. Note that
this changes as the schedule is constructed, as N is continually increasing.

It can be shown that in its cumulative form the response function to
which this is equivalent is a smooth, convex, bow-shaped curve. It
rises steeply at first, from about 1 at the first issue read, and is flat at
N issues where its value is approximately $N/2$. This is a reasonable
general-purpose shape for a response function. It lies between the
abrupt step functions which call for high cover and the linear function
which calls for low-cost insertions up to the permitted maxima. It is
of course inflexible: unlike Taylor's response function there is no parameter which can be adjusted to produce different schedules between
high cover and high OTS. It is also unsuitable where a sigmoid or
step function are thought to be appropriate for response.

The model has several interesting aspects, typical of most stepwise
construction methods. It would be suitable for handling media data
in most forms about individuals. It can start buying from any base,
not necessarily from zero, i.e. it can be told that some publications
must be included (mandatory insertions). It can be adapted to cope
with a step function response or other functions. It produces a sequence
of solutions at increasing cost so the effect (in media terms) of altering
the budget can be seen quickly. Finally, in this case the computer
program finishes with an analysis of the schedule produced, showing
the distribution of issue-readings obtained. This analysis can be
applied to any schedule, for example one written manually, so comparisons can be made between schedules; thus the method extends to
the assessment approach covered in §3.

(c) *Mediaplan.* Three French methods have been described by Boss

(1965) of CFRO. The latest is Mediaplan II, which was preceded by an assessment method (PUBLIRO) and by Mediaplan I.

Mediaplan is based on CESP media data incorporating the direct questions on reading frequency advocated by Agostini. The criterion for taking each step in construction is flexibly defined: it may include media weights, target weights and a response function, or it may be, for example, a very simple example of these: unduplicated cover. This objective is called the "norm" and the best addition is that with the lowest value of cost/norm. This is related to the score–cost ratio, being its reciprocal with a wider definition of "score".

In one important respect Mediaplan extends the normal stepwise approach. Instead of pursuing a single path up the effectiveness surface, it fans out and pursues a number of paths simultaneously; it can also retrace its steps to start another set of paths. The purpose of these complications is to try to jump the valleys mentioned at the beginning of this section: some paths not immediately profitable are followed up to see whether they later improve.

Naturally, the number of paths followed must remain comparatively small—say 10. From each of these paths, 30 (say) alternatives are investigated, making 300 variations in all. Of all these the 10 best are selected for the next stage. The process is then repeated. Another version allows for the worst advertisements (by a marginal cost judgment) to be deleted from the schedule at each stage.

We can use the example already quoted in §2.2 to show how a fanning-out method finds the optimum which the straightforward approach missed. Suppose we choose two simultaneous steps at first (i.e. to 5 and 4 on the diagram) and from each take two more (5 leads to 7 and 6; 4 leads to 6 and 7). We take the best two of these four (the two 7s). From each of these we again take two steps (to 9 and 8 or to 8 and 10) of which the best two are 9 and 10. If we now make a final choice we have arrived at the true optimum (10).

2.5. Likely Developments

(a) *COMPASS*. The most interesting development among individual models may be COMPASS (Anon, 1964); this stands for Computer Optimal Media Planning and Scheduling System and is supported by a group of agencies in the U.S. The programming of this ambitious project is in the hands of the Diebold Group which has published a brief outline of the "model of the future" (Zinn, 1965).

One interesting point is that this is a co-operative venture. A broad choice of methods of operating the system is being programmed. There is therefore no implication of complete conformity between the agencies in the way media problems are formulated: "Each individual will be working against the same computer model that evolves from our planning, but it will be a challenge to ingenuity as to how we will use the model." At the same time, costs are obviously reduced and duplication of effort saved.

Other technical aspects of the suggested model are worth summarizing here. The possibility of different responses by different individuals in the target population is allowed for. Individual multi-media and product usage data are used in their original complexity. The timing of the final plan is considered, as well as the vehicles and number of insertions in each. A Monto Carlo simulation method is used to move by a type of stepwise approach towards (hopefully) a single optimum. Reach and frequency analyses of this schedule are produced.

(b) *Formula or Individual Approach*. It is not likely that the next five years will see agreement over which approach—formula or individual— is superior. It is probable that both will continue. As already stated, we hope that by publication and co-operation it will become easier to determine whether and in what areas one of the two has overwhelming advantages or whether both should reasonably co-exist.

It would be pleasant to predict that the number of different models within each type will decrease. Certainly some models are being quietly pensioned off, giving little but embarrassment to their authors. However, others of both types are already pushing forward. Therefore the most likely position in 1970 is that there will still be some half-dozen active models of each type. To practitioners in the field one or two of each type will have emerged as the most reasonable; to the uninitiated the differences will appear obscure and irritating.

(c) *Input Improvement*. The reader of this paper must by now have asked himself the following questions more than once. Where do these models get their data? Is there some source of knowledge about advertising effectiveness and inter-media comparisons which is still concealed from lesser folk? Or do the models blithely use unrealistic, or even misleading, data?

The answer to these questions is that a reasonably detailed model certainly requires the quantification of many factors about which little is known with certainty. And the constructors and users of models have no access to information which is hidden from traditional media planners. But it is the latter who blithely go ahead. They write schedules based on equally imperfect knowledge—and they are quite justified in doing so, because time and space have to be booked although the ideal information is unobtainable. Media model users are probably more disturbed at this situation than traditional media planners—but they are doing something constructive about it.

Before we go on to explain why the media model users can be called constructive, it may be helpful to expand on the word "unobtainable" used above. We said that the ideal information—about advertising effectiveness, for example—could not be obtained. This is literally true if we mean what the advertiser really requires: measures of sales effectiveness for next year's campaign. For consider what this means. To obtain the sales effectiveness of advertisements in different media, different vehicles and of different sizes or lengths is an extremely laborious, lengthy and expensive research operation, even when feasible. The results of the research apply strictly to the time and other circumstances in which they were carried out. We cannot be sure they apply to next year's campaign in next year's circumstances. So even if we spent the large sums required on researching our own particular brand's current advertising effectiveness, we still have to make a judgment in extrapolating these results. Worse, we usually have to use research on other brands, based on measures other than sales. Thus to take practical decisions, with limited time and money available, judgment is inevitable. An advertising agency does not apologize for using it: judgment is its stock-in-trade.

Given that media decisions are based on judgment (as well as on a variety of hard data) how can the media model user be called constructive? In two ways, both of which will probably develop during the next five years.

First, media models require considered, consistent, explicit, quantified judgments. This means that at the least a model is a check-list which cannot be short cut. Opinions have to be brought out into the open, given numerical values and defended. This clarification and common language help the media planning process.

Second, sensitivity analyses with a media model show whether differences in these judgments, or differences which research might throw up, will alter media decisions. This means that executives can save their breath instead of disagreeing on some items, as a recent published example showed (Broadbent, 1965d). More importantly, sensitivity analyses may indicate which research is likely to be most useful.

To sum up, the input to models certainly and admittedly needs improvement. So does the input for media planning generally. The models themselves can show where the improvement is most needed.

(d) *Data for Media Models*. We have just discussed part of the information which media models—and media planners generally—require. The other part is more often taken for granted—the reading, viewing and listening data. Here again the models differ little from other planning methods—their requirements are for figures on the probability of exposing advertising to individuals in various vehicles. Therefore to list the data need is simply to list all the thorny problems in media research, which would be out of place here.

There is, however, one way in which the models differ from other planning methods. There is no need for simplicity in a computer system. This restriction has been removed. We can specify as complex a set of data as we please, and provided we tell it how to cope, the computer will do so.

This liberating effect of the computer will probably be felt most dramatically in all-media research. Most models restrict themselves to press but sometimes include TV. These are the most important media and therefore the ones usually tackled by the models we are describing. There is now no need from a processing point of view to be limited in this way. Further, by tradition a budget is first split between media, then each is planned almost independently. While inevitable when planning is manual, this could be very inefficient. Perhaps a poster campaign could be a better way of spending the tail-end of a TV budget; perhaps regional papers should supplement a national press campaign; cinema or radio might be planned to complement the main media. Also, the target weighting used in a media model emphasizes that advertising is rarely intended for all adults equally, or all housewives. The group in the population of most interest to the advertiser is often heavy users in a product group, or those with particular attitudes to a brand.

More precise data than now available would be needed to plan campaigns on the lines just suggested. For each individual in the data we would require her probability of being exposed to each of the five main media, in sufficient detail for broad planning. All-media data will give no difficulties in the computer, which regards a media vehicle as simply a probability of delivering a certain weighted impression to an individual, and which indifferently weights individuals by demographic or purchasing or attitude characteristics. The requirements do, however, raise formidable research technique problems.

One way is by panel methods (Parfitt, 1965). These have the advantage of validated purchase data and repeat information about the same individuals. They are at present restricted to housewives, will always set a limitation (at least for cheap data) on sample size, cannot measure attitudes. For these reasons, surveys plus short-term diaries which can guarantee a high response rate and so representativeness are being considered as a source and details of such a method piloted by Research Services have been published (Broadbent, 1965e). From the use made of some American systems, e.g. Simmons (A.R.F., 1965), brand rating index (Garfinkle, 1963), and media evaluations (Landis, 1965) and from the Institut für Demoskopie's All-Media Survey it is reasonable to predict that a service of this type will, perhaps quite shortly, be used in models here.*

3. Assessing Schedules

3.1. Description of the Problem

In the problem of constructing media schedules we noted two approaches, the formula and the individual. The second of these usually appears in the assessment of schedules. The objective here is to compare schedules already written with data representing the real world. We want to know, as accurately as our information allows, how these schedules will perform if they are actually bought. The approximations of a formula rarely satisfy us: we use the best comparison we can get.

The schedules to be assessed may come from any source. They may be alternatives prepared by one media planner or alternatives put

* *Added in proof*: The Research Services method—the All-Media Product Survey or AMPS—is now offered as a syndicated service.

forward by different people who disagree on which to select. They may even be schedules produced by one of the construction methods of the previous section.

The purpose of assessing various schedules is not a sterile one. It is not simply to describe what has already been decided on—although this is a valid use of assessments since schedules have to be justified to the agency's client as well as constructed. The main intention is to help decisions. These may be decisions on the size of the budget or its allocation. The point is that these decisions are here taken outside the computer. The computer has no operating rules to modify the schedule presented to it: it simply passes judgment by the standards it has been set.

To help in these decisions some methods do not stop at assessing the schedules themselves. They may also evaluate various alternatives to these schedules. But they do not act on these evaluations, they merely report them.

If methods of construction are available, why should anyone use assessment? Particularly if an optimum is attainable, is it not wasteful to do more than determine it? Here are some answers to these questions.

(i) We have stated that, to construct an "optimum" schedule, some simplification of the problem is inevitable. There is no such restriction on an assessment method: it may be as complex a description of the problem as we feel justified in writing down and can afford to programme and run.

(ii) An assessment does not need the controlling part of a construction programme nor the repetition of a large number of steps. There is no need for any search or decision procedures, no need to carry details of discount structures or of the limitations to the amount of advertising which can be bought in any vehicle. It is basically a simpler task to describe than to construct.

(iii) Assessments are familiar. As will be seen below, they are variants on accepted "analysis" procedures. Media planners have for years used assessments and taken decisions based on them. Schedule analyses have an important psychological advantage in leaving control clearly in the planner's hand: he is not asked to abdicate.

(iv) We need assessment methods to examine historical data after the event and see what the effectiveness was of the schedule we actually bought.

(v) An assessment may describe more of the effectiveness surface than the single point on it which a construction method states is optimum. This is specially true if alternatives to a schedule as planned cannot be bought. Perhaps the client insists on a certain vehicle or medium being included, perhaps the spaces or times the planner wants are unavailable, perhaps rates have changed. A good assessment method will indicate whether such changes are disastrous or relatively unimportant: a construction method cannot always comment.

3.2. Examples

(*a*) *Cover and OTS.* The most familiar methods of analysis give two measures for a schedule: *Cover*, the proportion of the target population who will read at least one of the publications on the schedule, or be rated as a viewer of at least one TV spot. *OTS*, the total opportunities to see, whether issue-readings or viewings, over the whole target population. These can be produced by various methods, of which punched-card sorting and a desk-calculator are the best known. The computer can also quickly produce these figures.

Cover is simply the complement of the first term (read none or see none) in the distribution of issue-readings or viewings; OTS is the total area of the distribution. From these two figures we can quickly find the average number of issue-readings or viewings for an individual who is exposed to the schedule at all. These are reasonable general descriptions of what a schedule is doing but they do not contain all the information which is in the full distribution. Indeed these measures are subject to serious disadvantages and can actually mislead. It is likely they will be replaced by other measures (such as impression cover and effectiveness, to use the LPE terms). Their defects are as follows:

(i) They stop at issue-reading or being rated as a viewer, while we are really interested in people seeing advertisements. They therefore do not distinguish between a small advertisement and a full-page advertisement, or a time when attention value is high and one when it is low.

(ii) Cover takes no account of the number of issues booked in one publication. For these two reasons it is easy, for example, to buy a schedule with ludicrously high cover for a few hundred pounds simply by taking one small advertisement in each of a large number of publications.

(iii) Data on regularity of reading will make nonsense of the old figures for cover. We cannot assume, for example, that an individual who reads one issue in six is necessarily covered when we take only one or two advertisements in a publication; on the other hand, when we take many advertisements, all those individuals who read the publication at all should be included as having a chance to see the advertising. Our readership data at present do not allow such considerations to enter.

(iv) The weighted target population is really what should interest us. The normal calculations of cover and OTS assume that all individuals have equal value.

(v) Media weights are not usually applied to the concept of cover, i.e. all publications, days and time-segments are treated as having equal value.

(vi) All these reasons can be summed up by saying that schedule effectiveness is a more accurate measure of a schedule's value. Every way in which cover and OTS differ from this concept leave open the possibility that a schedule which is satisfactory by these measures may nevertheless have low effectiveness.

For these reasons it is suggested that the efforts which have been put into mathematical approximations to cover and attempts to optimize on either cover or OTS are misguided. These measures, as now calculated, doubtless still have a long life in front of them, but their sickness will ultimately prove fatal.

(b) *All-combinations.* The calculation of cover for different combinations of publications (Shields, 1959) was one of the first published applications of a computer in media planning. The principle is attractive. The planner lists a number of publications (say up to 9); the computer then lists each possible combination of these (for example, there are 36 possible pairs); it then runs through the media data for a given target group (say housewives) counting the proportion covered by each combination. The resulting table allows the planner to see what five publications, say, have the highest cover and what additional cover is given by adding in turn each of the remaining four. This approach is subject to the criticisms already levelled at the measure of cover itself.

(c) *ICI Fibres* (*Mark* 1). A more realistic assessment method (Carpenter and Rawes, 1963) was published by British Nylon Spinners (as it then was). This corrected the two most glaring omissions already noted, namely it included an estimate of advertisement-noting (to reduce readers to people actually seeing advertisements) and the number of advertisements booked was taken into account. The method was a Monte Carlo simulation; it went further than assessing the schedule itself, it assessed the contribution of individual publications to the whole schedule so giving indications of ways to improve it.

(d) *SRDS.* Another approach which helps to replace the simple concept of cover is the media schedule iteration model, a service offered by Standard Rate and Data Service (Wenig, 1965) in the U.S. This method is based on data which measure product usage as well as demographic data, so the target audience can be more meaningfully defined. The method must be carefully distinguished from *unduplicated* cover as a means of constructing a schedule: the latter means that a publication is added if it increases most the net cover of a group of publications, which is the algorithm used with an all-combinations analysis. In contrast, this iteration procedure is based on the concept of *exclusive* cover, which means the audience reached by a publication or TV programme but not reached by any other vehicle on the schedule. This concept is used as a guide to *reducing* an initial long list of vehicles. The computer is used to print out the exclusive cover of each vehicle and those which fail to provide an adequate exclusive audience are eliminated. The choice can be made by the computer or outside it by examination. The new shorter list of vehicles is then re-analysed for the next iteration.

AS G*

(e) *TV Viewing Frequency Analyses.* Before press schedules were analysed in this country to produce distributions of issue-readings or ad-notings, TV data had been used to produce distributions of the numbers of people being rated as viewers of none, one, two . . . spots in a schedule. As already pointed out, cover and OTS are summary descriptions of such a distribution. The availability of the full distribution encouraged planners to set themselves more meaningful targets; for example, the proportion of housewives viewing four spots at least.

These distributions are produced by Television Audience Measurement. Once the spots and category of individual have been determined, it is straightforward to run through the individual viewing records to construct the distribution.

It is only a step from such *ad hoc* analyses to derive general observations about the distributions themselves. For example, Ogilvy and Mather (1965) stated that from 900 such analyses they have deduced a relation between the number of spots booked, their average rating and the reach and frequency (equivalent to cover and OTS) of a schedule. The problem found here by another agency is that cover depends considerably on the proportions of peak and off-peak spots, rather than on the average rating alone.

There are six difficulties attendant on TV viewing frequency analyses. As already noted, the weighted target population is the advertiser's real concern, whereas most analyses count all individuals within the category used as equal. Second, the data used inevitably suffer from some missing records (e.g. when a diary is incompletely or unacceptably filled in for one of the days required for the schedule). Third, such analyses stop at rated viewing and do not use the attention values which, it is now generally appreciated, should be taken into account to obtain advertisement exposure. Fourth, the schedules analysed conventionally run over four weeks only (for longer periods the problem of missing records becomes more acute) so that longer campaigns cannot be assessed. Fifth, the planner still has to consider a whole distribution which is difficult to judge in its entirety. Finally, the output lacks indications on the effect of possible changes.

The first two of these problems are tackled in the ICT service provided to subscribing agencies to the 1964–67 JICTAR contract. Here the missing records are replaced by substitution from other days (when available) and a target weighting of the different individuals in the records is allowed. These—and the speed and economy of a computer service—are improvements over the analyses usually made. The other difficulties seem to be dealt with in the LPE media model summarized below.

(f) *SCAL.* A model is currently under construction in France which differs from most others by introducing time into the assessment. The model is called SCAL (Simulation des Comportements Aléatoires de Lecture—Simulation of Stochastic Reading Habits) and is being built by SEMA. It is restricted to weekly, fortnightly, and monthly publications and goes as far as issue-exposure. Individuals' reading over a period of time is given by a simulation based on a model of individual behaviour by a Monte Carlo process. The basic data will come from a survey of some 2,000 individuals. It is impossible to obtain reliably full information over time by a survey method, so the hypotheses made in constructing a model of behaviour and the claims made of reading habits will be checked on a validating panel.

(g) *Media-Planex.* At the 1965 ESOMAR Conference, Steinberg of AUROC described a French assessment method entitled Media-Planex, in which Agostini collaborated. This is based on multi-media data (press, radio, cinema) collected on a pilot basis in the Paris region; the CESP Survey will provide similar data nationally. Target weights and media weights are employed; an estimated response function is also used. A "contact" distribution is produced by a simulation, and when weighted by this response function provides a single figure for the "efficacité" or effectiveness of the schedule.

The method of producing the distribution is a Monte Carlo simulation for each individual, which is then summed. The output allows for a comparison of several schedules by their effectiveness ratings. It also produces the contact distributions and effectiveness figures for different groups of vehicles in each schedule, and for each of these on different categories in the target population.

(h) *Institut für Demoskopie Allensbach.* Also at the 1965 ESOMAR Conference, Noelle-Neumann outlined a service based on the Institut für Demoskopie Surveys. We have already mentioned these surveys as an example of a source of all-media data: it is noteworthy that posters, cinema and radio are covered as well as newspapers, magazines and television. A pack representing individuals of interest to the advertiser from their demographic description is selected from the basic data. The effect of a given schedule on these people is shown by a distribution of issue-readings or the equivalent, produced by a programme based on an extensive study of cumulative audiences in 59 vehicles.

(i) *Media-Mix.* One of the largest computer applications to media planning was set up by the Simulmatics Corporation (Bernstein, 1961) in the United States. Media-Mix is a complex, dynamic simulation model of the media habits of a panel of 2,944 individuals representing the population of the U.S. It is used to produce various descriptions of the exposure of media schedules to people. There are two aspects of this model worth emphasizing here. First, since some of the data required are not known, mathematical methods have been used to construct a data bank, based on reasonable assumptions. Second, this approach is purely descriptive; it stops short at media exposure and is limited to the actual schedule. There is no direct guide to changes which might improve the schedule, or summary figures which assist in the choice between schedules.

(j) *CAM.* One of the most advanced assessment models appears to be the LPE media model, called CAM (Computer Assessment of Media). Comments on its use and the light it has thrown on other media problems have been published (Broadbent, 1965c, d) as well as a full technical description (Broadbent, 1956b).

The main points of CAM are briefly as follows. Full media weighting and target weightings are used. CAM covers both press, TV and mixed press and TV schedules; the basic NRS and TAM data are married together to enable mixed schedules to be dealt with. A probability of viewing ITV in different day-time segments is developed from the basic data so that schedules of more than four weeks can be assessed. Attention values are taken into account. The schedules submitted are assessed by their impression distributions, both on the whole target and on special sections of the population called key groups. The distributions are also summarized, by weighting with a response function, to give a single figure for effectiveness.

The method is a simulation on a panel of individuals; it is not a Monte Carlo simulation as no random elements are employed; the resultant distributions are all calculated. Other safeguards are introduced to ensure accurate results for the major uses of the model.

One use of CAM is the comparison of different media strategies, e.g. a long press list against a short list, a mixed schedule against pure TV, 30 second spots against 60 seconds. Another use is to compare different additions to and deletions from the schedules; each change is evaluated by its marginal rate of return, i.e. the change in effectiveness divided by the change in cost.

3.3. Likely Developments

It is safe to predict that whatever advances are made in schedule construction methods, schedule assessments will continue to be needed. The reasons advanced in §3.1 will remain true. Nor does one exclude the other—for example Masius, Wynne-Williams has stated (De Voss and Gent, 1965) that it has deliberately set out to construct both descriptive and optimization models. In addition, when there is not the time or money to carry out full constructions or assessments, rapid and approximate methods of analysis will be necessary.

These new methods will develop naturally from the present ones. They will change as the data change, for example the TAM individual data now available and the reading frequency data we hopefully expect will influence the type of assessment that can be carried out. Indeed reading frequency data not only requires a new type of summary—as suggested in §1.3(d)—it demands a new analysis method. Some methods of assessment, CAM for example, have been designed specifically with these data in mind. Essentially assessments produce distributions of impressions or impacts or issue-readings or TV ratings. These will be refined by greater use of target weighting, by media weighting and by evaluating possible changes to the proposed schedule. These improvements are common to several of the models already referred to and their use is certain to spread. The remarks on input and data in §2.5(c) and (d) apply equally to assessment methods.

We have already noted that construction methods can conclude with an assessment and that assessments can take and perhaps improve computer-constructed schedules. The link between the two approaches is closest when the construction is by the individual approach.

Each step of stepwise construction or modification is in effect preceded by an assessment. The computer weighs the relative values of various alternatives, taking into account the schedule already booked. This is exactly the comparison of changes which a good assessment method will carry out. The differences are: first, that the computer decides on the changes or additions in a construction method, automating the job the media planner carries out by the assessment method; second, the effort in programming the control system in a construction method generally goes into a fuller and hopefully more precise description of schedule effectiveness in the assessment method. The latter is not an inherent difference between the systems but a practical difference in emphasis. It is possible to imagine a construction method which is as detailed as an assessment method but more automatic and less completely in the control of the planner. Such a combination of the two complementary approaches may be the most powerful approach of all. It would give the most accurate description possible of selected points on the effectiveness surface, together with an efficient way of exploring it. While it could never guarantee, on a really complex surface, to find the absolute optimum, it would give reasonable assurance that better schedules were found than by any other method.

REFERENCES

ANON. (1964). Seven agencies pool efforts in computer research venture. *Advert. Age* (December 18).

ANON. (1965). Mather's TV advertising breakthrough. *World's Press News* (September 10).

A.R.F. (1961). *Towards Better Media Comparisons.*

A.R.F. TECHNICAL COMMITTEE (1965). *Analysis of Selective and Mass Markets and the Media Reaching Them—1964.* (Series of reports by W. R. Simmons and Associates Research Inc.)

BERNSTEIN, A. (1961). Simulation of media consumption. A.R.F. Operations Research Discussion Group.

Boss, J.-F. (1965). Selection models for publicity campaigns. 9th ESOMAR Conference.

BROADBENT, S. R. (1964). Computers and media schedules. *Commentary.* (Special media research issue.)

—— (1965a). Models in media planning. Seminar: Associazione Italiana Tecnici Pubblicitari, Milan.

—— (1965b). Computer assessment of media—the LPE media model. LPE.

—— (1965c). The LPE media model—some implications for research. 9th ESOMAR Conference.

—— (1965d). A year's experience of the LPE media model. A.R.F. 11th Annual Conference.

—— (1965e). A new type of media research: All-media and product surveys. *Advert. Wkly* (December 10).

BROADBENT, S. R., CHILTON, R. T. S. and PHILLIPS, D. H. (1965). Symposium. *admap* (October and November.)

CARPENTER, R. C. and RAWES, E. A. (1963). An approach to the assessment of press schedules. 16th ESOMAR Conference.

DE VOS, A. B. and GENT, G. (1965). The computer experience of a large agency. I.P.A. Seminar: Computers in Advertising.

GARFINKLE, N. (1963). A marketing approach to media selection. *J. Advert. Res.*, **3**, 7–15.

LANDIS, J. B. (1965). Exposure probabilities as measures of media audiences. *J. Advert. Res.*, **5**, 24–29.

MARKET RESEARCH SOCIETY (1963). *The Advertising Chain up to the Point of Reception.*

MORAN, W. T. (1962). Practical media models—what must they look like? A.R.F. 8th Annual Conference.

PARFITT, J. H. (1965). The use of consumer panels for media research. 9th ESOMAR Conference.

PHILLIPS, D. H. (1965). Schedule building for press and TV. I.P.A. Seminar: Computers in Advertising.

PHILLIPS, D. H. and WEBB, M. H. J. (1965). The computer in media planning. 9th ESOMAR Conference.

RAWES, E. A. (1965). Media models and budget decisions. I.P.A. Seminar: Computers in Advertising.

SHIELDS, R. M. (1959). The use of a computer for media research. *Commentary*, **2**, 1–6.

TAYLOR, C. J. (1963). Some developments in the theory and application of media scheduling methods. *Operat. Res. Quart.*, **14**, 291–305.

TAYLOR, G. P. (1964). The computer in media planning. *Scientific Business*, **2**, 287–294.

WENIG, P. W. (1965). Media schedule operations. *Data*, **1**, Nos. 1–6 (December 1964–April 1965).

WILSON, C. W. and MANELOVEG, M. (1962). Linear programming basics *and* A year of L.P. media planning for clients. A.R.F. Midwest Conference.

ZINN, M. (1965). *The Use of Computers in the Media Selection Process.* The Diebold Group.

Different Approaches to Advertising Media Selection

DENNIS H. GENSCH

Carnegie-Mellon University, Pittsburg, Pennsylvania

Research groups on both sides of the Atlantic are attempting to use the power of mathematics to aid the decision-maker in dealing with the complex media scheduling problem. This paper reviews, compares and critiques several possible approaches. The approaches reviewed are: linear programming, dynamic programming, marginal analysis, heuristic programming and simulation. At least one particular model of each approach is discussed in detail.

INTRODUCTION

THE PROBLEM of how to select the most "cost efficient" set of magazines, television programmes, newspapers and other available media vehicles for communicating a given advertising message to potential customers is basically the same problem for advertisers in any of the free enterprise markets.

Research groups on both sides of the Atlantic have attempted to use the power of mathematics to aid the decision-maker in dealing with the complex media scheduling problem. This paper is presented in the hope that more communication will be generated between the research groups working on the same problem in different countries.

The early computer models in media scheduling were essentially data generation models which all followed a general pattern. The available information a decision-maker felt to be important was read into the computer's memory and stored there. For each specific commercial message, the computer was required to select, arrange and print out the information the decision-maker desired. The decision-maker would then attempt to integrate the information and make his selection as objectively as possible.

Gradually, as advertising managers increased their ability to use the computer, they started using it to integrate and arrange the data. Thus the initial data generation models became subroutines for more advanced media selection models. The models that integrated the data would often actually select a media schedule.

Introduction of media selection models in the United States was highly publicized. In October 1962, *Advertising Age* carried the heading "Y & R, BBD & O Unleash Media Computerization".[1] One of these firms, Batten,

193

Barton, Durstine and Osborne, even placed full-page ads reading "Linear programming showed one BBD & O client how to get $1.67 worth of effective advertising for every dollar in his budget".

This author agrees with the judgement of Al Norelli of IBM that the initial integrated media selection models did not produce the "practical" results they advertised.

"We had a most unfortunate verbal storm over this subject in the States when models first burst into prominence. I believe that exaggerated and premature claims produced misunderstandings that are only now subsiding. A good case can be made for the fact that the negative impact of that storm possibly set back computer use in advertising by at least two years."[2]

Since 1962 the American advertising agencies have conducted most of their research behind closed doors on a trial-and-error basis. During this same time period the European groups, perhaps because they are publishing more openly, appear to be steadily increasing the level of sophistication in the media selection models they are using and proposing.

What has been learned in the past five years? How do the European and American mathematical approaches compare to one another? Is one mathematical approach more realistic than another? How does one model compare with another? Are computerized media selection models unrealistic toys? The remainder of this paper will constitute an attempt to answer the above questions.

CLASSIFYING THE ADVERTISING MEDIA MODELS

Many available media models are variations of the same basic approach. Various mathematical approaches that are feasible for media selection will be identified, and then each approach will be analysed.

It is not this author's intention to imply that the models and approaches described here are exhaustive sets. It is possible that there are other approaches, besides those reviewed. It is also recognized that various models are actually combinations of the approaches to be discussed.

In analysing a given mathematical approach, one of the models using it will be explained in detail. Other analogous European and American models belonging to the same set will also be mentioned.

There are two quite different approaches in models that attempt to analyse proposed media schedules. Some models take an optimizing approach. After the media data have been reduced to comparatively few parameters and various simplifying assumptions are made about how the vehicles actually reach people, a mathematical algorithm is used to determine the "best" possible media schedule. The second approach consists of heuristic and simulation models that evaluate the value of a given schedule, usually in comparison with other alternative schedules. The heuristic and simulation models are less rigidly constrained but do not yield optimum results.

Three main mathematical optimizing approaches have been applied to the problem of media selection:

1. Linear programming.
2. Iteration or marginal analysis models.
3. Dynamic programming.

Two major non-optimizing approaches can be applied to media scheduling:

1. Heuristic programming.
2. Simulation.

Most known media selection models fall into one of these six approaches. The following analyses attempt to explain each approach and its limitations.

LINEAR PROGRAMMING

The linear programming model is a well-known tool of mathematical analysis that can be formulated to allocate a scarce resource among several alternative uses to attain the best possible value of some stated criterion function. Stated in this way, it is clear that the media selection problem can be formulated to fit this structure. The advertising budget is the scarce resource. Various television shows and magazines are viewed as alternative means of using the budget allocation. The best combination is determined by some effectiveness criterion, usually stating that the objective is to get the most weighted advertising units for a given budget or the least cost for a given level of weighted advertising units. The weighting in the criterion function is an attempt to have factors—such as the advertisement's target population, the difference in prestige of the various media vehicles and the different exposure values of the various advertisement forms used by each vehicle—influence the decision of the linear programming model. Selection of media vehicles is limited by budget size, minimum and maximum allowable use of specific media vehicles and media categories, and type of advertisement form permitted.

The firm Batten, Barton, Durstine and Osborne brought out a linear programming model greatly publicised in November 1961.[3] Details of the model are in Robert D. Buzzell's *Mathematical Models and Marketing Management*.[4] In practice the model has not had the success BBD & O expected. Also, many journal articles in the early 1960's proposed different formulations of the media problem in linear programming terms.[5-11]

After reviewing these articles and the initial experience of BBD & O, the linear programming approach was found to contain several artificialities arising from the formulation that restricted the model's usefulness. Philip Kotler[12] summarized the five most important limitations.

1. Linear programming assumes repeat exposures have the same effect.
2. It assumes constant media costs (no discounts).
3. It cannot handle the problem of audience duplication.
4. It says nothing about when advertisements should be scheduled.
5. It often requires poor or non-existent data.

Recent articles have recognized these limitations and tried to suggest ways of approximating one or more of these problem areas so that linear programming models might provide more realistic results. Brown and Warshaw[13] suggested a piecewise approximation of the objective function.

Although it is possible to make the objective function non-linear, it is difficult to deal with the constraining equations non-linearly and still use the simplex algorithm. The real problem is that many constraints, such as discounts, estimates of audience duplication and value of repeat exposures, are either known or believed by media experts to be non-linear functions.

The problem is not that the linear programming model cannot deal with many constraints simultaneously,[14] but rather that the model cannot handle the constraints non-linearly.

Bass and Lonsdale[15] actually applied the linear programming model to an advertising media problem. Besides exploring the operational details of applying linear programming to advertising media selection, they also studied the influence of weighting systems and various constraint systems, using actual data as inputs.

Bass and Lonsdale reached some important conclusions on the applicability of the mathematical structure required by linear programming to the media problem:

1. "Linear models are crude devices to attempt to apply to the media selection problem. The linearity assumption itself is the source of much difficulty. Justifying an assumption of linear response to advertising exposures on theoretical grounds would be difficult. The restraints are fundamental judgments about the non-linearity of response. . . .
2. "On the basis of the investigation presented in this paper, it appears that attempts to impose meaningful restraints on the linear model would probably be unfruitful. When only the budget restraint and operational restraints on each vehicle are employed, the model is reduced to a simple cost per thousand model. The distribution structure of media audiences makes it difficult to develop useful restraints which allocate exposures to market segments. . . .
3. "Assumptions about the nature of response to advertising cause most difficulties in models of the type examined in this article. Models with non-linear response functions, although empirically demanding, would diminish most problems associated with the imposition of judgment restraints on a linear structure."[16]

The most recent published improvement of the basic linear programming approach to media selection is provided by Charnes *et al.*[17, 18] This model, called LP II, uses the concept of "goal programming" whereby the program seeks to minimize the distance from stated goals to reach 85 per cent of the kth audience segment at least twice by time t_2. It is possible to weigh the relative value of obtaining these two objectives. The procedure is to let u^+ and u^- represent the positive and negative variance from the first goal of 85 per cent reach and say v^+ and v^- the positive and negative variance from the second goal. These values are then weighted and minimized in the functional:

$$Z = W_1 (u^+ + u^-) + W_2 (v^+ + v^-).$$

Formulated in this manner the model states that to exceed the goal by 5 per cent is just as bad as falling 5 per cent below the stated goal. Say two media schedules produced identical results except for the fact that the first schedule reached 95 per cent of the kth segment in t_1 while schedule 2 reached 81 per cent. This model would select schedule 2 as the better schedule while in reality most media schedulers probably would prefer 95 per cent reach if they could get it for the same price as 81 per cent reach. This model recognizes the need for evaluating the trade-offs between inter-related and interdependent advertising goals. However, the linear programming algorithm forces the model to assume that the amount of penalty for deviating from the stated goal is linear. To miss the goal by 10 units is always 10 times worse than missing the goal by 1 unit.

The values for reach are obtained through the use of the following key equation:

$$1 - R_k (t) = \Pi_{ij} (1 - r_{kij} (t))$$

where:

Π—means the product of the indicated terms,

$R(t) =$ proportion of the net kth audience segment obtained by media purchases in period t.

$r_{kij}(t) =$ proportion of the kth net audience segment obtained by jth cumulative purchase of medium i in period t.

$X_{ij}(t) =$ the jth cumulative purchase of medium i in period t (usually $X_{ij}(t) =$ 0 or 1).

In effect this formula gives the proportion of the kth segment not reached in time period t. This is done in order that the "non-reach" value may fit into a minimizing objective function. Note, however, that this formula is still based upon the assumption of independence of reading and viewing patterns. The independence assumption is unsubstantiated and contradicts the published research on this topic.[†]

An improvement on previous linear programming programs is the attempt to use a frequency distribution in place of the customary single value for average frequency. The authors examined the existing approximating formulae for

[†]See p. 206 of this paper for discussion of this topic.

estimating frequency and decided that they were inadequate. They decided to use a log-normal distribution to approximate the frequency distribution. The mean and standard deviation are determined empirically from the data.

Why the log-normal is a better approximating device than alternative approximating methods is not explained. Furthermore, the method by which the mean and standard deviation are empirically determined is not explained. Thus the reader is asked to take the entire concept of frequency distribution on faith alone. The one example given by the authors shows a bi-modal distribution, yet the log-normal itself is not a bi-modal distribution.

In conclusion this model is indeed an improvement over the previous works, as it attempts to break down the aggregate values into market segments. It also attempts to deal with the problem of optimizing inter-related goals for an advertising schedule. While it is not clear that the LP II model has indeed solved these problems, it must be recognized that the model has moved on to new ground for linear programming in attempting to deal with these aspects of the media selection system. The authors seem to be aware that a number of problems exist with this model and point out that this is a step forward that will eventually lead to a LP III formulation of the problem.

ITERATION MODELS

Several presently operational models are called iteration models by advertising agencies using them. The underlying concept of the iteration approach is to try to bring one vehicle into the solution at a time. The vehicle with the highest value is selected first. The list is then re-examined, and the vehicle with the next highest value is selected. This process is repeated until enough media vehicles have been selected to exhaust the budget. Often values of the remaining vehicles are recomputed after every selection, and any duplication in values of the remaining vehicles is subtracted. Such recomputing ensures that the vehicles with the largest unduplicated value are selected. This kind of model, with various modifications, is used in several agencies and sometimes called by other names. Young and Rubican (American agency) calls its version "high assay". Other agencies usually call it an "iteration model". Another name for this group of models could be "marginal analysis models". Three groups using the iteration model are Standard Rate and Data Service (American), J. Walter Thompson (American) and Mather (British).

The Mather model was reviewed by the British media expert, P. I. Jones:[19]

"The mathematical technique used is known as iteration, meaning that successive solutions are reached each moving nearer to the optimum, until the optimum is reached. The model is confined exclusively to press planning.

The input

1. List of candidate media with space sizes to be used and maximum and minimum insertions in each.

2. Readership figures for each publication from the National Readership Survey broken down by requested subdivisions, e.g. age, sex, social class, etc.
3. A persuasion index for each publication allowing for a weighting of each medium by subjective factors.
4. The total appropriation available and a profile of desired advertising weight that reflects the marketing requirements.

The objectives

1. To allocate expenditure to the publication offering the best value for money in terms of cost/weighted readership rates.
2. To attempt to match the advertising weight profile to that of the desired profile.
3. To obtain alternative solutions by reducing the number of publications and increasing frequency.

The output

1. Details of the optimum schedule in terms of publication, space, size, number of insertions and total cost per publication.
2. A table of weighted costs per thousand by publication.
3. A comparison of advertising weight profiles including the required profile, the solution profile and the population profile.

"The major fault of this model is the failure to consider the way in which sections of the population are reached. By failing to take any notice of duplication between publications, the tendency could well be to concentrate advertising on certain sections of the population with high average opportunities to see while neglecting others."

An improvement on this approach is offered by the J. Walter Thompson model, in which the criterion for selecting the next vehicle is the net unduplicated audience. This model also incorporates weighting systems to evaluate both audience and media vehicles.

Similar is the Media Schedule Iteration Model used by Standard Rate and Data Service.[20] This model attempts to define the target population in terms of produce usage. Once the target population has been defined, the vehicle with the largest exclusive coverage is selected. The selected vehicle will then reach the greatest audience of previous product users who were not reached by any other vehicle. This decision algorithm is different from the all-combinations analysis algorithm of unduplicated audience used by J. Walter Thompson. The details of Young and Rubican's "high assay" model have never been made public. But from introductory statements by William Moran,[21] it appears that the "high assay" model is an iteration model similar in approach to the first three just listed. The iteration model described in greatest detail and perhaps the most sophisticated of the iteration models is S. H. Benson (British).[22] This model includes media weights, advertisement form weights, target coverage and a handicapping function used to adjust the probability of exposure in determining the total net unduplicated audience.

Douglas Brown[23] suggests a method for incorporating the cumulative effect of advertising into the criteria function. His weighting structure assumes a monotonic decreasing function for advertising effectiveness, i.e. $DE_1 \geqslant DE_2 \geqslant ... \geqslant DE_n$ ($i = 1,..., n$), where DE is the discounted effect of the ith exposure. To handle a situation in which the magazines have different media weights, Brown simply averages the DE's for the n magazines under consideration. This model has been criticized because of this averaging process and in the manner he assigns his basic probabilities.[24, 25] In addition, the assumption that all response functions are monotonic decreasing is questionable. If advertising is learning without involvement as Krugman[26] suggests, it might be that the first and second exposures become lost in the barrage of competing stimuli. It is not until the third, fourth and fifth exposures that the advertising starts to become effective. One could not use a learning curve as a basis for assigning the DE values since the basic learning curve is not a monotonic decreasing function. The flow diagram in Figure 1 indicates the basic structure of an iteration advertising media selection model.

Models using the iteration approach have five basic limitations:
1. The iteration approach does not always yield an optimal solution.
2. The model does not specify the timing of the advertising.
3. The criterion function is too limited for a general model.
4. The model does not use integrated television and magazine data.
5. The model does not take into account the effect of advertising from past periods.

An example of why the iteration process does not necessarily yield an optimum is presented by Broadbent.[27]

Broadbent's example

```
Vehicle A's cost
        3 │ 9
        2 │ 7   8
        1 │ 5   6   8
        0 │ 0   4   7   10
          └─────────────────
            0   1   2   3    Vehicle B's cost
```

The incremental solution will lead to the selection of 3 units of A while the optimum solution is to select 3 units of B. Since vehicle A offers the greatest increment at the first purchase it is purchased and this action thus precludes the possibility of over-reaching the "true" optimum solution of 3 units of vehicle B. This conclusion from the simple two-media situation can be generalized. Because the incremental approach chooses sequentially, it is "stuck with" all its earlier choices even though they may not appear "optimal" later on. All other things equal, the incremental approach will tend to include media options which have high gains in effectiveness on the first (or early) insertions and bias against media options having lower effectiveness in early insertions but which, because of accumulation and duplication (or lack thereof), exhibit increasing returns or less rapidly diminishing returns later.

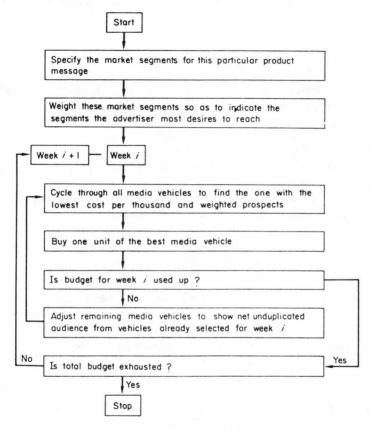

FIG. 1. *Iteration model.*

It is also interesting to note that the more dimensional the interactions between the components to be selected, the smaller the chance that a stepwise selection process based on a single criterion will discover the true optimum.

DYNAMIC PROGRAMMING

Dynamic programming is a useful technique if the problem can be limited so that the carry-over effect from one period to another can be expressed in terms of five or six variables, otherwise the problem very quickly becomes unmanageable, even with a computer.

The mathematics of a dynamic programming model are relatively straightforward and can be easily programmed for a computer. The trick is to simplify the problem so that only a limited number of variables are considered.

The objective function of the dynamic programming problem is to maximize:

$$\sum_{i=1}^{n} R_i,$$

where:

$$R_i = f(s_i\, d_i).$$

Here R_i stands for the reward of the process in Stage i. The second statement states that the reward is a function of the process state at Stage i and the decision made at Stage i.

The dynamic programming algorithm is a brute-force technique that takes into account all possible combinations of decisions and then selects the best alternative. By selecting the best decision in the nth stage and then working backwards to select the best decision in the $n-1$ stage, taking into account the decision made in the nth stage, dynamic programming can reduce the number of combinations that must be directly examined.

Let:

M = number of decisions at each stage,
S = number of states at each stage,
N = number of stages.

Dynamic programming will reduce the number of combinations the computer must consider from M^N to $(MS)N$.

Figure 2 shows a simple dynamic programming system, a serial system in which the output of one stage becomes the input for the next. This same basic system can be expanded to include branching decisions and random variables that affect each stage. At first the notation used may appear awkward; however, it is the standard notation used in dynamic programming literature. Remember, in the series of sequential decision periods (1, 2, ..., N) the dynamic programming algorithm analyses the last stage (N) first and then proceeds backwards through the decision stages until it finally analyses the first decision stage 1.

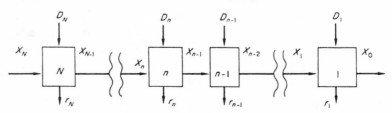

FIG. 2.

Each box represents a stage in the process. For the general stage n ($n = 1$, 2, ..., N) of the N-stage system:

D is the decisions made at each stage that controls the variables in the box.

X is the input for a stage that gives all relevant inputs to the box. The input for stage n is the output from stages $n-1$.

r is the reward or return for combined D_n decisions at a stage n with X_n inputs.

Richard Maffei published a media allocation problem solved by dynamic programming.[28] Keeping the problem small, he solves a problem that allocates a given advertising budget among *three* media in a test market.

John Little and Leonard Lodish considered a larger problem.[29] Although many of the assumptions need justification, their model represents an example of how skilled model builders attempt to fit the real world to meet the constraints of a given mathematical form. The authors first present a general model and then a specific application of it.

Little and Lodish first define market segments to be mutually exclusive and presumed to represent relevant groups with respect to sales potential and media usage. This statement implies that the members of a market segment are homogeneous. It is difficult to visualize mutually exclusive market segments for many major products. The target audience is usually defined in terms of past-purchase behaviour or a series of socio-economic traits. To divide this target population into groups that approximate internally homogeneous and externally mutually exclusive segments usually requires several groups. The dynamic programming algorithm quickly expands beyond the limits of the computer if several market segments are considered. "One place that computational limitations become serious is the number of market segments."[30] Yet, the segments must be approximately homogeneous because values for such things as sales potential, exposure value, exposure efficiency, retention of advertising and probability of media usage will be assigned to each market segment based on the assumption that the group is homogeneous. In the Little and Lodish example, only *one* market segment, consisting of people with American Express credit cards, was used. This segment was then treated homogeneously with respect to the assigned values just listed.

The method is further limited in respect to the number of vehicles that can be considered and the number of time periods. In the example, the media vehicles were limited to 15 magazines. The exact 15 magazines evaluated by the dynamic programming model were selected in advance, outside the scope of the model. The number of time periods was set at four. If weeks were the time units, the planning period would be 1 month. Again, if the number of vehicles or time periods is increased, the problem will quickly expand beyond the time and storage capacities of a computer.

This model also assumes the amount of sales is strictly a function of the number of exposures to an advertisement. Other variables that affect the sales decision, such as price, quality and competition, are disregarded.

In attempting to consider 15 media vehicles, this model is forced to limit other considerations and make some questionable assumptions; the most serious of which are:

1. Limit of only four time periods.
2. Assumption that the very limited number of market segments will each be homogeneous.
3. Assumption that sales are a function only of advertising exposures.
4. Limiting the model to consider only one media type (magazines).
5. Inability to handle the discounted cost structure of advertising media selection.

In summary, dynamic programming does not have the capacity to help select a media package that considers simultaneously all of the leading consumer magazines and television programmes available. The problem of fitting the complex structure of the media selection problem into the constraints of to handle a large-scale problem with the degree of complexity found in the media-scheduling system. It is my judgement that the assumptions required out. The basic problem with present dynamic programming models of media selection is that present computers simply do not have the storage capacity the dynamic programming algorithm is analogous to condensing a paper bag full of springs—push one thing into a smaller space and something else pops to limit the number of variables considered and thus condense the number of interactions between the variables not only simplifies but also distorts reality.

Little and Lodish have shifted their efforts into the development of a simulation model that enables them to increase the scope of their problem. An interesting facet of this model is the attempt to break the aggregate population data down into reading and viewing patterns for individual market segments.

"It is expected that audience duplication may only be available for the total population, but, as previously indicated, it can usually be broken down to individual market segments by empirically developing estimating equations."[31]

If one grants the questionable assumption that all individuals within a given demographic market segment have the same reading and viewing patterns, this still leaves a very extensive task of computing empirical equations. Developing estimating equations for all combinations of the 15 magazines used in their dynamic programming example would require 15! ($13,077 \times 10^8$) empirically derived equations per market segment. Working with this market segment in different time periods would increase the complexity still further.

This concludes the discussion of four optimizing approaches suggested as possible mathematical models for advertising media selection. Each model has a definite procedure or algorithm by which the model could predict the "best" media schedule from the various media schedules evaluated by it. The chief task of the model builder using one of these approaches is to fit the real-world situation into the constraints of the specific mathematical algorithm. He does this by defining the problem so that it will fit the form required by the algorithm. The obvious danger with optimizing approaches is that the model builder can become enamoured with the mathematics of his approach and distort reality to meet the constraints of his model.

NON-OPTIMIZING MODELS

Another approach is to identify what the model builder believes the relevant variables are and quantify the relationships between these variables without attempting to modify or adjust the model builder's view of reality to fit a specific solution algorithm.

This approach is not compelled to reduce the media data to comparatively few parameters by various simplifying assumptions used to represent how a media vehicle actually reaches and affects people. Rather, a non-optimizing kind of model often uses data about individual viewers in all of its complexity. Usually none of the standard optimizing solution algorithms can handle the complex form of the model which is basically descriptive and simulates the real-world situation. Hence, these descriptive models are often called *simulation models*. By manipulating a simulation, it is possible to infer how changing some system variable or relationship would affect the system's output.

It is also possible to construct decision rules that appear to improve the complex system's performance. The desirable decision rules are often called *heuristic decision rules*. By using heuristics, it is often possible to simplify the complex system.

A HEURISTIC MODEL

In 1958, a British trio of operations researchers, Lee, Burkart and Taylor, working for British European Airways, started work on a heuristic approach to scheduling advertising media.

A model was built, first for a static state and later expanded to render the model dynamic with respect to time. To evaluate media schedules, two criteria were established: (1) *coverage* was defined as the proportion of the population seeing at least one advertisement and (2) *impact* was defined as the average number of times an advertisement is seen. It was impossible to optimize more than one objective criterion at a time. Therefore, coverage or impact would be optimized under the constraint that a certain level of the other criteria would also be produced.[32] Through a process of constant refinement and further simplification, the model was eventually reduced to the key equation:

$$R = Q \sum_r W_r I_r,$$

where:

R = the response function indicating how positively the target population responds to given media schedule,

Q = a value indicating the effectiveness of the formats used,

W_r = a weighting factor measuring the proportionate response from these people who have received r impacts and who form a proportion I_r of the target population.

Through this equation, the model has been extended so that it can deal with coverage, impact and other effectiveness criteria simultaneously.[33]

To formulate the mathematical expressions that support this equation, the model builders were required to make several assumptions. The quality of this model is determined by the realism of the following assumptions:

1. The size and attention value of an advertisement is related by the square-root rule. "An advertisement of size $p = z^2$ in any publication is seen by a proportion z of the readers of that publication.[34]

2. The proportion of the target population who read both media M_i and M_j, say a_{ij}, is the product of the proportions a_i and a_j who read M_i and M_j respectively, that is, $a_{ij} = a_i a_j$.

3. There exists a set of mutually independent probabilities typified by Z_{nij} which represents the probability that the nth individual will look at the jth issue of the ith medium and that he will see the insertion in that issue.[35]

4. The chance a reader will see an advertisement in M_i is independent of whether he has seen an advertisement with the same format and content in M_i previously or in another medium M_j.

5. The expected response of a person to the advertisement campaign in terms of purchase behaviour is determined by the number of insertions he sees.

Assumption 1 states that the attention value of an advertising form is solely a function of advertisement size. It is possible to question the accuracy of the square-root functional relationship. More important, this assumption totally ignores such variables as use of colour, advertisement position and uniqueness of the given advertisement compared with competitive advertisements. In reality it is the interactions between these ignored variables and page size, rather than page size alone, that determines the attention value of the given advertisement.

To use probability theory in formulating their model, Lee, Taylor and Burkart were often forced to assume that the interactions between key variables were random, when in reality definite patterns of behaviour existed. This is true for assumptions 2, 3 and 4. Assumption 2 denies the existence of patterns in magazine reading, saying, in effect, that magazine selection is random. Assume that for a given target audience the a_i of *Glamour* equals the a_j of *Popular Mechanics*. If it is also known that a particular woman reads *Vogue*, *Ladies' Home Journal* and *McCall's*, is it correct to assume that the probability that this woman also reads *Popular Mechanics* is equal to the probability that she reads *Glamour*? This model answers "Yes" because the randomness assumption states that the probabilities of the woman reading *Glamour* and *Popular Mechanics* are independent of her other reading; thus, the probabilities should not be affected by other magazines she reads. This denial of reading patterns is unsubstantiated by the authors and is contradicted by the research in this area.[36-39] These researchers, working independently, found that definite reading patterns exist in France, the United States and Germany.

Assumption 3 states that a person's probability of looking at the *j*th issue of the *i*th medium is independent of whether this person has seen the last ten issues of the given medium or has seen none of the last ten issues. This assumption denies the existence of reading patterns of given magazines over time.

Assumption 4 states that people do not build recognition patterns in relation to advertisements. It seems unrealistic to assume that an advertisement format that you noticed in the last five issues should have the same probability of being recognized in the sixth issue as an advertisement format you have failed to notice in the first five issues.

Assumption 5 is that sales are solely a ...iction of the number of advertising exposures a person receives. Price, quality and actions of competition are among other factors generally felt to influence purchase decisions. These factors are completely ignored by the model. This again is unrealistic.

A sub-set of these assumptions exists in all of the models previously discussed as well as in the CAM, COMPASS and DYNAMO models to be discussed in the next section of this paper. Ellis[40] makes the point that lack of empirical data prompted these unrealistic assumptions and that as empirical data become available the independence assumptions should be dropped from all of the media selection models.

Work on removing these assumptions from media models has progressed rapidly. Taylor[41] used empirical exposure values and costs for each insertion size to move away from assumption 1. Marc[42] used panel data in determining individual readership probabilities thus avoiding assumptions 2 and 3. Gensch,[43] using syndicated sample data available to American agencies, has devised a system that avoids all four assumptions.

The use of duplication formula such as the IPC model's use of Metheringham duplication formula and other models using Agnosti's formula are on the way out. As integrated empirical data on an individual basis become available, the models will not have to rely on duplication formulae, rather the attention will turn to providing a model structure flexible enough to use these data and methods of optimizing the response surface generated by the non-linear, non-aggregate data. This type of data is presently available in the United States in the form of a computer tape supplied by either the Brand Rating Index Corporation or W. R. Simmons and Associates. The tapes contain reading and viewing records for 16,000 individuals as well as past purchasing records and socio-demographics by individuals.

This concludes the review of a mathematical heuristic approach. Another class of non-optimizing models is simulation models.

SIMULATION MODELS

The two most widely known simulation models are the Computer Assessment of Media (CAM) model of the London Press Exchange and the model of the Simulmatics Corporation of New York.

The CAM model became operational in 1954, representing 2 years' research by S. R. Broadbent, Director of Computer Operations, and his staff at the London Press Exchange. The model is used today and is influencing the spending of over £10 million per year. It attempts to simulate the process by which television and magazine advertisements reach individuals. This means that the steps in the communication process are described, and numerical values are attached to the various stages.

Viewing data come in 4-week periods from the Television Audience Measurement Ltd. (TAM). The data from the actual 4-week period are converted into probabilities of television viewing for a yearly period. The magazine data are supplied by the National Readership Survey (NRS). Because no detailed information is available on the viewing and reading of the same individuals, a marriage process is performed to link existing viewing and readership information. The individuals in the TAM and NRS samples are paired off on the basis of demographic characteristics, after which the NRS individual is allotted the viewing pattern of his TAM counterpart. Figure 3 is an example of how the marriage process operates.

A target population for a message is selected and weighed. A perception value is then determined for each vehicle. This perception value attempts to measure the impact a certain advertisement is expected to have on the viewer. It tries to indicate the percentage of people reading a magazine who have "open eyes in front of the advertisement".

It was felt that certain times of weekdays may be more suitable for television commercials. The same advertisement may have more prestige and influence when it appears in one publication than in another. To allow for these effects, a second series of weights called *selectivity weights* are used. A third series of weights, called *impact weights*, are then used to determine the advertisement's usefulness, its effect on a person seeing it.

The model's objective is to describe how an advertising campaign affects the defined target population. The single dimension used to describe how much

Television Audience Measurement			
Individual	Demo-graphic charac-teristics	Television viewing pattern	
1	1 4 5	112	
2	2 3 2	114	
3	1 2 1	000	
4	2 1 4	210	
5	3 6 2	101	

National Readership Survey			
Individual	Demo-graphic charac-teristics	Magazine reading pattern	
6	1 3 1	214	
7	1 4 5	863	
8	3 6 2	110	
9	2 1 5	002	
10	2 3 2	415	

Married individual	Television viewing pattern	Magazine reading pattern
1-7	112	863
2-10	114	415
3-6	000	214
4-9	210	002
5-8	101	110

FIG. 3. *Marriage process.*

advertising is received by an individual is called the campaign's impression value. For each individual, the probability of receiving an impression (*PRI*) is computed as:

PRI is the adjusted probability of seeing the magazine × perception × selectivity × impact.

With this approach, it is possible to obtain an impression distribution. Again a series of weights can be applied to the impression distribution to produce one number as the output of the entire model. This is what the CAM model has done. The weighting applied to the impression distribution is the model's response function. The single value that becomes the model's output is the schedule effectiveness value. This effectiveness figure, which is produced by the response function, is the criterion used for choosing between schedules.[44]

The approach taken by this model of trying to combine all judgments involved in evaluating a media package into a logical flow sequence is a major step in the right direction. There is an assumption of independence in regard to probabilities of repeat exposures. This could be remedied by using continuous empirical data, such as that generated by a small survey or panel, as the basis for assigning an individual's probability of exposure to medium *A* in time period *j* + 2 given that exposures have taken place in periods *j* and *j* + 1. There are no inherent simplifying assumptions that *must* be included to allow the model to function. The response surface defined by the schedule effectiveness is free to assume any non-symmetric shape dictated by the model inputs. The response surface will not require the simplifications needed for the usual mathematical approaches.

209

Two main criticisms have been levelled against this model. First, the initial reading and viewing data generated by the marriage process are poor. Critics and the model's proponents admit this.

The second major criticism of the model is that its entire output is in terms of one number. It is a practical problem for the conventional model user. Jones states the criticism:

> "The main broad criticism is that CAM gives a measure of effectiveness, but in what terms? The media planner is suddenly thrust from circumstances in which he uses his rather limited but understandable measurements of effectiveness into a new space age dimension which he cannot relate in any way to his traditional measurements. In making these criticisms, however, it becomes increasingly obvious that CAM is a model of the future. Most of the assumptions can be validated or modified by research."[45]

An American firm, the Simulmatics Corporation, generated its imaginary population representing an accurate national sample. The computer tape contains detailed information on 2994 imaginary individuals, representing a cross sample of the U.S. population over 4 years of age. They are properly, distributed with respect to age, sex, region, rural–urban–suburban residence, employment, education, race, family size, consumer purchasing power, etc. Each individual is described in regard to his social characteristics and media habits.

The computer steps hour by hour, through a day, week, month or year, as the client's needs dictate. For each hour it cycles through the entire population of 2994. The exact evaluation programme varies from medium to medium. For television, the computer starts with an initial figure on the probability of the individual being exposed to the given programme at the given time. This probability figure is based on audience data if available. The initial probability of exposure is then modified by functions representing habit, formation in television viewing, saturation with a given type of show and competition from other shows. For competition, it was claimed that the model had a method for simulating the decision process that goes on when an individual is faced with the choice between shows.

In summary, the main criticism of this model is that advertising theory is not sufficiently developed to allow a model to be as abstract as the Simulmatics model. Advertising agencies knew that their clients would demand evidence that the imaginary sample really corresponded to the national audience. It was feared that the interrelations programmed into the imaginary sample could easily become dated and no one would know the difference. Simulmatics could not really justify many of the functions it proposed to use to represent habit formation in television, saturation and competition between shows.

In an attempt to save the model by making it less abstract, the Simulmatics Corporation suggested getting the initial data inputs from a large national sample. It was also suggested that if the agencies desired, national samples could continue to serve as a check on the imaginary population. Although the agencies felt that continuing national samples were necessary, the cost of maintaining such a sample was more than they were willing to pay. Thus, the Simulmatics model was never adopted by agencies.[46] Perhaps it was too far ahead of its time and of the data needed to support it.

Broadbent reported on a simulation model under construction in France.[47] It differs from others in the manner it introduces time into the assessment. The model is called SCAL (Simulation des Comportements Aléatoires de Lecture— Simulation of Stochastic Reading Habits). It goes as far as issue exposure in analysing a schedule. A simulation of a person's reading over time is based on a model of individual behaviour by a Monte Carlo process. The basic data will come from a survey of some 2000 individuals. The reliability of the survey will be checked by a validating panel. The model is limited to magazines. Marc[48] reports that panel data are used in repeat exposures. Thus, the model is not required to assume independence between successive opportunities for exposure.

This model seems to have two major improvements over the CAM and Simulmatics models. First, the model introduces the timing of the advertisements into the decision process. Second, it proposes using a panel to serve as a check on the predicted reading habits.

Foote, Cone and Belding have been working hard along with nine other agencies to get a joint project model, Computer Optimal Media Planning and Selection System (COMPASS), operational. To the best of my knowledge there has not been any published description of the COMPASS model. In discussing the model with executives of various agencies the following description of the COMPASS model emerges. COMPASS functions by simulating the media exposures generated by alternative media schedules. These exposures are weighted by subjective judgements to establish the most effective reach and frequency criteria. A large sample is used to provide the media/marketing data by individual.

The project has been under development since 1965, with the Diebolt consulting firm acting as technical adviser and developer. Considerable time and effort has been extended in trying to develop target population and vehicle appropriateness weights.

The most perplexing problem is the attempt to optimize a single criteria function. The first problem is that the same criteria function is not appropriate for all advertising messages. Second, it is difficult to define a meaningful single criterion function that can later be validated. Effectiveness has been defined in terms of increasing the purchases or the probability to purchase. It is extremely difficult to get empirical measurements for this type of criteria on products, especially non-impulse products. The communication goals of exposure, perception and attitude change are difficult to incorporate into the single criteria function as a series of linear weights.

A third problem is that they are attempting to use a hill-climbing search technique to find *the* optimal schedule. The hill-climbing technique drops out the least effective vehicle and replaces it with the most effective vehicle currently not in the media schedule. The process continues until no improvement has been made in ten iterations. It is thus assumed that the peak of that particular segment of the response surface has been obtained. Sub-samples of the total population are used in this test so as to reduce the computer time needed. In theory, if one were to randomly start at a large enough number of points, the statistical probability of climbing the highest hill in the response surface would be approaching one or certainty. In practice the cost of checking this large number of points is too costly in terms of computer time.

There also seems to be difficulty in attempting to program in the discount structure. This is due to the bargaining relationships causing wide variances especially in television.

It is clear that substantial time, money and research effort has gone into the development of COMPASS. It appears that many of the inter-relationships between variables that are ignored, assumed independent or subjectively estimated in other models have been empirically measured. It is possible that when and if this model becomes operational it could set the standard for advertising media selection models.

An interesting combination of a simulation model coupled with an optimizing search routine is the DYNAMO model developed by the Operational Research Group of I.C.I. Limited.[49] The simulation model is used to generate the exposure probabilities and a dynamic programming search technique is used to explore the response surface.

The data needed to evaluate alternative media schedules are obtained in three steps:

1. Develop market weights for each individual on the basis of socio-demographic characteristics.
2. Obtain a stratified sample of individuals to get estimates of readership probabilities.
3. Estimate "impact" probabilities per person.

Four socio-demographic traits (e.g. age, sex, social grade and educational level) may be used to define the target group. A weight is assigned to each trait. Weights are then calculated multiplicatively for each informant.

Based upon these weights a sample of magazine readers is obtained. The sample is biased towards the inclusion of individuals with high market weights.

"Each informant's probability of selection is proportional to his market weight, so that the most efficient sample is selected."[50]

This type of sampling could lead to problems in projecting the results of the sample to the population. It is essential that one knows the percentage of the total population each individual or each sample stratum represents in order to project the results of a stratified sample to the population. It might be difficult to estimate the percentage of the total population represented by each weighted individual described above. A suggestion would be to define specific cells of high market weight groups, where the percentage of the total population conforming to each cell is known, then fill each cell with the number of individuals needed to achieve a desired level of statistical significance. The information from these cells could then be developed to represent the entire population.

The variable "impact" is the key variable in this entire system. This is the variable used in building the response functions and upon which the quality of alternative schedules will be ranked. It should be noted that this key variable is both *defined* and *measured outside* of the DYNAMO model. "The user may interpret 'impact' as he wishes." The quality of the magazine selection depends more on the definition and measurement of "impact" than on *all* of the manipulations performed by the computer programs.

In building a response function the advertiser wishes to know not only how many opportunities each given individual has to see his message, but also to what degree individuals are consciously reading, comprehending and remembering his message. This is the concept of perception which is usually measured in terms of recognition, recall and noting scores. Perception clearly precedes and greatly influences response. The users of the DYNAMO model are urged to consider impact as strictly a probability of viewing.

"It is emphasized that DYNAMO uses impact probability in a strictly probabilistic sense, and not as a measure of the size or value of an impact."[52]

An individual may perceive and remember more from one full-page colour advertisement than from four other one-half page black-and-white advertisements he has been exposed to. It is important to take into account the strength, depth and quality of each potential perception as well as the probability of such a perception occurring. Contrary to the quotation above, it is suggested that the user weights the probability of viewing by the value of the potential exposure.

Although it is possible to give the viewing probability a weighted value to account for the size of the impact, there is still a problem in that the impacts are treated as statistically independent events. This is contrary to the empirical evidence of Starch scores in the United States and Gallup–Robinson scores in the United Kingdom. Once a person perceives a message in one magazine and his interest is aroused, the probability of his perceiving this message in other magazines increases. There are carry-over influences from one magazine to another. The interaction between carry-over effects should be acknowledged measured and taken into account rather than ignored.

Once the data have been collected in the three steps mentioned above, alternative magazine schedules are analysed by the following procedure:

15   213

1. Calculate or estimate the probability of 0, 1, 2, ..., etc., number of impacts per individual.
2. Apply a specified response function to the distribution on an individual basis.
3. Apply each individual's market weight to his weighted response.
4. Sum the market weighted responses and select the schedule with the largest sum.

The response function is defined as:

$$R = \sum_i w_i r(n_i),$$

where:

w_i = market weights of the ith individual,

n_i = number of impacts received by the ith individual,

$r(g)$ = response value assigned to j impacts ($j = 1, 2, 3, ...,$ etc.).

The major shortcoming of this formulation is that the time dimension is ignored in assigning the response values to the impacts. Zielske[52] has shown that time makes a significant difference in terms of reinforcement, thus affecting the awareness and forgetting rates. There will be two quite different response patterns to twelve advertisements depending upon whether the advertisements are shown once per week for 12 weeks or once per month over a year's time. This response function should take into account the effect of the time period since the j-1 impact when defining the value of the jth impact.

To include the time dimension and carry-over effects of previous viewing in a dynamic programming algorithm means that the values for each combination of media vehicles over all possible insertion time schedules must be computed *before* the dynamic programming algorithm works its way backward through the data to find the optimum path.

Consider a simple example of evaluating 25 shows over a 13-week period. Each one of these combinations must be weighted by a combined function that estimates the effect of forgetting and carry-over. Of the $(25!)^{13}$ weighted combinations the dynamic programming algorithm must consider at least $(25!)^{13}$ of these values.

To compute only the weighted values needed to run this simple example will cost several thousand dollars of computer time on present machines. Furthermore, consider the fact that there are probably different carry-over and forgetting functions for various segments of the population. The cost becomes a multiple of the number of market segments considered.

Consideration of the complex time dimension is beyond the present capability of dynamic programming. It is *presently* an *inherent* limitation in a realistic media model formation. As the computer capacity expands by a factor of 50 or 100, as is expected within the '70's, the dynamic programming approach may not only become feasible, but the best approach to use in media models.

The DYNAMO program provides a dynamic programming search technique which attempts to optimize some nicely defined response surface by subdividing the budget into cost levels and then optimizing by cost level.

"The method of building up the new schedule will now be briefly described. Suppose the budget is £50,000 and we are using an interval of £2000 in our table, so that at the end of the previous stage we have schedules stored for £2000, £4000, £6000, ..., £50,000. New schedules for each level are built up as follows: Suppose we are at the £40,000 level, and the new publication we are considering costs £2500 per insertion and a maximum of six insertions is permitted in a new publication. The following alternatives will be examined in order to arrive at the 'new best schedule' for £40,000:

$$0 \text{ inserts} + \text{Previous best for £40,000,}$$
$$1 \text{ insert} + \text{Previous best for £36,000,}$$
$$2 \text{ inserts} + \text{Previous best for £34,000,}$$
$$3 \text{ inserts} + \text{Previous best for £32,000,}$$
$$4 \text{ inserts} + \text{Previous best for £30,000,}$$
$$5 \text{ inserts} + \text{Previous best for £26,000,}$$
$$6 \text{ inserts} + \text{Previous best for £24,000,}$$

where 'Previous best' means the schedule found at the end of the previous stage costing *no more* than the given amount of money. The best of these seven alternatives is selected as the 'new best schedule' for £40,000. The entire process is repeated for each cost level in the table (i.e. in the example, the calculation would proceed to the £42,000 level) until the table has been filled up. The calculation then proceeds to the next stage, i.e. the addition of a new publication, until the candidate list has been exhausted. It should be clear that a very large number of alternatives are examined by this procedure, the evaluation of £2000 schedules being normal."[53]

Again the search technique says little about the timing of the inserts. Should the given number of inserts in a magazine be run weekly, bi-weekly or monthly? The question of discounts is handled by this model as long as the discounts are series discounts or at least predictable and programmable. This might be sufficient for British magazines, but discounts become much more of a problem when they are determined in a bargaining situation such as with American television and to a lesser extent American magazines. Television discounts usually range from 10 to 50 per cent of the stated price depending on whom the agency is, for which client the time is being purchased and the competitive demand for this time. These discounts obviously will make a significant difference in any model that evaluates exposures or impacts on a per dollar basis, yet the bargained discounts are difficult to forecast for use in a model using a fixed algorithm to evaluate schedules or search feasible solution spaces.

215

In summary, the approach of generating the basic data by individual simulation model followed by an optimizing algorithm such as dynamic programming seems a modelling approach that will be of real value to the advertiser. Most of the limitations and problems associated with DYNAMO can be solved. The major limitations of DYNAMO as it now stands are the following:

1. Limited to magazines only.
2. Biased sampling procedure.
3. Lack of mechanism to incorporate perception values into the decision system.
4. *A priori* response surfaces fail to consider the time dimension.
5. Not designed to handle a flexible discount structure.

It should be noted that the dynamic programming algorithm, as pointed out in the Little and Lodish example, might not be able to cope with response surfaces that take into account the increased number of interactions between variables that are suggested in four of the above points.

CONCLUSION

The purpose of advertising research should be to identify and then measure the inter-relationships between the components of the advertising system. To use an optimizing algorithm which *a priori* denies the existence of possible inter-relationships seems to be a good way of guaranteeing that models so formulated will be of little practical value in aiding media schedulers to deal with their problems. Indeed this has probably been a major reason why many mathematically sophisticated models have failed to produce useful insights or results.

Two major trends are developing on both sides of the Atlantic. First, there is a definite movement toward simulation and heuristic models. Second, there are attempts to provide the basic input data in the form of an individual's reading and viewing pattern rather than aggregate totals for specified demographic segments of the population.

Both of these trends could be explained by the fact that model builders are using present media models more as learning devices than as problem-solving resource allocators. In other words, since the body of advertising theory does not contain a documented and commonly accepted explanation of how the key variables in the advertising process relate together nor research which measures the strengths and elasticities of these relationships, model builders are interested in the models that diagram their view of reality and explicitly state the axioms which they wish to test. Thus simulation and heuristic models which help the model builder to better understand the complex process are presently preferred to various optimizing models that attempt to abstract and simplify a decision process that is neither clearly understood nor defined.

Dennis H. Gensch – Advertising Media Selection

Knowledge gained through the use of non-optimizing models will eventually be put to good use in the construction of optimizing models in that the model user will have some insight into the *consequences* of the assumptions the various optimizing algorithms require.

Note: Five individuals in each sample are listed above with a code that identifies their demographic characteristics, and either their television-viewing pattern or their magazine-reading pattern. By matching the demographics, the ten individuals, five from each sample, are combined or "married". These "married" individuals now have a television-viewing pattern and a magazine-reading pattern.

REFERENCES

[1] Y & R, BBD & O unleash media computerization (1962) *Advertising Age*, October, 1, 1.
[2] A. NORELLI (1966) Can we learn from America? In *Computers in Advertising*, pp. 28–34. Institute of Practitioners in Advertising, London.
[3] Y & R, BBD & O unleash media computerization (1962) *Advertising Age*, October 1, 1.
[4] R. D. BUZZELL (1964) *Mathematical Models and Marketing Management*, Chap. 5, p. 52. Division of Research, Graduate School of Business Administration, Harvard University, Boston.
[5] D. W. MILLER and M. K. STARR (1960) *Executive Decisions and Operations Research*, pp. 190–209. Prentice-Hall, New Jersey.
[6] R. L. DAY (1962) Linear programming in media selection. *J. Advertising Res.* 2 (June), 40.
[7] L. M. GODFREY (1962) Media selection by mathematical programming. Speech at New York Chapter, The Institute of Management Sciences, 10 October.
[8] H. MANELOVEG (1963) A Year of Linear Programming Media Planning for Clients. Paper presented at the 9th Annual Conference of the Advertising Research Foundation, New York, October
[9] J. F. ENGEL and M. R. WARSAW (1964) Allocating advertising dollars by linear programming, *J. Advertising Res.* 4 (September), 42.
[10] C. W. WILSON (1962) Linear Programming Basics. Paper presented at the 8th Annual Conference of the Advertising Research Foundation, New York, October.
[11] D. LEARNER (1961) Mathematical Programming for Better Media Selection. Paper presented to the Region Convention, American Association of Advertising Agencies, New York.
[12] P. KOTLER (1964) Toward an explicit model for media selection. *J. Advertising Res.* 4 (March), 34.
[13] D. B. BROWN and M. R. WARSHAW (1965) Media selection by linear programming. *J. Marketing Res.* 2 (February), 83.
[14] S. F. STASCH (1965) Linear programming and space-time considerations in media selection. *J. Advertising Res.* 5 (December), 40.
[15] F. M. BASS and R. T. LONSDALE (1966) An exploration of linear programming in media-selection. *J. Marketing Res.* 3 (May), 179.
[16] F. M. BASS and R. T. LONSDALE (1966) An exploration of linear programming in media-selection. *J. Marketing Res.* 3 (May), 183.
[17] A. CHARNES, W. W. COOPER, J. K. DEVOE, D. B. LEARNER and W. REINECKE (1968) A goal programming model for media planning. *Mgmt Sci.* 14, 423.
[18] A. CHARNES, W. W. COOPER, D. B. LEARNER and E. F. SNOW (1968) Note on an application of a goal programming model for media planning. *Mgmt Sci.* 14, 431.
[19] P. I. JONES (1966) *The Thompson Medals and Awards for Media Research*, 1965. Tonbridge Printers, Kent.
[20] P. W. WENIG (1964) Media schedule operations. *Data* 1, 16.
[21] W. T. MORAN (1962) Practical Media Models: What Must They Look Like? Speech at Midwest Conference, Advertising Research Foundation, Chicago, November 1962.

[22] D. PHILIPPS (1966) Schedule building for press and TV. In *Computers in Advertising*, pp. 57–62. Institute of Practitioners in Advertising, London.

[23] D. B. BROWN (1967) A practical procedure for media selection. *J. Marketing Res.* **4** (August), 262.

[24] R. J. SCHREIBER (1968) A practical procedure for media selection: Comments. *J. Marketing Res.* **5** (May), 221.

[25] S. BANKS (1968) The true probability of exposure. *J. Marketing Res.* **5** (May), 223.

[26] H. E. KRUGMAN (1965) The impact of television advertising: Learning without involvement. *Public Opinion Q.* **XXIX**, 349.

[27] S. BROADBENT (1966) Media planning and computers by 1970: A review of the use of mathematical models in media planning. *Appl. Statist.* **15**, 240.

[28] R. B. MAFFEI (1960) Planning advertising expenditures by dynamic programming methods. *Ind. Mgmt Rev.* **1** (December), 94.

[29] J. D. C. LITTLE and L. M. LODISH (1966) A media selection model and its optimization by dynamic programming. *Ind. Mgmt Rev.* **8** (Fall), 15.

[30] J. D. C. LITTLE and L. M. LODISH (1966) A media selection model and its optimization by dynamic programming. *Ind. Mgmt Rev.* **8** (Fall), 23.

[31] J. D. C. LITTLE and L. M. LODISH (1968) A Media Selection Calculus, p. 32. Working Paper 304–68, MIT.

[32] A. M. LEE and A. J. BURKART (1960) Some optimization problems in advertising media planning. *Opl Res. Q.* **11**, 113.

[33] A. M. LEE (1962) Decision rules for media scheduling: Static campaigns. *Opl Res. Q.* **13**, 229.

[34] A. M. LEE (1962) Decision rules for media scheduling: Static campaigns. *Opl Res. Q.* **13**, 234.

[35] C. J. TAYLOR (1963) Some developments in the theory and applications of media scheduling methods. *Opl Res. Q.* **14**, 291.

[36] J. M. AGOSTINI (1962) Analysis of magazine accumulative audience. *J. Advertising Res.* **2** (December), 24.

[37] F. L. ENGELMAN (1965) An empirical formula for audience accumulation. *J. Advertising Res.* **5** (June), 21.

[38] W. KUHN (1963) Net audiences of German magazines: A new formula. *J. Advertising Res.* **3** (March), 30.

[39] S. BANKS and A. MANDANSKY (1958) Estimation of multimagazine readership. *J. Business* **31** (July), 235.

[40] D. M. ELLIS (1966) Building up a sequence of optimum media schedules, *Opl Res. Q.* **17**, 413.

[41] C. J. TAYLOR, *op. cit.*

[42] M. MARC (1968) Combining simulation and panel data to obtain reach and frequency. *J. Advertising Res.* **8** (June), 11.

[43] D. H. GENSCH (1969) A computer simulation model for selecting advertising schedules. *J. Marketing Res.* **VI** (May), 203.

[44] S. R. BROADBENT (1962) A Year's Experience of the LEP Media Model. Paper presented at the 8th Annual Conference, Advertising Research Foundation, New York, October.

[45] P. I. JONES (1966) *The Thompson Medals and Awards for Media Research*, 1965. Tonbridge Printers, Kent.

[46] A. BERNSTEIN (1961) Computer simulation of media exposure. In *A Report of the Sixth Meeting of the ARF Operations Research Discussion Group*. Advertising Research Foundation, New York. See also Simulmatics Media-mix I, General Description, Simulmatics Corporation, February 1962; Simulmatics Media-mix, Technical Description, Simulmatics Corporation, October 1962.

[47] S. BROADBENT (1966) Media planning and computers by 1970: A review of the use of mathematical models in media planning. *Appl. Statist.* **15**, 234.

[48] M. MARC, *op. cit.*

[49] UNIVERSITY OF LONDON ATLAS COMPUTING SERVICE, *Dynamo-media Scheduling Suite of Programs*, p. 1.

[50] UNIVERSITY OF LONDON ATLAS COMPUTING SERVICE, *Dynamo-media Scheduling Suite of Programs*, p. 11.
[51] UNIVERSITY OF LONDON ATLAS COMPUTING SERVICE, *Dynamo-media Scheduling Suite of Programs*, p. 5.
[52] H. A. ZIELSKE (1959) The remembering and forgetting of advertising. *J. Marketing*, 239.
[53] UNIVERSITY OF LONDON ATLAS COMPUTING SERVICE, *Dynamo-media Scheduling Suite of Programs*, p. 13.

Operational Research Quarterly
VOLUME 11 NUMBER 3 SEPTEMBER 1960

Some Optimization Problems in Advertising Media Planning†

A. M. LEE and A. J. BURKART

British European Airways

This is an account of the first stage of a multi-stage research programme in the planning of advertising media schedules. The problems of securing maximum impact and maximum coverage in an intense campaign of short duration for a fixed outlay are discussed. A precise solution of the Impact problem and an approximate solution of the Coverage problem are outlined. These solutions are currently being used, but test results are not yet available. This is, therefore, an interim statement and not a completed case history.

MANUFACTURERS of consumer goods or services usually determine, on grounds more or less *a priori*, the amount of money they believe they can afford to spend on advertising. The decision then facing the advertiser is how to maximize the effect of his advertising; given a fixed sum of money available, what is the most advantageous method of using it?

The criticality of this decision evidently varies from industry to industry, but in the airline case (and, we believe, in other transport industries) not spending more money on advertising than is required to fill the available capacity is of great importance.

For example, let us suppose the case of a flight undertaken daily in the evening from *A* to *B*, primarily for positioning purposes, in order to be able to fly from *B* to *A* the next day. The costings for the latter flight, *B* to *A*, will have already accounted for the need to position and, in order to fill the evening positioning flight at a commercially unattractive time, it is decided to create a special low fare, which will cover direct operating costs and make the positioning flight profitable. A programme of advertising is decided on to publicize the special low evening fare. Now if the aircraft operates at a load factor far below the break-even point, the effect of advertising expenditure will be to increase the loss; if, however, the advertising expenditure is highly successful, enough traffic may be stimulated to create a demand for an extra service, which of course destroys the basis on which the whole operation was predicated. We may leave out of account for this purpose errors in pricing policy, since in

† Paper read to the Operational Research Society, 30 December, 1959.

effect there will be a tendency to overprice and to compensate for this "playing safe" by advertising. Thus it is important to gauge exactly what level of expenditure on advertising is justified.

The advertiser, in making this decision, is confronted with two sets of choices: first, choices between media, involving inter-media comparisons (e.g. whether to spend so much on television, so much in the press, a lesser amount on posters, and so on); and secondly, choices within media (e.g. which newspapers to use and at what frequency of use, and so on). We are here concerned with the second case, namely, to determine which of a group of newspapers should be used and what size of advertisements should be used in order to get the largest possible effect for a given expenditure.

Empirical evidence of the effect of different sizes of advertisement is slender and, since we have it in mind to explore even less well-charted fields, we decided to examine the effect of different assumptions about the way in which advertising works, rather than wait until experimental evidence became available. Like other forms of economic investigation, it is often very expensive and laborious to confirm hypotheses in the field, and we felt it more profitable to build a model, recognizing its axiomatic character, and to judge its validity *ex post facto*.

Two further caveats must be entered. First, we are not concerned here with the contents of an advertisement nor with actual response to an advertisement in the shape of sales or coupon replies: we have not attempted to relate at this stage the seeing of an advertisement to the effect it scores. Secondly, in the case described in more detail below, we are concerned with a number of advertisements in a number of publications, but with the significant condition that each publication carries the advertisement just once. This happens to be a type of campaign which occurs quite frequently in our particular field.

PROBLEM FORMULATION

When we came to specify the problem which we had set ourselves more precisely, we realized that there were two different, but related, problems to be solved. The first of these was to maximize the *coverage* provided by an advertising schedule of given cost. Coverage is defined as the proportion of the population seeing at least one advertisement. The second problem was to maximize total impacts. By *impacts* we mean the number of times an advertisement is seen. This differs from coverage in that a person who sees n advertisements counts only 1 towards coverage, but n towards the total impacts. We decided to attempt to solve both problems. The first step which we took was to inspect the data which were available, and the assumptions which we could make, to formulate functional expressions for these factors.

The readerships of the leading daily and Sunday newspapers and of the leading magazines in Great Britain are available as a result of surveys carried out regularly by the Institute of Practitioners in Advertising[2]. This survey also gives what are known as "duplication tables". The duplication between news-paper A and magazine B, for example, is the number of people who read both A and B. It is possible to obtain information on higher order "duplications" such as the number of people who read all of any group of four of the publications included in the survey.

Secondly, and obviously, comprehensive cost figures for different sizes of advertisements in different periodicals are available from the publishers.

In addition to the basic factual information provided by these surveys, it was necessary to make certain assumptions regarding the attention value of advertisements. At the time we began this project the best attested relationship in our view appeared to be the square-root rule proposed initially by London Press Exchange Ltd. This says that an advertisement in any periodical which occupies a proportion p of a page is seen by a proportion $\sqrt{p}$ of the readers of that page. In any periodical, however, a whole page is not necessarily seen by all readers. However, for our purposes, we assumed initially that this would be so. In later work we may alter this assumption if it seems necessary.

One further assumption had to be made. Suppose that the attention value of a whole page in publication A_1 was a_1. Then the square-root rule says that the attention value of an advertisement occupying a proportion p_1 of a page in A_1 would be $a_1\sqrt{p_1}$. Similarly, for a publication A_2 with advertisement size p_2, the attention value would be $a_2\sqrt{p_2}$. But A_1 and A_2 duplicate, and the duplicated readership of A_1 and A_2 is, say, a_{12}. The question to be resolved is the proportion of the population who see both an advertisement of size p_1 in A_1 and p_2 in A_2. We assumed that there would be no predisposition for someone who had seen the advertisement in A_1 to see it also in A_2 or not to see it in A_2, and that the answer to this question would be

$$a_{12}\sqrt{p_1}\sqrt{p_2}.$$

This is the simplest assumption to make. If, however, it were proved that a person who reads both A_1 and A_2, and who had seen an advertisement in A_1, was more or less likely to see an advertisement in A_2 than another reader of both who had not seen an advertisement in A_2, then the answer would take some other form, say $ra_{12}\sqrt{p_1}\sqrt{p_2}$, where r is a correlation coefficient of some type. Evidence in support of any hypothesis is very sparse.

However, by considering the various combinations of publications which are possible, these hypotheses enabled us to write down a general expression for the proportion of the population (e.g. all adults, or all housewives, or all AB social group—the a's being chosen accordingly) under consideration seeing j advertisements, that is receiving j impacts given that advertisements have appeared in k publications. This expression is

$$I_j = \sum_{r=j}^{k} (-1)^{r+j}\binom{r}{j} H_r, \tag{1}$$

115

where I_j is the proportion of the population receiving j impacts and

$$H_r = \sum_{u_r > u_{r-1}} \sum_{u_{r-1} > u_{r-2}} \cdots \sum_{u_1 = 1}^{k} a_{u_1 u_2 \cdots u_r} z_{u_1} z_{u_2} \cdots z_{u_r}$$

with $z_i = \sqrt{p_i}$.

For two publications, for example, one has (introducing I_0 also, with obvious meaning):

No. of advertisements seen (x)	Proportion of people seeing x advertisements	Symbol
0 advertisements	$1 - a_1 z_1 - a_2 z_2 + a_{12} z_1 z_2$	I_0
1 advertisement	$a_1 z_1 + a_2 z_2 - 2 a_{12} z_1 z_2$	I_1
2 advertisements	$a_{12} z_1 z_2$	I_2

It is convenient to introduce identity labels w_j to attach to the expression for j impacts. Then, if the number of people receiving j impacts is denoted by I_j, one can define an expression E, which will be called the *effectiveness index*, thus

$$E = w_0 I_0 + w_1 I_1 + \ldots + w_k I_k.$$

The interpretation to be put on the effectiveness index E varies according to the values chosen for the w_j. For example, if $w_0 = 0$ and $w_i = 1$ for $i = 1, 2, \ldots, k$, then it is equal to the coverage; that is, it is a measure of the proportion of the population seeing at least one advertisement. If, however, w_j were put equal to j, where j takes the values $0, 1, 2, \ldots, k$, etc., then the effectiveness index would become exactly equivalent to the mean number of impacts.

In the work at present being described, we were interested in both factors: the mean number of impacts per person, denoted by $F(z_1, z_2, \ldots, z_k)$, and the coverage, denoted by $G(z_1, z_2, \ldots, z_k)$. Functional expressions for these can be derived without difficulty by using the quantities H_r. In fact,

$$F(z_1, z_2, \ldots, z_k) = H_1 = \sum_{i=1}^{k} a_i z_i \tag{2}$$

and

$$G(z_1, z_2, \ldots, z_k) = \sum_{j=1}^{k} (-1)^{j-1} H_j. \tag{3}$$

The problems which we had to consider, therefore, were special cases of one general problem. This was to maximize the effectiveness index, given the values of the w_j subject to a number of conditions on the values of the z's. As each z is a proportion, it is clear that all z's must lie between zero and unity. Furthermore, as the total sum of money available for advertising purposes is usually limited to, say, £c, and as the costs of full-page advertisements are known to be £c_1, £c_2, ... and so on, there is a cost condition on the z's also.

The conditions may be summarized thus:

Nature of Restriction	Mathematical Expression
Proportionality of z's (no advertisement is less than zero or more than unity as proportion of a page)	$0 \leqslant z_i \leqslant 1 \ (i = 1, 2, ..., k)$
Cost (the total sum spent must equal £c)	$\sum_{i=1}^{k} c_i z_i^2 = c$
(The problem is non-trivial)	$\sum_{i=1}^{k} c_i \geqslant c.$

The method of solution of problems of this type is well established and need not be described. A good, short account is given by Saaty[1]. The difficulty of obtaining solutions in particular cases depends upon *the exact form of the function E to be maximized.*

THE MAXIMIZATION OF IMPACTS

The problem can be solved in fairly simple algebraic terms when the function E being maximized is, in fact, F, the mean number of impacts. In this case the solution is given by carrying out the iterative calculations outlined below.

Solution of impacts maximization problem:

(1) Compute

$$x_i = (ca_i^2/c_i^2)\left\{\sum_{i=1}^{k} (a_i^2/c_i)\right\}^{-1} \quad (i = 1, z, ..., k).$$

(2) Arrange x_i in ascending order of magnitude and re-label as x_i (re-label z_i correspondingly).

(3) If no $\qquad x_i \geqslant 1$, then $z_i^2 = x_i$;

If $\qquad\qquad x_i < 1$ for $i = 1, 2, ..., (k-a)$,

$\qquad\qquad\qquad x_i \geqslant 1$ for $i = (k-a+1), ..., k.$

Then $\qquad\qquad z_i^2 = 1$ for $i = (k-a+1), ..., k,$

and compute

$$u_i = \left(c - \sum_{i=k-a+1}^{k} c_i\right)(a_i^2/c_i^2)\left\{\sum_{i=1}^{k-a} (a_i^2/c_i)\right\}^{-1} \quad \{i = 1, 2, ..., (k-a)\}.$$

(4) Go back to (2), operating on u_i as formerly on x_i.

The meaning of this result is that to maximize impacts when advertising in a number of publications, advertising space should be bought in them in inverse proportion to the square of the cost per thousand readers, except that the maximum permissible size of advertisement in any one publication is a whole page.

117

THE MAXIMIZATION OF COVERAGE

When the function to be maximized is the coverage G, however, the problem cannot be solved in simple algebraic terms except in the case $k = 2$, that is, when only two publications are involved. Furthermore, the number of terms in the expression for G is $2^k - 1$, and in practical cases, when 10 or more publications may be under consideration, the sheer size of the equations (4) becomes alarming. Even the evaluation of G in such cases would be a lengthy process.

However, an approximation to G was suggested by an examination of IPA data. This was to write $a_{ij} = a_i a_j$, $a_{ijl} = a_i a_j a_l$, and so on. We plotted

$$x_{ij} = a_{ij} - a_i a_j,$$

$$x_{ijl} = a_{ijl} - a_i a_j a_l,$$

for the same group of 15 periodicals mentioned above, and obtained histograms which suggested that *in the case of publications suitable for this type of advertising* we could write

$$a_{ijl \ldots p} \sim a_i a_j \ldots a_p,$$

and it is apparent that in this case,

$$G \sim \left\{ 1 - \prod_{i=1}^{k} (1 - a_i z_i) \right\}. \tag{4}$$

This convenient-looking expression is, in fact, useful for calculating the coverage obtained, given values for the z_i. But it is difficult to use in determining what the optimal z_i are.

It seemed necessary, therefore, to find some other form of approximation—albeit cruder—to the coverage expression which could be used in practical applications. The obvious course of action was suggested by making the first approximation rather more general. Further examination of IPA figures showed that if

$$\bar{a} = \frac{1}{k} \sum_{r=1}^{k} a_r = a, \quad \text{say,}$$

in the case of 15 periodicals considered by us as most suitable for a certain campaign, then

$$\bar{a}_{..} = \frac{1}{k(k-1)} \sum_{j=i+1}^{k} \sum_{i=1}^{k} a_{ij} \sim a^2,$$

$$\bar{a}_{...} = \frac{1}{k(k-1)(k-2)} \sum_{(ij+1)} \sum_{j=i+1}^{k} \sum_{i=1}^{k} a_{ijl} \sim a^3.$$

In fact, we found that
$$\bar{a} - a^2 = 0 \cdot 0002,$$

$$\bar{a} - a^3 = -0 \cdot 0002.$$

We supposed, on the basis of this evidence, that $\bar{a}_n \sim a^n$ for all $n = 1, 2, ..., k$, so long as k was reasonably large (say $k \geqslant 10$). Consequently, if for the sake of seeing where it would lead, we assumed that the advertisements in the various publications were chosen to have equal attention values z, then the coverage would be, roughly,

$$G^* = \{1 - (1 - az)^k\}. \tag{6}$$

Remembering that what was desired was to reduce the number of terms to be handled in the coverage expression, we considered the quality of approximation to G^* given by taking the sum of terms up to and including those of order r in (az), by examining the *relative difference*

$$G_r^*/G^*$$

where
$$G_r^* = \sum_{i=r+1}^{k} (-1)^{i-1} \binom{k}{i} a^i. \tag{7}$$

This relative difference was tabulated for various values of a, z, k and r, and the results showed that in the region of values of a, z and k of interest to us, the proportionate error would not exceed 10 per cent for $r = 3$. In other words, a reasonably satisfactory approximation could be obtained to the coverage expression by truncating it after third-order terms in the z's.

We realized that this was a far from rigorous procedure, and as we have described it, it represents a written equivalent to thinking aloud. But such approximate analyses are very useful in operational research and, according to Polya, are indispensable in most mathematical work.

Thus we decided that we should consider the approximate form

$$G' = H_1 - H_2 + H_3.$$

Even so, G' would be a very large expression, and still too awkward to allow the equations (4) to (7) to be solved in simple algebraic terms. An iterative type of calculation, an extension of Newton's method for finding the zeros of functions by means of successive approximations, was employed. This method also is described by Saaty[1].

The calculation was programmed for an IBM 650 computer, and a number of optimizations were carried out, using as the initial trial solution in every case the solution to the corresponding impacts maximization problem. We noticed at once that the differences between the initial and final solutions were in many cases very small. In the course of a series of 12 optimizations, each involving 10 publications, only 1 in 4 of final values of z's differed from the initial values by a factor of more than 5 per cent. This made us wonder whether by merely solving the fairly easy impacts problem we could not obtain, almost always, a satisfactory, though not necessarily absolutely optimal, solution to the coverage problem.

It seemed desirable to establish the conditions under which the solutions to the two problems would, in fact, be identical, and after a little time we managed to prove the following theorem:

Theorem. The set of values z_i' $(i = 1, 2, ..., k)$ which maximize

$$\sum_{i=1}^{k} a_i z_i$$

subject to the conditions $\quad \sum_{i=1}^{k} c_i z_i^2 = C$

and $\qquad\qquad\qquad 0 \leqslant z_i \leqslant 1 \quad (i = 1, 2, ..., k),$

also maximizes $\qquad\qquad G = \sum_{r=1}^{k} (-1)^{r-1} H_r$

subject to these conditions if

(i) $\qquad\qquad a_{u_1 u_2 \, ... \, u_j} = \prod_{r=1}^{j} a_{u_r} \quad (j = 1, 2, ..., k),$

and if

(ii) $\qquad\qquad (a_i^2 / c_i) = \lambda \qquad (i = 1, 2, ..., k),$

where λ is some constant.

It had been demonstrated previously that to secure the maximum number of impacts, advertising space should be bought in inverse proportion to the square of the cost per thousand readers of each publication. As, however, the solutions to the coverage and impacts maximization problems are identical under the conditions of the above theorem, we had in fact verified the rule:

Rule. When, for any group of publications,

(i) $\qquad\qquad a_{u_1 u_2 \cdots u_j} = \prod_{r=1}^{j} a_{u_r} \quad (j = 1, 2, ..., k),$

and if

(ii) $\qquad\qquad (a_i^2 / c_i) = \lambda \qquad (i = 1, 2, ..., k).$

The optimum schedule is obtained by both as regards coverage and impacts by buying space in inverse proportion to the square of the cost per thousand for each publication, subject to the qualification that no advertisement should occupy more than one whole page.

We had already shown that the first condition for the theorem to be valid was satisfied, approximately, by most publications of interest to us. The next step was to see how well the second condition was satisfied. The values for

15 publications are given below, ranked in ascending order:

i	(a_i^2/c_i)	i	(a_i^2/c_i)
1	0·01	9	0·03
2	0·01	10	0·03
3	0·01	11	0·03
4	0·02	12	0·04
5	0·02	13	0·05
6	0·02	14	0·11
7	0·02	15	0·14
8	0·02		

The variation appeared somewhat large, and we examined the "tail" values from 0·04 upwards to see if these publications numbers 12–15 were in any sense different in type from the others. It would be impolitic to divulge the identities of these publications, or to enable them to be identified. It must suffice to say that numbers 14 and 15 were high-cost, high-prestige publications, whereas numbers 12 and 13 were different in make-up to the other publications in having more, but smaller, pages.

Our experience has been that variability such as that existing among the (a^2/c) values for periodicals 1–11 is not too great to prevent the application of the theorem, and even when publications with larger values, such as numbers 12 and 13, were included in iterative calculations, the initial and final answers rarely differed by much.

Consequently, the procedure which we have adopted to determine accurately the allocation of money to maximize impacts, and determine approximately but quickly the allocation to maximize coverage, is as follows. First, if the information is not already available, we check that the conditions of the theorem are satisfied, at least to a reasonable approximation. Secondly, we obtain the values $(z_1^0, z_2^0, ..., z_k^0)$ which maximize impacts. Finally, we calculate the corresponding (approximately maximal) coverage

$$G = \left\{ 1 - \prod_{i=1}^{k} (1 - a_i z_i^0) \right\}.$$

This method, which is suitable for our use, is not of course so in general, as the necessary conditions are not always satisfactorily met.

DISCUSSION AND CONCLUSIONS

The optimization procedure which we have developed, it is plain, does not in general produce an advertising schedule which maximizes coverage. The resulting schedule will, within the limits of our assumptions, produce maximum total impacts and, probably, a high level of coverage. Generally speaking, total impacts and coverage cannot be simultaneously maximized for a fixed cost.

The difficulties in solving some of these problems are computational rather than mathematical, and our method has been to develop approximate working rules. To do this we have not found it necessary to use any out-of-the-way methods. For this reason, mathematical derivations have been deliberately omitted from this paper. It is hoped at a later date, when some results of applying these methods are to hand (and practical applications are being made now), to publish a more detailed account, which will for completeness include mathematical proofs where required.

We think it proper to mention what we propose to do at the next stage of our investigations. First, we propose to take into account the effect of a series of advertisements in one or more publications; this will display, we intend, the effect of decay and rejuvenation throughout a series of advertisements. Secondly, we propose to carry out a similar investigation for television advertising and to combine both into an inter-media comparison where both the press and television are used simultaneously. Thirdly, we hope to investigate the effect of varying intervals between advertisement appearances, both within one medium and in the inter-media situation. We are, however, still in the contemplatory stage at the moment.

ACKNOWLEDGEMENTS

It is impossible to mention individually the many members of the advertising profession who have helped us with their comments (but who are not responsible for our conclusions). We are, however, particularly indebted to the Media Department of Colman, Prentis & Varley Ltd. and to the Research and Statistics Department of Associated Newspapers Ltd. for showing us their work in this field.

We wish to thank the Board of British European Airways for permission to publish this paper.

REFERENCES

[1] T. L. SAATY, *Mathematical Methods of Operations Research*, McGraw-Hill (1959).
[2] INSTITUTE OF PRACTITIONERS IN ADVERTISING, National Readership Survey, The Institute (1958).

Decision Rules for Media Scheduling: Static Campaigns

ALEC M. LEE

INTRODUCTION

THIS paper is the first of three concerned with the problem of constructing advertising media schedules which are, in some sense, optimal. The research which the series embodies originated in a problem posed to the author by A. J. Burkart, and consists of both an expansion and a number of extensions to the studies described in an earlier paper.[1] The problem was to devise decision rules which Burkart could use in planning media schedules for his company's advertising campaigns. The objective was practical. Unfortunately the theoretical means of attaining it did not seem to exist, and had to be devised. This proved difficult for two reasons: the irrelevance of most advertising research for our purpose, and its inconsistency.[2] Thus the theory which was built up to serve our immediate practical purpose rests upon postulates which are, in part, conjectural. Nevertheless, many of the decision rules based upon this theory are being put to use.

This paper begins with a statement of the media scheduling problem. It then presents an advertising model and from it derives decision rules applicable to static campaigns, i.e. those intended to evoke a maximum response, the time of attainment being unimportant. The second paper will be concerned with dynamic campaigns, e.g. those in which the rate of generation of response over a specified time period is paramount. The third and final paper will be in two parts. The first will be devoted to the problem of advertising strategy; the second will be a discussion of some unresolved problems.

Once more: the objective of this research was strictly practical. There is nothing so practical as a theory.

THE PROBLEM

An advertising campaign is usually carried out with one or other of two objectives: to persuade some portion of the population to take some definite course of action, or to create and maintain an idea or an attitude in their minds. Whatever the objective may be, the essence of advertising is that a message must be conveyed from the advertiser to some class of people whom we call the target population. The message must be expressed in coded form; words, pictures, ideograms and so on. The method of expression is called the format. The message, in whatever format, needs a carrier—that is a medium through which it can be transmitted to the target group. This medium might be the press (including magazines), television, hoardings or any one of many other means of mass communication. We shall confine ourselves for the moment to press media.

An advertiser has to remember that whatever medium or group of media he chooses to carry his message will be shared by other advertisers whose messages are different and perhaps competitive. His message therefore has not only to be clear, but must be transmitted strongly if it is to be perceived. The strength necessary to get his message across will of course be influenced by the "set", in the psychological sense, of the target population.[3] In some circumstances this could make the advertiser's task easier. In this paper, it is assumed that the members of the target population do not have any set which predisposes them to receive an advertiser's message, and that in order to transmit it to them he must choose his media carefully, put his message in an effective format and transmit it with sufficient strength to ensure an adequate degree of reception. Nothing less will do.

The specification of the target population will not concern us. We shall assume that, as a result of motivational studies, market surveys and economic analyses, the advertiser has decided what he wants to say and whom he must say it to. The advertiser has two residual tasks: the encoding of his message into an effective format[4] and the specification of a media schedule. A media schedule defines the media in which advertisements are to appear, the size and frequency of repetition of advertisements in each medium and the dates on which they are to appear. The format and the media schedule between them will largely determine how many of the target population receive the advertiser's message, and how often they receive it. We shall not be much concerned with the design of formats; this is an art which is still in an early stage of translation into a science.[5] Its importance is recognized nevertheless, and although no rules will be given for improving the effectiveness of formats, a measure of their effectiveness will be discussed.

The characteristics of media will be considered in relation to the reception of messages they provide in the target group. Each medium possesses a readership, which is defined as the average proportion of people in the population who see each issue. The readership of a medium M_i can be analysed into components such as "the readership of M_i in population sub-group P_j", and can therefore be defined in relation to various target populations. We shall denote the readership of one newspaper or magazine, M_i, in our specified target population by a_i. In the case of Great Britain, the National Readership Survey of the Institute of Practitioners in Advertising (IPA) provides quarterly estimates of the a_i for a large range of media M_i. Readership in the IPA sense is proportional to readership as defined here.[6] Similar data are available in Canada, U.S.A. and France,[7] though not quite in so convenient a form.

The advertiser has usually a large choice of media, which have different readerships in the target population, and different costs. This wide range of available media can be quickly reduced to manageable proportions by considering the readership of each medium in the target group in relation to the cost of a whole-page advertisement. If the actual number of people (or family units, or automobile owners, or whatever unit the population is counted in) is known to be N for the target group, and a_i is the readership of the medium M_i in this group, then if C_i is the cost of a whole-page advertisement in M_i, the cost per potential 1000 readers for M_i is

$$\frac{C_i}{Na_i} \times 1000.$$

Media with high values of this criterion[8] can often automatically be excluded from the schedule. But the selection of appropriate media does not have only an economic basis. To some extent it is also intuitive; all media possess individual qualities of character and prestige. One can think that all media generate random noise which is more likely to obscure some messages than others. And in the crude, real world there may, in Burkart's phrase, be "secular" reasons, or subjective reasons or both, why some of the favourable media should be eliminated and others re-introduced.[9] In any event the result of these non-quantitative judgements is that the range of possible media is defined. We shall assume that it comprises k newspapers and magazines; but we may not undertake, in the last analysis, to use them all.

As soon as this is done, the potential audience is reduced from all the members of the target population to those who belong to the readership of at least one of the k feasible media. The potential audience provided by these media is not the sum of their readerships, for some of them may be read by the same people.[10] If for convenience we define the proportion of people in the target population who are included in the readerships of all of the r media M_{u1}, M_{u2}, M_{ur} by $a_{u1u2...ur}$ then the potential audience is a proportion of the target which will be denoted by A:

$$A = \sum_{j=1}^{k} (-1)^{j-1} H_j$$

where

$$H_j = \sum_{ur>ur-1} \sum_{ur-1>ur-2} \cdots \sum_{ui=1}^{k} a_{u1u2...ur}.$$

For two media, for example, this formula gives $A = a_1 + a_2 - a_{12}$.

Whether any member of the potential audience will respond to the advertising depends upon whether or not he sees an advertisement, how often he sees it and at what intervals of time. It is primarily the format of the advertisement which determines its attention value.[11] The merits of position, left-hand page or right-hand page, bleed and so on are all questionable. We shall dismiss them as being either economically unjustifiable or factors over which in practice one has no control. We shall stipulate the importance of colour, illustrations and simplicity, but the aspect of format which shall concern us most is size. To isolate this, suppose that all messages consisted of four nonsense syllables,[12] and all formats consisted of these syllables arranged vertically and enclosed in a rectangular border, the whole being printed in black or white. Then a single insertion of this advertisement in one magazine would be seen by more readers of that magazine if it occupied a whole page than if it occupied a half page.[13] The implication of this for a mathematical theory is that if we define the size of an advertisement as the proportion of a whole page which it occupies and denote this by p, the proportion of the readers of the page who will see the advertisement is some function of p which we shall signify by $z = f(p)$.

Furthermore, if the same "neutral" advertisement that we have postulated were repeated in subsequent issues of the same magazine, the proportion of the readership who had seen at least one advertisement would be increased.[14]

In general then, if all formats and messages were equally appealing, which we will presently assume, the proportion of the potential audience reached by the advertiser would be determined by the size and frequency of his advertisements.

The potential audience would contain many people who would be capable of seeing the campaign advertisements several times due to their readership of several publications. In point of fact, the proportion of the target population who would have exactly j "opportunities to see"[15] would be

$$S_j = \sum_{r=j}^{K} (-1)^{r+j} \binom{r}{j} H_r.$$

Not all of these opportunities to see might be realized, due to inadequate size and frequency. But by choosing size and frequency carefully the number of "impacts" actually scored on the potential audience could be fixed at some desired level. This is important as there is a tendency for response to be higher when impacts are higher.

The ultimate[16] proportion of a target population who have seen—or been reached by—at least one advertisement of a campaign is called the "ultimate coverage" or "reach" of the campaign whereas the average number of advertisements seen by each member of a target population is called the "ultimate impact" of the campaign. These are the measures of dispersion and intensity respectively. The magnitudes of ultimate coverage and ultimate impact are not affected by the times at which the advertisements of a campaign appear.

The dates at which advertisements appear do, however, affect the time taken for ultimate coverage and ultimate impact to be achieved. In this respect other characteristics of the media are important. When an issue of a publication appears, the people who see it do not all do so at the same time. Some see it on the day of issue, some on the second day, others on the third and so on. As time passes, the number of people who have seen it tends to the readership. In other words, the readership growth curve is asymptotic and in the case of some magazines a long period elapses before the limit is closely approached. Thus the coverage and impact of a campaign may take some time to reach their ultimate values.[17]

Furthermore, as soon as a number of people have seen an advertisement they begin to forget it.[18] When this effect is combined with the asymptotic growth characteristic of readership, it is clear that at any point in time the target population consists of three classes of people:

(1) those who have not yet seen the advertisement,
(2) those who have seen it but have forgotten it,
(3) those who have seen it and recall it.

Thus in addition to coverage and impact we may define one further important factor: the awareness, which is the third of the above groups.

A media schedule therefore produces a certain ultimate coverage of, and ultimate impact in, the target population and a pattern of awareness varying with time. The advertiser's problem is to determine which media he should use to transmit his message, what size the advertisement should be in each medium, how often it should be repeated and on what dates. To decide which of the innumerable possible schedules he should select, the advertiser needs a criterion of optimality. And this must depend upon the type of advertising campaign which he intends to mount. The remainder of this paper is devoted to static campaigns.

STATIC CAMPAIGNS

Static advertising campaigns are not carried out to generate awareness in a certain target group. The objective is to stimulate active responses from the members of the target group. We shall ignore the dynamics of awareness and rate of change of audience in this type of campaign. Impact and coverage are all that is required to define the direct effect on the target group of a campaign based upon a specified media schedule. They may be used to determine the optimal media schedule for a campaign if the objectives of the campaign, specified in terms of required values of these factors, are known. A schedule which satisfied these requirements at least cost would be optimal.

The paramount problem, however, is then to determine the desirable values of these factors. They could be chosen arbitrarily. If this were done, the objectives might be mutually inconsistent. This possibility will be examined later. It would, however, be better to relate these factors to, or supplant them by, a response function. Then if the total sum of money available for buying space were limited, the optimization to be carried out would be to maximize response for a given cost. This is at first sight very difficult because in the real world there are no "neutral" formats.

A realistic treatment of response ought to account for the effects of different formats. We may in fact conceive of a relationship between response and a parameter related to the format and content of advertisements, which we call their efficiency. One can imagine that an approximation to this relationship might be obtained by means of an elaborate, controlled series of pre-tests of different advertisements, or by a comprehensive statistical analysis of all such pre-tests ever carried out in, say, the United Kingdom, but if such has been done at all, the results are not available. Indeed, relatively little that can be expressed mathematically appears to be known about the effectiveness of a format.[19] This implies that all the endeavour invested in producing an optimal media schedule might be nullified by a catastrophically bad format, or increased in value by a good one. Pre-testing of advertisements is not, therefore, a waste of money if the campaign is sufficiently big to warrant the cost.

We shall, therefore, at first beg the question by excluding format from consideration. We can justify this expedient, at least temporarily, by conjecturing that the structure of the response function is

$$R = Q \sum_{r=1}^{n_1+n_2+...+n_k} W_r I_r,$$

where R is the response as a proportion of the target population; Q is an as yet undefined measure of effectiveness of the format, which can range from zero to unity; W_r is a weighting factor which measures the proportionate response from those people who have received r impacts and who form a proportion I_r of the target population. The validity of this conjecture will be discussed in the sequel.

The implication of this model is that as $\Sigma W_r I_r$ cannot exceed unity, Q, the format criterion, is the maximum response that can be obtained, and further that no amount of repetition or size can offset the disadvantage of a bad format. But as $\Sigma W_r I_r$ can vanish, a poorly planned media schedule can fail to secure an advantage from a good one.

MATHEMATICAL FORMULATIONS

In order to formulate mathematical expressions we have to make a number of assumptions. The first of these is that the size and attention value of an advertisement are related by the square root rule:

(1) An advertisement of size $p = z^2$ in any publication is seen by a proportion z of the readers of that publication.

This assumption is based upon some experimental work carried out by London Press Exchange and implies that an advertisement of size 1, that is a whole page, is seen by every reader of a publication.[20]

(2) The proportion of the target population who read both media M_i and M_j, a_{ij} say, is the product of the proportions a_i and a_j who read M_i and M_j respectively, i.e. $a_{ij} = a_i a_j$.

This assumption is an approximation to the truth, which may not always be valid. But in much press and magazine advertising, in Great Britain at least, it is a good enough approximation, as the IPA data show.[21]

The third assumption says that

(3) The chance that a reader will see an advertisement in M_i is independent of whether or not he has seen an advertisement with the same format and content in M_i previously or in another medium M_j.

This assumption requires discussion. It would be untrue if a reader could deliberately avoid seeing an advertisement which he had previously seen. He could only do this by ceasing to look at any advertisements at all. Otherwise to avoid it he would have to know where it would appear, which is unlikely.[22]

A series of advertisements of size $p = z^2$ in any medium M, appearing one at a time in each of n issues, will be called a multiple sequence of dimension (z^2, n). The ultimate coverage of such a multiple sequence is defined as the expected proportion of persons in the target population who will see at least one advertisement of the series, and is denoted by $G(z, n)$. A campaign consisting of k multiple sequences in k media $M_1, M_2, ..., M_k$ where the dimension of the sequence in M_i is (z_i, n_i), $i = 1, z, ..., k$, will generate an ultimate impact $F(z_i, n_i; k)$ and an ultimate coverage $G(z_i, n_i; k)$.

IMPACT AND COVERAGE

Now, if an insertion of size $p_i = z_i^2$ is made the basis of a sequence of n_i repetitions in medium M_i and the readership of M_i is a proportion a_i of the target population, then

(1) the ultimate impact of one insertion in M_i is $a_i z_i$,

(2) the ultimate coverage of one insertion in M_i is $a_i z_i$,

(3) the cost of one insertion in M_i is $C_i z_i^2$, where C_i is the cost of a whole page.

Furthermore,

(4) the ultimate impact of the sequence in M_i is $n_i a_i z_i$,

(5) the ultimate coverage of the sequence in M_i is

$$a_i[1 - (1 - z_i)^{n_i}],$$

(6) the cost of the sequence in M_i is $n_i C_i z_i^2$.

The third basic assumption permits us to derive from these results:

$$F(z_i, n_i; k) = \sum_{i=1}^{k} n_i a_i z_i,$$

$$G(z_i, n_i; k) = 1 - \prod_{i=1}^{k} \{1 - a_i[1 - (1 - z_i)^{n_i}]\},$$

$$C(z_i, n_i; k) = \sum_{i=1}^{k} n_i C_i z_i^2.$$

RESPONSE

The proportion of people in the target population who will see exactly r advertisements in a multiple sequence $(z_i, n_i; k)$ is the coefficient of s^r in the expansion in powers of s of:

$$\prod_{i=1}^{k} \{(1-a_i)+a_i[1-(1-s)z_i]^{n_i}\}.$$

The coefficient of s^r will be denoted by $I_r(z_i, n_i; k)$.
The structure of the response function is:

$$R(z_i, n_i; k) = Q \sum_{r=0}^{m} W_r I_r(z_i, n_i; k)$$

where
$$m = \sum_{i=1}^{k} n_i.$$

It is noteworthy that if $W_r = r$, the right-hand side becomes $Q.F(z_i, n_i; k)$. If however $W_0 = 0$ and $W_r = 1$ for $r = 1, 2, 3, ..., m$ then it becomes $Q.G(z_i, n_i; k)$. For the response function, however, we shall postulate that:

(4) The chance that a person capable of response to a campaign will respond after having received r impacts is W_r where

$$W_r = (1-P^r)$$

where P is some parameter to be determined.[23]
The response to the campaign is therefore:

$$R(z_i, n_i; k) = Q \sum_{r=0}^{m} (1-P^r) I_r(z_i, n_i; k).$$

This can be written more explicitly.

First of all,
$$\sum_{i=0}^{m} I_r(z_i, n_i; k) = 1$$

by definition. And secondly,

$$\sum_{i=0}^{n} P^r I_r$$

is the generating function for I_r with s replaced by P so that

$$\frac{1}{Q} R(z_i, n_i; k) = 1 - \prod_{i=1}^{k} \{(1-a_i)+a_i[1-(1-P)z_i]^{n_i}\},$$

or
$$= 1 - \prod_{i=1}^{k} \{1 - a_i[1-\{1-(1-P)z_i\}]^{n_i}\}.$$

This expression is comparatively compact and is similar in form to the expression previously derived for coverage, namely

$$G(z_i, n_i; k) = 1 - \prod_{i=1}^{k} \{1 - a_i[1-(1-z_i)^{n_i}]\},$$

but with z_i in the latter replaced by $(1-P)z_i$ in the former, and Q appearing as a scale factor. The significance of this result is that coverage and response can be given similar mathematical treatments.

OPTIMIZATION PROBLEMS[24]

One of the perennial problems in media scheduling is to decide whether to plan for maximum impact or maximum coverage. The search for optimal media schedules will begin, therefore, with the study of two relatively simple problems.

The first of these, which is called the Impact Maximization Problem, may be stated as follows: Let $F(z_i, n_i; k)$ be the average impact on the target population of r_i repetitions of an advertisement of size $p_i = z_i^2$ in the K media M_i ($i = 1, 2, ..., K$), and H be the total cost. Find the values of n_i and z_i which maximize impact for this cost.

The second, the Coverage Maximization Problem, is, if $G(z_i, n_i; k)$ is the coverage of the target population achieved by r_i repetitions of an advertisement of size $p_i = z_i^2$ in the k media M_i ($i = 1, 2, ..., k$), to maximize coverage subject to the cost equalling H.

We shall then consider whether it is possible:
(1) to maximize impact and coverage simultaneously,
(2) to maximize coverage subject to the condition that the mean impact will not be less than I.

THE IMPACT MAXIMIZATION PROBLEM

Suppose that a media schedule consists of k multiple sequences of advertisements to which corresponds the ultimate impact $F(z_i, n_i; k)$. The money available is H so that the cost restriction on the campaign is represented by $C(z_i, n_i; k) - H = 0$. The advertisement sizes are subject to the restrictions

$$0 \leqslant z_i \leqslant 1 \quad (i = 1, 2, ..., k).$$

To maximize $F(z_i, n_i; k)$ subject to these restrictions, the method of undetermined multipliers is used.[25] The maximization is achieved with the values of z_i and n_i which satisfy ($4k + 1$) equations:

$$n_i a_i + 2\lambda n_i C_i z_i + 2\psi_i z_i = 0 \quad (i = 1, 2, ..., k), \tag{1.1}$$

$$a_i z_i + \lambda C_i z_i^2 = 0 \quad (i = 1, 2, ..., k), \tag{1.2}$$

$$\psi_i v_i = 0 \quad (i = 1, 2, ..., k), \tag{1.3}$$

$$z_i^2 + v_i^2 - 1 = 0 \quad (i = 1, 2, ..., k), \tag{1.4}$$

$$\sum_{i=1}^{k} n_i C_i z_i^2 - H = 0, \tag{1.5}$$

where $\lambda, \psi_1, \psi_2, ..., \psi_k$ are undetermined multipliers,

$v_1, v_2, ..., v_k$ are slack (dummy) variables.

As a general rule the money available, H, would not suffice to buy one whole page in every medium, but would be large enough to do so in at least one. Assume therefore that $v_i = 0$ and therefore $z_i = 1$ for $i = 1, 2, ..., h$; and that $v_i \neq 0$, and therefore $\psi_i = 0$, for $i = h+1, ..., k$. Then the equations clearly imply that for $i = h+1, ..., k$, $n_i = 0$, $z_i = 0$. In other words, buy whole pages where possible. The next question is: in which media? We can suppose without loss of generality that the answer will be: in media $M_1, M_2, ..., M_f$. So $n_i \neq 0$ for $i = 1, 2, ..., f$ and $n_i = 0$ for $i = f+1, f+2, ..., h$. Then,

$$\lambda = -\frac{a_i}{C_i} \quad (i = 1, 2, ..., f).$$

Which implies that the only media included in the schedule have equal costs per thousand readers (this is inversely proportional to a_i/C_i). Subject to the cost condition being satisfied, it is immaterial how many insertions are placed in each medium. Clearly the media selected must be the cheapest.

This result is intuitively obvious. In practice it would mean to secure maximum mean impact, spend all the money available on advertisements in the cheapest medium. The consequence of this result in the case of the multiple unit campaign is interesting. In such a campaign, fix $n_i = 1$ in advance. The previous result suggests that one would begin by ranking the media in order of ascending cost per thousand and would move down the list, buying whole pages until the money was all allocated. It is not clear what one would do on reaching say the $(h+1)$th publication to find for the first time that the money remaining unallocated was less than the cost of a whole page in it. Is the best policy to spend it all on the $(h+1)$th publication? The answer, surprisingly, is no. It is better to allocate the surplus money over all remaining media than to spend it all on the cheapest one. These results may be summarized into optimization procedures relevant to two cases as follows:

Case 1. No restrictions placed on values of n_i other than that they must be integral.

The only media included in the schedule are those for which C_i/a_i (proportional to the cost per thousand readers) are equal and minimal. Say there is only one of these M_i. Then the number of insertions n_i and the size z_i^2 may take any values satisfying $n_i C_i z_i^2 = T$ so long as n_i is integral and $z_i^2 \leq 1$ for $i = 1$. And $n_i = 0$, $i \neq 1$.

Case 2. The n_i are restricted to the values $n_i = 0$ (one insertion or no insertion must appear in one issue of each medium).

(1) Compute $\quad x_i = (Ca_i^2/C_i^2) \left\{ \sum_{i=1}^{k} (a_i^2/C_i) \right\}^{-1} \quad (i = 1, z, ..., k)$.

(2) Arrange x_i in ascending order of magnitude and re-label as x_i (re-label z_i correspondingly).

(3) If no $x_i \geq 1$, then $z_i^2 = x_i$.

If $\quad x_i < 1 \quad$ for $\quad i = 1, 2, ..., (k-a)$,

$\qquad x_i \geq 1 \quad$ for $\quad i = (k-a+1), ..., k$.

Then $z_i^2 = 1$ for $i = (k-a+1), ..., k$

and compute

$$u_i = \left(C - \sum_{i=k-a+1}^{k} C_i\right) (a_i^2/C_i^2) \left\{\sum_{i=1}^{k-a} (a_i^2/C_i)\right\}^{-1} \quad [i = 1, 2, ..., (k-a)].$$

(4) Go back to (2), operating on u_i as formerly on x_i.

THE COVERAGE MAXIMIZATION PROBLEM

This problem is similar to the Impact Maximization problem except that the function to be maximized is the ultimate coverage, $G(z_i, n_i; k)$ instead of $F(z_i n_i; k)$. A set of $(4k \neq 1)$ simultaneous equations in $(4k \neq 1)$ unknowns is again obtained. By similar methods to those employed in the case of ultimate impact, the following results are obtained:

(1) No n_i should exceed unity (i.e. not more than one insertion per medium).
(2) The values of z_i which provide maximum coverage are the solution of the k equations $(i = 1, 2, ..., k)$,

$$\frac{Ha_i}{1-a_i z_i} = C_i z_i \sum_{j=1}^{k} \frac{a_j}{1-a_i z_i} \quad (i = 1, 2, ..., k).$$

Except that if this requires $z_i > 1$ for an i, then the z_i shall be put equal to 1 and the corresponding media be removed from the calculation which will be repeated for the remaining media and money.

The difficulty in this instance is that the k equations have no algebraic solution in general. However, in any real situation, they may be solved by numerical methods.[25]

SIMULTANEOUS MAXIMIZATION OF IMPACT AND COVERAGE

In general it is not possible to maximize ultimate coverage and ultimate impact for a fixed cost. For example, consider the case where $H < C_i$ $(i = 1, 2, ..., h)$ which in the case of ultimate impact does not give a requirement for whole-page advertisements. The optimal advertisement sizes require

$$z_i = \frac{a_i}{C_i} \cdot \sqrt{\frac{H}{\sum_{i=1}^{k} (a_i^2/C_i)}}.$$

These values only satisfy the equations which give the solution to the maximum coverage problem if

$$\frac{a_1^2}{C_1} = \frac{a_2^2}{C_2} = \frac{a_3^2}{C_3} = ... = \frac{a_k^2}{C_k}.$$

It was shown in a previous paper[26] that these conditions are in fact almost satisfied by some groups of media in Great Britain, but it is clear that this is unusual.

CONDITIONAL MAXIMIZATION OF COVERAGE
SUBJECT TO IMPACT EXCEEDING A FIXED MINIMUM

It is intuitively obvious that if the amount of money to be spent on a campaign is fixed, schedules which provide a high coverage will provide a low impact and vice versa. For example, if a sum of money H_i is allocated to a medium M_i in which there is to be a multiple sequence of advertisements of dimension (z_i, n_i). the following relationships hold:

$$n_i C_i z_i^2 = H_i, \tag{1}$$

$$n_i a_i z_i = F(z_i, n_i), \tag{2}$$

$$a_i[1 - (1 - z_i) n_i] = G(z_i, n_i), \tag{3}$$

by use of (1), (2) and (3) may be expressed as

$$F(z_i, n_i) = \sqrt{\left(\frac{a_i^2}{C_i}\right)} n_i H_i,$$

$$G(z_i, n_i) = a_i \left\{ 1 - \left[1 - \sqrt{\left(\frac{H_i}{C_i n_i}\right)} \right]^{n_i} \right\}.$$

As n_i increases, $F(z_i, n_i)$ increases but $G(z_i, n_i)$ decreases. When k media are under consideration, there are many possible schedules which will provide the same impact, and it may be that one of these will provide greater coverage than the others. Now, the example quoted above for one medium shows that so long as the money available is finite, the impact can be made to exceed any desired value, by increasing the number and decreasing the size of advertisements in the medium. The same conclusion obviously applies when there are k media, for in this case it is only necessary to put $n_2, n_3, ..., n_k = 0$ and let n_1 be as great as necessary. Consequently it is reasonable to seek for that schedule which whilst providing a fixed minimum impact will maximize coverage. In this case it is necessary to maximize

$$G(z, n; k) = 1 - \prod_{i=1}^{k} \{1 - a_i[1 - (1 - z_i)^{n_i}]\} \tag{1}$$

subject to the conditions

$$\sum_{i=1}^{k} n_i a_i z_i - J = 0. \tag{2}$$

and
$$z_i^2 + t_i^2 - 1 = 0 \quad (i = 1, 2, ..., k) \tag{3}$$

and
$$\sum_{i=1}^{k} n_i C_i z_i^2 - H = 0. \tag{4}$$

By our customary procedures we arrive at two sets of k equations each, which constitute $2k \neq$ equations in $2k$ unknowns:

$$\phi(z_i, n_i - 1) = \frac{C_i}{H} \sum_{j=1}^{k} n_i z_j \phi(z_j, n_j - 1) \quad (i = 1, ..., k),$$

$$\phi(z_i, n_i - 1)(1 - 2z_i) = \frac{a_i}{J} \sum_{j=1}^{k} n_j (1 - 2z_j) \phi(z_j, n_j - 1) \quad (i = 1, ..., k)$$

where $$\phi(z_i, n_i - 1) = \frac{a_i(1-z_i)^{n_i-1}}{\{1 - a_i[1 - (1-z_i)^{n_i}]\}}.$$

These equations are not capable of solution in general in terms of algebraic expressions, but a solution in any practical case can be obtained by numerical methods.

MAXIMIZATION OF RESPONSE

We conclude by noting that as the expressions for response and coverage are identical except for the potential response Q, which acts as a scale factor which we ignore, and the occurrence of $(1-P)z_i$ in the former instead of z_i in the latter, response is maximized in the same way as coverage. Immediately therefore, one can obtain for $n_i = 1$ (all i) that maximum response is obtained when the z_i satisfy the k simultaneous equations

$$\frac{H(a_i/C_i)}{1 - a_i(1-P)z_i} = \sum_{i=1}^{k} \frac{a_i(1-P)z_i}{1 - a_i(1-P)z_i}.$$

The practical problem of assigning a value to P remains.

CONCLUSION

It has been shown that subject to several assumptions media schedules can be obtained by mathematical methods which will, for fixed expenditure, maximize either ultimate impact or ultimate coverage. In general both cannot be maximized simultaneously, but ultimate coverage can be maximized whilst maintaining any arbitrarily chosen value for ultimate impact. Furthermore, given a certain response model, a quantity defined as response can also be maximized for fixed expenditure.

The paper, one might say, has raised more questions than it has attempted to answer. But it is hoped that it has at least suggested how some conceptual framework might be erected to assist in the construction of media schedules for static campaigns. The next stage in the progress of this inquiry will be to consider the problem of the construction of schedules for dynamic campaigns, which involve the spacing of advertisements in time. Such campaigns are more complex, but it can be shown that by use of mathematical programming techniques media schedules can, in principle at least, be devised which will provide any arbitrary awareness pattern at least cost, or will minimize the deviation of actual awareness levels from those desired whilst maximizing ultimate coverage at fixed cost.

ACKNOWLEDGEMENTS

The incentive to write this paper was given by John Burkart, Advertising Manager of British European Airways, and Bill Ellis of Cockfield Brown Ltd. of Montreal who has provided constant encouragement and advice. The two referees are thanked for their helpful comments and suggestions.

NOTES ON SOURCES AND REFERENCES

[1] A. M. LEE and A. J. BURKART (1960) *Operat. Res. Quart.* **11**, 3.

[2] H. J. RUDOLPH (1947) Attention and interest factors in advertising. *Printer's Ink*, pp. 29–31.

[3] N. MUNN (1956) *Psychology.* Harrap, London.

[4] "Effective" means "will produce the desired response". For comments see R. REEVES (1961) *Reality in Advertising*, pp. 114–119. Knopf.

[5] H. J. RUDOLPH, loc. cit.; H. HENRY (1958) *Motivation Research*, Ch. 9. Crosby Lockwood. Also REEVES, loc. cit.

[6] INSTITUTE OF PRACTITIONERS IN ADVERTISING, *National Readership Survey.* London.

[7] NEWSPRINT INFORMATION COMMITTEE, *A National Study of Newspaper Reading* (1961). New York. CENTRE D'ÉTUDE DES SUPPORTS DE PUBLICITÉ, *Press Readership Study* (1957).

[8] The "cost per thousand" readers is a commonly used criterion of the relative expensiveness of different media.

[9] I.e. reasons of policy. See also L. BOGART, Media research: a tool for effective advertising. *J. Marketing* **20**, 4; and W. M. WEILBACHER, The qualitative values of advertising media. *J. Adv. Res.* **1**, 2.

[10] "When two media possess readers in common, they are said to duplicate." See *IPA National Readership Survey*; also M. AGOSTINI, How to estimate unduplicated audiences. *J. Adv. Res.* **1**, 2.

[11] H. J. RUDOLPH, loc. cit.; BURKART's personal experiences with copy testing and the Hulton Readership Survey influenced this judgement.

[12] N. MUNN, loc. cit.; Nonsense Syllables are meaningless letter-triads, e.g. GEJ, QUD, LIW. Used extensively by EBBINGHAUS in his experiments on forgetting.

[13] H. J. RUDOLPH, loc. cit., pp. 32–35.

[14] D. STARCH, What is the best frequency of advertisements? *Mediascope*, Dec. 1961; BENJAMIN *et al.*, Operational research and advertising—theories of response. *Operat. Res. Quart.* **11**, 4.

[15] This term is commonly used for the total of all readerships of the media included in a schedule. As long ago as 1958, R. M. SHIELDS of Associated Newspapers Ltd., London, had a computer programme for evaluating any proposed media schedules in terms of the frequency distribution of O.T.S. and costs.

[16] "Ultimate" is used to mean "the asymptotic value reached after a long lapse of time".

[17] BENJAMIN *et al.*, loc. cit.; R. W. JASTRAM, A treatment of distributed lags in the theory of advertising. *J. Marketing* **20**, 1. Also reports issued by individual publishers: e.g. *Readers' Dig.*

[18] Sir F. BARTLETT, *Remembering*, Cambridge; EBBINGHAUS's work on forgetting—also research by Hobson, Bates and Partners, London, for Granada Television.

[19] R. REEVES, loc. cit.

[20] The London Press Exchange data were privately communicated to the author. But see also JIRO YAMANAKA (1960) *A Method of Prediction of Readership Scores.* Dentsu Advertising, Tokyo.

[21] LEE and BURKART, loc. cit. This approximation was suggested to the author by Mr. F. MONKMAN, Colman, Prentiss and Varley Ltd., London.

[22] See also *Psychological Review* (1913).

[23] BENJAMIN *et al.*, loc. cit. The problem is also discussed in *J. Marketing*, Jan. 1959.

[24] The mathematical derivations in this section have been curtailed at the suggestion of the referees. More detailed accounts are obtainable from the author, on request.

[25] T. L. SAATY (1958) *Mathematical Methods of Operations Research.* John Wiley, New York; also W. S. DORN (1961) On Lagrange multipliers and inequalities. *Operat. Res.* **9**, 1.

[26] LEE and BURKART, loc. cit.

Operational Research Quarterly

VOLUME 14 NUMBER 4 DECEMBER 1963

Decision Rules for Media Scheduling: Dynamic Campaigns

ALEC M. LEE

Trans-Canada Air Lines, Montreal, Quebec

1. INTRODUCTION

THIS is the second paper in a series of three concerned with the problems of constructing advertising media schedules that are, in some sense, optimal. The previous paper[1] began with a statement of the media scheduling problem. It then presented an advertising model and from it derived decision rules applicable to *static* campaigns, i.e. those intended to evoke a maximum response, the time of attainment being unimportant.

This treatment ignored—deliberately—the existence of advertising campaigns of one further type: those which are intended to generate and maintain a specific awareness level in a predetermined target population throughout a certain period. These will be called *dynamic* campaigns. They are the subjects of concern in this paper.

2. SOME DEFINITIONS

The reader is referred to the previous paper for a description of the attitudes towards media scheduling which underly the present analysis. To prevent misunderstanding, the definitions of three of the principal concepts used are restated below:

(1) The ultimate† proportion of a target population who have seen—or been reached by—at least one advertisement of a campaign is called the "ultimate coverage" or "reach" of the campaign.

(2) The number of advertisements seen by each member of a target population is called the "ultimate impact" of the campaign.

These are measures of dispersion and intensity respectively.

(3) The *awareness* generated by a campaign is at any point in time that proportion of the target population consisting of persons who have already seen at least one advertisement in the campaign and not yet forgotten it.

---

† It is usual to omit the qualifying adjective "ultimate" in advertising literature and this practice will be followed when no ambiguity can result.

3. DYNAMIC CAMPAIGNS

When an issue of a publication appears, the people who see it do not all do so at the same time. Some see it on the day of issue, some on the second day, others on the third and so on. As time passes, the number of people who have seen it tends to the readership. In other words, the readership growth curve is asymptotic and in the case of some magazines a long period elapses before the limit is closely approached. Thus the coverage and impact of a campaign may take some time to reach their ultimate values.

It is necessary to begin an analysis of dynamic campaigns by formulating a function which specifies how the readership of a single issue of a publication accumulates with time. There is some evidence on this point, though of a some-what oblique type,[2] which will be examined in the final paper of this series. For the present, we shall postulate that:

The increment in readership of M_i on day r given that publication was on day 1 is:

$$\alpha_i(r) = a_i(1-p_i)p_i^{r-1},$$

assuming that 100 per cent readership is only achieved after the lapse of a very long (infinite) time.

One meaning which can be put upon this postulate is that a person has a finite probability $(1-p_i)$ of reading the publication on any day, so that the probability of his doing so for the first time on day r is $\alpha_i(r)$ as defined.

With the aid of this *postulate* the readership provided by a single advertisement of size z_i^2 in medium M_i, on day r given that it appeared on day 1, can be expressed as:

$$\alpha_i(r)z_i.$$

The accumulated readership of such an advertisement in M_i up to and including day r, $A_i(r)$, is then:

$$A_i(r) = a_i(1-p_i^r)z_i.$$

To evaluate the accumulated impact and coverage up to day r of a multiple sequence of advertisements, we introduce the variables $x_i(j)$, which take the values 0 or 1 only, as follows:

$x_i(j) = 1$ if the issue of medium M_i on day j carries an advertisement.

$x_i(j) = 0$ if the issue of medium M_i on day j does not carry an advertisement.

We can write down an expression for total impact up to day r of a multiple sequence. The impacts provided on the rth day only may be written:

$$f_r(z_i, n_i; k) = \sum_{i=1}^{k} \sum_{j=1}^{r} x_i(j)\alpha_i(r-j+1)z_i,$$

where:

$$\sum_{j=1}^{r} x_i(j) \leqslant n_i \quad (i = 1, 2, ..., k).$$

Consequently the accumulated impact up to and including the day may be expressed as:

$$F_r(z_i, n_j; k) = \sum_{m=1}^{r} f_m(z_i, n_i; k)$$

$$= \sum_{i=1}^{k} \sum_{j=1}^{r} A_i(r-j+1) x_i(j) z_i,$$

where:

$$\sum_{j=1}^{r} x_i(j) \leqslant n_i \quad (i = 1, 2, \ldots, k).$$

In a similar way we can derive the accumulated coverage up to the rth day:

$$G_r(z_i, n_i; k) = \prod_{i=1}^{k} \left\{ 1 - a_i \left[1 - \prod_{j=1}^{r} [1 - x_i(j)(1 - p_i^{r-j+1}) z_i] \right] \right\},$$

where:

$$\sum_{j=1}^{r} x_i(j) \leqslant n_i \quad (i = 1, 2, \ldots, k).$$

At this point we may pause to consider one of the classes of advertising campaign which stimulated the study and of which part is the basis of the present paper. This class of campaign, not uncommon in the travel industry, has as its objective to persuade people to travel during a specific period to certain places. The message (e.g. "Fly to Jamaica for Winter Sunshine") must be conveyed to the target group (e.g. snowbound Canadian families) while its period of effectiveness—and while the airline's winter Caribbean schedule—lasts. The unplanned stimulation of massive additional traffic to Jamaica during July could prove embarrassing. In such cases, therefore, one would like to know what accumulated coverage or accumulated impact would be attained by any media schedule by the end of the *effective* period of the campaign. The above formulae may be used for this purpose.

However, we must note that although these expressions can be extremely useful in making evaluations of accumulated coverage and impact, they are in themselves of no merit for devising optimal schedules. The reason is that any attempt to maximize the accumulated impact or coverage attained before a specified time necessarily results in all advertisements appearing as early as possible. Thus we are led to look for some measure of the dispersion in time, throughout the planned life of a campaign, of the effectiveness of the advertising schedule. One such measure is provided by the concept of *awareness*.

It was pointed out in the previous paper that as soon as a person has seen an advertisement he begins to forget it, and when this effect is combined with the asymptotic growth characteristic of readership, discussed above, at any point in time the target population consists of three classes of people:

(1) those who have not yet seen the advertisement,
(2) those who have seen it but have forgotten it,
(3) those who have seen it and recall it.

Thus in addition to coverage and impact we defined the further important factor: *awareness*, which is the third of these groups.

If the *levels of awareness* which are desired at different times during the life of a campaign are specified, an appropriate media schedule can be composed. For example, if it was desired to run a campaign for 8 weeks, and it had been decided that a high level of awareness in the population during the first 2 weeks, then a constant, lower level during the remaining 6 was required, the criterion might be written thus:

Week number	1	2	3	4	5	6	7	8
Acceptable minimum average level of awareness (percentage of population aware)	30	30	15	10	10	10	10	10

However, at the same time it might have been specified that the total accumulated coverage of the campaign should be at least 70 per cent. In general, the number of insertions required to satisfy both criteria would not be equal, and it would be necessary to satisfy the more stringent one. To compute quickly the adequacy of a schedule of media to satisfy the awareness criterion, use may be made of the concept of *awareness units*. An awareness unit (or AU) is 1 per cent of the population aware, on one day, of an advertisement. Thus if the level of awareness for a newspaper advertisement varied thus:

Day after publication	1	2	3	4	5	6	7
Awareness level (percentage of population aware)	10	7	5	3	1	$\frac{1}{2}$	0

then this newspaper advertisement would generate a total of:

$$10+7+5+3+1+\tfrac{1}{2} = 26\tfrac{1}{2}\,\text{AU (awareness units)}.$$

It can be seen that the minimum requirement of the 8-week campaign specified above is for:

$$210+210+105+70+70+70+70+70 = 875\,\text{AU}.$$

And owing to wastage of AU through having involuntarily to overprovide in some weeks, even this number might not suffice.

4. MATHEMATICS OF AWARENESS

To formulate a mathematical expression for the level of awareness at a certain time after the commencement of a campaign, we first postulate a "rule of forgetting" which, in a discrete-time model, is:

The proportion of those people who saw an advertisement on day r who remember it during a subsequent day d is:

$$mq^{d-r} \quad (q<1).$$

m and q are two "memory" parameters.

This is, in effect, the well-known Ebbinghaus Law in a different guise.[3] The validity of this application will be considered in some detail in the final paper of the series, but it should be noted here that we do not assume that the sum of infinity of these proportions is unity. In other words, allowance is made for the contingency that some people might not remember seeing an advertisement at all. By making suitable choice of the value of m, contingency can be discounted.

Then the proportion of the readership of M_i who are *aware* of the advertisement during the day d is, in awareness units:

$$\epsilon_i(d) = \sum_{r=1}^{d} a_i \, mq^{d-r}(1-p_i)\, p_i^{r-1} z_i.$$

We shall make use of this expression in studying the optimization of media schedules for dynamic campaigns. But first we shall clear up one side-issue. It is clear that in planning multiple sequences of advertisements, the cost per awareness unit must play an equivalent role to that of cost per thousand in more conventional calculations. If a set of publications were ranked in ascending order of cost per thousand, and this turned out to be a different ranking to that given by ascending cost per awareness unit, difficulties would arise in selecting media to satisfy total coverage and level of awareness requirements simultaneously at least cost. Publications which should be selected to give a cheap total coverage would be rejected on the basis of cheap awareness units. However, mathematical analysis shows that so long as the (memory) decay constant is independent of publications (as may perhaps be assumed) the ranking by cost per thousand is exactly the same as that by cost per awareness unit. In fact:

(cost per awareness unit) $\propto$ (cost per thousand).

This is an interesting result. It means that if there is a universal memory decay constant one can still choose media for inclusion in a schedule solely on the basis of cost per thousand (subject to secular considerations). We now turn our attention once more towards the mathematical formulation and solution of the problem of dynamic campaigns.

5. OPTIMIZATION PROBLEMS INVOLVING AWARENESS

The basic problem is this: given a number of advertisements of predetermined size in several media, how to space their appearances in time so that a predicted level-of-awareness pattern is generated. In other words, a campaign is supposed to begin at a certain time, and it is desired that at any time thereafter the level of awareness in the target population should be not less than a specified figure.

In mathematical terms, the number of awareness units required on the dth day of a campaign $d = 1, 2, ..., D$ is L_d and so the total AU provided on day d must not be less than L_d.

To meet this objective one has, say, n_i advertisements of size z_i^2 in medium M_i and there are k media altogether. The z_i are assumed to be predetermined.

Now if it is assumed that a coverage maximization has already been carried out:

the number of issues of medium M_i carrying advertisements n_i is not to exceed n_i^0.

And with this is naturally associated the objective, I:

the total AU's used during the campaign must be a minimum.

But if it is not assumed that maximum coverage is of prime importance and there are no restrictions on the values of n_i the natural objective seems to be, II:

the total cost of providing AU's during the campaign must be minimal.

We introduce again the variables $x_i(j)$, which take the values 0 or 1 only as follows:

$x_i(j) = 1$ if the issue of medium M_i on day j carries an advertisement,

$x_i(j) = 0$ if the issue of medium M_i on day j does not carry an advertisement.

It is now possible to formulate the problem mathematically. The AU's provided on the first day may be written:

$$\sum_{i=1}^{k} x_i(j)\, \epsilon_i(1)\, z_i,$$

and these must be such that:

$$\sum_{i=1}^{k} x_i(j)\, \epsilon_i(1)\, z_i \geqslant L_1.$$

Similarly for the second day:

$$\sum_{i=1}^{k} \sum_{j=1}^{2} x_i(j)\, \epsilon_i(3-j)\, z_i \geqslant L_2,$$

and in general:

$$\sum_{i=1}^{k} \sum_{j=1}^{d} x_i(j)\, \epsilon_i(d+1-j)\, z_i \geqslant L_d \quad (d = 1, 2, ..., D).$$

These equations represent a set of D linear constraints, where D is the planned time-span of the campaign.

Now if a coverage maximization has already been carried out, we have, additionally, for Model I:

$$\sum_{j=1}^{D} x_i(j) \leqslant n_i^0 \quad (i = 1, 2, ..., k),$$

a further set of k linear constraints. Furthermore, for the objective function:

$$\sum_{d=1}^{D} \sum_{i=1}^{k} \sum_{j=1}^{d} x_i(j) \, \epsilon_i(d+1-j) z_i,$$

which is linear in the $x_i(j)$.

Thus the problem of determining the $x_i(j)$ which minimize this subject to the linear constraints given above is one in linear programming. Model I is therefore an integer linear programming allocation model.

Now if no coverage maximization has been carried out, there is no restriction on the n_i and only the constraints apply. But the objective function is:

$$\sum_{i=1}^{k} \sum_{j=1}^{D} x_i(j) \, C_i z_i^2.$$

The costs $C_i z_i^2$ may be assumed known if the advertisement size is predetermined, and again the objective function is linear. Model II is also, therefore, one of integer linear programming.

Maximization of coverage subject to restrictions on awareness levels

Of the problems not discussed so far the most outstanding is the maximization of accumulated coverage up to the end of the effective life of a campaign, subject to restrictions upon cost and the attainment of a specified awareness pattern. This problem will be stated, but no solution will be given. The author is not able at the present time even to suggest how a solution might be obtained by any method other than the extensive use of computing facilities to search for a solution in any particular case of practical interest. The problem is to maximize:

$$F_D(z_i, n_i; k) = 1 - \prod_{i=1}^{k} \prod_{r=1}^{D} \left\{ 1 - a_i \left[1 - \prod_{u_i=1}^{n_i} [1 - \delta(u_i, r)(1-p_i)^{D-r} z_i] \right] \right\},$$

in the notation previously introduced, but where additionally:

$\delta(u_i, r) = 1$ if the u_ith advertisement in M_i appears in the issue of M_i on day r

$ = 0$ otherwise.

Subject to:

$$\sum_{i=1}^{k} \sum_{u_i=1}^{n_i} \sum_{r=1}^{d} \delta(u_i, r) \, \epsilon_i(d-r+1) \geqslant L_d \quad (d = 1, 2, ..., D),$$

and

$$\sum_{i=1}^{k} n_i \, C_i z_i^2 = H,$$

371

where there is at least one solution of the inequalities L_d and the equation for H.

The solution to this problem requires the determination of the z_i $(0 \leqslant z_i, \leqslant 1)$, n_i and $\delta(u_i, r)$ which achieve the maximization. It would have to be preceded by ensuring that the inequalities for L_d could be satisfied subject to the cost condition for H.

This problem is proposed in the hope that someone may find it of interest and be able to suggest a solution.

CONCLUSION

The work on which this paper, like its forerunner, has been based, has gone forward in uncertain and widely spaced steps, interrupted frequently by more pressing concerns. Both papers have raised more questions than they have attempted to answer. But it is hoped that they have suggested some bases for a conceptual framework to assist in the construction of media schedules.

The first drafts of these two papers were quite widely circulated and have been the subject of a certain amount of discussion and correspondence. As a result, the next and final paper in this series is being rewritten with new objectives in mind. It will be devoted to the major questions embedded in the first two: the nature of the evidence, the difficulties in formulating a coherent theory, and their importance for the strategy of advertising research.

ACKNOWLEDGEMENTS

The author wishes to acknowledge his indebtedness to John Burkart for constant encouragement and advice, and to Bill Ellis for supplying basic data on North American media.

REFERENCES

[1] A. M. LEE (1962) Decision rules for media scheduling: static campaigns. *Operat. Res. Quart.* **13**, 229–242.

[2] Discussion of the evidence is deferred to the third paper. A typical example of the better research in this area is *How Reading Days Accumulate; A Study of Seven Publications* by ALFRED POLITZ RESEARCH INC., published by Reader's Digest Association Inc.

[3] The Ebbinghaus Law was originally derived from experiments using nonsense syllables; cf. N. MUNN (1956) *Psychology*, Harrap, London. Its approximate validity in advertising has been confirmed by many experimenters. Discussion of the evidence is deferred to the third paper. See, however, JAMES P. WOOD (1962) *Advertising and the Soul's Belly*, University of Johns Hopkins Press.

Linear Programming
in Media Selection

RALPH L. DAY

Carnegie Institute of Technology

Dr. Day explains, in plain language, how an elsewhere useful mathematical technique may help select advertising media—provided three key tasks can be done first.

THE MEDIA SELECTION PROBLEM is to allocate a scarce resource among a large number of alternative uses so that the best possible contribution is made to a central objective. The "scarce resource" is, of course, the advertising appropriation. The alternative uses of the appropriation are the

RALPH L. DAY is a visiting assistant professor in the Graduate School of Industrial Administration at the Carnegie Institute of Technology for the 1961-62 academic year, on leave of absence from the University of Texas where he is an associate professor of marketing administration. He received a B.S. in 1950, and an M.S. in 1955, both from the Georgia Institute of Technology, and a Ph.D. in 1961 from the University of North Carolina for which his dissertation was "A Study of Mathematical Programming as a Tool for Marketing Management." He has since served on the faculties of both universities. Consultant to a large petroleum refiner, Dr. Day is the author of *Marketing in Action: A Dynamic Business Decision Game* (Homewood: Richard D. Irwin, Inc., 1962).

many "advertising units"[1] which must be considered before a specific media schedule is adopted. The objective to be maximized is the marketing effectiveness of the advertising program, i.e., obtaining the maximum possible impact on the pertinent marketing target with a given budget.

When stated in this way, the media mix problem clearly fits the basic structure of the linear programming model, a well known tool of mathematical analysis which has been applied to many business problems in the past ten years. Yet the first announcement of a serious effort by a U.S. advertising agency to use linear programming in media selection was made in recent months. (See *Mathematical Programming for Better Media Selection*, papers from the 1961 regional conventions of the American Association of Advertising Agencies.)

---

[1] As defined in *Toward Better Media Comparisons*, by the Audience Concepts Committee of the Advertising Research Foundation, New York, 1961.

Before one either condemns agencies as laggards in the use of new mathematical tools or concludes that mathematical analysis has little to offer the advertising business, he should take a careful look at the linear programming model, its promise and its problems. Such an appraisal will be undertaken here, intended for the reader who knows advertising but has only a layman's knowledge of mathematics.

What Is Linear Programming?

Linear programming is a particular type of mathematical model. In the sense used here, a model is an abstract representation of some real world process or group of interrelated activities. Linear programming is a mathematical model since the pertinent features of the real world situation are expressed in mathematical terms and cast into a mathematical structure. This structure can be solved to reveal the effects on some specified central objective of various alternative programs for operating the real world process. It is a particularly useful kind of model since it can specify the optimal (best possible) program for achieving the stated objective. But the optimal solution to a programming model gives the best possible solution to the problem *as it is depicted in the mathematical structure.*

Since a model is an abstract representation of a real world process, it cannot be expected to reflect perfectly all complexities in the actual situation. The optimal solution of the model should be considered an approximation to the optimal course of action. The solution should be carefully examined with regard to any simplifications or inaccuracies which might be contained in the model which produced it.

One of the most appealing features of the linear programming model is that it provides, as a by-product of the solution process, a means of evaluating the solution to see if errors in the assumed values of the model could have a significant effect on the solution. Through such "sensitivity analysis," it can often be seen that even sizable errors in values such as unit cost figures would not affect the optimal solution. In other cases, slight changes in these values might alter the optimal solution. In such instances, either further studies can be made to improve the values used in the model or a decision can be made outside of the model on the basis of subjective judgment.

The use of a linear programming model should

never be thought of as a way of turning a problem over to a mystical black box which gives instant solutions to thorny problems. The greatest value of a mathematical model is that it provides an organized and methodical approach to the study of complex relationships. When teamed with an electronic computer, the programming model provides an efficient way to study *simultaneously* a large number of interrelated variables, hence can reveal significant relationships likely to be overlooked in more casual, piecemeal analysis. Only routine relationships can be reduced to routine computations. Linear programming can best be considered as a way of organizing, analyzing, and presenting large quantities of information in such a way that a theoretically optimum starting point is provided for the solution of a complex problem.

Media Mix Model

While the mathematics needed to solve a large-scale programming model is rather complex, an intuitive understanding of the basic structure does not require advanced mathematics. However, it is very difficult to talk about a mathematical structure without using symbols. The programming model can be expressed in the notation of ordinary algebra and involves only one kind of relationship which is likely to be unfamiliar. This relationship is the conditional inequality signified by the symbols $\geq$ and $\leq$ which mean, respectively, "the quantity on the left *is equal to or greater than* the quantity on the right" and "the quantity on the left *is equal to or less than* the quantity on the right."

Below is the linear programming model in symbolic notation. The meaning of the symbols when the model is applied to the media mix problem will be explained. A later section will discuss in more detail how specific values are assigned to those elements which do not vary in the solution process.

(1) Maximize: $P_1X_1 + P_2X_2 + \cdots + P_nX_n$
Subject to: $A_{11}X_1 + A_{12}X_2 + \cdots + A_{1n}X_n \leq C_1$
(2) $\qquad\qquad A_{21}X_1 + A_{22}X_2 + \cdots + A_{2n}X_n \leq C_2$

$$\vdots$$

$$A_{m1}X_1 + A_{m2}X_2 + \cdots + A_{mn}X_n \leq C_m$$
(3) $\qquad\qquad X_1, X_2, \ldots, X_n \geq 0$

The subscripted X's represent the particular advertising units which are being considered for inclusion in the media schedule. All "candidate" advertising units are arbitrarily numbered consecutively from 1 and are represented in the model by the letter X with that number as a subscript. The X's are the "variables" of the model. When the model is completed and solved, the numerical values assigned to the X's will indicate how many times each advertising unit will be used.

The P's represent the contributions which each use of the corresponding advertising unit would make to the objective. In other words, the P's represent the advertising values of the corresponding advertising units. A specific value must be assigned to each P in formulating the model. The sum of the products of the corresponding P's and X's, as shown in expression (1), is the objective function which is to be maximized in solving the model.

Each conditional inequality in (2) represents a restriction on the way in which values may be assigned to the X's. This system of inequalities reflects the fact that achievement of the objective is limited by availability of resources and by certain environmental conditions. The C's either represent the maximum possible use of some resource or specify some other relationship which must be preserved. The A's in each inequality represent the rate at which each X uses up that particular scarce factor. For example, if C_1 is the amount of the total advertising budget, then A_{11} will be the cost of each insertion of advertising unit 1, A_{12} the cost of each insertion of advertising unit 2, etc. This conditional inequality then specifies that when values are assigned to the X's, the total cost of the designated media purchase will be equal to or less than the budget. At the same time, the values of the X's must satisfy the other inequalities. Since any information which affects the solution must be explicitly stated in the model, the maximum number of insertions of each advertising unit must also be reflected in the constraints. For example, if X_2 represents a two page spread in a monthly magazine and the planning period is one year, the constraint, $X_2 \leq 12$, must be included to avoid the possibility that the solution will specify more insertions than are possible in 12 months. If the client specifies maximum or minimum use of any advertising units or combinations of units, then these restrictions on the solution are also incorporated in the constraints.

The relationships specified in (3) are called the non-negativity requirements. Since buying negative insertions does not make sense, these requirements must be built into the mathematical structure. In the final solution of the model, all X's must take either a value of 0, indicating that the corresponding advertising unit should not be used, or some positive number of insertions.

Solving the Model

In the linear programming media mix model, the objective function shows how particular advertising units contribute to "total advertising effectiveness." The system of inequalities reflects the restrictions imposed on the solution values of the variables by the budget, the characteristics of available media, and other environmental conditions. The non-negativity requirements prevent infeasible solutions involving negative values of the variables. Solution of a correctly formulated model will then indicate the particular advertising units to be included in the media schedule and the number of uses of each which will result in the greatest "total advertising effectiveness" obtainable from a given budget.

Once the basic structure has been formed in accordance with mathematical requirements, and specific values have been assigned to the P's, C's, and A's, the solution of the model to obtain the optimal media schedule is a routine computational problem when computer facilities are available. An explanation of the mathematical process of solution will not be undertaken here. It is simply a systematic search among the usually large number of possible solutions permitted by the structural characteristics built into the model. After finding any solution which does not violate any of the restrictions of the model, the solution process (algorithm) systematically investigates alternative solutions to see if they give better answers (a higher level of total advertising effectiveness). This process is continued until the set of values for the variables which yields the highest possible level of advertising effectiveness is found.

The optimal solution is precise and exact; there is no better solution to the media choice problem as it is depicted in the linear programming model. The usefulness of the solution as a guide to the real situation depends on the care with which the model has been formulated and the extent to which necessary simplifications of actual relationships distort the real world relationships. If the model can closely depict real values and relationships, it clearly offers great promise as an analytical tool for media buyers.

The following sections will consider the major

conceptual and measurement problems involved in giving meaning to the mathematical structure described above. There are three major tasks: (1) the selection of candidate advertising units; (2) the recognition of the significant relationships and restrictions in the real world, and the depiction of them in the system of constraining inequalities; (3) the establishment of an effectiveness measure for each candidate advertising unit.

Selecting Candidate Advertising Units

Though the computational capacity of modern electronic computers staggers the imagination, a model which could handle *every* possible media alternative is still inconceivable. Thousands of alternatives could be found within each of the major media types. Obviously the choices to be considered in a programming model must be limited to a workable number: dozens rather than thousands. Some method apart from the model must be used to select the candidate advertising units.

Pre-selection of a limited number of candidate advertising units is but one of the ways in which the experience and judgment of media experts are required in formulating a linear programming media selection model. Although some promising alternatives may be missed, the selection of candidate units will not be regarded as a serious problem by most media departments. General knowledge of the client's product, his marketing target, and advertising strategy allows the elimination of great numbers of advertising units as clearly inappropriate. But care should be exercised to ascertain that all reasonably promising alternatives are considered. If the range of choice left to the model is overly narrow, much of its potential value may be lost.

Forming the System of Inequalities

The system of constraining inequalities must reflect all restrictions on the solution values of the variables. That the budget not be exceeded is perhaps the most important such restriction, but it is only one of many which must be explicitly stated. Without other constraints, the solution might be to spend the entire budget on one particular advertising unit, leading to such programs as "use 238 back covers of *Life* Magazine this year." Besides the budget restriction there are two other types of restrictions on the solution values of the variables: specified values must not exceed the available number of units of a particular media vehicle; and

standards of advertising practice and client preferences must not be violated.

The budget restriction is simply a matter of expressing the cost of each advertising unit and the budget figure in an inequality of the form, $A_{11}X_1 + A_{12}X_2 + \ldots + A_{1n}X_n \leq C_1$, where A_{11} is the cost in dollars of one insertion of advertising unit 1, etc., and C_1 is the total budget in dollars. (Remember that when the model is solved, the X's will appear either as zeroes or some positive number of insertions of the corresponding advertising unit.)

There will usually be at least one specific restriction on the number of uses of each candidate advertising unit. For periodicals the uses may simply be restricted to the number of issues published during the planning period. If X_3 is a particular type of insertion in a particular weekly magazine, then the restriction $X_3 \leq 52$ would be required unless some more restrictive limit was specified by client preferences or agency policy. Similar limits will usually be established in the process of defining the advertising units of other media types, particularly when the units are defined in terms of specific network programs or packages of spot commercials.

Often the basic media strategy developed for the client will generate restrictions which must be included in the model. These can refer to specific media vehicles or to general media types. For example, the client might specify that if advertising unit X_3 is used, it should not be used more than 10 times, instead of the possible 52 times, i.e., $X_3 \leq 10$. Or it might be specified that no more than 30 per cent of the budget should be used for magazines. Then an inequality restricting the combined amount spent on all magazine units to 30 per cent of the budget would be included.

Subjectively determined constraints are usually a necessary part of the model but should be established with great care. There is always the danger that biases or misunderstandings can limit the model's effectiveness through arbitrary constraints which largely predetermine the solution values. It is advisable to keep subjectively determined restrictions to a minimum in the initial formulation of a model. Then if the model produces clearly unreasonable levels of use for certain advertising units, arbitrary maximum levels can be inserted and the model can be recomputed. In any event, the effects of subjectively determined constraints should be carefully studied to determine their effect on the resulting optimal program.

Establishing Effectiveness Measures

While the determination of a list of candidate advertising units and the formulation of a system of constraining inequalities are not easy, they are not insurmountable tasks for knowledgeable media people working with a model building specialist. The question on which the ultimate usefulness of a media mix model seems to depend is *whether it is possible to establish meaningful effectiveness measures for alternative advertising units.*

One approach to estimating effectiveness values for particular advertising units (the P's in the objective function) can be outlined as follows:

1. Identify the target consumers. This is sometimes referred to as constructing a "market profile." It may involve picking a particular population subgroup as the only relevant target, or involve weighting several relevant subgroups according to their importance as consumers of the product.

2. Obtain data on the total circulation or audience of each media vehicle and the composition of this circulation or audience according to population characteristics.

3. Establish the "effective circulation" of each media vehicle, i.e., the number of actual prospects reached.

4. Evaluate the relative effectiveness of an "exposure" to a single target consumer for each of the candidate advertising units. Some form of rating scale is useful in establishing these values.

5. Adjust the "effective circulation" by the value rating for each candidate unit and use this as the effectiveness value for each insertion.

Aside from the formidable measurement problems posed in the above steps, one must consider duplications of individuals reached and the effects of repeats in a given media vehicle as opposed to "one shot" insertions.

Usable measures of these effects are essential if a media selection model is to be meaningful. Such measures are difficult to obtain reliably, but remember that they are tacitly *assumed* whenever a media schedule is made up by current methods. If nothing else, explicit consideration of these measures brings out and explains such hidden assumptions.

Summary

It has been shown that conceptually the linear programming model provides a useful approach to the media selection problem. Although technical problems of model construction and solution have not been discussed, some of the measurement problems involved in the practical application of programming techniques have been considered.

Clearly linear programming offers media directors no panacea. Rather, it is an invitation to hard work and rigorous thinking about the problem of selecting the best possible media schedule for a client.

If approached with full realization of the difficulties and dangers involved in using complex mathematical models, media selection models can aid in the development of sounder media practices. But if models are used so that an agency can say, "look how scientific we are," then the results are likely to be harmful to all concerned.

In vain the sage, with retrospective eye,
Would from the apparent what conclude the why.

—Alexander Pope

Allocating Advertising Dollars
by Linear Programing

JAMES F. ENGEL   and   MARTIN R. WARSHAW
The Ohio State University   The University of Michigan

The authors present simple examples to show precisely how to implement L.P. They also discuss the advantages and limitations of L.P.

ADVERTISERS AND ADVERTISING AGENCIES alike have recently shown increased interest in the use of mathematical programing to allocate advertising

JAMES F. ENGEL is an associate professor of business organization at the College of Commerce and Administration, The Ohio State University. He also has taught at The University of Michigan and the University of Illinois. He received his B.S. from Drake University, and his M.S. and Ph.D. in marketing and psychology from the University of Illinois. He has published several articles, including one in this journal. Dr. Engel is a member of the American Marketing Association and the American Association for Public Opinion Research.

MARTIN R. WARSHAW is an associate professor of marketing at the Graduate School of Business Administration, The University of Michigan, where he received both his M.B.A. and Ph.D. He received his bachelor's degree from Columbia University. He has participated in a faculty mathematics seminar co-sponsored by the Ford Foundation and the Michigan Business School, and has published several journal articles and a book, *Effective Selling Through Wholesalers*. He also has edited *Changing Perspectives in Marketing Management*.

expenditures to media, and the technique of linear programing has received special attention. Indeed, about a year ago full-page ads in the *Wall Street Journal* stated that linear programing had shown one client how to get "$1.67 worth of effective advertising for every dollar in his budget."

Ralph Day (1962) led the way in explaining how L.P., as we shall call it, might be applied to the allocation of the advertising appropriation. We attempted to implement Day's suggestions, and it became quite clear that the difficult problems in the L.P. approach pertained to the identification and evaluation of important marketing variables. A great deal of this delineation and quantification was, of necessity, judgmental in nature. Once these definitions and subjective appraisals of marketing variables had been made, however, the mathematical problem was rather straightforward and presented no major difficulties.

It is our purpose to delve more deeply into the problem, beginning where Day and others leave off, by suggesting through simple examples how one might implement the L.P. approach. Also, the strengths and weaknesses of L.P. will be stressed to help the thoughtful advertiser judge how this promising tool might be used in his organization.

Since the mathematical model of L.P. and the methods of solution have been well documented in technical terms by Spivey (1963), Churchman, Ackoff, and Arnoff (1957), Dorfman, Samuelson, and Solow (1958), and others, we shall proceed directly to a simple statement of the mathematical model.

(1) Maximize (or minimize)
$$f = p_1x_1 + p_2x_2 + \cdots + p_nx_n$$
(objective function)

(2) subject to
$$a_{11}x_1 + a_{12}x_2 + \cdots + a_{1n}x_n \leqq b_1$$
(linear constraints)
$$a_{21}x_1 + a_{22}x_2 + \cdots + a_{2n}x_n \leqq b_2$$
$$\overline{\phantom{a_{21}x_1 + a_{22}x_2 + \cdots + a_{2n}x_n \leqq b_2}}$$
$$a_{m1}x_1 + a_{m2}x_2 + \cdots + a_{mn}x_n \leqq b_m$$

(3) and $x_i \geqq 0$ $(i = 1, \ldots, n)$.
(non-negativity constraint)

Hence L.P. is uniquely applicable to problems where the purpose is to maximize (or minimize) a given linear function under several constraining conditions represented by linear inequalities.

Equation (1) is called the objective function. The x's represent the variables in the problem, while the p's express the contribution or value of each x to the objective function. If, for example, the objective function to be maximized is the number of prospects reached by a given media assortment, the x's would be "dollars invested in individual media," and the p's "prospects reached by each medium per dollar invested."

The first constraints are designated by the inequalities (2). The symbol $\leqq$ means "less than or equal to," and $\geqq$ means "greater than or equal to." The b's refer to maximum quantities of resources or capacities available, and the a's indicate the extent to which each x uses up or consumes the resource or capacity b. For instance, b_1 may refer to the total advertising budget, which cannot be exceeded by the number of dollars invested in the various media. Factor b_2 may specify the number of insertions allowed in magazine x_2. The flexibility allowed in placing constraining conditions is one

of the real strengths of the L.P. approach. Finally, inequality (3) specifies that all x's in the optimal solution either must assume a value of 0 or some positive number.

Day (1962) indicates more specifically the manner in which the general L.P. model is applied to allocation of advertising dollars:

In the linear programing media mix model, the objective function shows how particular advertising units contribute to "total advertising effectiveness." The system of inequalities reflects the restrictions imposed on the solution values of the variables by the budget, the characteristics of available media, and other environmental conditions. The non-negativity requirements prevent infeasible solutions involving negative values of the variables. Solution of a correctly formulated model will then indicate the particular advertising units to be included in the media schedule and the number of uses of each which will result in the greatest "total advertising effectiveness" obtainable from a given budget (p. 42).

The rest of this article analyzes two examples to show how one moves from the general L.P. problem to a specific application. The simplest application of L.P. to media allocation is illustrated in the solution of the McGraw-Edison case (1961). The Pennsylvania Transformer Division of McGraw-Edison manufactures transformers used by industrial plants, schools, public institutions commercial construction projects, and hospitals. The plant engineer usually makes the purchase decision, so the objective is to maximize the number of plant engineers reached, given budgetary and other constraints. The company has $25,000 to spend on industrial advertising, and data are available on markets reached by various media. Since ten media are available for analysis, the objective function assumes the following general form:

$$\text{Maximize } f = p_1x_1 + p_2x_2 + \cdots + p_{10}x_{10}$$

where the x's are the number of dollars invested in the various media and the p's represent the number of plant engineers reached in each magazine per advertising dollar invested.

We computed the values of the p's by dividing the total number of plant engineers reached by the six-time bulk page rate in each medium. The data shown in Table 1 were gathered:

TABLE 1

Magazine		Plant Engineers Reached/ Cost per Insertion		Plant Engineers Reached per Dollar
x_1	Consulting Engineer	0/475	p_1	0
x_2	Electrical Construction	12,000/792	p_2	15.15
x_3	Electrical World	24,000/730	p_3	32.87
x_4	Power	44,000/890	p_4	49.44
x_5	Plant Engineering	52,000/918	p_5	56.65
x_6	Electrical West	8,000/456	p_6	17.54
x_7	Electrified Industry	44,000/756	p_7	58.20
x_8	Public Power	0/700	p_8	0
x_9	Electric Light and Power	16,000/680	p_9	23.53
x_{10}	Transmission and Distribution	23,000/575	p_{10}	40.00

Thus the objective function becomes:

Maximize $f = 0x_1 + 15.15x_2 + 32.87x_3 + 49.44x_4 + 56.65x_5 + 17.54x_6 + 58.20x_7 + 0x_8 + 23.53x_9 + 40.00x_{10}$.

With only $25,000 to spend, a budgetary constraint must be established:

$$x_1 + x_2 + \cdots + x_{10} \leqq \$25,000.$$

In addition, constraints must be fixed to prevent more dollars being invested in any one monthly magazine than is necessary to buy 12 insertions. (*Electrical World* is published weekly but insertions have been limited to 12 for purposes of exposition.) Therefore, these constraints are added:

$x_1 \leqq$	5,700	$x_6 \leqq$	5,472
$x_2 \leqq$	9,504	$x_7 \leqq$	9,072
$x_3 \leqq$	8,760	$x_8 \leqq$	3,300
$x_4 \leqq$	10,680	$x_9 \leqq$	8,160
$x_5 \leqq$	11,016	$x_{10} \leqq$	6,900

This problem is of the general L.P. form and can be solved by the Simplex method (see Spivey, 1963; Garvin, 1960), a procedure which moves the objective function from one feasible solution to the next until a solution is reached in which the objective function has the greatest value given the constraining conditions. An IBM 7090 computer was programed for the Simplex method, and an optimal solution indicated that an investment of $4,912 (roughly 5.5 pages) in *Power* (x_4), $11,016 (12 pages) in *Plant Engineering* (x_5), and $9,072 (12 pages) in *Electrified Industry* (x_7) would maximize the number of plant engineers reached for $25,000.

Obviously, we do not need a computer to solve such a simple problem (which suffers from lack of necessary refinements). It is apparent that some media are better than others for reaching desired objectives, and we need some form of "effectiveness rating." In other words, the media buyer must be certain that he has chosen the media which best match the audience as specified by his objectives. Audience dimensions such as age, income, location should be included in the objective function so that an "optimal" solution maximizes not only the number reached but readers who are likely to be prospects. Let us call this phase of effectiveness rating the "audience profile match."

In addition, media must be analyzed in terms of certain qualitative characteristics, such as the appropriateness of their editorial climate for the product advertised and their proven past ability to provide advertising readership. This second phase of effectiveness rating will be called the "qualitative rating."

Another problem was formulated to illustrate an approach to effectiveness rating. Here the problem is to spend $1,000,000 on advertising of women's electric razors in consumer magazines using full-page, four-color, non-bleed advertisements. Twelve media were singled out for analysis: *Cosmopolitan* (x_1), *Mademoiselle* (x_2), *Family Circle* (x_3), *Good Housekeeping* (x_4), *McCall's* (x_5), *Modern Romances* (x_6), *Modern Screen* (x_7), *Motion Picture* (x_8), *True Confessions* (x_9), *Woman's Day* (x_{10}), *Seventeen* (x_{11}), and *Ladies' Home Journal* (x_{12}).

The first step in effectiveness rating is to determine what parts of the market to reach. Suppose that we discovered through multiple correlation analysis that the desired market is composed of women who are: (1) white; (2) 18 to 44; (3) have incomes of $7,000 or more; and (4) live in metropolitan areas. Using the Starch Consumer Magazine Report, we next analyze various media possibilities in terms of these characteristics to arrive at the "audience profile match." In addition, we estimated each magazine's ability to deliver a good potential audience through data on the number of electric shavers bought by readers in the past year. A large percentage of purchases was considered a favorable indication, and these data were useful in the qualitative rating.

If the problem were approached in a manner similar to the McGraw-Edison case, the objective function would be framed in terms of the number of women reached by each magazine divided by the page rate. With the introduction of the effectiveness rating a great many different schemes could be employed. What we did, though, was to devise a rating scale, ranging from 0 to 1.00, to encompass both the profile match and qualitative rating. The total number of women reached by each medium is multiplied by this factor value to arrive at total "effective audience."

Assume that a multiple correlation analysis showed age to be the most important discriminator of prospects. Age would be assigned a weight in the total rating to reflect its relative importance, as would other factors. In the problem at hand we specified what each factor should contribute to the effectiveness rating as follows:

	Maximum Contribution:
Age (18-44)	.40
Bought shaver	.30
Income ($7,000 or over)	.15
Metropolitan location	.10
White	.05
Total	1.00

The rating scheme could be modified to reflect any additional values which management assumes to be important. For instance, we could have employed another scale ranging from 0.5 to 1.0 to reflect ratings of the appropriateness of editorial climate. The actual form of the effectiveness rating, then, is entirely dictated by the tasks to be accomplished and the data available.

The profile match is obtained by analyzing each magazine's audience on the various dimensions and then assigning a factor weight. A conversion system, of course, is necessary for this purpose, and in a sophisticated approach one perhaps would derive the conversion scale by expressing the various magazines' characteristics in terms of standard deviations of their distributions. Thus, if the proportion of readership aged 18-44 for the magazines under consideration averaged 50 per cent with a standard deviation of five per cent, a specific magazine with 55 per cent of its readership aged 18-44 might be assigned a $+1$ (one standard deviation above the mean). Another magazine having only 40 per cent of its audience in the 18-44 bracket would be assigned a -2. To eliminate negative weights, -3 standard deviations might be termed a zero with the scale running up to a $+6$ for a magazine three standard deviations above the mean.

A much simpler conversion scale is used here for expository purposes. Here is the conversion scale for each factor:

Age (18-44) (0 to .4)		Income ($7,000 or more) (0 to .15)	
Under 50%	0	Under 25%	0
50-55	.1	26-30	.03
56-60	.2	31-35	.06
61-65	.3	36-40	.10
66 or over	.4	41 or over	.15

White (0 to .05)		Metropolitan area (0 to .1)	
Under 85%	0	Under 50%	0
85-90	.01	51-55	.03
91-95	.03	56-60	.06
96 or over	.05	61 or over	.10

Previously Bought Shaver (0 to .3)	
Under 4%	0
5-6	.1
7-8	.2
9-10	.3

To illustrate the effectiveness rating procedure, let us take a hypothetical magazine, *Woman's World*. Assume that the audience data shown below are available on market coverage (from Starch Magazine report or the individual medium). Converting the data, these weights would be applied:

	Audience	Weights
Age 18-44	59%	.20
Income $7,000 or over	31	.06
White subscribers	96	.05
Metropolitan coverage	61	.10
Purchased shaver in last 12 months	7	.20
		.61

Suppose this magazine reaches 5,070,492 women. Multiplying this total by a factor of .61 gives an effective audience of 3,093,000 women. Dividing this by the four-color, full-page rate ($29,100) gives "effective readings per dollar spent" of 106. This final figure will appear in the objective function as the coefficient of the variable (x).

Using the above procedure for each magazine produced the following objective function:

$$\text{Max } f = 158x_1 + 263x_2 + 106x_3 + 108x_4 + 65x_5 + 176x_6 + 285x_7 + 86x_8 + 120x_9 + 51x_{10} + 190x_{11} + 101x_{12}.$$

With the budgetary constraint:

$$x_1 + x_2 + \ldots + x_{12} \leq 1,000,000.$$

And the usual non-negativity constraint:

$$x_1 \geq 0 \qquad (i = 1, \ldots, 12).$$

Also constraints again were established to prevent assigning more than 12 insertions to any of these monthly magazines. Suppose, however, that management had good reason to limit the maximum insertions to less than 12 for media x_2 and x_{12} (for example, 7 and 2 insertions respectively). Thus the constraints are:

$x_1 \leq 58,080$	$x_7 \leq 52,380$
$x_2 \leq 30,075$ (7)	$x_8 \leq 53,580$
$x_3 \leq 349,000$	$x_9 \leq 57,960$
$x_4 \leq 288,000$	$x_{10} \leq 333,000$
$x_5 \leq 407,400$	$x_{11} \leq 72,360$
$x_6 \leq 52,380$	$x_{12} \leq 81,200$ (2)

Suppose further that the client company has specified certain minimum expenditures in magazines x_2, x_3, x_5, and x_{10}. Therefore:

$$x_2 \geq 13,275$$
$$x_3 \geq 58,166$$
$$x_5 \leq 33,950$$
$$x_{10} \geq 27,750$$

Finally, management declared a maximum expenditure of $280,000 in magazines x_3, x_9, x_{10}, and x_{12} and specified the investment of exactly $85,870 in magazines x_1 and x_8. Thus:

$$x_3 + x_9 + x_{10} + x_{12} \leq 280,000$$
$$x_1 + x_8 = 85,870$$

The above problem is obviously more complex than the McGraw-Edison case, and it is no longer possible to visualize a solution readily. Imagine the difficulties if 50 media were employed with a more complex set of constraints! Also, a variety of subjective restrictions could have been used as alternatives to those shown above. The strength of L.P. is that for every configuration of subjective constraints, we can readily solve the corresponding problem. Indeed, management might be presented with two or more solutions showing the impact of changes in the subjective constraints upon the optimal solution.

The Simplex method of solution was used on the computer, and an optimal solution to the above problem directed that we make these purchases:

Medium	
x_1 *Cosmopolitan*	$ 58,080
x_2 *Mademoiselle*	30,075
x_3 *Family Circle*	194,290
x_4 *Good Housekeeping*	288,000
x_5 *McCall's*	180,484*
x_6 *Modern Romances*	52,380
x_7 *Modern Screen*	52,380
x_8 *Motion Picture*	27,790
x_9 *True Confessions*	57,960
x_{10} *Woman's Day*	27,750
x_{11} *Seventeen*	72,360
x_{12} *Ladies' Home Journal*	0

* Includes reinvested discounts.

After the initial allocation it was necessary to reconsult Standard Rate and Data Service to find the extent of volume discounts which the firm had earned. We discovered that an additional $41,549 was available for expenditure. The Simplex solution indicates, within bounds, where to invest these additional funds. In the problem at hand, it was indicated that the additional dollars should be invested in *McCall's*.

An important point to keep in mind is that quantity discounts could not have been built into the original statement of the problem. The cost function would then have been nonlinear, and L.P. would no longer have been applicable. Nonlinear programing methods are available, but the solution would become decidedly more complex (see Dorn, 1963; Wolfe, 1959).

As suggested earlier, management should not view the Simplex solution as the final phase in the L.P. approach. It might be quite useful, for example, to engage in a sensitivity analysis by changing the weights used in the effectiveness rating, especially those based on subjective evaluation. If rather large changes can be made in these weights without changing the optimal solution, it is evident that the solution is not dependent on precise evaluations of qualitative characteristics. If, however, the optimal solution changes with slight variations in these weights then it is obvious that the quality of the solution can be little better than the quality of the effectiveness rating procedure.

Let us now state more specifically the steps in a well-conceived L.P. media allocation procedure:

1. Establishment of specific advertising objectives.
2. Procurement of data on the relative importance of various characteristics of the market to be reached through multiple correlation analysis or other means.
3. Procurement of data on audiences of various candidate media. Often these data are stored in the computer, thus permitting quick access.
4. Application of an effectiveness rating procedure encompassing two phases: audience profile match and qualitative factor rating.
5. Quantification of all constraining conditions, including budgetary limits, limits on media availability, and other environmental factors.
6. Application of an L.P. computational procedure.
7. Analysis of the resulting media plan to determine its sensitivity to various factors in the effectiveness rating and to changes in constraint conditions.

The L.P. approach has important strengths and weaknesses which must be recognized by all potential users, and each point will be examined.

Advantages of L.P. Approach

1. L.P. forces management to make precise definitions of markets to be reached. Instead of guesses or hunches, data must be developed which characterize markets along several dimensions. The net result of such analysis cannot help but increase the effectiveness of media allocation.

2. L.P. requires a quantification of factors which are highly qualitative in nature. Editorial climate is perhaps a highly subjective factor yet management must take this media characteristic and others of a similar nature into account when engaging in media selection.

3. L.P. creates a definite need for audience profiles of various media. The occasional media audience study no longer will suffice, and instead careful audience profile information must be provided with the regularity of ABC sworn circulation data. L.P. is certain, therefore, to stimulate the collection of a wealth of previously unavailable facts.

4. L.P. can be applied to problems involving a variety of media. Although we have discussed only magazines, there is no reason why all possible media cannot be included in the L.P. approach. If data are available, all media can be considered in the same terms, making it feasible to consider vastly more media at a time than would be possible without the aid of a computer.

5. L.P. can be used by advertisers and agencies

of *any* size. No mumbo jumbo in the methodology limits this approach only to large firms. Furthermore, it is not necessary to confine L.P. to allocations approaching astronomical sums. Indeed, the allocation of a few thousand dollars can become sufficiently complex to warrant use of the computer, especially when one considers the potential costs of an ineffective allocation.

6. L.P. allows the blending together of many factors. As Maneloveg (1962) points out:

In the past we have worked at it with stubby pencils and people, many people. However, no matter how much time and how many people, we have had too many factors to contend with. The real advantage of an electronic computer to us then—its principal purpose—is to give us an opportunity to change these relationships, to juggle with them, to work with them while at the same time keeping all of them in the forefront of the operation and to end up with an effort that examines the whole not individual pieces of media . . . the way, incidentally, our customers view the campaign that we're putting together (p. 6).

Limitations

1. L.P. is applicable only if all relationships in the problem are linear or if it is appropriate for management purposes to regard them as so. This is a marketing decision, not a mathematical one. As noted above, the requirement of linearity in cost functions did not permit inclusion of quantity discounts in the initial allocation. Yet the resulting allocation may fail to achieve the maximum discount which might have become available if dollars were allocated differently. It is difficult to maximize discounts unless constraints require only large purchases of individual media, but, on the other hand, such constraints may unduly limit the solution space to large buys and thereby force an ineffective allocation.

The assumption of linearity becomes more crucial in another respect. Although the cost functions in both examples required purchases of full pages, fractional page purchases appeared in the allocation. The problem arises because the Simplex approach does not guarantee the purchase of only full pages. The cost of a half page, for example, is not half of the page rate, so it may be incorrect to assume that purchases of fractional pages are optimal. In other words, the cost function for various page sizes is actually nonlinear. Then what is the advertiser to do when his answer calls for 4.83 pages? Is he safe in rounding this figure to 5.00? He probably would not err greatly if he does, but he still must recognize the danger of arriving at a non-optimal allocation if he rounds off on a large scale. Furthermore, cost structures may not depart

so far from linearity as to preclude meaningful answers. The only feasible way in which to guarantee nonfractional purchases, however, is to use "integer programing," and we are experimenting with this approach.

Finally, it is assumed that successive purchases in a media all contribute the same value to the objective function. It must be recognized that multiple exposure of a given prospect may become increasingly less effective, thus introducing nonlinearity into the response function. This problem may be crucial, but we cannot avoid it without resorting to more complex nonlinear programing methods.

2. Solutions were arrived at without consideration of audience duplication and accumulation. Because of audience overlap, purchase of two or more magazines should result in a total audience that is less than the sum of the individual audiences. Although the Agostini (1961) constant may permit estimates of nonduplicated audiences, his approach requires data that are not available on a consistent scale, especially if one is comparing a magazine and a television show. Furthermore, whereas duplication and accumulation of *prospects* are the only truly relevant considerations, existing data are confined entirely to total audiences. Thus at present the L.P. approach cannot solve effectively the duplication and accumulation problems.

3. Comparable data are not always available for various media in terms of audience dimensions. More and better media data are required before L.P. can achieve its potential.

4. Finally, resulting solutions give a very misleading illusion of definiteness. Solutions are only as good as the data and assumptions upon which they are built. Weaknesses in data or in analysis of the problem will be compounded, so good judgment is vital.

CONCLUSION

The approach to L.P. and media allocation described here obviously needs considerable refinement. And it should be abundantly clear that the major problems arise in identifying and quantifying the important marketing variables—not in application of the L.P. computational procedure. L.P. is not a magical device that relegates responsibility for management decisions to computers and their programers. Indeed, the successful use of L.P. involves three essentials: (1) defining market targets; (2) rating media in terms of their effectiveness in reaching these targets; (3) developing and quantifying monetary and non-monetary 'constraints which limit feasible solutions. Thus judgment responsibilities of the media executive are *sharpened*, not eliminated. The only thing eliminated is laborious clerical work.

Let us conclude by observing that L.P. is not a breakthrough and that it involves very little more than systematizing steps which have long been followed by successful advertisers. The real gain comes in the time saved and the ability to handle complex problems with greater ease and to deal quickly with alternative subjective evaluations of constraints and weighting factors. We hope the glamor which quantitative methods now hold does not cause advertisers to overlook the inescapable difficulty of identifying and evaluating the important marketing variables. If this problem is fully recognized, then L.P. is not likely to be blighted in its infancy, as was motivation research, by exaggerated and commercially-motivated claims of a few zealous spokesmen.

REFERENCES

AGOSTINI, J.-M. How to Estimate Unduplicated Audiences. *Journal of Advertising Research*, Vol. 1, No. 3, March 1961, pp. 11-14.

CHURCHMAN, C. WEST, RUSSELL L. ACKOFF, AND LEONARD E. ARNOFF. *Introduction to Operations Research*. New York: John Wiley, 1957.

DAY, RALPH L. Linear Programming in Media Selection. *Journal of Advertising Research*, Vol. 2, No. 2, June 1962, pp. 40-44.

DORFMAN, ROBERT, PAUL A. SAMUELSON, AND ROBERT M. SOLOW. *Linear Programming and Economic Analysis*. New York: McGraw-Hill, 1958.

DORN, W. S. Non-Linear Programming—A Survey. *Management Science*, Vol. 9, No. 2, January 1963, pp. 171-208.

GARVIN, W. W. *An Introduction to Linear Programming*. New York: McGraw-Hill, 1960.

MANELOVEG, HERBERT. Linear Programming. Paper presented at Eastern annual convention, American Association of Advertising Agencies, November 1962, New York.

McGRAW-EDISON COMPANY. *ICH 6m67*. Boston: Intercollegiate Case Clearing House, 1961.

SPIVEY, W. ALLEN. *Linear Programming: An Introduction*. New York: Macmillan, 1963.

WOLFE, PHILIP. The Simplex Method for Quadratic Programming. *Econometrica*, Vol. 27, No. 3, July 1959, pp. 382-398.

A Ballade of Multiple Regression

If you want to deal best with your questions,
　Use multi-regression techniques;
A computer can do in a minute
　What, otherwise done, would take weeks.
For 'predictor selection' procedures
　Will pick just the ones best for you
And provide the best-fitting equation
　—For the data you've fitted it to.

But did you collect the *right* data?
　Were there "glaring omissions" in yours?
Have the ones that score highly much *meaning*?
　Can you tell the effect from the cause?
Are your 'cause' factors ones you can act on?
　If not, you've got more work to do;
Your equation's as good—or as bad—as
　The data you've fitted it to.

But it's worse when new factors have entered
　The field since your survey was made,
Or even the old ones have varied
　Beyond all the bounds you surveyed.
Has your leading competitor faltered?
　Have you got, with old brands, one that's *new*?
This won't have come in your regression
　Or the data you've fitted it to.

So 'get with' the Efroymson programme,
　And list out your factors with zeal,
With their sesquipedalian labels
　And wonderful client-appeal.
But, brothers, please always remember,
　Be you Marplan, or Schwerin, or who—
Your optimum only is bonum
　For the data you've fitted it to.

—TOM CORLETT
(Taken from paper read at Market Research Society Conference, February 1964)

Media Selection by Linear Programming

DOUGLAS B. BROWN

and

MARTIN R. WARSHAW*

➤ Linear programming models for media selection have limited application because the function describing the aggregate response to additional inputs of advertising effort is generally non-linear. The authors present a general media mix model which assumes linear response and illustrate how the model can be modified to accommodate non-linearity while still using the revised simplex method as a solution algorithm.

Great interest is being shown currently in the use of linear programming (L.P.) as a tool to allocate advertising appropriations to various media. Evidence of this interest can be found scattered throughout the advertising industry. The subject of the sixth meeting of the Advertising Research Foundation Operations Research Discussion Group was "Mathematical Methods of Media Selection" [3]. A series of papers dealing with "Mathematical Programming for Better Media Selection" was presented at the 1961 Eastern Annual Conference of the American Association of Advertising Agencies [4]. Indeed, linear programming seems to have become an advertising industry fashion to the extent that late in 1962 full-page ads in the *Wall Street Journal* and elsewhere stated that linear programming had shown one client how to get ". . . $1.67 worth of effective advertising for every dollar in his advertising budget."

A statement like the one above may lead the potential user of the L.P. approach to underestimate the technical difficulties which arise in the application of linear programming to media mix problems. Foremost among these obstacles is the typically non-linear response to additional inputs of advertising in a single medium. The purpose of this paper is to demonstrate how a linear model can be adapted to solve many media mix problems involving non-linear responses to advertising. This is not to say that all of the difficulties have been overcome; however, the problems remaining are of a different sort. These remaining issues, implicit in the models to be presented, involve determining appropriate values for the coefficients of the variables in the

objective function and making an allowance for audience duplication. These and other questions are discussed later.

Two models are presented: The first, a very simple one, illustrates the general linear programming method. It is essentially a refined version of a model developed by Engel and Warshaw [2]. The second, a slightly more complex model, shows how a non-linear objective function can be treated within the framework of a linear model under certain conditions.

THE FIRST MODEL—LINEAR RESPONSE

Institutional Constraints

Let N_i ($i = 1, 2, \cdots, n$) be the number of times the i_{th} advertising alternative is used per period. Thus, N_i could be the number of insertions in a national magazine, or it could be the number of 3:00 p.m., WJBK, 30-second spot television commercials used, or it could be the number of full-page black and white ads to be placed in the *Detroit News* in any given period. Alternative uses of the same medium require different N_i's. If one is considering both half-page and full-page insertions in the *Detroit News*, a different N_i is needed for each alternative. Different media of the same type also require different N_i's. For instance, full-page insertions in the *Ann Arbor News* and the *Detroit News* require different N_i's. Suppose N_1 is to be the number of full-page, four-color advertisements to be placed in the *Saturday Evening Post* per year. Since there are only 52 issues of the *Post* per year, clearly,

$$N_1 \leq 52.$$

Suppose N_2 is to be the number of 30-second 12:15 p.m. commercials on "Love of Life," a television soap opera. Since this program has only 260 broadcasts per year,

$$N_2 \leq 260.$$

* Douglas Brown is currently a Ford Fellow in the doctoral program at the Graduate School of Business Administration, University of Michigan. Martin Warshaw is an associate professor of marketing at the same institution. Both authors wish to thank James F. Engel, associate professor of business organization at Ohio State University, for his help in laying the groundwork for the research upon which this article is based.

In general, $\Sigma N_i \leq$ the maximum number of times it is possible (or it is allowable) to use the particular medium in the time period under consideration. The subscript i relates to a particular medium.

Budgetary Constraint

Let the advertising budget be M dollars, and let the cost of one use of media i be c_i. Then,

$$c_1 N_1 + c_2 N_2 + c_3 N_3 + \cdots + c_n N_n \leq M.$$

Subjective Constraints

The advertiser may decide that it is desirable to have at least 6 insertions in *Fortune* (N_3) which is a monthly magazine. Thus,

$$N_3 \geq 6.$$

Or he may want to use either *Life* (N_{17}) or *The Saturday Evening Post* (N_1) in a particular way at least once each month. Then

$$N_1 + N_{17} \geq 12.$$

In addition, he may want to use these two publications no more than 16 times:

$$N_1 + N_{17} \leq 16.$$

Within the framework of this model, one is free to impose subjective constraints which reflect management's or the agency's conception of the limits to be placed on the media program. However, because of the possibility of mistaken judgment on the part of advertising managers and agency account executives it is probably best to minimize the use of such constraints. Such subjective constraints may be responsible for defects in many advertising programs. At the very least, a solution not involving such constraints may cause the executive concerned to reconsider his judgment if the solution indicates that a medium should be used in quantities different from those originally considered. A comparison of optimal programs both with and without constraints will help illustrate the effect of the inclusion of the constraints. Such information may be of use in the formulation of constraints and, when combined with good judgment, could be of substantial help in developing better advertising programs and allocation models.

Objective Function for the First Model

Although there is a less than perfect relationship between the number of reader exposures to advertising and the sales response to advertising, it is reasonable to choose the objective of maximizing the number of "effective" exposures that can be attained given the advertising budget. The key word in this assertion is the word effective. The objective is not to maximize the number of exposures of all readers to the advertising; on the contrary, it is to maximize the potential buyers exposed to the advertising, and in some cases to maximize the number of exposures to the advertising of

potential buyers and persons having major purchase influence.

Needless to say, some media are better than others for reaching desired audiences, and the need arises for some form of "effectiveness rating." In other words, the media buyer must be certain that he has chosen media which best match the audience he must reach as specified by his promotional objectives. A number of audience characteristics such as age, income, location, and other attributes should be considered in the objective function if this goal is to be attained.

In order to illustrate the idea of effectiveness rating, a simple example will be used. The problem is to spend M dollars on advertising of a women's hair coloring product in consumer magazines using full-page, four-color, non-bleed advertisements.

Assume that consumer research has established that the desired market is composed of women with the following characteristics weighted in importance as indicated.

Age (18–44)	.50
Income ($7,000+)	.25
Metropolitan location	.15
White	.10
Total	1.00

Suppose the following data are available on the readership of one of the magazines under consideration:

Age (18–44)	60%
Income ($7,000+)	33%
Metropolitan location	70%
White	95%

Assume that 5,000,000 women are reached by this magazine. Note that the number of women reached by the magazine is not the same concept as the number of women subscribers. The former information may in fact be very difficult to obtain for some publications, although Daniel Starch and Staff determine readership by sex for a number of publications.

In order to determine the effective readership of this magazine, we multiply the total readership by a positive number which is less than or equal to one. This number can be determined by multiplying the maximum weight assigned to each demographic purchase determinant by its corresponding percent incidence in the readership of the magazine, summing the numbers so calculated, and dividing by 100:

$$\frac{(60 \times .50) + (33 \times .25) + (70 \times .15) + (95 \times .10)}{100}$$
$$= .583$$

The effective readership of this magazine is therefore $.583 \times 5,000,000$, or 2,915,000 readers. In general, it is possible to calculate an effectiveness rating coefficient, e_i, like the number .583 determined above for each medium under consideration. Let the total readership for the particular medium associated with i be r_i.

(Note that if a single medium is used in more than one way, e_i and r_i will have the same magnitudes for each of the i's associated with this medium.) A preliminary estimate for the objective function for this model is then:

$$\max z = e_1 r_1 N_1 + e_2 r_2 N_2 + \cdots + e_n r_n N_n$$
$$(0 \leqq e_i \leqq 1).$$

However, additional refinements should be made. Media must be analyzed in terms of certain qualitative characteristics such as appropriateness of editorial climate for the product being advertised and demonstrated past ability to produce successful advertising readership. For instance, on this basis a manufacturer of home furnishings would probably prefer *House Beautiful* over *Life* as an appropriate vehicle to carry his advertising message. This type of analysis should also be reflected in the objective function.

Suppose that management on the basis of experience determines that both the demonstrated past ability to produce successful advertising readership and the appropriateness of the editorial climate should each carry 10 percent of the weight in the decision-making process. (In some cases it may be possible to make a quantitative determination of the appropriate weights.) Let x_i be the number of points assigned to demonstrated past ability of alternative i to produce successful advertising readership. Let y_i be the number of points assigned to the appropriateness of the editorial climate of the medium corresponding to i. Note that the following inequalities hold:.

$$0 \leqq x_i \leqq 10$$
$$0 \leqq y_i \leqq 10$$

The final adjusted effective readership for this magazine is

$$\frac{80 + x_i + y_i}{100} \, (e_i r_i N_i).$$

It is obvious that the model is not limited to the use of two qualitative characteristics; and depending on the situation, any of a number of such characteristics would be appropriate for inclusion in the model. Define the qualitative characteristics rating coefficient q_i corresponding to the i_{th} alternative as a coefficient which is determined in the manner described above. The objective function for this first model can now be stated as:

$$\max z = q_1 e_1 r_1 N_1 + q_2 e_2 r_2 N_2 + \cdots + q_n e_n r_n N_n$$
$$(0 \leqq q_i \leqq 1), (0 \leqq e_i \leqq 1).$$

In some cases one or two additional refinements are necessary. If both color and non-color advertisements are being considered (a different N_i corresponding to each alternative) the relative effectiveness of a color versus a non-color presentation must be considered. Unless this is done the lower-priced non-color advertisements will always be selected before the higher priced

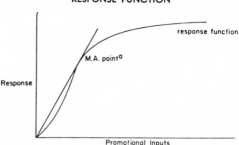

Figure I

RESPONSE FUNCTION

[a] This is the point at which the average response is equal to the marginal response.

color advertisements. Suppose that in the particular application being considered, the black and white ad is deemed to be 70 percent as effective as a four-color ad, and suppose that N_1 and N_2 correspond to black and white and four-color advertisements in the *Saturday Evening Post*. Then the first two terms in the objective function just presented would be modified as follows:

$$\max z = .70 \, q_1 e_1 r_1 N_1 + q_2 e_2 r_2 N_2 + \cdots$$

In general, when both black and white and color advertisements are being considered, the objective function must be modified to appear as follows (c_i represents the relative effectiveness of the color characteristics of the advertisement under consideration compared with the most effective color advertisement available, expressed as a decimal):

$$\max z = c_1 q_1 e_1 r_1 N_1 + c_2 q_2 e_2 r_2 N_2 + \cdots + c_n q_n e_n r_n N_n$$
$$(0 \leqq c_i \leqq 1), (0 \leqq q_i \leqq 1), (0 \leqq e_i \leqq 1).$$

If placements of different size ads are being considered, the relative effectiveness of such placements must also be evaluated. For example, if both half and full page ads are being considered, and if the relative effectiveness of these two alternatives was neglected, the lower priced half-page ads would always be selected before the full page ads. Let s_i represent the relative effectiveness of the size of ad i under consideration when compared with the largest size ad under consideration, expressed as a decimal. For instance, a half-page ad may be deemed 25 percent as effective as a full-page ad, or a 15-second TV spot commercial may be deemed 35 percent as effective as a full-minute spot.

The final objective function would appear as:

$$\max z = s_1 c_1 q_1 e_1 r_1 N_1 + \cdots + s_n c_n q_n e_n r_n N_n,$$
$$\text{with } (0 \leqq s_i \leqq 1), (0 \leqq c_i \leqq 1), (0 \leqq q_i \leqq 1),$$
$$\text{and } (0 \leqq e_i \leqq 1).$$

First Model—Summary

The institutional constraints, the budgetary constraint, and the subjective constraints described earlier, and the objective function just developed together describe a linear programming problem. Problems of a size likely to be considered by most advertisers can be solved by means of the revised simplex method on a properly programmed digital computer.[1]

THE NATURE OF ADVERTISING RESPONSE

The objective function derived above is probably a satisfactory approximation in some cases. But, in general the response to advertising as a function of the number of insertions in a particular medium is nonlinear. The use of one term of the form $s_i c_i q_i e_i r_i N_i$ in the objective function for each considered use of a medium implies that the marginal value of each additional unit of advertising is the same regardless of the level of the advertising. However, many informed observers feel that a curve representing the individual's response to steadily increased promotional activity probably will have the form shown in Figure 1 [6]. According to Zentler and Ryde:

> The opinions of the publicity experts we have consulted seem to confirm this. Such a curve embodies the following ideas: When the promotion is first started, the response is very small, but once the required 'softening up' process has been performed there is a range in which the response rises rapidly as promotional activity is increased. Ultimately, as promotion is increased to much higher levels, the rate of increase in response tails off again and a point is reached at which further promotion produces little additional effect [6].

Conditions Necessary for the Use of the First Model

When the bow of the lower portion of the curve in Figure 1 is not too great, a straight line such as the one

---

[1] The simplex method provides a way of solving linear programming problems. A very simplified explanation of how it works is that it enables the objective function to be evaluated at different corner points of the set of feasible solutions as determined by the constraining conditions. A theorem states that the objective function will have an optimum value (maximum or minimum) when it passes through one of these points. Through an iterative process the simplex method tests each "corner point" until the optimum value of the objective function is reached.

Without the computer the time element alone would place most linear programming problems beyond solution. However, by using a computer programmed to apply the simplex solution algorithm, even the larger L.P. problems can be solved in a matter of minutes.

The revised simplex algorithm is a more efficient version of the simplex method requiring fewer iterations and, therefore, less computer time to reach an optimum solution. The original simplex program is available through the IBM Share program reference number 863 RSM 1. The revised simplex is available under IBM Share number 1037 SCM 2.

For a highly readable basic approach to linear programming the reader is referred to W. A. Spivey, *Linear Programming: An Introduction*, New York: Macmillan, 1963.

illustrated is a good approximation to this part of the curve. If the institutional or subjective restrictions of the first model are such that at most a small section of each medium's curve above the point M.A. is included in the objective function, then the first model will be a good approximation provided, of course, that the bow in the lower portion of the curve is not too pronounced.[2] However, even when these conditions do not hold, the model is frequently appropriate. This model will yield accurate results when the solution values for the N_i's are not large enough to correspond to points above the M.A. points on the response functions for the various media. It seems likely that this will often be the case, since promotional budgets are generally restricted to an amount which will yield a high return for the last dollar spent.

Reasonable Approximations to the Curve of Figure 1

Zentler and Ryde use curves of the form of Figure 2 as an approximation to the curve in Figure 1 [6]. Vidale and Wolfe have achieved excellent results using an aggregate response function of exponential form [5]. Their article presents an interesting derivation of this result based on the differential equation

$$dS/dt = rA(t)(M - S)/M - \lambda S$$

where λ is the exponential sales decay constant, M is a saturation level, and r is a response constant. They present empirical evidence to support their conclusions. Thus, the curve in Figure 2 appears to be a valid approximation to the form of the response function and the Vidale-Wolfe article provides a method for deriving such curves in many cases.

THE SECOND MODEL—NON-LINEAR RESPONSE

It is indeed fortunate that such approximation is possible, because for each medium a non-linear function (a) of the form shown in Figure 2 can be incorporated into the objective function, and the linearity of the model will be maintained. Figure 2 further illustrates that two or three or more straight lines (b) can be used to approximate a function like the one shown in Figure 2 to any desired degree of accuracy. (Since little more than the general shape of the response function is presently known, a two- or three-line approximation is all that is justified.) For the purpose of illustration, consider the function illustrated in Figure 2 and assume that the slopes of the three lines which approximate this function are 8,000,000, 5,000,000 and 2,000,000, where these slopes are expressed in the units response per unit input of promotional activity. Note that the slope of this function never increases as

---

[2] Note the assumption here that the aggregate-response-to-advertising function for a medium has a shape similar to the individual's function.

Figure 2

APPROXIMATION OF RESPONSE FUNCTION

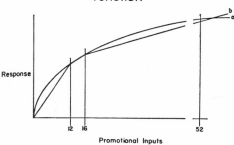

Promotional Inputs

promotional activity increases, and that it changes to a lower value at two points as promotional activity increases. To be even more specific, assume that the advertising placement under consideration is N_1 and that $N_1 \leq 52$. Assume that the response function changes slope at the points $N_1 = 12$ and $N_1 = 16$ as illustrated in Figure 2. Define N_{11}, N_{12}, and N_{13} as follows:

for the region

$$0 \leq N_1 \leq 12, \qquad \begin{aligned} N_{11} &= N_1 \\ N_{12} &= 0 \\ N_{13} &= 0; \end{aligned}$$

for the region $\qquad\qquad\qquad\qquad\qquad\qquad (1)^3$

$$12 < N_1 \leq 16, \qquad \begin{aligned} N_{11} &= 12 \\ N_{12} &= N_1 - 12 \\ N_{13} &= 0; \end{aligned}$$

and for the region

$$16 < N_1 \leq 52, \qquad \begin{aligned} N_{11} &= 12 \\ N_{12} &= 4 \\ N_{13} &= N_1 - 16. \end{aligned}$$

It follows from the definitions of N_{11}, N_{12}, and N_{13} that

$$N_1 = N_{11} + N_{12} + N_{13}.$$

Replace the term $s_1 c_1 q_1 e_1 r_1 N_1$ in the objective function of the first model by the terms $s_1 c_1 q_1 e_1 r_1 N_{11}$ + 5,000,000/8,000,000 $s_1 c_1 q_1 e_1 r_1 N_{12}$ + 2,000,000/ 8,000,000 $s_1 c_1 q_1 e_1 r_1 N_{13}$ which can be simplified to

$$s_1 c_1 q_1 e_1 r_1 N_{11} + .625 s_1 c_1 q_1 e_1 r_1 N_{12} + .25 s_1 c_1 q_1 e_1 r_1 N_{13}$$

Although the above equations and inequations as well as the objective function appear to be complex, their net effect is simple. It is that media insertion numbers 1 through 11 are of equal and unit value but insertions 12 through 15 are discounted 37.5 percent $(1 - .625)$ and insertions 16 on up to 52 are discounted 75 percent $(1 - .25)$.

Replace the institutional restriction

$$N_1 \leq 52$$

by the inequations[3]

$$(2) \qquad \begin{aligned} 0 &\leq N_{11} \leq 12 \\ 0 &\leq N_{12} \leq 4 \\ 0 &\leq N_{13} \leq 36 \end{aligned}$$

in the first model. In all the remaining constraints of the first model involving N_1 replace N_1 by $N_{11} + N_{12} + N_{13}$. The resulting system of constraints and the modified objective function compose the second model. This model involves only the variables N_{11}, N_{12}, N_{13}, $N_2, \ldots, N_n$.

If the solution algorithm used for the second model guarantees that for an optimum solution all available N_{11} is used if any N_{12} or N_{13} are used, and that if any N_{13} is used, all of N_{11} and N_{12} are used, then inequations and equations (1) will be satisfied. But the revised simplex method for solving linear programming problems guarantees that inequations and equations (1) will be satisfied. Since the coefficient of N_{11} in the modified objective function is greater than the coefficients of N_{12} or N_{13}, it will always increase the value of the objective function to move some N_{12} or N_{13} to N_{11} when this is possible. Hence, for an optimum solution, $N_{11} = 12$ if N_{12} or N_{13} are greater than zero. This is true because the only way in which N_{11}, N_{12}, and N_{13} enter the constraints of the modified model is in the form $N_{11} + N_{12} + N_{13}$ other than in inequations (2), and units can interchange between N_{11}, N_{12}, and N_{13} provided that their sum is unchanged and inequations (2) are satisfied. Similarly, for an optimal solution, if N_{13} is greater than zero, then $N_{11} = 12$ and $N_{12} = 4$ since it always increases the value of the objective function to exchange N_{13} for N_{11} or N_{12} when this is possible. The preceding reasoning shows that for an optimal linear programming solution to the modified first model, all available units of N_{11} will be used before any N_{12} is used, and that all available N_{12} will be used before any N_{13} is used.

If this procedure is repeated for each N_i ($i = 1, 2, 3, \cdots, n$) by introducing each particular use of a particular medium i in sequence, the first model is replaced by a new linear programming model. (Note that the equations and inequations (1) for each i are not formally introduced into the new model.) This procedure can easily be generalized such that any N_i ($i = 1, 2, \cdots, n$) can be replaced by a set of variables N_{ij} ($j = 1, 2, \cdots, m$), where m can be chosen as large as is necessary to sufficiently approximate the response to advertising function for i. However, if $S_1, S_2, \cdots, S_m$ are the slopes corresponding to $N_{i1}, N_{i2}, \cdots, N_{im}$, the following inequality must hold:

$$S_m < S_{m-1} < S_{m-2} < \cdots < S_1.$$

---

[3] These bounds on N_{11}, N_{12}, and N_{13} follow from equations and inequations [1].

This is just another way of saying that this method can only be used for a response-to-advertising function of the form shown in Figure 2. The inequalities imply that the response-to-advertising function which is being approximated by straight-line segments must have a non-increasing first derivative as the amount of promotion increases.

Although the second model takes into account the relative effectiveness of the various media, certain qualitative observations about the media, and a declining response to advertising in each media with increased use, it is still less than perfect. However, it should be accurate enough for use in a wide variety of situations and for a number of different products. But before concluding this discussion, some of the limitations of this model should be pointed out.

One complication occurs when more than one N_i per medium is used. Although the model presented considers the decreasing effectiveness of additional insertions of the same type in a particular medium, it does not consider the fact that when two or more different types of advertisements are placed in the same medium their cumulative effect may be different from the sum of their individual effects. For example, the combined effect of a series of black and white and color ads placed over a campaign period in a single medium may be different from the sum of the effects achieved by each type of ad if placed in the same medium unaccompanied by the other type.

Of course it remains to be answered how one obtains the response to advertising function for each proposed use of each medium under consideration. Such functions can be derived by an analysis of past sales and advertising data for the product under consideration or for similar products, provided the media under consideration have previously been used. Even if the firm has no such data of its own, it may be able to use competitors' data, since the sales performance and advertising history of competing products can frequently be determined. Our intention is not to underemphasize the problem of collecting current and valid aggregate response data. Nevertheless, until such time that better methodology allows more accurate derivation of response functions, we feel that workable approximations can be made.

One of the most serious shortcomings of the model is that it does not take into account audience duplications for the media being considered. An optimal linear programming solution might indicate heavy use of two magazines whose readerships have a large audience duplication. Thus, it might be possible to reach individual readers' M.A. points much more rapidly than the model would indicate. In this event, a true optimum solution might dictate the choice of an alternative magazine which has less audience duplication with the other than the originally selected magazine.

Agostini and others have found methods for estimating the unduplicated audiences of groups of media, but the authors have not been able to apply these approaches to programming problems [1]. However, it may be possible that the individual's response to advertising curve tails off less rapidly when the message is presented in a variety of media and in a variety of ways than when the message is always presented in the same style in the same media. To the extent that this is true, there will be a compensatory effect.

The fact that a linear programming solution to the model will, in general, result in non-integer values for N_i may cause difficulty. However, considering the approximate nature of the objective function, round-off error in many cases should not appreciably increase the degree of non-optimality. In any event, integer programming methods are available for the solution of problems of this type.

One final reservation should be mentioned. The coefficients in the budgetary constraint were treated as constants. In reality large placements in certain media may result in quantity discounts. However, if such discounts are a small percentage of the total budget, the solution to the dual problem indicates where a modest additional amount of a scarce input can best be used. If discounts are a large part of the total budget, other means would have to be devised to handle the nonlinear cost functions.

It has been suggested that it might be useful to engage in a sensitivity analysis by changing the weights used in the effectiveness rating (and the qualitative ratings), especially those based on subjective evaluation [2]. If rather large changes can be made in these weights without significantly altering the optimal solution, this solution is probably not dependent on the precise evaluation of the rating coefficients used to modify the objective function. If however the optimal solution changes with slight variations in these weights, the quality of the solution can be little better than the accuracy of these coefficients.

REFERENCES

1. J. M. Agostini, "How to Estimate Unduplicated Audiences," *Journal of Advertising Research,* 1 (1961), 11-14.
2. James F. Engel and Martin R. Warshaw, "Allocating Advertising Dollars by Linear Programming," *The Journal of Advertising Research,* 4 (1964), 42-48.
3. *Mathematical Methods of Media Selection. A Report of the Sixth Meeting of the ARF Operations Research Discussion Group,* New York, Advertising Research Foundation, Inc.
4. *Mathematical Programming for Better Media Selection,* Papers from 1961 region conventions, 1961. American Association of Advertising Agencies.
5. M. L. Vidale and H. B. Wolfe, "An Operations-Research Study of Sales Response to Advertising." *Operations Research,* 5 (1957), 370-81.
6. A. P. Zentler and Dorothy Ryde, "An Optimum Geographical Distribution of Publicity Expenditure in a Private Organization," *Management Science,* 2 (1956), 337-53.

Linear Programing and Space-Time Considerations in Media Selection

STANLEY F. STASCH

Northwestern University

Two problems in media selection are when and in which markets advertisements should appear. The author shows how to refine a linear program to incorporate these considerations.

THE PURPOSE of the present article is to point out one possible method of extending the linear programing technique to include certain time and space considerations in media selection.

Relevant previous papers are few, and none deal with the time and space considerations discussed here. Miller and Starr (1960) and Day (1962) provide a good basic discussion of the principles of linear programing as applied to media selection. Like Day and most of the other articles, the present article will attempt to provide the reader with

STANLEY F. STASCH has been assistant professor of marketing, Northwestern University, since 1963. Before that he worked in product and market planning for the Communications Division of Motorola, Inc., where his final position was marketing manager, closed circuit television department. In addition to M.B.A. and Ph.D. degrees from Northwestern University, Professor Stasch also holds degrees in electrical engineering from Notre Dame. This engineering background combined with his business experience led to his interest in the application of quantitative techniques to marketing problems. He is a member of the AMA and TIMS.

an intuitive understanding of space and time considerations, rather than develop the mathematics associated with the linear programing algorithm. Engel and Warshaw (1964) presented two examples of media selection, and Brown and Warshaw (1965) suggested a method of dealing with non-linear response functions through the use of approximations of the non-linear response. Only one paper (Lee, 1963) deals with either problem discussed in the current article. Lee asked: given the length of the campaign and the number of advertisements to be placed, how should their appearance be spaced in time to assure a certain level-of-awareness pattern? He did not include the space consideration.

A linear program can attempt to maximize the value of the objective function, or it can attempt to minimize the value of the objective function. Because the approach of minimizing media selection costs permits the incorporation of space and time considerations into the linear programing model, it will be used in this paper. Also, since the objective will be to minimize costs, it is necessary to express the costs associated with a particular medium in terms of a standard unit such as cost per page, cost per minute, and so on. The expression "cost per unit" will be used because the models to be developed will be stated in general terms and hence applicable to many media. However, it should be clear to the reader that this is not the same problem as that associated with discounts due to advertisers placing many ads in a single publication. This paper does not deal with either the discount problem or the duplication problem. The reader interested in descriptions of either of these problems is referred to Miller and Starr.

Finally, all of the models discussed in this paper will be presented in terms of only two alternate media. It should be obvious, however, that essentially the same linear programing models could be applied to more than two media.

A Basic Model

Consider first a rather simple linear programing model wherein it is desirable to minimize the media costs associated with the achievement of certain objectives. The type of input data required is shown in Table 1. It is assumed that Table 1 is

TABLE 1

MEDIA INFORMATION

	Medium One B/W	Medium One Color	Medium Two B/W	Medium Two Color
Total exposures/issue	a_1	a_1	a_2	a_2
Total exposures/issue by readers whose income exceeds \$5,000/year	d_1	d_1	d_2	d_2
Total exposures/issue by readers with a high school education or better	e_1	e_1	e_2	e_2
Cost/unit for a single issue	$c_{1,1}$	$c_{1,2}$	$c_{2,1}$	$c_{2,2}$
Co or effectiveness adjustment	$f_{1,1}$	$f_{1,2}$	$f_{2,1}$	$f_{2,2}$

representative of the type of information which might be expected to be available for each alternate medium being considered. Furthermore, the following might be a representative listing of the objectives to be achieved by the media selection.

B_1: The total number of effective exposures resulting from the media selection should equal or exceed B_1.

B_2: The total number of effective exposures by readers whose income exceeds \$5,000/year should equal or exceed B_2.

B_3: The total number of effective exposures by readers with a high school education or better should equal or exceed B_3.

B_4: The minimum number of units to be placed in medium one should equal or exceed B_4. (This might be construed as a lower limit dictated by competition or experience.)

B_5: The maximum number of units to be placed in medium one should be less than or equal to B_5. (This may result because of the combination of a managerial decision to place no more than one unit per issue in any

medium and a fixed number of issues of medium one during the time period of the campaign.)

B_6: The maximum number of units to be placed in medium two should be less than or equal to B_6. (This may result because of the combination of a managerial decision to place no more than one unit per issue in any medium and a fixed number of issues of medium two during the time period of the campaign.)

The problem can now be formally stated as:

Minimize:

$$c_{1,1}X_{1,1} + c_{1,2}X_{1,2} + c_{2,1}X_{2,1} + c_{2,2}X_{2,2} \quad (1)$$

Subject to:

$$a_1f_{1,1}X_{1,1} + a_1f_{1,2}X_{1,2} + a_2f_{2,1}X_{2,1} + a_2f_{2,2}X_{2,2} \geqq B_1 \quad (2a)$$

$$d_1f_{1,1}X_{1,1} + d_1f_{1,2}X_{1,2} + d_2f_{2,1}X_{2,1} + d_2f_{2,2}X_{2,2} \geqq B_2 \quad (2b)$$

$$e_1f_{1,1}X_{1,1} + e_1f_{1,2}X_{1,2} + e_2f_{2,1}X_{2,1} + e_2f_{2,2}X_{2,2} \geqq B_3 \quad (2c)$$

$$X_{1,1} + X_{1,2} \geqq B_4 \quad (2d)$$

$$X_{1,1} + X_{1,2} \leqq B_5 \quad (2e)$$

$$X_{2,1} + X_{2,2} \leqq B_6 \quad (2f)$$

The purpose of the problem is to minimize expression (1)—the sum over all media considered, of the product of the cost/unit for each medium times the number of units placed in each medium—while at the same time satisfying or achieving each of the objectives of the media selection—shown as constraints (2a) through (2f) respectively. All of the parameters are assumed to be known from Table 1 and from the objectives of the media selection. The various values of X are the unknowns—the number of black and white units and/or color units to be placed in medium one and/or medium two respectively. The problem is to solve for the values of X in such a way that expression (1) will be minimized while satisfying all of the conditions found in expression (2). These optimum values can be found through the use of linear programing.

It is appropriate that some comments be made with respect to the meaning of the term "effective exposures" as used in the media selection objectives. The reader should note that black and white units in a medium are treated separately from color units in a medium. Referring to medium one, it is seen that the cost/unit for black and white is designated as $c_{1,1}$ while the cost/unit for color is designated as $c_{1,2}$. (In general, the first subscript refers to the medium while the second subscript refers to the option of black and white, or color.

When the second subscript is 1, this will refer to the black and white option. When the second subscript is 2, this will refer to the color option.) Presumably some benefits will accrue from using color as compared to black and white. If this were not the case, there would be little reason to include the color option in the model since the cost of color units ($c_{1,2}$) is likely to be greater than the cost of black and white units ($c_{1,1}$), and hence the former would find little use. The effect of these benefits could be incorporated into the model by using the color effectiveness adjustment. Thus, if a color unit of medium one was evaluated as being twice as effective as a black and white unit of medium one, this could be incorporated into the model by letting $f_{1,1} = 1$ and $f_{1,2} = 2$. The use of such a color effectiveness adjustment is illustrated in expressions (2a), (2b) and (2c).

The reader should also note that color, or the lack thereof, should be taken into consideration when satisfying the fifth objective. Thus, if no more than B_5 units are to appear in medium one, this objective can be assured by stipulating that

$$X_{1,1} + X_{1,2} \leqq B_5. \qquad (2e)$$

A similar statement applies to the fourth objective.

This knowledge of the basic model will now be used as the foundation for the discussion of time and space extensions of the model.

A Time and Space Extension

Two problems encountered in media selection are those concerned with when the advertisements should appear and the markets in which they should appear. The problem of when an advertisement should appear can be illustrated by using as an example a particular merchandising season, say Easter. Assume, for the sake of convenience, that Easter falls on the last Sunday of March, and that the advertising campaign managers would like the campaign to run at different levels of intensity during different time periods within the thirteen week campaign period. If this were the case, such a time period consideration should be incorporated into the media selection procedures.

The second problem—that of where an advertisement should appear—arises when a product's potential stems from many markets, but the potential of the various markets does not occur in proportion to the circulation of the various media serving those markets. To best appreciate this problem, it is first necessary to visualize the situation which calls for selecting media which reach markets scattered throughout geographic space. If each available medium reaches only one market, a space extension of the model is of no use because the previous model can be applied to each market separately. This situation might be characterized by markets wherein the only media available are local media such as local newspapers. On the other hand, if media are available which simultaneously reach more than one market, then the space extension of the model can be of some use. An example of this might be a national magazine which does not offer to advertisers the option of advertising in certain regional issues only. Another example might be found in the regional issue of a national magazine if that regional issue reaches two or more metropolitan markets within the region it serves. These space considerations should also be incorporated into the media selection procedures.

In order to accommodate these two extensions into the linear programing model, a number of adjustments and modifications must be made. The first such modification has to do with the use of subscripts. Subscripts were used above to identify each medium and whether the option was color or black and white. The first subscript was associated with medium identification and the second subscript with the color or black and white option. Thus, $c_{1,2}$ and $X_{1,2}$ were associated with the color option of medium one. In order to incorporate time into the model, it is necessary to add a third subscript, the purpose of which will be to identify the particular time period in which an advertising unit is to appear in a particular medium. For example $X_{1,2,1}$ and $X_{1,2,7}$ will indicate the number (unknown) of color units to be placed in medium one during week one and week seven respectively. If medium two were a monthly publication, $X_{2,2,1}$, $X_{2,2,5}$, and $X_{2,2,10}$ would indicate the number (unknown) of color units to be placed in medium two during the first month's issue, during the second month's issue, and during the third month's issue respectively. The third subscripts in these cases are shown as 1, 5 and 10 because it is assumed here that the respective monthly issues appear in those week numbers.

In order to extend the previous model to include the space consideration, a fourth subscript will be used to identify the particular market area of interest. For example, if medium one reaches two markets—call them north and south—$X_{1,2,3,n}$ will indicate the number (unknown) of color units to be placed in medium one in week three in the north market. In general then, the first subscript associated with X will indicate the individual medium identification, the second subscript will indicate color or black and white, the third subscript will indicate the time period, and the fourth subscript will indicate the market. This subscripting approach permits complete identification with respect to these four variables.

A second modification to the linear programing model has to do with the objectives of the media selection. The objectives of the basic model did not include time or space considerations. In the practical media selection problem, this could not be permitted. Therefore, both space and time must be identified, and in such a way that the needs of a particular market at a particular time will be taken into consideration. For example, utilizing the same six objectives of the basic model, the reader can see that it would be necessary to write each of these six objectives for each of the six month-market combinations being considered here—the two markets (north and south) and the three months (January, February and March). This would only be a simple extension of the objectives used in the basic model. For example, by identifying BJN_1 to be the equivalent of the first objective as it applies to the north market during the month of January, that particular space-time consideration can be incorporated into the model. Similarly, BFS_2 can identify the equivalent of the second objective as it applies to the south market during the month of February. Since the writing of the other space-time objectives should be obvious to the reader, they need not be further discussed. The final outcome of this is that there are now thirty-six properly stated time-space objectives rather than the original six.

It is pointed out that time and space extensions require more information than that used in developing the basic model. As the reader saw in the last paragraph, the objectives of the media selection must now be stated in terms of a particular time period and a particular market. This means that the date of appearance of each issue of a publication must be known. This also means that it is necessary that the various issues of the publications being considered be stated in terms of time periods compatible with the time periods used in the media selection objectives. In this paper, the appearance of an issue has been stated in terms of the week in which it appears. These, of course, can be

identified with particular months, and hence the two time periods are compatible. In order to incorporate space considerations, it is necessary that each medium's audience be broken down according to the characteristics of the audience reached in each market served by that medium. This means, for example, that the type of information available for medium one in the first two columns of Table I would now have to be available for each market reached by medium one. This represents a substantial increase in the amount of information required, but this is to be expected when dealing with a problem as complex as the selection of multi-market media.

The completion of the expressions of all the objectives associated with each month-market combination does not signal the completion of the model. Two components of the model still require attention. The objective function has yet to be written, and it will also be necessary to describe what might be called constraints which are internal to the model. Because they are related, these two components will be treated simultanously.

Procedures normally followed in constructing an objective function would also apply when incorporating time considerations into a linear programing model. That is, a variable—one which is identified with a particular time period—should appear in the objective function only if the medium represented by the variable does in fact appear in the designated time period. Referring to the example of medium two given earlier, the variable $X_{2,2,7}$ could not be included if medium two appears only in weeks numbered one, five and ten. In short, if a time and medium designation associated with a variable actually exists, that variable should be included in the objective function; otherwise the variable should not be included.

Turning now to the adjustments which must be made in order to incorporate space variables, consider that portion of the objective function concerned with both medium one and two, color as well as black and white, and both the north market and the south market. For the sake of convenience in presentation, however, consider only the time period spanning the first two weeks in January. It will become obvious that a two week example is sufficient to display the consistent pattern that is present in the objective function of this model. Expression (3) represents the sample portion of the objective function if it were written in the normal manner used in writing objective functions.

Minimize:

$$c_{1,1}X_{1,1,1,s} + c_{1,2}X_{1,2,1,s} + c_{2,1}X_{2,1,1,s} + c_{2,2}X_{2,2,1,s}$$
$$+ c_{1,1}X_{1,1,2,s} + c_{1,2}X_{1,2,2,s}$$

. .

. .

. .

$$+ c_{1,1}X_{1,1,1,n} + c_{1,2}X_{1,2,1,n} + c_{2,1}X_{2,1,1,n} + c_{2,2}X_{2,2,1,n}$$
$$+ c_{1,1}X_{1,1,2,n} + c_{1,2}X_{1,2,2,n}$$

. .

$$\tag{3}$$

It must be pointed out that expression (3) is not an accurate representation of the costs which are to be minimized. Numerous pairs of terms in expression (3) are comparable except for the fact that one term is for the north market and one term for the south market. For example, $c_{1,1}X_{1,1,1,s}$ and $c_{1,1}X_{1,1,1,n}$ are two such terms, as are $c_{2,1}X_{2,1,1,s}$ and $c_{2,1}X_{2,1,1,n}$. In general, there will be m such comparable terms for each medium which serves m different markets, where $m \geqq 2$. Because the cost/unit ($c_{1,1}$ and $c_{2,1}$) appears in both terms in each such pair, an erroneous cost will be calculated. It is in error to calculate $c_{1,1}X_{1,1,1,s}$ and add it to $c_{1,1}X_{1,1,1,n}$ because this has the effect of a double charge. If the advertiser purchases one black and white unit of medium one during period one, the advertiser pays a price of $c_{1,1}$. For this price he gets one unit in the north market *and* one such unit in the south market. This is not equivalent to letting $X_{1,1,1,s} = 1$ and letting $X_{1,1,1,n} = 1$ and substituting into the first and seventh terms in expression (3). If this were the only advertisement placed, expression (3) could be written as expression (4).

$$c_{1,1}X_{1,1,1,s} + c_{1,1}X_{1,1,1,n} = 2c_{1,1}. \tag{4}$$

If $c_{1,1}$ is the true cost, since $2c_{1,1}$ does not equal $c_{1,1}$, it is obvious that expression (3) includes some inaccuracies. This points out the problem that can exist in the space extension of the linear programing model if care is not taken in constructing the objective function. To overcome this potential problem, two adjustments are necessary.

An accurate expression for the objective function can be written if one bears in mind which medium reaches more than one market for the cost/unit associated with that medium, and if one then makes certain that this cost value prefixes *only one* of the unknown variables associated with that medium. For example, in expression (4) the cost value $c_{1,1}$ should prefix either $X_{1,1,1,s}$ or $X_{1,1,1,n}$ but not both. The other unknown variable should be prefixed with a zero coefficient. Furthermore, if there were also an east market and a west market, the cost value should prefix only one of the four unknown variables. The other three unknown variables should be prefixed with a zero coefficient. In terms of correcting expression (3), if $c_{1,1}$ prefixes $X_{1,1,1,s}$ it should not prefix $X_{1,1,1,n}$. Also, if $c_{2,1}$ prefixes $X_{2,1,1,s}$ it should not prefix $X_{2,1,1,n}$, and so on. In other words, the model designer should permit no double, triple, or multiple counting in the objective function.

The procedure described in the above paragraph is not the only one which can be used for writing objective functions in which multiple counting is to be avoided. All of the other procedures with which the author is familiar display the same characteristic—one or more of the cost coefficients in the objective function are either reduced to zero or made to appear relatively less expensive than they actually are.

An objective function written according to the above rules displays the weakness of having a zero cost coefficient in some of the terms of the objective function. Because the linear program is designed to minimize costs, it would sense this fact and have a tendency to assign large values to the variables associated with those zero cost coefficients. This would be unrealistic because, from the foregoing, it is known that those units are not available at zero cost. They are available for a real and specific cost/unit, but that cost is shown elsewhere in the objective function. It is possible to overcome this tendency on the part of the linear program to assign large values to the variables associated with these artificial zero cost coefficients, by writing constraints which are internal to the model. For example, if $c_{1,1}$ prefixes $X_{1,1,1,s}$ in the objective function, $X_{1,1,1,n}$ will be prefixed with a zero. The linear program will then unrealistically assign large values to $X_{1,1,1,n}$. However, this can be prevented by specifying within the model that $X_{1,1,1,n} = X_{1,1,1,s}$. This is tantamount to saying that if the model assigns a positive value to $X_{1,1,1,n}$ it must also assign the same positive value to $X_{1,1,1,s}$ which is the variable prefixed with the appropriate cost coefficient value ($c_{1,1}$). That is, if the model designer adds the internal constraint that the same number of units assigned to $X_{1,1,1,n}$ must also be assigned to $X_{1,1,1,s}$, the model would accurately reflect the fact that the advertiser must purchase the same number of units in each market reached by medium one. However, since the appropriate cost coefficient only prefixes one of these variables, the

44

internal constraint also assures that the exact cost will be calculated by the objective function.

Furthermore, if both an east and a west market were also reached by medium one, the proper internal constraint could then be written as expression (5).

$$X_{1,1,1,n} = X_{1,1,1,s} = X_{1,1,1,e} = X_{1,1,1,w} \tag{5}$$

Similar expressions could also be written for other media which reach more than one market, independent of the number of markets they reach. Referring now to the more general case represented by expression (3), it is seen that an entire set of internal constraints—such as expression (6)— would have to be written.

$$\left. \begin{aligned} X_{1,1,1,n} &= X_{1,1,1,e} \\ X_{1,2,1,n} &= X_{1,2,1,s} \\ X_{2,1,1,n} &= X_{2,1,1,s} \\ \quad\cdot\quad &\quad\cdot \\ \quad\cdot\quad &\quad\cdot \\ \quad\cdot\quad &\quad\cdot \end{aligned} \right\} \tag{6}$$

Having properly written these internal constraints to prevent the assignment of large values to variables with zero coefficients, the time and space extensions of the linear programing model

FIGURE 1

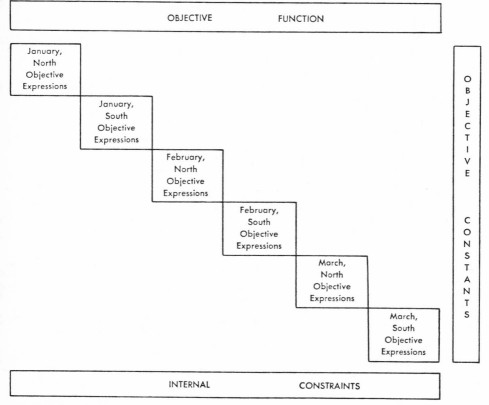

for media selection would be complete. It is impractical to show the final model in its complete form because of size. However, Figure 1 does show the layout of the model, and this should help the reader visualize the model in its final form.

Comments

The problem of incorporating space and time considerations into the linear programing media selection model has not been treated in the literature concerned with the subject. The current article illustrates one method by which these considerations can be incorporated into a linear programing model. Because it seems appropriate for the space and time dimension problem, the approach taken was one of minimizing the costs associated with the media selection. The method itself has three main components. First, it is necessary to identify the unknown variables and the

media selection objectives in terms of both time and space. Second, the objective function of the linear programing model must be modified to assure no multiple counting. Finally, because of the modified objective function, it is necessary to add certain internal constraints to prevent understating the costs associated with the media selection.

REFERENCES

BROWN, D. B. AND M. R. WARSHAW. Media Selection by Linear Programming, *Journal of Marketing Research*, Vol. 2, No. 1, February, 1965, pp. 83-88.
DAY, R. L. On Methods: Linear Programming in Media Selection, *Journal of Advertising Research*, Vol. 2, No. 2, June 1962, pp. 40-44.
ENGLE, J. F. AND M. R. WARSHAW. On Methods: Allocating Advertising Dollars by Linear Programing, *Journal of Advertising Research*, Vol. 4, No. 3, September 1964, pp. 42-48.
LEE, A. M. Decision Rules for Media Scheduling: Dynamic Campaigns, *Operational Research Quarterly*, Vol. 14, No. 4, December 1963, pp. 365-372.
MILLER, D. W. AND M. K. STARR. *Executive Decisions and Operations Research*. Englewood Cliffs, N. J.: Prentice-Hall, Inc., 1960, pp. 190-209.

Mathematics is the only science where one never knows what one is talking about nor whether what is said is true.

—BERTRAND RUSSELL

An Exploration of Linear Programming in Media Selection

FRANK M. BASS

and

RONALD T. LONSDALE*

> This article explores operational details of the application of linear programming to advertising media selection. The influence of weighting systems used to adjust audience data and various restraint systems is examined with actual data as inputs.

Recent attention to development of formal models and procedures for advertising media selection has provoked widespread comment and controversy. Much comment has centered on variation in conceptual detail of the various models while operational details and output behavior have received relatively little discussion. In this article, the operation of specific linear models will be examined in detail using actual data.

THE MODEL

The problem is to select from among various media alternatives the "best" set. The total amount of money available, the budget, is a restraint. Alternatives include not only media, but specific choices within a given medium as well. For a given magazine, for example, there is the choice of page size, colors and the like. Thus, choices available include all media vehicles capable of carrying an advertisement. A vehicle is any possible carrier of advertising. Each vehicle will yield a certain number of exposures per dollar. Clearly, the term exposure should be defined in such a way that exposures among various alternatives can be compared. The problem of developing weights for this purpose will be discussed later.

Assume that one wishes to make a selection from among n vehicles. If c_j is the number of exposures per insertion in vehicle j $(j = 1,2,\ldots, n)$, then one will wish to choose a vector x such that $c'x$ is a maximum subject to some set of restraints, where x_j $(j = 1,2,\ldots, n)$ is the number of units of vehicle j. One of the important restraints is, of course, the budget. Thus, $\Sigma\theta_j x_j \leq B$, where θ_j is the cost per unit of vehicle j.

Additionally, because of this model's linearity features, certain operational restraints may be necessary

to prevent the most "efficient" vehicles from running away with the program. An operational restraint will restrict the program, for example, so that no more than one advertisement will appear in each issue of a medium.

Another type of restraint may be employed when the advertiser has decided the maximum proportion of the budget he wishes to allocate to each of the major media classifications, but is uncertain which vehicles to select within a media group. Thus, an advertiser may specify that no more than 50 percent of his budget is to be allocated to newspapers and no more than 25 percent to magazines.

Another type of restraint controls allocation of exposures to market segments. If twice as many women as men buy the product advertised, it may be wise to impose a restraint set which allocates twice as many exposures to women as men.

In the following analysis, the effects on the solution vector of various weighting systems as applied to exposures and various restraint systems will be examined. This will permit examination of the behavior characteristics of the linear model with realistic data inputs.

STRUCTURE AND SOURCE OF DATA

Data used here were developed in connection with planning the media schedule for an oral hygiene product for a six month period in 1963. Two million dollars were available for advertising during this period. Audience and cost data for the 63 vehicles considered in this problem were obtained from a major advertising agency and are thought to be realistic for the period. Table A1, in the appendix shows the 63 vehicles included in the analysis, the cost per advertisement for each vehicle and the various audience measures used.

In addition to data in Table A1, data were available for audience figures broken down by socioeconomic

* Frank M. Bass is professor of industrial administration, Krannert Graduate School of Industrial Administration, Purdue University. Ronald T. Lonsdale is assistant professor of marketing, School of Business, Marquette University.

179

segments for each vehicle. These socioeconomic breakdowns included sex, age, geographical location, county size and income level. Units of measurement for the first classification were individuals, while those used for the other three classifications were households. For reasons of conciseness, these data are not reproduced here.

WEIGHTS

Three types of audience data are explored. First, the adjusted audience, is simply the total circulation, or audience of the vehicle, less that part of the audience among segments not thought to be customers for the product. Adjusted audience is restricted to the audience of the vehicle who are also prospective customers.

The second type of audience statistics used here are weighted audience figures, arrived at by applying two sets of weights to the adjusted audience data. First of these, an exposure factor, is the fraction of the audience one expects to see the advertisement. This weight is arrived at by applying typical Starch or Nielsen ratings for advertisements of product types being considered. The second type of weight is a subjective evaluation factor scored on a 0–1 scale by an advertising expert. It represents an attempt to evaluate the appropriateness of the vehicle's editorial content, tone, *etc.* for the product advertised. The product of exposure factor, subjective evaluation factor and adjusted audience yields weighted audience.

The third type of audience data, weighted exposure units (WEU), is arrived at by further weighting the weighted audience data to give greater weight to vehicles whose audience distribution is similar to the market distribution of potential customers and less weight to vehicles whose audience distribution is unlike the distribution of the product. For the product under consideration (an oral hygiene product) a product profile is developed representing the assumed distribution of the product among the various socioeconomic segments. The fraction of the potential customers thought to fall in a given socioeconomic segment is multiplied by the weighted audience for that segment and summed over all segments to arrive at the weighted exposure units for a vehicle. Since the socioeconomic segments being considered are not mutually exclusive, this weighting system results in double counting of exposures. The rationale for this is to provide heavier relative weights for vehicles whose audience distribution more closely matches the distribution of potential customers of the product, than for vehicles whose audience distribution is less like the profile of potential buyers.

PROGRAM SOLUTIONS

Altogether, 33 different linear programs were tried, eleven with each of the three different audience units: Adjusted Audience (AA), Weighted Audience (WA), and Weighted Exposure Units (WEU). One primary

area of interest is the effect of the weighting system on the solution. Effects of weights are explored by holding the restraints constant and varying the audience measures. An additional interest area is the influence of the restraint structure on the value of the objective function. Several programs were run, therefore, with different restraint sets. In all cases the number of vehicles considered was 63.

OPERATIONAL RESTRAINTS

In the first set of programs the budget restraint is used and the operational restraints on the media are introduced sequentially. This procedure is followed for all three audience measures. In the first program, A001, where A indicates that adjusted audience units were used and 001 indicates the program number, there was only one restraint, the budget. For this program obviously only one variable emerged in the solution. This is the one which has the highest ratio of coefficient in the objective function to cost (audience/cost ratio). The variable which entered the solution in this program was then restrained, and in program A002 we have two restraints, the budget and the variable which entered the solution in program A001. The process of constraining the variable which entered the solution in previous programs is repeated until in program A006 we have six restraints.

The process of introducing restraints sequentially has been carried out with each of the three different audience measures. Table 1 indicates the restraints, the solution and the value of the objective function for programs A001 through A006, W001 through W006 and E001 through E006. Throughout this article the following operational restraints were used: day television, 26; night television, 13; spot radio, 13; spot television, 26; magazines, 3 or 4.

The similarity of these results in each of the three different audience measures is the most noteworthy feature of results of the programs in Table 1. Solutions for programs using adjusted audience and weighted audience data are in fact identical, including the order in which the variables enter the solution. The solution for E006 yields the same set of variables as the solutions in A006 and W006 and the order in which variables enter the solution differs only slightly between programs using weighted exposure units and adjusted audience and weighted audience. Therefore, we find that the *weighting system has very little influence on the solution.*

While it is not possible to generalize on the basis of the results obtained here beyond these data and these programs, it is strongly suspected that this conclusion has general validity. If so the conclusion is significant since it suggests that sophisticated weighting systems tend to be "washed out" in linear models. This suggests that cruder models such as cost per thousand will produce media schedules not very different from those

Table 1

RESTRAINTS AND SOLUTIONS FOR SEQUENTIALLY INTRODUCED OPERATIONAL RESTRAINTS

Program no.	Constraints	Solution variable—no. of insertions	Value of objective
		Adjusted audience	
A001	Budget	58—1481.5	14840.0
A002	Budget 58 ≤ 26	58—26 62—1455.5	14723.5
A003	Budget 58 ≤ 26 62 ≤ 26	58—26 62—26 17—839.0	14008.9
A004	Budget 58 ≤ 26 62 ≤ 26 17 ≤ 26	58—26 62—26 17—26 15—935	13907.0
A005	Budget 58 ≤ 26 62 ≤ 26 17 ≤ 26 15 ≤ 26	58—26 62—26 17—26 15—26 61—1038.8	13690.8
A006	Budget 58 ≤ 26 62 ≤ 26 17 ≤ 26 15 ≤ 26 61 ≤ 26	58—26 62—26 17—26 15—26 61—26 13—805.7	13600.8
		Weighted audience	
W001	Budget	58—1481.5	4488.9
W002	Budget 58 ≤ 26	58—26 62—1455.5	4446.6
W003	Budget 58 ≤ 26 62 ≤ 26	58—26 62—26 17—839.0	4237.9
W004	Budget 58 ≤ 26 62 ≤ 26 17 ≤ 26	58—26 62—26 17—26 15—935	4206.5
W005	Budget 58 ≤ 26 62 ≤ 26 17 ≤ 26 15 ≤ 26	58—26 62—26 17—26 15—26 61—1038.8	4147.8
W006	Budget 58 ≤ 26 62 ≤ 26 17 ≤ 26 15 ≤ 26 61 ≤ 26	58—26 62—26 17—26 15—26 61—26 13—850.7	4113.5

Table 1—Continued

Program no.	Constraints	Solution variable—no. of insertions	Value of objective
		Weighted exposure units	
E001	Budget	58—1481.5	83109
E002	Budget 58 ≤ 26	58—26 62—1455.5	78779
E003	Budget 58 ≤ 26 62 ≤ 26	58—26 62—26 15—964.9	78195
E004	Budget 58 ≤ 26 62 ≤ 26 15 ≤ 26	58—26 62—26 15—26 17—816.4	75561
E005	Budget 58 ≤ 26 62 ≤ 26 15 ≤ 26 17 ≤ 26	58—26 62—26 15—26 17—26 13—826.3	75483
E006	Budget 58 ≤ 26 62 ≤ 26 15 ≤ 26 17 ≤ 26 13 ≤ 26	58—26 62—26 15—26 17—26 13—3 61—1035.1	73960

produced by linear models. It is possible, of course, to study the sensitivity of solutions to various weighting systems, but results suggest that this sensitivity is not great.

To further assess the influence of weights on the solution structure, programs must be run in which all variables are restrained. This is accomplished in programs A011, W012 and E013. Table 2 indicates the constraint structure used in these programs. Altogether there are 44 restraints. Some variables are restrained individually, while others are restrained as part of a group. Solutions to these programs may be found in Table A2. Results are summarized in Table 3.

There were 24, 26, and 28 variables appearing in the solutions to programs A011, W012, and E013, respectively. Since seventeen variables appeared in all three programs, these were uninfluenced by the variation in the three different weighting systems. When all restraints are imposed simultaneously, weights yield somewhat different results between the three weighting systems, but examination of "shadow prices" in the duals indicates that the value of the objective function changes little among the three different solutions. In this case, the primary effect of weighting is to reduce the importance of nighttime television vehicles. One can conclude, however, that solutions are not as sensitive to weights as might be expected. It is particularly apparent that the weights applied to weighted audience to arrive at weighted exposure units have negligible influence. Solutions to programs W012 and E013 (shown in Table A2) are similar.

ADDITIONAL BUDGETARY RESTRAINTS

As long as the restraint set is limited to a single budget restraint and operations restraints, as was the case in the programs discussed in the previous section, a computer is hardly needed to develop solutions to linear programming models, since the program simply

Table 2
RESTRAINTS USED IN PROGRAMS A011, W012, AND E013, 44 RESTRAINTS, BUDGET AND 43 OPERATIONAL RESTRAINTS

Variables		Value of constraint
Budget	≤	2,000,000
1	≤	4
2	≤	4
3	≤	3
4	≤	4
5	≤	3
6	≤	3
7	≤	3
8	≤	3
9	≤	3
10	≤	3
11	≤	3
12	≤	3
13	≤	26
14	≤	26
15	≤	26
16 + 61	≤	26
17	≤	26
18 + 19	≤	26
20	≤	3
21	≤	3
22	≤	3
23	≤	3
24 + 25 + 26 + 27	≤	78
28	≤	13
29 + 30 + 31 + 32 + 33 + 36 + 37	≤	21
34	≤	3
35	≤	3
38 + 39 + 40 + 41 + 59	≤	15
42 + 49	≤	52
43 + 44	≤	6
45	≤	3
46 + 47	≤	13
48	≤	26
50	≤	13
51	≤	13
52	≤	26
53	≤	3
54 + 55 + 56	≤	52
57	≤	26
58	≤	26
60	≤	13
62	≤	26
63	≤	26

Table 3
ANALYSIS OF PROGRAMS A011, W012 AND E013

Program numbers combinations	Number of vehicles which appear in programs indicated
A011, W012, E013	17
A011, W012	18
A011, E013	17
W012, E013	25

Table 4
ANALYSIS OF PROGRAMS A014, W015, AND E016

Program numbers combinations	Number of vehicles which appear in the programs indicated
A014, W015, E016	22
A014, W015	23
A014, E016	23
W015, E016	29

selects the most efficient variables, *i.e.*, the variables with the highest audience cost ratio, until the budget is exhausted. Additional restraints, however, complicate the solution procedure.

An advertiser may at times wish to restrict the proportion of his budget spent in a certain media class such as magazines, newspapers or television. Effects of this type restraint will be explored in this section. Programs A014, W015 and E016 use the 44 restraints employed in programs A011, W012 and E013 and the following additional restraints:

The sum of all expenditures in magazines ≤ $800,000.

The sum of all expenditures in day television ≤ $350,000.

The sum of all expenditures in spot television ≤ $270,000.

The sum of all expenditures in spot radio ≤ $100,000.

The sum of all expenditures in night television ≤ $700,000.

The purpose of imposing the operational restraint set was to prevent linearity in the program from overloading one vehicle. The purpose of applying a restraint set such as the one above, however, is to superimpose additional judgment criteria for allocation on the linear model. While the restraints indicated above were chosen arbitrarily, results apparently do not depend crucially on the particular numbers chosen.

As indicated in Table A2, there were 30, 30 and 31 vehicles, respectively, in the solutions to A014, W014 and E016. Table 4 summarizes the results. Again, the influence of weights is not as great as might be expected. The primary result of these added budgetary restraints has been to diminish the number of day television vehicles appearing in the solutions, and to increase the number of vehicles in other media classes such as nighttime television, spot television and radio.

Table 5 shows the values of the objective function for various programs expressed as a percentage of the objective function value when only a single budgetary restraint is employed. The figures clearly suggest the peculiar character of the problem of applying linear programming to the media selection problem. Ordinarily, in linear programming applications, the restraints are imposed by the physical environment. In applying linear programming to media selection problems, however, restraints are imposed by the decision maker based on judgment, essentially because he lacks faith in the linearity assumptions in linear models. The peculiar result is that the attempt to improve efficiency of programs by adding restraints, necessarily reduces the value of the objective function. One might add in defense of linear programming that it does produce schedules which appear useable on a judgment basis. Solutions are not very different from those one might derive from judgment alone. The extent to which the solutions differ from judgment may suggest fruitful avenues for exploring alternatives.

MARKET SEGMENT RESTRAINTS

One may be dissatisfied with the distribution of exposures among market segments which a given media schedule yields. Restraints which may be introduced to remedy this weakness are considered here. For programs discussed in this section the 49 constraints of programs A014, W015, and E016 are used. In addition, restraints are imposed upon distribution of exposures to certain segments of the market, as indicated in Table 6.

The number of exposures going to each of the three segments considered: women, men, and teens in programs A014, W015, and E016 was calculated by multiplying the number of exposures per advertisement within each segment by how often the vehicle appeared in the solution. These values were called the "original allocation." The purpose was to study how restraints which sought to change original allocation influenced the solution. It was discovered that for restraints listed in the programs in Table 6, no solution existed. Several at-

Table 6
SEGMENTATION RESTRAINTS

Program no.	Description of constraint		Value
AW23	Sum of exposures to women	≥	1,400,000
AM30	Sum of exposures to men	≥	1,000,000
AT31	Sum of exposures to teens	≥	350,000
WW32	Sum of exposures to women	≥	600,000
WM33	Sum of exposures to men	≥	350,000
WT34	Sum of exposures to teens	≥	150,000
EW35	Sum of exposures to women	≥	1,500,000
EM36	Sum of exposures to men	≥	500,000
ET37	Sum of exposures to teens	≥	100,000

tempts to lower the restraining values produced the same results.[1] Solutions existing at the time of the error stops are presented in Table A2. Table 7 summarizes the results. In no case was the segmentation restraint satisfied, but it was possible to increase the exposures allocated to a segment slightly. Thus it appears that because of the structure of audience distribution among media, controlling the allocation of exposures among market segments is difficult. The new restraints did have an influence in introducing certain media into the solutions. The women's restraint, for example, pulled in more women's magazines, and the men's restraint pulled in more men's magazines. Even with these changes in the solution vector, it was not possible to greatly alter the allocation of exposures to segments of the market.

Table 8 indicates the duplication of vehicles in solutions using the three audience measures. Again, weighting systems apparently have only a limited influence on the solutions.

CRITIQUE AND SUMMARY

Linear models are crude devices to apply to the media selection problem. The linearity assumption itself is the source of much of the difficulty. Justifying an assumption of linear response to advertising exposures on theoretical grounds would be difficult. In applying linear programming to media selection problems, it has been observed that a restraint structure must be imposed which is essentially judgmental. The restraints are fundamental judgments about the nonlinearity of response. Hence, restraints are imposed on media, or on the allocation of exposures to market segments, in order

[1] The data were processed on the IBM 1620 and the instruction manual "Linear Programming Code for the Card 1620 with Punch Card Option" reads as follows (p. 8):
5. Error stops
 a. 02545 Dual algorithm—inconsistent matrix
 b. 02665 Simplex algorithm—unbounded solution
It may be possible to obtain the solution existing at the time of either of these stops by Non Process Runout. . . .

Table 5
OBJECTIVE VALUES EXPRESSED AS PERCENTAGES OF PROGRAM 001

Adjusted audience		Weighted audience		Weighted exposure units	
A001	100.0	W001	100.0	E001	100.0
A006	91.64	W006	91.64	E006	88.99
A011	50.35	W012	68.05	E013	69.66
A014	42.04	W015	53.76	E016	54.98

Table 7
ANALYSIS OF MARKET SEGMENT RESTRAINTS IN PROGRAMS 23 TO 37

Program	Original allocation	Restriction value	Solution result	Percentage of total exposures going to the segment		
				Original	Restriction	Result
AW23	1,179,000	1,400,000	1,199,687	55.93%	66.38%	56.87%
AM30	703,560	1,000,000	765,929	33.35	47.41	36.31
AT31	223,598	350,000	256,412	10.72	16.59	12.16
WW32	471,324	600,000	481,498	56.1	71.46	57.35
WM33	271,686	350,000	310,130	32.3	41.69	36.94
WT34	96,600	150,000	111,620	11.5	17.87	13.29
EW35	1,392,147	1,500,000	1,473,440	79.9	86.21	84.63
EM36	302,654	500,000	459,887	17.3	28.72	26.42
ET37	45,743	100,000	55,843	2.6	5.74	3.21

Table 8
COMPARISON OF SOLUTIONS UNDER DIFFERENT WEIGHTING SYSTEMS

Program number combinations	Number of vehicles which appear in the programs indicated
AW23, WW32, EW35	19
AW23, WW32	24
AW23, EW35	19
WW32, EW35	20
AM30, WM33, EM36	10
AM30, WM33	14
AM30, EM36	12
WM33, EM36	13
AT31, WT34, ET37	13
AT31, WT34	14
AT31, ET37	14
WT34, ET37	17

to express some judgment about limits of effectiveness within these categories.

On the basis of the investigation presented in this paper, it appears that attempts to impose meaningful restraints on the linear model would probably be unfruitful. When only the budget restraint and operational restraints on each vehicle are employed, the model is reduced to a simple cost per thousand model. The distribution structure of the media audiences makes it difficult to develop useful restraints which allocate exposures to market segments. Finally, the weighting system used to adjust audience data for variations in "quality" and audience composition does not seem to influence solutions greatly.

Crude as these models are, they suggest possible avenues for examining alternatives. As a point of departure, these models serve a useful purpose. It is clear, however, that much more theoretical and empirical work will be necessary in order to permit significant improvement in media selection. Assumptions about the nature of response to advertising cause most difficulties in models of the type examined in this article. Models with non-linear response functions, although empirically demanding, would diminish most problems associated with the imposition of judgment restraints on a linear structure.

Table A1

VEHICLES, COST AND AUDIENCE DATA USED IN THE ANALYSIS

Vehicle number	Vehicle	Cost	AA^a	WA^b	WEU^c
1	TV Guide, 4 clr. pg.	20710	69900	39144	75589
2	Life, 4 clr. pg.	49616	101333	50159	93595
3	Cosmopolitan, 4 clr. pg.	4865	10190	5502	11557
4	True Confessions, 4 clr. pg.	4589	11785	5303	10163
5	Modern Romances, 4 clr. pg.	3210	10541	4743	9361
6	Motion Picture, 4 clr. pg.	4242	11630	5235	10282
7	Modern Screen, 4 clr. pg.	3136	12300	5535	10960
8	Sport, 4 clr. pg.	2605	8220	3020	7230
9	Redbook, 4 clr. pg.	16895	30967	18115	36088
10	McFaddens Women's group, 4 clr. pg.	18736	49600	22320	44136
11	N. Y. Times Magazine, 4 clr. pg.	4625	7430	4792	10198
12	American Weekly, 4 clr. pg.	14921	23267	15007	31340
13	First Impressions, day 30 secs.	2200	14885	4502	8272
14	Password, day 30 secs.	3942	22759	6884	13266
15	Loretta Young, day 30 secs.	2000	13872	4196	7809
16	Price is Right, day 60 secs.	3500	11952	6095	10849
17	Truth or Consequences, day 30 secs.	2300	16078	4863	8658
18	Monday Night Movie, prime 60 secs.	34000	42471	26756	53630
19	Eleventh Hour, prime 60 secs.	35000	40749	27098	52884
20	Good Housekeeping, 4 clr. pg.	23546	48191	27468	61492
21	American Home, 4 clr. pg.	19389	34496	19662	39178
22	McCall's, 4 clr. pg.	37523	59747	36893	72316
23	Better Homes and Gardens, 4 clr. pg.	34115	60008	34204	65857
24	Truth or Consequences, day 60 secs.	4600	16078	8199	14593
25	Loretta Young, day 60 secs.	4000	13872	7074	13159
26	Password, day 60 secs.	7883	22759	11607	22359
27	First Impressions, day 60 secs.	4600	14885	7591	13942
28	Saturday Night Movie, prime 30 secs.	18000	40236	15430	30912
29	Family Weekly, 4 clr. pg.	17664	21920	15080	26824
30	This Week, 4 clr. pg.	58270	72209	46574	87435
31	Sports Illustrated, 4 clr. pg.	9455	17100	8464	15366
32	U. S. News & World Report, 4 clr. pg.	10555	18200	9009	16200
33	Time, 4 clr. pg.	22130	33900	16780	31358
34	Newsweek, 4 clr. pg.	13285	26240	12988	23965
35	McFadden's Men's group, B & W. pg.	2201	14100	2270	5743
36	Playboy, 4 clr. pg.	11685	20100	8844	15452
37	New Yorker, 4 clr. pg.	4988	8500	4590	9252
38	Parents, 4 clr. pg.	12181	19103	10315	21696
39	Woman's Day, 4 clr. pg.	27220	36054	19469	40148
40	Family Circle, 4 clr. pg.	30576	43743	23621	48651
41	Ladies Home Journal, 4 clr. pg.	33271	50955	31464	62275
42	Who do you Trust, day 60 secs.	2700	9937	5067	8704
43	Saturday Evening Post, 4 clr. pg.	42923	70942	40436	74243
44	Look, 4 clr. pg.	49664	90221	44659	81998
45	Newspapers Top 100 Markets, 2400 lines, 2 clr.	210000	136741	39381	72090
46	Spot Radio Top 100, day 60 secs.	3000	4600	878	1712
47	Spot Radio Top 100, prime 60 secs.	3000	5745	502	963
48	Queen for a Day, day 30 secs.	1350	9082	2747	4726
49	CBS Morning Plan, day 60 secs.	3200	9599	4895	9455
50	Wagon Train, prime 30 secs.	19500	51055	19579	33653
51	Tonight Show, fringe 30 secs.	6500	15582	5570	11356
52	Spot TV, fringe top 25 markets, 60 secs.	8000	8777	4212	8599
53	Readers Digest, 4 clr. pg.	45720	110545	46981	82766
54	Spot TV, day top 50 markets, 60 secs.	11600	12350	5928	11970
55	Spot TV, prime top 50 markets, 20 secs.	21400	30444	6545	12814
56	Spot TV, prime top 25 markets, 20 secs.	15300	22080	4747	9488
57	Spot TV, day top 50 markets, 60 secs.	5300	7520	3609	7512
58	Seven Keys, day 30 secs.	1350	10017	3030	5608
59	Parade, 4 clr. pg.	40513	56841	3662	73106
60	International Showtime, prime 30 secs.	18000	43239	16582	27976
61	Price Is Right, day 30 secs.	1750	11952	3615	6433
62	Who Do You Trust, day 30 secs.	1350	9937	3000	5312
63	Seven Keys, day 60 secs.	2700	10017	5108	9454

[a] Adjusted Audience: Audience of the vehicle among relevant market segments.

[b] Weighted Audience: Adjusted audience times an "exposure" factor and a subjective "evaluation" factor.

[c] Weighted Exposure Unit: Weighted audience adjusted for the distribution of the audience among market segments relative to the assumed distribution of the product among market segments.

PROGRAM SOLUTIONS

Vehicle no.	vehicle	Numbers of units of vehicles appearing in solutions to programs														
		A011	W012	E013	A014	W015	E016	AW23	WW32	EW35	AM30	WM33	EM36	AT31	WT34	ET37
1	*TV Guide*, 4 clr. pg.	4	4	4	4	4	4	4	4	4	4	4	4	4	4	4
2	*Life*, 4 clr. pg.		3	0.7	4	4	2.6				4	4	4	4	4	4
3	*Cosmopolitan*, 4 clr. pg.		3	3	3	3	3	3	3	3						
4	*True Confessions*, 4 clr. pg.	4	4	4	4	4	4	4	4	4				4	4	4
5	*Mod. Romances*, 4 clr. pg.	3	3	3	3	3	3	3	3	3			3	3	3	3
6	*Motion Pic.*, 4 clr. pg.	3	3	3	3	3	3	3	3	3				3	3	3
7	*Mod. Screen*, 4 clr. pg.	3	3	3	3	3	3	3	3	3				3	3	3
8	*Sport*, 4 clr. pg.	3	3	3	3	3	3				3	3	3			
9	*Redbook*, 4 clr. pg.		3	3	3	3	3	3	3	3						
10	*McFaddens Women's group*, 4 clr. pg.	3	3	3	3	3	3	3	3	3				3	3	3
11	*N. Y. Times Mgzn.*, 4 clr. pg.		3	3			3	3					3	3		
12	*Am. Weekly*, 4 clr. pg.			3		3	3									
13	First Impressions, day 30 secs.	26	26	26	26	26	26	26	26	26	26		26	12.5		
14	Password, day 30 secs.	26	26	26	7.6			16.5	16.5	26	7.6					
15	Loretta Young, day 30 secs.	26	26	26	26	26	26	26	26	26	26			26	26	26
16	Price Is Right, day 60 secs.		26	26												
17	Truth or Consequences, day 30 secs.	26	26	26	26	26	26	26	26		26	26	26	26		
18	Mon. Nt. Movie, prime 60 secs.									11.2		6.2		6.2	6.2	
19	Elev. Hr., prime 60 secs.															
20	*Good Houskpg.*, 4 clr. pg.		3	3	3	3	3	3	3	3						
21	*Am. Home*, 4 clr. pg.		3	3		3	3	3	3	3						
22	*McCall's*, 4 clr. pg.			3			3	3	3	3						
23	*Better Homes & Gardens*, 4 clr. pg.			3		0.3	3	3								
24	Truth or Consequences, day 60 secs.	78											35.4			
25	Lor. Young, day 60 secs.									25.8						
26	Password, day 60 secs.		78	78												
27	First Imp., day 60 secs.															
28	Sat. Nt. Mov., pr. 30 secs.	5.3			7.1	11.8	13	7.1	7.1	13	7.1	11.8	13	13	13	13
29	*Fam. Weekly*, 4 clr. pg.															
30	*This Week*, 4 clr. pg.															21
31	*Sports Ill.*, 4 clr. pg.											21		21	21	
32	*U. S. News & World Report*, 4 clr. pg.															
33	*Time*, 4 clr. pg.															
34	*Newsweek*, 4 clr. pg.				3						3	3	3			
35	*McFadden's Men's group*, B & W. pg.	3	3	3	3	3	3	3			3	3	3	3		3
36	*Playboy*, 4 clr. pg.										21		21			
37	*New Yorker*, 4 clr. pg.															
38	*Parents*, 4 clr. pg.															
39	*Woman's Day*, 4 clr. pg.															
40	*Fam. Circle*, 4 clr. pg.															
41	*Ld. Hm. Jour.*, 4 clr. pg.							1.7	9.1	9.1						
42	Who do you Trust, day 60 secs.	52	52	52								25.6		52	52	52
43	*S. E. Post*, 4 clr. pg.											2.6	4.5			
44	*Look*, 4 clr. pg.				1.7						1.6			1.4	4.3	4.1
45	*Newspapers, Top 100 Mkts.*, 2400 lines, 2 clr.															
46	Spot Radio Top 100, day 60 secs.				13											
47	Spot Radio Top 100, prime 60 secs.				13			13			13			13		
48	Qu. For a Day, day 30 secs.	26	26	26	26	26	26				26	26		26		
49	CBS Morn. Plan, day 60 secs.															
50	Wg. Train, pr. 30 secs.	13			13	13	13	13	3		13	13	13	13	13	13
51	Ton. Show, fringe 30 secs.	13			13		13	13	13	13	13					

Table A2—Continued

Vehicle no.	Vehicle	A011	A012	A013	A014	W015	E016	AW23	WW32	EW35	AM30	WM33	EM36	AT31	WJ34	ET37
						Numbers of units of vehicles appearing in solutions to programs										
52	Sp. TV, Fr. top 25 mkts., 60 secs.					1.5	1.5		1.5	1.5		18.7	18.7			
53	Rd. Dig., 4 clr. pg.	3	3		3	3		3			3	3		3		
54	Sp. TV, day top 50 mkts. 60 secs.														1.0	1.0
55	Sp. TV, pr. top 50 mkts., 20 secs.													5.2		
56	Sp. TV, pr. top 25 mkts. 20 secs.					4.7					7.2					
57	Sp. TV, day top 50 mkts. 60 secs.					26	26	20.9	26	26					26	26
58	Sev. Keys, day 30 secs.	26	26	26	26	26	26	26	26	26	26	26	26			
59	*Parade, 4 clr. pg.*															
60	Int. Shtm., pr. 30 secs.	13			13	13	7.1	13	13		13	13		11.8		
61	Pr. Is Rt., day 30 secs.	26			26	26	26	26	26		26	26				
62	Who Do You Trust, day 30 secs.	26		26	26	26	26	26	26		26	26	26	26	26	26
63	Sv. Keys, day 60 secs.	26	26	26		11.8	11.2				26					

Linear Models Examined in the Analysis

In the first set of programs, A001, ··· A006, W001, ·· W006, and E001, ·· E006, the model was

$$\text{Max} \sum_j C_j x_j,$$

subject to:

$$\sum_j \ominus_j x_j \leq B.$$

Where C_j is the number of exposures per unit of vehicle j, x_j is number of units of vehicle j, and $\ominus_j$ is cost per unit of vehicle j. An appropriate set of C_j values corresponded to each of the three weighting systems. In the first set of programs, additional restraints were introduced sequentially over the x_j values. Thus, if $x_{58} = 1{,}481.5$ was the optimal solution to program A001, x_{58} was restrained in program A002 to be less than or equal to 26. The process of restraining the variables appearing in the previous solution was carried out for each of the three different weighting systems through six solutions. The results are summarized in Table 1.

In the second set of programs, A011, W012, and E013, restraints were imposed over variables, in some cases individual restraints; in others collective restraints, simultaneously. Thus, the program was

$$\text{Max} \sum_j C_j x_j,$$

subject to:

$$\sum_j \ominus_j x_j \leq B$$
$$x_1 \leq b_1$$
$$x_2 \leq b_2$$
$$\vdots \qquad \vdots$$
$$x_{15} \leq b_{15}$$
$$x_{16} + x_{61} \leq b_0 \qquad etc.$$

The restraints are shown in Table 2.

In the third set of programs, A014, W015, and E016, the program was

$$\text{Max} \sum_j C_j x_j,$$

subject to:

$$\sum_j \ominus_j x_j \leq B$$
$$x_1 \leq b_1$$
$$x_2 \leq b_2$$
$$\vdots \qquad \vdots$$
$$x_{15} \leq b_{15}$$
$$x_{16} + x_{61} \leq b_0$$
$$\sum_{j \epsilon j_1 *} \ominus_j x_j \leq B_1$$
$$\vdots \qquad \vdots$$
$$\sum_{j \epsilon j_k *} \ominus_j x_j \leq B_k \qquad etc.$$

Where in the final set of restraints, the number of dollars spent in a certain type of medium is restrained. Thus, if B_1 is an upper bound on the dollars to be spent in magazines, $j \epsilon j_1 *$ indicates that the j index is to run over those vehicles which are magazines.

In the final set of programs, in which restraints are placed over the number of exposures going to different segments of the market, we have:

$$\text{Max} \sum_j C_j x_j,$$

subject to:

$$\sum_j \ominus_j x_j \le B$$
$$x_1 \le b_1$$
$$x_2 \le b_2$$
$$\vdots \qquad \vdots$$
$$x_{15} \le b_{15}$$
$$x_{16} + x_{61} \le b_0$$
$$\sum_{j \in j_1 \cdot} \ominus_j x_j \le B_1$$
$$\vdots \qquad \vdots$$
$$\sum_{j \in j_k \cdot} \ominus_j x_j \le B_k$$

$$\sum_j a_{1j} x_j \ge \lambda_1$$
$$\sum_j a_{2j} x_j \ge \lambda_2$$
$$\sum_j a_{3j} x_j \ge \lambda_3 \qquad etc.$$

Where in the final set of constraints, the number of dollars spent in a certain type of medium is restrained and, in addition, the number of exposures going to different segments of the market are also restrained. λ_i is the minimum number of exposures to be allocated to market segment i, and a_{ij} is the number of exposures in segment i per unit of vehicle j. The particular restraints are shown in Table 6.

STANLEY F. STASCH*

Because efficient media selection is a complex process, and because media costs are essentially linear, the most promising technique for media selection is linear programming. To improve its usefulness, it will first be necessary to collect more detailed readership data and to utilize more realistic restraints.

Linear Programming and Media Selection: A Comment

In a recent article, Bass and Lonsdale [1] explored the use of linear programming in media selection. In particular, they examined the influence of various methods of weighting the audience data to be used in the linear program. The article was the first of its kind to use actual data, and for this the authors are to be complimented, but they made statements which raise some interesting questions.

VALUE OF WEIGHTING SYSTEMS

The conclusions reached by the authors that the weighting systems had little influence on the solution is properly qualified by a statement that a sensitivity analysis may lead to a somewhat different conclusion. Although it may be true that a sensitivity analysis will indicate that certain weighting systems can have a meaningful influence on solutions, their findings may have many different causes. Consider the "subjective evaluation factor" used in the "weighted audience" figures. If the 63 media used in the linear program were subjectively selected by a decision maker, it may be reasonable to assume that the subjective evaluation factor mirrors the decision maker's original selection of the 63 media. If this were true, finding the weighting systems to have little influence on the solution merely reflects the fact that the subjective evaluation of media duplicates the original selection of them.

Conflicting Restraints

The authors recognized that a trivial case exists when the only restraint used is the budget restraint. When individual medium and budgeting restraints are added to the program, the weighting systems more strongly

influence the linear program solutions. When market segment restraints were added, the authors discovered that no solution existed.

A "no solution" output in linear programming can result only if the restraints are conflicting. Although the cause of the difficulty cannot be pinpointed, some information indicates that the lack of a solution is caused by an inconsistency in the following restraints. The individual media class restraints had the form:

$$a_1 \, x_1 + a_2 \, x_2 \leq \$800,000.$$

The market segment restraints had the form:

$$b_1 \, x_1 + b_2 \, x_2 \geq 1,400,000 \text{ exposures.}$$

The symbols are as follows:

x_1, x_2 are the number of insertions to be made in media one and two,

a_1, a_2 are the cost per insertion in media one and two, and

b_1, b_2 are the number of exposures in a particular market segment for media one and two.

Depending on the values assigned to the restraint coefficients (the a's and b's), the two restraints could be conflicting. For example, if $(a_1 > b_1)$ and $(a_2 > b_2)$, the restraints would conflict, and no solution would result. This can be observed by graphing the two restraints.

The authors' findings indicate that weighting systems have little effect on the solution when only budget and operational restraints are used in the linear program. Their Table A2 reveals that weighting systems affect the solutions when limitations on media classes are added to the previous set of restraints, that is, when the set of restraints are more complex.[1] The addition of

---

* Stanley F. Stasch is assistant professor of marketing, Graduate School of Business Administration, Northwestern University.

[1] A simple example illustrates the meaning of complexity of restraints. Assume that the total audience (50,000 readers) of a

Journal of Marketing Research,
Vol. IV (May 1967), 205-7

market segment restraints led to the "no solution" situation. However, if the conflicting restraints which caused the situation were rectified, the result might possibly have been solutions that would have indicated that weighting systems become more influential as the set of restraints becomes more complex. This, of course, is unknown, but the findings of Bass and Lonsdale seem to indicate a trend in that direction.

Because of this and the foregoing comments, it appears that their tentative conclusion that "attempts to impose meaningful restraints on the linear model would probably be unfruitful" can be questioned.

Judgment in the Use of Restraints

The authors also suggest that the role of judgment reduces the effectiveness of linear models. Judgment is an important aspect of all models. In particular subjective judgment abounds in linear programming; this applies not only to restraints, but also to the criterion function. The authors chose to maximize exposures subject to a maximum budget restraint. Is this advantageous when compared with a linear program that minimizes media costs subject to a minimum number of exposures restraint? The answer to this question depends on a number of things. In one instance the question, "How much can we get for X dollars?" is asked, while in the other the question "How much will it cost to get Y number of exposures?" is asked.

The same kind of subjectiveness applies to restraints. It even applies to the selection and number of variables in the linear program. For example, why were 63 media used, and why were those 63 media selected? Linear programming begins with a great deal of subjectiveness. After the subjective judgments are made, linear programming is a tool designed to arrive at optimal decisions *within the framework* of those judgments. Consequently, if linear programming is to be useful in media selection problems, more attention should be given to the subjective judgments required for the operational use of linear programming.

FUTURE OF LINEAR PROGRAMMING IN MEDIA SELECTION

The eventual utility of linear programming in solving media selection problems is currently unknown. However, there are three developments that appear to

media breaks down into 50 percent males and 50 percent adults over 40 years of age, with the two groups not necessarily congruent. It is a simple matter to satisfy a restraint that requires either a minimum of 20,000 exposures to male readers or a minimum of 20,000 exposures to adults over 40. However, it may not be possible to satisfy a single restraint requiring a minimum of 20,000 readers who are both males and adults over 40 because the information given above does not guarantee that 20,000 readers with these qualifications can be found. That is, the latter restraint is more complex than either of the first two and may be more difficult to satisfy.

be essential in order for linear programming to attain a high level of practical utility.

1. Improved readership data will have to be available for various media.
2. Media selection objectives, which are translated into restraint constants, should be based on more supplementary research to reduce subjectiveness.
3. Complex restraints, which more accurately reflect the real world, should be developed.

Media Data

If linear programming is to approach its ultimate utility an improvement in the available media data is necessary. The circulation or readership data of media is available nationally, and in some cases by age, sex, and income. But, such data should be available for *each* metropolitan area served by *each* media vehicle. Education and family data should be included and cross-classifications of all these data made available. Duplication of audiences among media is also necessary if this factor is to be included in the analysis.

Improved Restraint Objectives

Why should the advertising budget not exceed $2,220,000? Why should the number of insertions in *Life* be limited to four? Why should women be subjected to at least 1.5 million exposures? Each of these values reflects an objective of the overall media selection program. But how were the values selected? If only guesswork was used, applying these figures to a linear program is much like using a precision cutting tool to make a nail. The tool is too sophisticated for the job or the raw materials. However, if back-up research is used to arrive at the values mentioned, then the level of sophistication of the tool and its inputs are more nearly justified.

As more supporting research is used in determining the values to be assigned to restraints, the level of subjectiveness will decline and linear programming will be more useful.

Realistic Restraints

The no solution situation provides a good example of an unrealistic restraint. Supplementary research of the audience data associated with the media used in the linear program would probably have indicated that the two restraints were in conflict. It is likely that further analysis of these data would result in more realistic restraints.

As more realistic and necessarily more complex restraints are applied to the linear program, its utility in media selection will be enhanced. The work of Bass and Lonsdale demonstrates that media selection becomes more difficult as more realistic restraints, such as budget restraints, restraints on the number on insertions in individual vehicles, budget restraints on different media classes, and market segmentation restraints, are added.

Other phases of the media selection problem that could be incorporated are the timing of insertions, the number of insertions to be directed at individual market areas, the effect of quantity discounts, and the role of audience duplication of various combinations of media.

Although sophisticated techniques are not required for the solution to simply-stated media selection problems, it seems fairly obvious that intuitive solutions become more questionable as the media selection problem is stated more realistically. It is then that linear programming or some other sophisticated technique will reach its fullest usefulness.

OTHER WORK

Others have made some interesting contributions to the linear programming approach to the media selection problem. Usually their interest has been in modifying linear programming in some small way to more realistically adapt it to the media selection problem. Although what they are doing may no longer be considered linear programming, it is nevertheless related to linear programming.

Brown and Warshaw [2] have suggested a method for dealing with nonlinear response functions by using segmented linear approximations of the nonlinear response. Another article [5], shows how linear programming can be modified to incorporate restraints for individual market areas and restraints for different time periods. Lee [4] modifies linear programming to deal with the problem: given the length of the campaign and the number of insertions to be placed, how should their appearance be spaced in time to assure a certain level of awareness pattern? Though not complete, my research [6] indicates that the problem of quantity discounts can be coped with by modifying the linear programming algorithm.

Finally, anyone interested in the media selection problem would also want to consider some of the work done in England. Lee and Burkart [3] and Taylor [7] have made some useful contributions to this area. Al-

though they depart somewhat from the strictly linear programming approach, this is not serious enough to warrant overlooking what they have done.

These researchers have attempted to use basically linear models to deal with nonlinearities and discontinuities in the media selection problem. Though the ideal media selection model does not yet exist, the results of the work mentioned are encouraging. They indicate that a useful media selection model may result from modifying, rather than abandoning, the standard linear programming model. They also indicate that the level of input data required is far more detailed than that currently available from standard sources. Furthermore, the restraints used are far more realistic and, hence, far more complex than those normally associated with simple linear programming models. This is to be expected because of the complex nature of the media selection problem.

Until these developments have been incorporated and tested, it seems premature to conclude that what are basically linear models should be abandoned as being deficient in their practical utility.

REFERENCES

1. F. M. Bass and R. T. Lonsdale, "An Exploration of Linear Programming in Media Selection," *Journal of Marketing Research*, 3 (May 1966), 179–88.
2. D. B. Brown and M. R. Warshaw, "Media Selection by Linear Programming," *Journal of Marketing Research*, 2 (February 1965), 83–8.
3. A. M. Lee and A. J. Burkart, "Some Optimization Problems in Advertising Media Planning," *Operational Research Quarterly*, 11 (September 1960), 113–22.
4. A. M. Lee, "Decision Rules for Media Scheduling: Dynamic Campaigns," *Operational Research Quarterly*, 14 (December 1963), 365–72.
5. S. F. Stasch, "Linear Programming and Space-time Considerations in Media Selection," *Journal of Advertising Research*, (December 1965), 40–6.
6. ———, "Media Selection, Quantity Discounts and Linear Programming," Unpublished working paper.
7. C. J. Taylor, "Some Developments in the Theory and Application of Media Scheduling Methods," *Operational Research Quarterly*, 14 (September 1963), 291–305.

MANAGEMENT SCIENCE
Vol. 14, No. 8, April, 1968
Printed in U.S.A.

A GOAL PROGRAMMING MODEL FOR MEDIA PLANNING*

A. CHARNES,[1] W. W. COOPER,[2] J. K. DeVOE,[3] D. B. LEARNER,[4]
AND W. REINECKE[5]

A goal programming model for selecting media is presented which alters the objective and extends previous media models by accounting for cumulative duplicating audiences over a variety of time periods. This permits detailed control of the distribution of message frequencies directed at each of numerous marketing targets over a sequence of interrelated periods. This is accomplished via a new logarithmic non-reach device and a continuous lognormal generation of the discrete message frequencies.

In November 1961 a session of the American Association of Advertising Agencies was devoted to an exposition and examination of the first linear programming model[6] which, by explicit announcement and design, was directed toward operational use and actual implementation in choosing media plans.[7] This was followed by a variety of still further expositions of this model and its associated developments.[8]

This first model was soon placed into the operational use for which it had been designed while, at the same time, care was taken to initiate further research designed to improve or strengthen various parts of the original model and also to extend its use via suitably designed dual evaluator and sensitivity analyses, etc. It was expected that such a first model would contain simplifications and would confront data gaps and other deficiencies as a result of a preceding history which depended solely on a variety of different ways of organizing (more or less well) the judgments and practices of a constantly changing mix of media executives.[9] Indeed it was expected that this first model and the associated research program would in themselves supply a systematic basis for assessing and repairing some of these difficulties. It was also supposed that at some point it

---

* Received March 1967.
[1] Northwestern University
[2] Carnegie-Mellon University
[3] Cargill, Wilson & Acree, Inc.
[4] Batten, Barton, Durstine & Osborn, Inc.
[5] Henderson Advertising Agency, Inc., Greenville, South Carolina.

[6] In particular the papers in this session were all organized around D. B. Learner's presentation of his work on the analytical model and its conceptual framework as subsequently implemented via the computer codes which he developed in cooperation with Milton Godfrey of CEIR, Inc. See [4].

[7] A still earlier announcement of a media mix model may be found in D. Miller and M. Starr [30] pp. 190 ff. Apparently, however, their model was not intended for actual use but was designed rather to illustrate some of the possibilities and difficulties of model development in this area of management activity.

[8] A succinct history of the background and objectives of this research may be found in [10].

[9] See remarks of D. B. Lucas in [4.6].

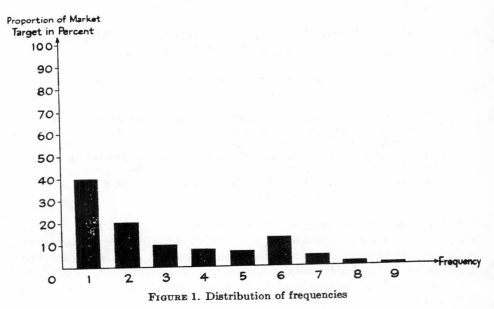

FIGURE 1. Distribution of frequencies

would become worthwhile to undertake further work in model development in order thereby to replace the initial LP Media Mix Model.

It is the purpose of this paper to report the results of such research and, in order to facilitate the discussion, we shall refer to this as LP II and thereby distinguish it from the first model, which we shall designate as LP I.

As was the case for LP I, the strategy here is again twofold: (a) to obtain a model which can be operationally implemented over a wide variety of situations in which optimally selected media plans are of interest and (b) to lay a foundation for continued assimilation of data and experience so that systematically we may on the one hand (i) improve the LP II model and on the other hand (ii) provide a start toward an LP III and possibly even further new models as the necessary background materials are accumulated. A case in point, for instance, would be the development of sales-and-profit-response data which would make it worthwhile to proceed toward media dynamics[10] as distinguished from media selection (e.g., to fit into already existing seasonal patterns of behavior).

Also, as was the case for LP I, it is desirable to stay as close as possible to the knowledge, insight—and hence practices—of experienced media executives. This is vital if developments of the kind already outlined are to be secured. To this end, LP II is oriented primarily in the direction of goal programming models[11] whereas this was not the case for LP I. On the other hand, we replace the idea of REU's (Rated Exposure Units) which were initially developed for LP I in order to compress a variety of advertising measures into an overall composite

[10] E.g., as is done in the DEMON Models where explicit provision is made for collecting the needed data when pertinent. See, e.g., [13].

[11] See Appendix B ff. of [12].

index. In LP II, however, we now extend the bounds of common practice which has heretofore relied on average frequency[12] as an adequate measure and as an adequate control. That is, in LP II we replace this with the entire distribution of frequencies.

Such distributions make it necessary to consider the cumulative audience of a single medium as well as the duplication of audiences among many different media cumulatively and over a variety of different time periods. This in turn made it necessary for us to experiment with a variety of approximating devices which would be sufficiently accurate and sufficiently convenient and economical for day-to-day use on computers, or otherwise. An important new development here is a method for the generation of net audience by means of a logarithmic device involving the idea of "non-reach."

To conclude this introductory section it is useful to refer once more to the original LP I presentation [4] in order to observe that such further development possibilities were predicted not only by reference to the possibilities in marketing and advertising but also by reference to experience with linear programming in other areas such as production, finance, etc.[13] That is, as predicted, this initial presentation was subsequently responded to in a variety of ways by others who, *inter alia*, undertook extensions and improvements via their own research. We hope and expect that even more of this will occur and, indeed, LP II is itself directed to this end.

Mathematical Model

To make the sense of all this more precise, we now proceed to develop relevant aspects of BBDO's LP II Media Model as follows. Let

(1) $d_{kij}(t)$ = gross k^{th} audience segment obtained by the jth cumulative purchase of medium i in period t;[14]

$x_{ij}(t)$ = the jth cumulative purchase of medium i in period t

where, usually, $x_{ij}(t)$ = 0 or 1. We approximate this generally by requiring

(2) $$\sum_j x_{ij}(t) \leqq 1, \qquad x_{ij}(t) \geqq 0.$$

Thus, the gross k^{th} audience segment obtained by media purchases in period t may be written

(3) $$\sum_i \sum_j d_{kij}(t)x_{ij}(t).$$

Next we consider the net audience or "reach." Let

(4) $r_{kij}(t)$ = proportion of the kth net audience segment obtained by j^{th} cumulative purchase of medium i in period t

---

[12] Defined as Gross Audience divided by Net Audience. See [7].

[13] See, e.g., [4.2].

[14] For instance, a specific $d_{kij}(t)$ might refer to the number (= d) of women aged 25 to 34, as subscripted by k (= demographic characteristic) obtained via a purchase of j issues of LIFE when i refers to the latter as the relevant media vehicle. See, e.g., [7].

and $R_k(t)$ = proportion of the net k^{th} audience segment obtained by media purchases in period t.

Then

(5) $$\ln (1 - R_k(t)) = \sum_i \sum_j \ln (1 - r_{kij}(t)) x_{ij}(t)$$

since

(6) $$1 - R_k(t) = \prod_{i,j} (1 - r_{kij}(t))^{x_{ij}(t)}$$

where "$\prod$" means "product"—of the indicated terms—and the $x_{ij}(t)$ conform to (2) for each t.[15]

Turning next to the question of estimating the distribution of frequencies for the net k^{th} audience segment, let

(7) $H_{ks}(t)$ = proportion of the net k^{th} audience segment which is reached s or more times in period t.

For instance, refer to Figure 1, wherein a specific audience segment, k, is represented. The scale on the vertical axis refers to the proportion of this segment which is reached. The scale on the horizontal axis refers to various frequencies. Thus, in this case the distribution of frequencies as charted shows 20% of the net k^{th} audience segment are reached exactly twice, 10% are reached exactly 3 times, and so on.

Note that this elaboration of significant detail replaces customary usages in which a single number, such as average frequency,[16] is used to represent entire distributions such as the one depicted in Figure 1. Note also that (7) is defined so that it decumulates as s increases.

Of course in practical applications a large number of combinatorial possibilities must generally be considered. Recourse to suitable approximating devices is therefore in order.[17] After some experimentation it was found that the already available devices were inadequate for use in this context, however, and it therefore became necessary to consider and test a variety of alternatives from which a type of approximation utilizing the log-normal distribution was finally deemed to be most satisfactory. That is, we obtain the discrete distribution of frequencies for each kth audience segment by suitably determining the parameters of a log-normal distribution.

It was found possible to accomplish this by replacing the usual (exact) relation between means and variances of normal and log-normal distributions[18] by the following approximations:

---

[15] This device is analogous to the way the nonlinear properties of octane numbers were treated by transforming them logarithmically to performance numbers as was done in the first industrial application of linear programming in the U.S. See [14] and [11].

[16] Defined as gross audience divided by net audience or, alternatively, as gross impressions divided by reach. See BBDO Glossary of Media Terms [7].

[17] See, e.g., any of the recent discussions as in Agostini [1], et al.

[18] See, e.g., [3].

$$\text{(8)} \qquad \mu_k(t) = A + B \sum_i \sum_j P_{ki}(t)x_{ij}(t) + C \sum_i \sum_j jx_{ij}(t)$$

$$\sigma_k(t) = D + E \sum_i \sum_j jx_{ij}(t)$$

with $\quad P_{ki}(t) = \dfrac{d_{ki1}(t)}{U_k}$

and $\qquad U_k = $ total number in universe for the kth audience segment,

where μ_k and σ_k are, respectively, the mean and standard deviation of the associated normal distribution and the A, B, C, D and E are constants determined empirically.

The correspondence with the discrete distributions is made via

$$\text{(9)} \qquad \frac{\ln (s - 0.5) - \mu_k(t)}{\sigma_k(t)} = Z_{(1 - H_{ks}(t))}$$

where Z is the studentized normal variate—viz., $N(0, 1)$. Employing (8), and effecting algebraic rearrangements, then

$$\text{(10)} \qquad Z = \frac{\ln (s - 0.5) - A - B \sum_{i,j} P_{ki}(t)x_{ij}(t) - C \sum_{i,j} jx_{ij}(t)}{D + E \sum_{i,j} jx_{ij}(t)}$$

where Z is the fractile associated with $1 - H_{ks}(t)$ for $N(0, 1)$.

The constraints on media choices are of various types such as, for instance, those on gross k^{th} audience segments at specified times—viz.,

$$\text{(11.1)} \qquad \sum_i \sum_j d_{kij}(t)x_{ij}(t) \geqq D_k(t)$$

as well as over selected time intervals,

$$\text{(11.2)} \qquad \sum_{t \in T} \sum_i \sum_j d_{kij}(t)x_{ij}(t) \geqq D_k(T).$$

Similarly for the net k^{th} audience segment we might require

$$\text{(12.1)} \qquad R_k(t) \geqq N_k(t)$$

or

$$\text{(12.2)} \qquad \ln (1 - R_k(t)) \leqq \ln (1 - N_k(t))$$

so that, via (5),

$$\text{(12.3)} \qquad \sum_i \sum_j \ln (1 - r_{kij}(t))x_{ij}(t) \leqq \ln (1 - N_k(t))$$

where $N_k(t)$ is some prescribed fraction of the kth audience segment at time t.

Turning now to controls for the distribution of frequencies we may wish to specify constraints such as, e.g., "at least 80% of the kth audience segment must be reached at least twice at specified times, t." Then

$$\text{(13.1)} \qquad Z_{1 - H_{k,2}(t)} \leqq Z_{1 - .8} = Z_{.2} = N^{-1}(.2)$$

where N is the distribution function for $N(0, 1)$. Thus, from (9) typical constraints of this type may be represented by

$$(13.2) \qquad \frac{\ln (s - 0.5) - \mu_k(t)}{\sigma_k(t)} \geqq Q$$

or, from (10),

$$(13.3) \quad (C + EQ) \sum_{i,j} j x_{ij}(t) + B \sum_{i,j} P_{ki}(t) x_{ij}(t)$$

$$\leqq \ln (s - 0.5) - A - DQ.$$

Other types of constraints such as those found in LP I may also be included.

From the constraints a specific subset may be selected to be fulfilled as close to equality as possible in the sense of "goal programming."[19] For instance, it may be desired to come as close as possible to reaching, say, 85% of the kth audience segment in time t_1 . Thus referring to the development leading into (12.3) we would write

$$(14.1) \quad \sum_i \sum_j \ln (1 - r_{kij}(t_1)) x_{ij}(t_1) + u^+ - u^- = \ln (1 - .85)$$

where the term $u^+ + u^-$ would also appear in the functional to be minimized. Similarly if it were desired to establish a goal for the frequency constraint, from (13.3) we could write

$$(14.2) \quad (C + EQ) \sum_{i,j} j x_{ij}(t_1) + B \sum_{i,j} P_{ki}(t_1) x_{ij}(t_1) + v^+ - v^-$$

$$= \ln (s - 0.5) - A - DQ$$

and, $v^+ + v^-$ would appear in the functional. Of course, weighting systems could be employed and various combinations of constraints could thus be handled in terms of a goal programming format. For example, if the goals were to have relative weights W_1 , W_2 the functional to be minimized would be

$$(15) \qquad z \equiv W_1(u^+ + u^-) + W_2(v^+ + v^-)$$

in the above example. That is, in this case, the objective would be to minimize z as in (15) subject to constraints of the form (11), (12), and (13), plus others of LP I type, including non-negativity, and so on. Media costs including discounts, etc., are introduced as in LP I by inserting them as appropriate for each application with possible supplementary sensitivity and dual evaluator analyses. As before these same techniques are available including dual evaluator analyses and associated interpretations with allowance, of course, for the fact that LP II is formulated as a goal programming model.[20]

Conclusion

The salient aspects of the LP II model and the machinery of approximation have now been set forth in adequate detail and this, in fact, is the way it is now being implemented. As indicated in the opening section of this paper, however, it is expected that further improvements and refinements will be effected in this model, from time to time, but that its main essentials will remain unaltered until,

[19] See, e.g., [12], Appendix B ff.
[20] See Appendix B and Chapter X ff. in [12].

at some future date, it becomes worth undertaking an LP III. In any case, however, the present paper is only the first in a series of reports on LP II and, in fact, another in this series will shortly be issued in order to provide interpretative detail with accompanying numerical illustrations that can help to provide insight and understanding of the properties and possibilities of these LP II developments.

References

1. AGOSTINI, J. M., "Analysis of Magazine Accumulative Audience," *Journal of Advertising Research*, 2, No. 4 (Dec. 1962), pp. 18–23.
2. ——, "How to Estimate Unduplicated Audiences," *Journal of Advertising Research* 1, No. 3 (March 1961), pp. 11–14.
3. AITCHISON, J. AND BROWN, J. A. C., *The Lognormal Distribution*, University Press, Cambridge, 1957.
4. AMERICAN ASSOCIATION OF ADVERTISING AGENCIES, Papers from 1961 Regional Conventions, Group IV. *Mathematical Programming for Better Media Selection*
   4.1 WILSON, C. L., "Introduction," pp. 1–3.
   4.2 CHARNES, A. AND COOPER, W. W., "Budgeting and Planning Media Schedules," pp. 5–24.
   4.3 LEARNER, D. B., "The Translation from Theory to Practice," pp. 25–32.
   4.4 GODFREY, M., "Computer Processing and Computer Results," pp. 33–42.
   4.5 MANELOVEG, H. D., "How the Practical Media Man Handles the Output," pp. 43–50.
   4.6 LUCAS, D. B., "A Summary Perspective—Some Implications, Questions and Comments," pp. 51–58.
5. ASSOCIATION OF NATIONAL ADVERTISERS, INC., *Defining Advertising Goals for Measured Advertising Results*, Association of National Advertisers, Inc., New York, 1961.
6. BASS, F. M. AND LONSDALE, R. T., "An Exploration of Linear Programming in Media Selection," *Journal of Marketing Research*, 3, No. 2 (May 1966), pp. 179–188.
7. BATTEN, BARTON, DURSTINE & OSBORN, INC., *Glossary of Media Terms*, BBDO, Inc., New York, 1966.
8. ——, "The Mathematics of Linear Programming for Advertising Men Who Hate Mathematics," BBDO, Inc., New York, 1963.
9. BROWN, D. B. AND WARSHAW, M. R., "Media Selection by Linear Programming," *Journal of Marketing Research*, February 1965, pp. 83–89.
10. BUZZELL, R. D., "Mathematical Models and Marketing Management," Ch. V., Harvard University, Division of Research, Graduate School of Business Administration, Cambridge, 1964.
11. CHARNES, A., Rejoinder to A. S. Manne's "The Strong Independence Assumption—Gasoline Blends and Probability Mixtures," *Econometrica*, 20, No. 4 (Oct. 1952), pp. 668–669.
12. —— AND COOPER, W. W., *Management Models and Industrial Applications of Linear Programming*, John Wiley & Sons, Inc., New York, 1961.
13. ——, ——, DeVOE J. K., AND LEARNER, D. B., "DEMON: Decision Mapping Via Optimum Go-No Networks—A Model for Marketing New Products," *Management Science*, Vol. 12, No. 11 (July 1966), pp. 865–887. (See also further references to other reports in the DEMON series as cited.)
14. ——, —— AND MELLON, B., "Blending Aviation Gasoline: A Study in programming Interdependent Activities," *Econometrica*, 20, No. 2 (April, 1952), pp. 135–139.
15. CRISTUREANU, T., "Application of Some Mathematical Methods to the Choice of Publicity Means and to Determine the Efficiency of Commercial Advertising," *Economic Computation and Economic Cybernetic Studies and Research*, No. 3, Bucharest, Romania, 1967, pp. 103–114.

16. DANTZIG, G. B., *Linear Programming and Extensions*, Princeton University Press, Princeton, N. J., 1963.
17. DAY, RALPH L., "Linear Programming in Media Selection," *Journal of Advertising Research*, II, No. 2 (June 1962), pp. 40–44.
18. ENGEL, J. F. AND WARSHAW, M. R., "Allocating Advertising Dollars by Linear Programming," *The Journal of Advertising Research*, 4, 1964, pp. 42–48.
19. ENGELMAN, F. L., "An Empirical Formula for Audience Accumulation," *Journal of Advertising Research*, 5, No. 2 (June, 1965), pp. 21–28.
20. GODFREY, M. L., "Advertising Media Decisions and the Computer," American Marketing Association, Annual Conference, Chicago, Nov., 1963.
21. ——, "Media Selection by Mathematical Programming," New York, Mediatrics, Inc., 1962.
22. IJIRI, Y., *Management Goals and Accounting for Control*, North Holland Publishing Co., Amsterdam, 1965.
23. KOTLER, P., "Toward an Explicit Model for Media Selection," *Journal of Advertising Research*, 4, No. 1 (March 1964), pp. 34–41.
24. KRAMER, R. L., "Mathematical Models for Media Selection: An Appraisal and Extension," Bankers Trust Co., Inc., New York, Nov., 1966.
25. LEARNER, D. B., "Mathematical Models of Media Selection," Advertising Research Foundation, Operations Research Discussion Group, New York, 1961.
26. LEE, A. M., "Decision Rules for Media Scheduling: Dynamic Campaign," *Operational Research Quarterly*, XIV, No. 4 (Dec. 1963), pp. 365–372.
27. LITTLE, J. D. C., "Extensions of the Linear Programming Models for Media Selections," Massachusetts Institute of Technology, Cambridge, 1964.
28. MANELOVEG, H., "Linear Programming" (Speech presented at AAAA Eastern Annual Conference, Nov., 1962), Batten, Barton, Durstine & Osborn, Inc., New York.
29. —— AND WILSON, C. L., "Year of Linear Programming Media Selections," Advertising Research Foundation, 8th Annual Conference, New York, 1962.
30. MILLER, D. AND STARR, M., *Executive Decisions and Operations Research*, Prentice-Hall, Inc., Englewood Cliffs, N.J., 1960).
31. MORAN, W. T., "Practical Media Models—What Must They Look Like?" *Proceedings: Eighth Annual Conference*, Advertising Research Foundation, New York, 1962, pp. 30–38.
32. NATIONAL INDUSTRIAL CONFERENCE BOARD, *Studies in Business Policy No. 121, Evaluating Media*, NICB, New York, 1967.
33. RICHARDS, ELIZABETH AND MENDELSON, M., eds., *The Marketing Plan in Action* (Workshop Sessions, 1963–1964), New York Chapter, American Marketing Association, 1964.
    32.1 DEVOE, J. K., "Media Selection and Linear Programming," pp. 43–47.
    32.2 WILSON, C. L., "Some Basics of Linear Programming," pp. 48–53.
34. SIMULMATICS CORPORATION, "Simulmatic Media-Mix I, General Description," February, 1962.
35. ZANGWILL, W. I., "Media Selection by Decision Programming," *Journal of Advertising Research*, 5, No. 3 (Sept. 1965), pp. 30–36.

MANAGEMENT SCIENCE
Vol. 14, No. 8, April, 1968
Printed in U.S.A.

NOTE ON AN APPLICATION OF A GOAL PROGRAMMING MODEL FOR MEDIA PLANNING*

A. CHARNES,[1] W. W. COOPER,[2] D. B. LEARNER,[3] AND E. F. SNOW[3]

An illustrative example is developed from an actual application of goal programming to media planning over a period of time. These goals involve distributions of frequencies by demographic and other characteristics as well as budget and other constraining limitations.

This report develops an example to illustrate and explain the model described in the preceding article.[4] Based on an actual problem—which has been run for a client of Batten, Barton, Durstine & Osborn, Inc.—the product involved is a seasonal, packaged consumer product that is marketed nationally. In this case, the product is an addition that is supposed to supplement the client's existing line. Computations were effected by electronic computers utilizing a matrix generator developed for use in connection with these models by Haverly Associates.

The product is assumed to be especially appealing for housewives with children and the target market is defined as "Ladies of the House for Families of Three or Larger." In the underlying "data bank," relevant demographic cells are identified which contain the audience for media vehicle i during any specified time interval t. In particular, cell 2866 consists of "Ladies of the House for Families of Three to Four Persons," and cell 2896 consists of "Ladies of the House for Families of Five or More Persons." The gross k^{th} audience segment is composed of these two cells and the total number in these two cells defines the value of U_k for this audience segment to be utilized in expression (8).

In addition to the audience segment which has just been described (and which represents the primary target group) there are additional segments, indexed by new k values, which represent secondary prospects.[5] For this illustration we are defining these other target groups as "all housewives and women with annual incomes over \$5,000." Thus, in this case we have to consider these three audience segments indexed as U_1, U_2, and U_3. See (8).

We assume that goals for each of these 3 audience segments have been specified. For the first quarter they are given in Table 1.

It should be observed that in this case no first-quarter goals have been established for the audience segment indexed by $k = 3$—viz., women from families with annual incomes greater than \$5,000.

---

* Received January 1968.
[1] Northwestern University
[2] Carnegie-Mellon University
[3] Batten, Barton, Durstine & Osborn, Inc.
[4] The expressions (in parentheses) and the references [in brackets] are also keyed to this article, viz., "A Goal Programming Model for Media Planning," by A. Charnes, W. W. Cooper, J. K. DeVoe, D. B. Learner, and W. Reinecke.
[5] In this illustration, however, we shall not use unequal weights of the kind admitted by (15).

TABLE 1
Quarterly Goals for Audience Segments 1 and 2

	"Ladies of the House for Families of Three or More" k = 1						All Housewives k = 2	
	% Reach	Freq.	%*	Freq.	%*	Freq.	% Reach	Freq.
Total Reach	90	1+	80	4+	55	8+	90	1+
Print	75	1+	80	2+	50	4+	75	1+
Television	75	1+	80	2+	50	4+	75	1+

* % of Audience Reached.

TABLE 2
Media Available for Selection

Medium	Cost		Maximum Per Mo.
	Winter	Summer	
Print			
$i = 1$	$41,817	Same	2
$i = 2$	43,347	Same	2
$i = 3$	31,200	Same	2
$i = 4$	48,961	Same	1
$i = 5$	26,220	Same	2
$i = 6$	53,100	Same	2
$i = 7$	48,150	Same	2
$i = 8$	20,330	Same	2
$i = 9$	13,993	Same	1
$i = 10$	33,686	Same	1
$i = 11$	28,560	Same	1
$i = 12$	25,412	Same	1
$i = 13$	23,765	Same	1
$i = 14$	38,692	Same	1
$i = 15$	12,132	Same	1
$i = 16$	18,006	Same	1
$i = 17$	27,180	Same	1
Television			
$i = 18$	$6,167	Same	25
$i = 19$	8,667	Same	25
$i = 20$	5,100	4,600	4
$i = 21$	3,400	2,900	4
$i = 22$	5,100	4,300	4
$i = 23$	5,100	4,600	4
$i = 24$	3,400	2,900	4
$i = 25$	4,500	3,900	4
$i = 26$	6,900	Same	4
$i = 27$	7,300	Same	4
$i = 28$	6,500	Same	4
$i = 29$	48,000	38,000	4
$i = 30$	45,000	35,000	4

TABLE 3
Monthly Goals for Audience Segments 1, 2 and 3

Month	"Ladies of the House for Families of Three or More"						"All Housewives"		"Women Over $5,000"	
	% Reach	Fr.	%	Fr.	%	Fr.	% Reach	Fr.	% Reach	Fr.
3	75	1+	65	4+	30	8+	65	1+	65	1+
4	70	1+	65	4+			60	1+	60	1+
5	60	1+	65	4+			50	1+	50	1+
6	60	1+	65	2+			50	1+	50	1+
7	60	1+	65	2+			50	1+	50	1+
8	60	1+	65	2+			50	1+	50	1+
9	60	1+	65	2+			50	1+	50	1+
10	60	1+	65	2+			50	1+	50	1+
11	50	1+	60	2+			25	1+	25	1+
12	50	1+	60	2+			25	1+	25	1+
1	50	1+	60	2+			25	1+	25	1+
2	50	1+	60	2+			25	1+	25	1+

TABLE 4
Media Mix Schedule

i	t												Total
	3	4	5	6	7	8	9	10	11	12	1	2	
Print													
2		2											2
3		1											1
5	1					1	1						3
8	1												1
9	1												1
11			1	1	1	1	1	1	1			1	8
13				1	1	1	1	1		1	1		7
15	1												1
Total	4	3	1	3	2	3	3	2	1	1	1	1	24
Television													
18	18												18
19	1												1
20	4	4	4	1									13
21	4	4	4										12
22	4	4	4										12
23	4	4	4	1	1	1	1	1	1	1	1	1	21
24	4	4	4										12
25	4	4	4										12
26	4												4
27	4												4
28	4												4
Total	55	24	24	2	1	1	1	1	1	1	1	1	113
Grand Total	59	27	25	4	3	4	4	3	2	2	2	2	137

TABLE 5
Comparison of Reach Achievements with Goals

	$k = 1$			$k = 2$			$k = 3$		
	Goal	Achievement	Difference	Goal	Achievement	Difference	Goal	Achievement	Difference
Quarterly									
Total Reach	90%	94%	+4	90%	94%	+4	(No goals were specified)		
Print	75	74	−1	75	74	−1			
Television	75	76	+1	75	75	0			
Monthly									
Month									
3	75%	75%	0	65%	79%	+14	65%	71%	+6
4	70	70	0	60	71	+11	60	65	+5
5	60	60	0	50	59	+9	50	53	+3
6	60	54	−6	50	50	0	50	50	0
7	60	55	−5	50	50	0	50	50	0
8	60	54	−6	50	50	0	50	50	0
9	60	54	−6	50	50	0	50	50	0
10	60	54	−6	50	50	0	50	50	0
11	50	30	−20	25	25	0	25	25	0
12	50	27	−23	25	25	0	25	25	0
1	50	27	−23	25	25	0	25	25	0
2	50	30	−20	25	25	0	25	25	0

In this case we see that there are goals involving Print Media and TV Media, separately as well as in combination, and also for "Ladies of the House for Families of Three or More" ($k = 1$) as well as "All Housewives" ($k = 2$). Consider, for example, the goals for $k = 1$ as described under the columns headed by "Ladies of the House for Families of Three or More." Opposite the row labeled "Print" we find the goal which is prescribed for reach stated as a percentage of U_1, the total number of women in the demographic cells associated with $k = 1$. This reach percentage of 75% is, however, only one of the goals to be achieved with the Print Media that might be used.

Additional goals are stated to be a frequency of 2 or more for 80% of those who are thus reached and a frequency of 4 or more for 50% of those reached via the Print Media utilzed.

Now refer to expressions (14.1) and (14.2) and note that the range of the summations for i and j in these expressions may vary according to the goals—e.g., the goals for "Print" for "Television" and for "Print Plus Television." Thus expressions (14.1) and (14.2) delineate the form of such expressions, which admit different ranges of summation. It is important further to note, by contrast, that the index t is handled in a different manner in expressions (14.1) and (14.2).

TABLE 6

Comparison of Frequency Achievements with Goals

$k = 3$

	"Ladies of the House for Families of Three or More"					
	Reach and Freq. Goals	Achievement	Difference	Reach and Freq. Goals	Achievement	Difference
Quarterly						
Total	70% (4+)	74%	+4	50% (8+)	42%	−8
Print	60 (2+)	65	+5	40 (4+)	17	−23
Television	60 (2+)	75	+15	40 (4+)	58	+18
Monthly						
Month						
3	50% (4+)	41%	−9	25% (8+)	14%	−11
4	45 (4+)	25	−20			
5	40 (4+)	20	−20			
6	40 (2+)	47	+7			
7	40 (2+)	48	+8			
8	40 (2+)	47	+7			
9	40 (2+)	47	+7			
10	40 (2+)	47	+7			
11	30 (2+)	26	−4			
12	30 (2+)	23	−7			
1	30 (2+)	23	−7			
2	30 (2+)	26	−4			

In this example, for instance, separate controls were established for different and overlapping intervals of time. Each of these time intervals is indexed as a different period. When, as in this case, a separate control is to be established for the first quarter as well as for each of the three months composing this quarter, then four different t indexes are assigned—one for each of these three months and a separate one for the quarter in its own right.

In this case the i indexes which have been assigned to Print and TV Media are displayed in Table 2 along with seasonal (i.e., summer and winter) costs. The upper limit for the index j associated with each medium is also displayed in the last column of Table 2. As already observed, these j values admit of different ranges, in this case as well as in general. In any event, the data of Table 2 may be used to formulate budget and other constraints of LP I type,[6] and in this case the budget limit for expenditure on all media was established as $1,200,-000.

As was observed above, monthly and quarterly goals may be independently established in the context of such a goal programming model. Furthermore, an

[6] See [4], and the discussion following (15).

application of this model may be initiated at any time. In this case the application is initiated in month 3, as shown in Table 3, and there is no requirement that the goals in Table 1 and 3 be consistent. In fact, when inconsistent, or when inconsistent with other constraints (e.g., of LP I type) then the objective of goal programming is to meet all requirements "as closely as possible."

Optimizing in this goal-programming sense while staying within the budgeted $1,200,000, a mix of media was selected and scheduled with the results portrayed in Table 4. The total cost of this schedule is $1,195,917. A next best buy would raise the insertions for Print $i = 5$ from its present zero amount to a value of 1 in month 4. I.e., we would then have for this Print $x_{ij}(t) = x_{51}(4) = 1$ and, by extension, it can be discovered that a still further increase in the budget would produce $x_{52}(4) = 1$ and $x_{51}(4) = 0$. That is, the number of insertions of media vehicle $i = 5$ in month $t = 4$ is given by the index $j = 2$. See expression (2) which was developed in this fashion so that precisely one of the $x_{ij}(t)$ could be unity in which event all of the other $x_{ij}(t)$ for this same i and t would be zero. This was done to accommodate cumulative reach and distribution of frequencies over contiguous and consecutive time periods and the expressions (2) were formulated accordingly. In cases where fractional $x_{ij}(t)$ are encountered, either round-off or sensitivity analysis routes may be utilized to adjust to integer values when required.

Having now served the purposes of illustration to a sufficient degree we do not propose to pursue this example into the further topics that would relate it to the dual-evaluation and the sensitivity analyses that are also pertinent for applications of these kinds of media mix models.[7] Instead we bring this discussion to a close by referring to Tables 5 and 6 which compare the goals and their achievement, as determined by the LP II Model for this particular example.

[7] See, e.g., Appendix B and Chapter 10 in [12] as well as [4].

A Media Selection Model and its Optimization by Dynamic Programming

John D. C. Little and
Leonard M. Lodish
Massachusetts Institute
of Technology

An advertiser can select media to spend a given budget in a large number of different ways. By selecting media we mean specifying the time, place, outward format, and type of medium for a schedule of advertising insertions. Advertisers and their agencies have evolved rules of thumb and aggregative procedures for reducing the number of possibilities and simplifying the selection process. More or less elaborate calculations of audience size, demographic composition, sales potential, media reach, frequency, and cost per exposure are often made in the course of developing a schedule. Nevertheless, the pieces of the problem are seldom put together in a unifying framework that permits overall comparison among alternatives.

In recent years attempts have been made to formulate the media selection problem in ways suitable for machine computation. Such a formulation has several advantages. First, the steps in the process must be made explicit, and so the underlying assumptions become conspicuous and subject to a healthy concern. Second, because computers are enthusiastic clerks, much more detail can be handled and far more alternatives examined within reasonable time and cost limits. Finally, consistent criteria and methods can be applied across all alternatives. This means that, although subjective inputs are currently important and are likely to remain so, computer solutions are not as subject to extraneous influences and momentary time pressures as are solutions developed by less formal methods.

The steps in setting up an advertising campaign include (1) identifying the desired audience, (2) picking the message, (3) preparing the copy treatment and (4) selecting the media. The steps are not independent; message, copy, and media all depend on the audience. However, once the characteristics of the audience have been specified, the questions of message and copy can be separated to a reasonable degree from the media question of how to reach the audience efficiently. Only the media question will be considered here. Provision is made, however, for including in the selection process a rating of each media vehicle and, if the information is available at the time the media are to be chosen, this could be extended to message and copy.

A formal selection process requires (1) a model that relates media choices to a measure of schedule effectiveness and (2) a search procedure for finding the best schedule, or at least a good one. In building the model two directions are open. One is to construct a relatively simple model that seeks to embody the key phenomena of the process and yet tries to remain within the capabilities of present computers in terms of optimization. This is the direction we take here. The other is to build more complicated models containing more detailed representations of various phenomena and to simulate the process. Then, to a degree depending on the length of time required for a single simulation, multiple runs can be made simulating different schedules. The components of the schedule can be varied by human intervention or by the computer using heuristic programming methods, i.e., by methods that seek to find improved but not necessarily optimal results. This latter approach, although worthwhile, is not taken up in the present paper.

The paper is divided into five parts: (1) a brief review of published models, (2) a model, (3) a dynamic programming method for optimizing the model, (4) a worked-out solution to a problem provided by a Boston advertising agency, and (5) a brief discussion of the merits of the model.

Review of Published Models

Among the earliest mathematical formulations of the media selection problem is the linear program developed jointly by BBDO and CEIR. Descriptions have been given by Wilson [1], and Buzzell [2]. The linear programming approach has been further discussed by Day [3], Engel and Warshaw [4], and Bass and Lonsdale [5]. In all these formulations, the objective function is linear in the number of exposures. This implies that the value of ten exposures to one person equals that of one exposure to each of ten people. This does not seem reasonable, particularly at high levels of exposure, where additional exposures are ordinarily believed to have less value than previous ones. The effect of the linearity on the solution is that the most efficient medium for generating exposures will usually be bought until some upper limit is reached, then the next most efficient is bought until its limit is reached, and so on. Upper limits must be provided to prevent unreasonable schedules, but then this starts to look similar to picking a schedule without a model except for the important point that the methods are systematic and employ an explicit objective function.

To get away from strict linearity, several models have introduced diminishing returns with increasing exposure. In an unpublished paper reporting the BBDO-CEIR model, Godfrey [6] presents a method of dealing with certain types of nonlinearities. Wilson [1] refers briefly to a method and presumably it is the same one. More recently, Brown and Warshaw [7] have published essentially the same thing. The basis of the method is a standard device for converting a nonlinear program into a linear one in the case that the objective function is separable and (for a maximization problem) concave. By separable is meant that the objective function is the sum of functions, each of a single variable. By concave is meant that the functions show diminishing returns (or are linear) but never show increasing returns. Methods are available for solving such a problem. See for example, Hadley [8], chapter 4.

Both Godfrey's and Brown and Warshaw's formulations have a serious drawback in that the nonlinearities of each medium are separate. Thus, a person's increase in response from seeing a TV commercial is the same whether he has seen zero, one, or ten ads in some other medium. It would seem more reasonable to expect diminishing returns with total exposure, especially at high levels.

Two further difficulties beset the above formulations. First, the timing of the insertions over the planning period is usually ignored, or at least is set outside the linear program. Second, a linear program permits variables to take on fractional values, whereas the number of insertions must always be an integer.

Zangwill [9] suggests handling the integrality problem by the use of integer programming. However, the current state of the art in this field is not encouraging for media problems of moderate size. Zangwill's evaluation of the effectiveness of a media choice is done almost entirely outside the model. This offers great flexibility, but much of the appeal of a model lies in having it synthesize the effectiveness of the various media combinations by consideration of what is happening in the customer population.

Lee and Burkart [10], Taylor [11], and Lee [12, 13] have developed a series of models motivated especially by print media. These models are much more explicit in their treatment of exposure probabilities and customer response to exposure than those previously mentioned. Under certain sets of assumptions, easily applied rules for optimal media selection are worked out. In the more recent and more complicated models, which take into account market response to the advertising schedule over time, the optimization is left as an integer linear program.

Moran [14] and Kuehn [15] discuss simulation models and heuristic programs for the selection or improvement of a media

JOHN D. C. LITTLE AND LEONARD M. LODISH

schedule. Neither of these papers goes into much detail.

Model Description

Our model may be described briefly as follows: The population is divided into *market segments*. Each segment has its own sales potential and media habits. A media schedule consists of *insertions* in *media vehicles* (examples of media vehicles would be: a full color page in LIFE, a 60-second spot in a particular TV show, etc.). An insertion brings about *exposures* in the various market segments. The exposures serve to increase what we shall call *exposure value* in the market segments. However, people are subject to *forgetting*, and so the retained exposure level decays with time in the absence of new exposures. The *anticipated sales* to a market segment increase with exposure level but with diminishing returns.

To develop the model in detail, let

M = number of media vehicles under consideration

T = number of time periods in the planning horizon

S = number of market segments

x_{jt} = number of insertions in media vehicle j in time period t

u_{jt}, l_{jt} = upper and lower limits on the value of x_{jt}, i.e.,
$$l_{jt} \leq x_{jt} \leq u_{jt}.$$

k_{ijt} = exposure efficiency: the expected number of exposures per person produced in market segment i by one insertion in media vehicle j in time t (exposures/capita/time period)

Thus, $k_{ijt}x_{jt}$ is the expected number of exposures per capita that the insertions x_{jt} develop in market segment i during t. Although we shall use per-capita units, some products would more appropriately be set up in other units, for example, per household. Market segments are defined to be mutually exclusive and are presumed to represent relevant groups with respect to sales potential and media usage.

The exposure efficiency k_{ijt}, can be built up from other constants; let

g_{ij} = fraction of people in market segment i who are in the audience of vehicle j (average value over a year).

s_{jt} = seasonal index of audience size for vehicle j (average value = 1.0)

h_j = probability of exposure to an ad in vehicle j given that a person is in the audience of the vehicle.

We take

$$k_{ijt} = h_j g_{ij} s_{jt}.$$

As may be seen, we have broken k_{ijt} into three factors. These involve average audience, seasonality of audience, and the probability of exposure for a person in the audience. The factor g_{ij} reflects the circulation of magazines, the sets tuned into a TV show, etc., in a given market segment. The factor s_{jt} represents the seasonal variation in the audience. Whether a person sees, hears, or is in some way exposed to the ad depends considerably upon its size, color, position, length of time, and so forth. Such characteristics will be called the format of the media vehicle. The probability of exposure, h_j, is presumed to depend primarily on format.

Next we must recognize that the value of an exposure is not the same for every media vehicle. One reason is format differences: A larger ad, besides being more noticeable, may convey more information. Even more important are intermedia differences: An exposure to a 30-second radio spot must be rated on the same scale as an exposure to a half page newspaper ad. At present there is a large subjective element in such appraisals but any final media schedule, however arrived at, implicitly includes such an evaluation. Other reasons that can be cited for exposure-value differences are the editorial climate of the vehicle, its usefulness in obtaining retailer support, and the copy opportunities within the vehicle, e.g., the capacity for demonstrating a product or the need for a faithful rendering of color. We shall let

e_j = exposure value conveyed by one exposure in vehicle j.

The units here are arbitrary except that they must be tied in later to a response function. One vehicle can be assigned a reference value and the others related to it.

It is assumed that an exposure increases some desirable quantity that we shall call the level of exposure value per capita. The amount of increase is the sum of the contributions from each media vehicle:

$$\Sigma_{j=1}^{M} e_j k_{ijt} x_{jt} =$$

increase in exposure level/capita in market segment i during time period t.

The level of exposure value is not conceived of as being a directly observable quantity. Perhaps something akin to it is observable and, if so, this would be very helpful. Quite likely, however, the communications process and the state of an individual involve a complex of quantities. If so, they are deliberately aggregated here.

In any case we suppose that the effect of advertising wears off as a result of forgetting. Specifically, it is assumed that, in the absence of new input, exposure value decreases by a constant fraction each time period. Let

y_{it} = exposure value/capita in segment i in time period t.
α = fraction of y_{it} retained from one time period to the next.

Then

$$y_{it} = \alpha y_{i,\ t-1} + \Sigma_{j=1}^{M} e_j k_{ijt} x_{jt}.$$

A typical pattern of y_{it} over time might look as follows:

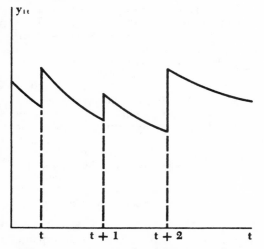

For some empirical evidence on decay, see Rohloff [17]. If desired, the decay constant α can be made to depend on i and t and various other factors. An interesting approach would be to let its value for each market segment and time period depend on the anticipated competitive advertising to that segment at that time. In some situations it would be expected that competitive advertising would erode a customer's level of exposure value faster than ordinary forgetfulness. In other situations, competitive advertising may slow down decay by increasing general product class awareness.

The next step is to specify the sales response of the market segments. We suppose that sales is a nonlinear function of exposure value/capita. Let

p_{it} = sales potential of market segment i in time period t (dollars/capita/time period).
$p_{it}f(y_{it})$ = anticipated sales rate to market segment i in time t when exposure value/capita is y_{it}.

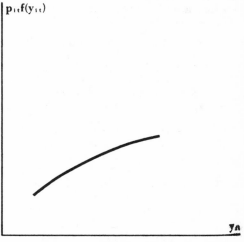

Conceivably, a different function $f(y_{it})$ could be used for each i and t but until evidence dictates otherwise it seems adequate to reflect differences between market segments and time periods simply by using sales potential as a scale factor.

Notice that sales have been expressed as a nonlinear function of an exponentially weighted sum of past exposures in the market segment. This could have been done without reference to the non-observable quantity, exposure value. We are actually trying to relate two observable quantities, exposures and sales. In some cases it may be possible to determine the relationship between these partly by field experimentation. In any case, the relationships used in the model should be in a range consistent with whatever empirical evidence is available. However, under present conditions, subjective estimates will have to play an important role in specifying sales response and, as an aid for forming these judgments, it seems helpful to use a concept such as exposure value for combining the effects of different media vehicles.

To calculate the total anticipated sales in the planning period, let

n_i = number of people in market segment i.

Then
$$\Sigma_{i=1}^{S} \Sigma_{t=1}^{T} n_i p_{it} f(y_{it}) =$$
total sales over the planning period (dollars).

To bring in costs, let

c_{jt} = cost per insertion in media vehicle j at time t (dollars/insertion).
b = total budget for the planning period (dollars).

The total cost of the schedule is then $\Sigma_{j=1}^{M} \Sigma_{t=1}^{T} c_{jt} x_{jt}$, which must be less than or equal to the budget. The cost is taken to be linear in the number of insertions. The published advertising rates are considerably more complex than this, and, worse yet for planning, the prices of many media purchases are negotiated. In practice, a media schedule is often not a single commitment but rather a series of them. Under these circumstances it can be anticipated that a media model might be re-run several times, each time incorporating the latest commitments and cost estimates.

Pulling everything together, we can express the model as the following mathematical program:

MP1. Find x_{jt} and y_{it} to
$$\max \Sigma_{i=1}^{S} \Sigma_{t=1}^{T} n_i p_{it} f(y_{it})$$

subject to

$$y_{it} = \alpha y_{i, t-1} + \Sigma_{j=1}^{M} k_{ij} e_j x_{jt}$$
i = 1, . . ., S
t = 1, . . ., T

$$l_{jt} \le x_{jt} \le u_{jt}$$
j = 1, . . ., M
t = 1, . . ., T

$$\Sigma_{j=1}^{M} \Sigma_{t=1}^{T} c_{jt} x_{jt} \le b$$

$$x_{jt}, y_{it} \ge 0$$

MP1 is a nonlinear program with linear constraints and a separable objective. We note that, if the function $f(y_{it})$ is concave (i.e., it shows diminishing returns or is linear, but is not, for example, S-shaped), then standard methods will reduce MP1 to a linear program. However, the difficulty of obtaining integer values for the x_{jt} would still remain.

There is a minor problem in how to handle end effects in MP1. Each market segment starts the planning period with some kind of exposure value, say y_{i0} and ends with y_{iT}. Presumably, reasonable values can be specified for y_{i0}. However, if we are not careful, the value of a large y_{iT} will be underrated because some of its effect comes in time periods after T and out of the analysis. A variety of approaches can be taken. A few extra periods can be added onto T without scheduling more media. Alternatively, a special $f_T(y_{iT})$ can be constructed to approximate the discounted value of future operations starting at T.

Dynamic Programming Formulation

MP1 can be set up as a dynamic program and problems of modest size can be solved fairly easily. For a dynamic programming solution, it does not matter whether $f(y_{it})$ is concave.

We reindex the media n = 1, . . ., N, counting each media vehicle-time period combination as a separate medium. Then N = MT. Furthermore, we arrange the order so that the first M are the media vehicles in the first time period, the second M, the media vehicles in the second time period, etc. Then n becomes a pseudo time index that puts the media choices in an orderly sequence.

The effect of the new "time" is to permit a recursion in the exposure values whereby one medium is introduced at a time. Let

y_{in} = the exposure value/capita in market segment i at time n
$$\alpha_n = \begin{cases} \alpha & \text{if } n = Mt, \ t = 0, \ldots, T \\ 1 & \text{otherwise} \end{cases}$$
Then
$$y_{in} = \alpha_{n-1} y_{i, n-1} + e_n k_{in} x_n.$$

Under the new subscripting, the objective function is (except for the end effect):

$$\Sigma_{i=1}^{S} \Sigma_{t=1}^{T} n_i p_{i, Mt} f(y_{i, Mt})$$

In other words, only every M^{th} value of n is used in the objective function. However, we would like to express the objective function in terms of individual contributions attributable to each x_n. This can be done by defining

$$f_{1n}(y_{1,\,n-1}, x_n) = \begin{cases} f(\alpha\, y_{1,\,n-1} + e_n k_{1n} x_n) \text{ if} \\ n = Mt + 1,\ t = 0, \ldots, T \\ f(y_{1,\,n-1} + e_n k_{1n} x_n) \\ -f(y_{1,\,n-1}) \text{ otherwise} \end{cases}$$

$$= \begin{cases} f(y_{1,\,n}) \text{ if} \\ n = Mt + 1,\ t = 0, \ldots, T \\ f(y_{1,\,n}) - f(y_{1,\,n-1}) \\ \text{otherwise} \end{cases}$$

Then the objective function becomes

$$\Sigma_{i=1}^{s}\ \Sigma_{n=1}^{N}\ n_i p_{1n} f_{1n}(y_{1,\,n-1}, x_n).$$

The dynamic programming recursion can now be developed. Let

$G_n(z;\ y_1, \ldots, y_8)$ = maximum sales that can be achieved over the planning period with a budget of z dollars allocated optimally over the media n, n + 1, ..., N when $y_{1,\,n-1} = y_1$, i = 1, ..., S.

$G_{N+1}(y_1, \ldots, y_8)$ = end effect, i.e., future sales attributable to leaving the customer population with exposure values, $y_{1,\,N} = y_1$, i = 1, ..., S.

Then

$$G_n(z;\ y_1, \ldots, y_8) = \begin{matrix} \max \\ l_n \le x_n \le u_n \\ c_n x_n \le z \end{matrix}$$

$$\{\Sigma_{i=1}^{8}\ n_i p_{1n} f_{1n}(y_1, x_n)$$
$$+ G_{n+1}(z - c_n x_n;\ y_{1n}, \ldots, y_{8n})\}$$

where, in the argument of G_{n+1},

$$y_{1n} = \alpha_{n-1} y_1 + e_n k_{1n} x_n,\ i = 1, \ldots, S.$$

The calculation starts with n = N and works back to n = 1. At each step, the maximizing value of x_n is stored as $x_n(z; y_1, \ldots, y_8)$ so that the optimal policy can later be determined. This is done by starting at n = 1 with z = b and whatever the starting values, y_{1o}, may be. Substitution gives the optimal x_1. Knowing this, we can deplete the budget by the amount spent and calculate the values of y_{11} brought about by the exposures of x_1. These new values can be put into $x_2(z, y_1, \ldots, y_8)$ to determine optimal x_2. The process is re- peated for each n.

The optimization can be programmed for a computer in a fairly straightforward manner. The time and storage requirements increase rapidly with the number of market segments, media vehicles and time periods but it appears that problems of a size large enough to be useful can be solved.

An Example of the Application of the Model

The dynamic programming solution has been developed for a problem supplied by the media director of the Boston branch of a medium-sized advertising agency. The problem concerned the nationwide introduction of a new service. The first four months' media schedule was to be determined.

Steps in the Determination of the Parameters

Media. The 15 media vehicles considered by the media director as viable alternatives were all included in the study. They are listed in Table 1.

Market Segments. Typical users of the service were expected to be males with high income, professional people, travellers, salesmen, and businessmen. The media director felt that people holding American Express credit cards would have the same characteristics as the potential users of the service. These credit card holders were therefore defined to be the target market. Without doubt, the number of people holding American Express credit cards is smaller than the actual market; however, it was felt that qualitatively (education, income, profession) the people comprising the two groups would be the same and that media reaching one group would tend to reach the other. The only market segment, then, comprised the 1,524,000 people holding American Express cards.

$k_{1,\,j,\,t}$ *Determination.* $g_{1,\,j}$, the fraction of people in group i in the audience of vehicle j was obtained from Simmons' figures and is shown in Table 1. The seasonal index was considered as 1.00 for all media, as was h_j, the probability of exposure to an ad in media j, since intermedia differences

JOHN D. C. LITTLE AND LEONARD M. LODISH

Table 1 The Media Considered

Media	J	Cost/ Insertion (B and W) ($)	Cost/ Insertion Rounded to $1400 Intervals	Audience Among AECC Holders (000)	$k_{ijt} = g_{ij}$	Intermedia Differences Out of 10	$e(j)$
Life	1	35,200	35,000	742	.486	9	1.3
Look	2	34,750	35,000	517	.350	6	.86
Readers' Digest	3	50,800	50,400	546	.360	8	1.1
Post	4	26,000	26,600	358	.235	7	1.0
Time	5	17,900	18,200	519	.348	9	1.3
Newsweek	6	10,435	9,800	305	.198	8	1.1
U.S. News	7	7,900	8,400	382	.252	7	1.0
Sports Il.	8	7,885	8,400	230	.151	7	1.0
New Yorker	9	3,700	4,200	242	.159	8	1.1
Holiday	10	7,690	7,000	179	.118	6	.86
Playboy	11	16,500	16,800	161	.105	7	1.0
Esquire	12	7,350	7,000	224	.147	6	.86
Bus. Week	13	5,730	5,600	263	.173	8	1.1
Fortune	14	6,430	7,000	196	.129	7	1.0
Wall St. Journal	15	14,492	14,000	369	.242	8	1.1

in probability of exposure were considered minimal by the media director. Therefore, in the example $k_{i,j,t} = g_{i,j}$.

e, Determination. Subjective determination in quantitative terms of the effectiveness of the editorial climate in each media was the hardest value to obtain. The media director responded best to the question, "If you were sure of reaching an average person in your target market with identical ads in media C and media D, how much, more or less, would you pay for an ad in D as opposed to C because of intermedia differences and editorial climate?" In this manner the effectiveness of each media in terms of editorial climate was judged on a scale from 1 to 10. As the values all fell between 5 and 9, 7 was considered average. e_j values were calculated as ratios of the scale factor to 7. The scale factor and the corresponding e_j is given in Table 1.

Diminishing Returns Curve. For the function $f(y_{i,t})$, the equation $A(1 - e^{-By_{it}})$ was chosen as a reasonably good fit to the media director's judgment. He made subjective estimates of the probability of purchase by an average person in the target market at exposure levels of 1, 2, 3, and 10 ads in an average medium. The values of A and B that gave a reasonable fit were A

= .35 and B = .245.

Decay Constant. α, the fraction of $y_{i,t}$ retained from one month to the next was estimated at .2.

u_j Determination. The maximum number of insertions in each vehicle in each month was limited to one, i.e., $u_j = 1$ for all j by the agency's policy.

Starting y_{it}. Since the service was new, $y_{io} = 0$.

Last Time Period's Effects. The problem of advertising effects after the fourth month was handled by having the model allocate media over four periods but having the effects of the allocations be calculated over 8 periods. This method results in some preference for the latter time periods because of the diminishing returns characteristic of the objective function and because the periods 5-8 do not become as saturated with exposures as do periods 1-4. However, in practice this preference has little effect on the final allocation.

Budget Level Determination. As the budget level desired by the media director could vary from $75,000 to $100,000, a budget top of $105,000 was used in the problem solution. Costs/insertion were given by the media director for one-page black and white insertions which were considered appropriate a priori.

Market Potential. The potential assigned to each person was set to one. Since a person who subscribes to the service remains a subscriber, or at least would remain so over the planning period, our measure of potential ignores the depletion of potential when a sale is made. However, for planning periods of the length considered, this is not a serious approximation.

Table 2 shows the results of the media allocation for the example for three different budget levels and gives the value of the objective function at each level. Sometimes the model changes the content of the allocation fairly drastically between two relatively close budget levels. This is due to the manner in which the various combinations of media costs combine to reach the different levels. It is interesting to observe that this same phenomena was referred to by the media director in a remark that at "certain budget levels instead of just adding new media I have to rethink the whole allocation."

Discussion

The model we have presented has several strong points. It is fairly simple and flexible but still embodies certain key phenomena. Nonlinearity of response is firmly introduced. The problem of spreading media over time is faced, principally by bringing in forgetting but also by letting sales potential depend on time, as it would for a seasonal product. The model is simple enough that considerable computation can be afforded.

On the other hand, the amount of calculation increases rapidly with problem size. It seems likely that an initial screening would have to be performed to reduce the number of alternatives under consideration to some interesting but limited set. The model requires a certain number of subjective estimates of relative value, and this may be regarded as a disadvantage. When better advertising measurements are developed, more complicated models can be justified and better data developed to use in them. At present, subjective evaluation is always introduced at some stage of the process. The use of a model permits specialized judgment to be applied to the parts and assembled along with various objective

Table 2   Solution to the Problem for Three Different Budget Levels
Media Allocation

Time Period	$105,000 Budget 466,067 Projected Sales	$100,800 Budget 457,329 Projected Sales	$75,600 Budget 362,917 Projected Sales
1	New Yorker U.S. News Bus. Week	New Yorker U.S. News Bus. Week Time	New Yorker U.S. News
2	U.S. News Bus. Week Time	New Yorker U.S. News Bus. Week	New Yorker U.S. News Time
3	New Yorker U.S. News Bus. Week	New Yorker U.S. News Bus. Week	New Yorker U.S. News
4	New Yorker U.S. News Bus. Week Time	U.S. News Time	New Yorker U.S. News Bus. Week

JOHN D. C. LITTLE AND LEONARD M. LODISH

data into an organized whole.

One place that computational limitations become serious is in the number of market segments. It would be desirable to define market segments partly by media use. This facilitates the introduction of media overlap considerations. Notice that if media segmentation is carried to an extreme, each individual becomes a market segment and we have a cell simulation of the market. The schedule can then be based on a sample of simulated people. For reasonable sample sizes, the dynamic programming approach would have to be abandoned but heuristic methods could be developed. One interesting possibility is to use heuristic methods to screen a large number of alternatives down to a likely few and then use exact methods to determine the final selection.

References

1 C. L. Wilson, "Use of Linear Programming to Optimize Media Schedules in Advertising," *Proceedings of the 46th National Conference of the American Marketing Association*, Henry Gomez, ed., 1963, pp. 178-191.

2 R. D. Buzzell, Chapter 5 in *Mathematical Models and Marketing Management*, Graduate School of Business Administration, Harvard University, Boston, 1964.

3 R. L. Day, "Linear Programming in Media Selection," *Journal of Adv. Research*, 2, 40-44, June 1962.

4 J. F. Engel and M. R. Warshaw, "Allocating Advertising Dollars by Linear Programming," *Journal of Advertising Research*, 4, 42-48, September 1964.

5 F. M. Bass and R. T. Lonsdale, "An Exploration of Linear Programming for Media Selection," *Journal of Marketing Research*, 3, 179-88, May 1966.

6 M. L. Godfrey, "Media Selection by Mathematical Programming," Talk before the Metropolitan New York Chapter of the Institute of Management Sciences, October 10, 1962.

7 D. B. Brown and M. R. Warshaw, "Media Selection by Linear Programming," *Journal of Marketing Research*, 2, 83-88, Feb. 1965.

8 G. Hadley, *Nonlinear and Dynamic Programming*, Addison-Wesley, Reading, Mass., 1964.

9 W. I. Zangwill, "Media Selection by Decision Programming," *Journal of Advertising Research*, 5, 30-36, Sept. 1965.

10 A. M. Lee and A. J. Burkart, "Some Optimization Problems in Advertising Media Planning," *Operational Research Quarterly*, 11, 1960, p. 113.

11 C. J. Taylor, "Some Developments in the Theory and Application of Media Scheduling Methods," *Operational Research Quarterly*, 14, 291-306, Sept. 1963.

12 A. M. Lee, "Decision Rules for Media Scheduling: Static Campaigns," *Operational Research Quarterly*, 13, 229-242, Sept. 1962.

13 A. M. Lee, "Decision Rules for Media Scheduling: Dynamic Campaigns," *Operational Research Quarterly*, 14, 365-372, Dec. 1963.

14 W. T. Moran, "Practical Media Models— What Must They Look Like," *Proceedings of the 8th Conference of the Advertising Research Foundation*, New York, 1962.

15 A. A. Kuehn, "Models for the Budgeting of Advertising," Chapter 6, in P. Langhoff, ed., *Models, Measurement and Marketing*, Prentice-Hall, Englewood Cliffs, N. J., 1965.

16 P. Kotler, "Toward an Explicit Model for Media Selection," *Journal of Advertising Research*, 4, 34-41, March 1964.

17 A. C. Rohloff, "Quantitative Analysis of the Effectiveness of TV Commercials," *Journal of Marketing Research*, 3, 239-246, August 1966.

John D. C. Little, Ph.D., *Associate Professor of Management, Sloan School of Management, Massachusetts Institute of Technology.* Formerly Associate Professor of Operations Research at Case Institute of Technology. A Fellow of the American Association for the Advancement of Science. Author of various papers in operations research and marketing.

Leonard M. Lodish, A.B., *Doctoral Candidate, Sloan School of Management, Massachusetts Institute of Technology.* Formerly Operations Research Analyst for Mead Corporation. Woodrow Wilson Fellow.

Toward an Explicit Model for Media Selection[1]

Philip Kotler
Northwestern University

A media planner must always rely partly on subjective beliefs unsupported by solid data. Kotler shows how these beliefs can be quantified to produce the "best" decision consistent with them.

ALTHOUGH THE QUALITY of media data has improved considerably over the last 30 years, the procedures used in media selection have not. Media selection is still largely intuitive. Media planners or committees are guided by previous experience, knowledge, and personal preferences. Their plans look plausible, but so would other plans. Beneath the surface lurk several implicit assumptions. Objective debate over the plans' merits is difficult.

Advertising agencies and their clients are showing an increased interest in more explicit models for media selection. An explicit model does not

eliminate subjectivity, but rather exposes the assumptions being made about the relative effectiveness of color, different sizes of advertisements, the editorial climate of the magazine, and so forth. The result is a media plan whose merits can be debated in terms of explicit criteria. Furthermore, the effect on the plan of modifying the assumptions can be readily determined.

In the search for more explicit models of media selection, agencies have turned for inspiration to management science models. Three different models have been developed: linear programing, dynamic programing, and simulation. These models provide interesting starting points for the analysis of the media selection problem, but in no way represent ultimate solutions.

An outline of a still different mathematical approach will be presented here. It starts from the premise that the advertising budget should be initially divided up among the major media and among the months in the year. In this way the

PHILIP KOTLER is an assistant professor of marketing in the Graduate School of Business Administration at Northwestern University, where he teaches courses on mathematical models in marketing. He also has taught at Roosevelt University. He received his Master's degree from the University of Chicago and his Ph.D. in economics and statistics from the Massachusetts Institute of Technology. In 1956, he studied in the behavioral sciences at the University of Chicago, and in 1959-1960 was a Ford fellow in the Institute of Basic Mathematics for Application to Business at Harvard University.

[1] I am indebted for helpful comments to both the research staff at Needham, Louis, and Brorby, Inc., and to the participants in the Ford Research Workshop in Marketing, held at the University of California at Berkeley last summer.

media planner knows what funds he can work with in each month and in each media category. He selects the vehicles in each media category according to *rated exposure value (r.e.v.)*.

In this model the r.e.v. of media does not remain static but rather changes with additional use of the media. This introduces a dynamic element in the media scheduling process. As media choices are made month by month, various indices are updated to reflect achievement in the way of gross r.e.v., frequency, cumulated r.e.v., and r.e.v. per dollar.

There are two steps in constructing a mathematical model for media selection. First, an effectiveness criterion must be defined and measured. Second, a procedure for selecting media using the effectiveness criterion must be designed. These two phases are discussed respectively.

MEASURING EXPOSURE VALUE

The concept of *r.e.v. per dollar* will be used as the effectiveness criterion. But what is meant by the r.e.v. of a particular advertisement placed in a particular media vehicle? It will be shown that r.e.v. will be affected by: 1) audience size and characteristics, 2) intermedia differences, 3) intramedia differences, and 4) advertising unit differences.

Audience Size and Characteristics

The purpose of an advertisement is to increase sales, or at least increase brand preference. To succeed, the advertisement must be both seen and motivating. The task of arranging that the advertisement be seen by the right people is the media problem, and the task of arranging that it be motivating is the copy problem. The copy problem will not be discussed here.

It becomes clear at the outset that trying to estimate in advance the number of viewers who will see and be motivated by an advertisement is not a feasible approach. The number of exposures which "take" in this sense is related to the vehicle's audience size, but the problem is that only an unknown fraction will perceive the advertisement, a smaller (unknown) fraction will pay attention to the message, and a still smaller (unknown) fraction will be impressed positively.

Instead of trying to estimate the fraction of the vehicle's audience who will experience increased brand preference, it would be better to adjust audience size by audience composition data as related to market segmentation goals. A million readers of a magazine equal a million possible exposures, but

the *exposure value* depends on the readers' characteristics and how closely they match those of the consumer target groups. For a baby lotion advertisement, the exposure value might be 1,000,000 if the readers were all women and 0 if the readers were all men. The exposure value depends as much on audience composition as on audience size.

The consumer target groups are defined by the client. As a first step, the client distinguishes between characteristics of potential buyers and nonbuyers and then further examines the potential buyer class to discern those segments where high brand penetration has been achieved. The client decides whether to concentrate on these segments or go after new groups. The measurement of exposure values crucially depends upon the market segmentation strategy defined by the client.

Various characteristics can be used to segment a market. Demographic-economic characteristics are the most popular basis although social and psychological characteristics have also been employed.

The client can define the target groups in two conceptually different ways.

The first consists of defining mutually exclusive target groups. Suppose the target groups are, in order of importance,

1. mothers between 18-34 with large families and low incomes;
2. mothers between 18-34 with large families and average incomes;
3. mothers between 35-49 with large families and average incomes;
4. etc.

The client would supply a numerical rating of the importance of each target group. For example, the first group may be rated 1.0, the second group 0.8, the third group 0.5, etc. Thus the first group serves as a norm. An exposure to a member of the second group has 80 per cent of the value of an exposure in the first group. An exposure in the third group has 50 per cent of the value of an exposure in the first group.

These ratings are based on per capita consumption data and the segmentation strategy of the client. They enable the media planner to convert audience composition data into a meaningful indicator of the vehicle's exposure value.

There are, however, a number of practical difficulties in using mutually exclusive target groups:

1. There is no practical limit on the number of meaningful groups which could be created. In the example, there were four relevant characteristics: motherhood, age, family size, and income. If there are two breakdowns of age, family size, and income, respectively, eight different combinations are possible. The number of groups grows very rapidly as the

number of characteristics and the number of their breakdowns multiply.

2. The market potential of the various target groups is difficult to establish objectively because market data are generally not cross-classified by more than three characteristics.

3. Nor is audience data for a media vehicle generally cross-classified by more than three characteristics.

Instead of identifying mutually exclusive groups, the client can *use single characteristics as the basis*. Suppose the media planner wishes to compare the exposure value of the same advertisement placed in magazines X and Y. Suppose both magazines have 6,000,000 female readers, but that audience composition differs with respect to age, income, and geographical distribution. Table 1 shows the difference in age distribution.

TABLE 1

A COMPARISON OF THE AGE DISTRIBUTION
OF THE AUDIENCE OF TWO MAGAZINES

	Magazine X	Magazine Y
18-34	3,000,000	1,000,000
35-49	2,000,000	3,000,000
50 and over	1,000,000	2,000,000
	6,000,000	6,000,000

The readers of magazine X are younger. Suppose the particular product brand makes a stronger appeal to younger women. Intuitively, magazine X would be the preferred vehicle. But how much more effective is it likely to be? This question would arise especially if advertising rates were higher for magazine X than for Y.

The task is to find scale values to multiply against audience size to reflect how effective each vehicle is in delivering the desired age profile, income profile, etc. A scale value, say for age, can be derived in the following manner. Suppose the age data in Table 2 were available from the A. C. Nielsen Company and the Market Research Corporation of America.

Now the question is, what is the relative importance of an exposure in each age group? An age group is important to a manufacturer to the extent that its members are heavy users of the product and heavy users of his brand. The relative product penetration by age group can be found by comparing columns 1 and 2 in Table 2. For example, the 18-34 age group accounts for 33 per cent of adult women and 35 per cent of product sales. If an average woman buyer is assigned 1.00, then an 18-34 year old woman should be assigned a slightly higher number because she accounts for a slightly higher percentage of product sales. This number can be called the *product penetration ratio* and is

TABLE 2

PRODUCT AND BRAND PREFERENCE
BY AGE OF BUYER

Age	Adult Women in Population %	Product Sales %	Brand Sales %
18-34	33	35	49
35-49	30	40	36
50 and over	37	25	15
Total	100	100	100

derived by dividing the value in column 2 by that in column 1. The resulting ratio is shown in the first column of Table 3.

TABLE 3

PRODUCT AND BRAND PENETRATION RATIOS

Age	Product Penetration Ratio	Brand Penetration Ratio	Average Penetration Ratio
18-34	1.06	1.40	1.23
35-49	1.33	0.90	1.11
50 and over	0.68	0.60	0.64

Next, it should be observed from Table 2 that the brand's sales in the three age groups did not conform to the product sales. The brand seems to have scored exceptional penetration in the youngest age group. This could be the result of natural brand appeal or deliberate segmental strategy. If the client wants to preserve this pattern of differential penetration, the following reasoning applies. The age class 18-34 is important not only because it shows higher than average product penetration, but also because it shows higher than average brand penetration. The *brand penetration ratio* can be derived from Table 2 by dividing the value in column 3 by that in column 2. The resulting ratio is shown in the second column of Table 3.

Both the product penetration ratio and the brand penetration ratio have a bearing on the value of an exposure in the various age groups. Somehow the two ratios must be averaged. A weighted mean could be used if one factor is deemed more important than the other. Otherwise, a simple mean can be employed and this is shown in the third column of Table 3. The average penetration ratio reflects the relative importance of each age group to this manufacturer. Why, for example, are women between 18 and 34 assigned the highest ratio? Because this age group shows more than average susceptibility to the product *and* more than average susceptibilty to this brand. Why does the age group 35-49 show a ratio slightly above the average? Because this group shows very high product susceptibility but below average brand susceptibility. The combined result is somewhat above 1.00. Finally the age group 50 and over shows a low ratio because of both low product susceptibility and low brand susceptibility.

Now that a measure exists of the relative importance of different age groups, it is possible to estimate the respective values of an advertisement placed in magazine X and magazine Y. The procedure is illustrated in Table 4.

TABLE 4

ADJUSTING AUDIENCE SIZE BY
AVERAGE PENETRATION RATIOS

Magazine X

Age	Female Readers	Average Penetration Ratio	Adjusted Number of Readers
18-34	3,000,000	1.23	3,690,000
35-49	2,000,000	1.11	2,220,000
50 and over	1,000,000	0.64	640,000
Total	6,000,000		6,550,000

Age scale value: $\frac{6,550,000}{6,000,000} = 1.09$

Magazine Y

Age	Female Readers	Average Penetration Ratio	Adjusted Number of Readers
18-34	1,000,000	1.23	1,230,000
35-49	3,000,000	1.11	3,330,000
50 and over	2,000,000	0.64	1,280,000
Total	6,000,000		5,840,000

Age scale value: $\frac{5,840,000}{6,000,000} = 0.97$

In Table 4, the number of readers in each age group is multiplied by the average penetration ratio for each age group to derive an adjusted number of readers. The adjusted number of readers is then summed for all age groups for each magazine. The total adjusted audience for a magazine is then taken as a ratio to the original audience and this ratio becomes the age scale value. For magazine X the age scale value is 1.09; for magazine Y it is 0.97. Thus magazine X delivers a more appropriate age distribution of readers than magazine Y for the particular product brand.

Other magazine characteristics can be analyzed in the same way. A scale value can be derived for a vehicle's relative effectiveness with respect to income, regional distribution, etc. Suppose that for magazine X the scale values for age, income, and region were 1.09, 1.05, and 0.94, respectively. These values can be used to develop an adjusted audience

figure for magazine X's 6,000,000 adult female readers. If the three factors are of equal importance, one procedure is to multiply the original audience size by the three scaled values; e.g.,

$$6,000,000 \times 1.09 \times 1.05 \times 0.94 = 6,454,980$$

The product, 6,454,980, is 7.6 per cent above the original audience size figure and can serve as a measure of the exposure value of magazine X — before additional adjustments described below.

The major caution about using scale values for various characteristics is that the characteristics should be fairly independent of each other. To show the danger, suppose the exposure value of a vehicle is scaled up because of a large proportion of high income readers and further scaled up because of a high proportion of older readers. But income and age are positively correlated and too much scaling up results. The problem of adjusting for the usual intercorrelation between characteristics will have to be investigated further.

The method outlined is only one of several conceivable methods of adjusting the audience size of a vehicle by the audience characteristics. In the limit, the media planner could simply assign a direct audience composition factor to the magazine's audience, based on his best judgment. The purpose here has been mainly to stimulate thought of possible approaches rather than to dogmatize on one.

Intermedia Differences

The five major media are magazines, newspapers, television, radio, and outdoor. Their relative effectiveness will vary with the product. Polaroid cameras, for example, are best advertised through live demonstration; hence television is probably the most effective medium. If color is important, as it is with many food products, then magazines are likely to be more effective than radio. While it is not easy to quantify relative media merits with respect to a particular product, it must be conceded that effectiveness will differ.

The media planner will have to find values which reflect intermedia differences in effectiveness. At the present time there are no reliable objective methods for establishing the relative effectiveness of different media. The media planner will supply, as he has done in the past, subjective values derived from his intuitive knowledge of the product and the media. Suppose for this product he assigns the values 1.15, 1.00, 0.85, 0.80, and 0.60 for magazines, television, radio, newspapers, and outdoor, respectively. Recall that magazine X emerged earlier with an adjusted audience figure of 6,454,980. This figure should now be scaled up an additional 15 per cent because magazines are deemed to have the greatest effectiveness for advertising this product.

Likewise, an adjusted audience figure for the advertisement placed in a newspaper might be scaled down by 20 per cent. If the intermedia adjustment was omitted, this would imply that an advertisement has the same effect whether it appears in, say, a magazine or a newspaper. But this would be wrong because the major media have different potentialities for demonstration, visualization, explanation, believability, and color.

Intramedia Differences

Suppose the problem was whether to place an advertisement in *Life* or *Look,* and the adjusted audience figure for each magazine was computed. Suppose these figures were also scaled by the effectiveness of magazines for this product. Should an additional adjustment be made for differences in the editorial image of the two magazines? A recent study by *Life*, under independent auspices, indicated that an advertisement in *Life* carried more impact than an advertisement in *Look*. There are a number of grounds which might warrant the assignment of a subjective value to represent a magazine's unique quality in relation to other magazines in advertising a particular product brand. Some of the grounds are:

1. *Believability:* For example, *Good Housekeeping* has succeeded in lending an aura of believability to the claims of its advertisers.
2. *Prestige:* This emanates from the magazine's slickness and professional quality.
3. *Noting scores:* The readers of certain magazines may be more ad-conscious. Magazines such as *Vogue* and *Glamour* are purchased for their advertisements as much as for their editorial content.

Whatever the source, if it is felt that the editorial image of the magazine makes a difference, the agency is obliged to assign a scale value. Some media vehicles may be assigned 1.00, while others which seem better or worse in editorial image may be assigned a relative number. Investigators are continually searching for more objective ways to derive these values. But the adjustment should be made, or otherwise the implicit assumption is that women are not influenced by which particular magazine carries the advertisement.

Advertising Unit Differences

A decision must be made concerning not only which media vehicles to use, but also what advertising units to buy. Different page sizes are available and so are different time lengths, different colors, etc. Each advertising unit will differ in cost and effectiveness.

Suppose the brand is to be advertised in a magazine. The media planner compares the effectiveness and cost of different advertising units. If a particular unit, say a full-page black-and-white advertisement, is used consistently in all magazines, there is no problem. But if the planner also uses other units, there will be a difference in effectiveness, making it necessary to consider some advertising unit as the norm, and rate the others accordingly.

Summary of r.e.v.

Rated exposure value (r.e.v.) is a quantitative measure designed to express the anticipated impact of a particular advertising unit placed in a particular vehicle of a particular medium. The starting point is the vehicle's audience size. This audience size is then adjusted by scale values reflecting: 1) audience characteristics in relation to segmental strategy, 2) intermedia differences, 3) intramedia differences, and 4) advertising unit differences.

The result is an adjusted audience size figure which is called r.e.v. This quantitative measure then serves as a guide for selecting media, the objective being to develop a schedule which maximizes the total r.e.v. for the given budget.

Much work remains to be done in refining the measurement of r.e.v., especially for media other than magazines. This section attempted to suggest some approaches.

A Model for Media Selection

Having decided on a procedure for obtaining rated exposure values, the next step is to develop decision rules for actual media scheduling. The basic strategy will be to develop a separate schedule for each media category and then to compare the separate schedules for further adjustment. In order to develop a schedule for a media category, it will be necessary to decide in advance how much of the budget is to be spent on each medium.

There are several bases on which to make an initial intermedia allocation. The nature of the brand and segmental strategy provide some guidelines. The history of media usage also provides some definite impressions as to the relative effectiveness of the different media. Finally, the client often expresses strong media preferences which delimit the agency's range of choice.

Suppose the advertising budget is $1,200,000 and the agency decides to confine advertising to two major media, television and magazines. Furthermore, judging the intermedia effectiveness, the agency allocates 80 per cent of the budget to television and 20 per cent, or $240,000, to magazines.

The next task is to develop a schedule for each medium separately. This step will be illustrated with monthly magazines for ease of exposition.

If the $240,000 were to be spent equally each month, the monthly magazine budget would be $20,000. But there are many reasons why a constant expenditure rate would be undesirable. Each product tends to have its own seasonal demand pattern. It is held by many that proportionately more money should be spent during or just preceding the months of high demand. An opposite view calls for contraseasonal advertising. Still another view favors "burst" advertising, which may not be timed according to the seasonal demand pattern. Production and distribution factors also should be considered in phasing advertising expenditures. The point here is that various factors will warrant the establishment of dissimilar monthly budgets. For the purpose of illustration, suppose the client and the agency agree to spend $20,000 in January, $10,000 in February, $20,000 in March, and $30,000 in April.

The next step calls for determining which magazines would be most effective in advertising this product. Most magazines can be dismissed from consideration on intuitive grounds or on a rough calculation of r.e.v. per dollar. Suppose four magazines remain in the running and the advertising unit has already been chosen. Suppose also that the r.e.v.'s for a first insertion of this advertisement in magazines V, W, X, and Y are 7,000,000, 8,000,000, 7,500,000, and 6,000,000, respectively. Will these r.e.v.'s remain constant regardless of how often the magazines are used? This is the very questionable assumption of linear programing. When an advertisement first appears in, say, magazine V, it attains an r.e.v. of 7,000,000. When it appears a second time, its impact is likely to be different. The advertisement on the second round is seen by some people for the first time and by others for the second time.

Some advertising men hold that additional exposure is a virtue, indeed that an advertisement seen only once is wasted. Under this theory, r.e.v. on the second round may exceed r.e.v. on the first round. But even the strongest advocate of repeated

exposure will admit that diminishing marginal returns, and possibly negative returns, will eventually set in as the frequency of exposure is increased within a given time period.

Others argue that a good advertisement need be seen but once, and therefore reach is all important. The r.e.v. attained with a second insertion is treated as less than that attained with the first.

This is not the place to examine the merits of frequency versus reach in guiding media selection. Fortunately, for any particular product, the client and agency will generally come to some accord as to when and at what rate diminishing returns will set in with the repeated use of the same media vehicle. Here the objective is to describe how this accord can be expressed mathematically.

Figure 1 shows three different general conceptions of how r.e.v. behaves with issue replication. Figure 1a shows r.e.v. falling continuously as n, the number of issues, increases; but the rate of decline itself decreases and thus r.e.v. may never reach zero. Figure 1b shows r.e.v. first rising and later falling, but at a diminishing rate. Figure 1c shows a constant r.e.v. for the first few insertions and then a decline at a diminishing rate.

Other conceptions are possible but these are the most common. The conception shown in Figure 1a can be represented by an exponential equation of the type

$$r.e.v. = ab^{n-1}$$

where

r.e.v. = rated exposure value with the nth insertion
a = rated exposure value with the first insertion
b = that fraction of the rated exposure value which is preserved from one insertion to the next
n = the number of the particular insertion being considered.

Suppose 90 per cent of the r.e.v. of magazine V is preserved between successive insertions. Then the equation for magazine V would read:

$$r.e.v. = 7,000,000 (.9)^{n-1}$$

Accordingly, the first four insertions in magazine V would achieve an r.e.v. of 7,000,000, 6,300,000, 5,670,000, and 5,103,000, respectively.

Suppose the agency assumes that r.e.v. for the other magazines also decays at the rate of 10 per cent per insertion. (A variable decay rate could, of course, be used.) Table 5 shows the r.e.v. for the first four insertions in all four magazines.

All these figures are based on the conception of the r.e.v. function shown in Figure 1a. The conception in Figure 1b could have been used, although this requires a more complicated mathe-

FIGURE 1
EFFECT OF INSERTIONS ON R.E.V.

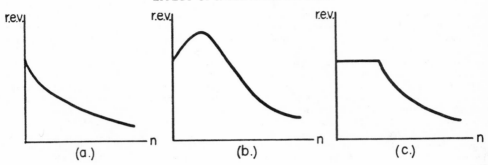

(a.)   (b.)   (c.)

TABLE 5
R.E.V. FOR THE FIRST FOUR
INSERTIONS IN FOUR MAGAZINES

Magazine	Insertion			
	1	2	3	4
V	7,000,000	6,300,000	5,670,000	5,103,000
W	8,000,000	7,200,000	6,480,000	5,832,000
X	7,500,000	6,750,000	6,075,000	5,467,500
Y	6,000,000	5,400,000	4,860,000	4,374,000

matical equation. The conception in Figure 1c requires a discontinuous equation. The major problem is not that of finding an equation to express a particular curve, but of settling on a plausible curve in the first place. Additional complications arise because of lagged effects in advertising impact and because the particular dating of the n insertions may make a difference in impact.

The next realization is that cost also varies with the number of insertions. Quantity discounts are common in the media field. Table 6 presents the hypothetical behavior of cost for the first four insertions in the four magazines.

TABLE 6
INCREMENTAL COST FOR THE FIRST
FOUR INSERTIONS IN FOUR MAGAZINES

Magazine	Insertion			
	1	2	3	4
V	$ 9,500	$ 9,000	$ 8,000	$8,000
W	$10,000	$10,000	$10,000	$7,000
X	$ 9,000	$ 9,000	$ 9,000	$9,000
Y	$10,000	$ 9,000	$ 8,000	$7,000

Now it is possible to derive *rated exposure value per dollar (r.e.v./$)* and it will be seen that this function changes with increased usage of particular

media. The measure is found by dividing the values in Table 5 by the corresponding values in Table 6. The results are shown in Table 7.

R.e.v./$ will serve as the effectiveness criterion for developing the media schedule. How should the $20,000 budget for January be spent? This budget will allow the purchase of only two magazines. Which two? According to Table 7, a first insertion in magazine X delivers the highest r.e.v./$, namely 833. Second-place magazine W delivers 800 r.e.v./$. The two magazines together cost $19,000 ($9,000 and $10,000 respectively) which virtually exhausts the January magazine budget. Thus the media schedule for January will consist of an advertisement placed in both magazines X and W.

TABLE 7
R.E.V. PER DOLLAR FOR THE FIRST
FOUR INSERTIONS IN FOUR MAGAZINES

Magazine	1	2	3	4
V	737	700	709	638
W	800	720	648	833
X	833	750	675	607
Y	600	600	608	625

Which magazine should be purchased with February's budget of $10,000? It is possible to make a first purchase of V or Y or a second purchase of W or X. According to Table 7, a second issue of X will offer the maximum r.e.v./$, 750, and hence an advertisement should be placed in X for $9,000.

The budget for March is $20,000 and this permits the purchase of approximately two magazines. According to Table 7, the purchase should consist of a first issue of V (r.e.v./$ = 737) and a second issue of W (r.e.v./$ = 720) at a cost of $19,500.

The $30,000 budget for April permits using approximately three magazines. According to Table 7, the purchase should consist of a second issue of V (r.e.v./$ = 700) and a third issue of X (r.e.v./$ = 675) and W (r.e.v./$ = 648) at a combined cost of $28,000. Notice that V had the highest r.e.v./$ for two successive insertions, but it cannot be used twice in the same month.

The magazine selections for the first four months, along with some indicators of achievement, are presented in Table 8.

TABLE 8

SUMMARY OF MAGAZINE SELECTIONS
FOR THE FIRST FOUR MONTHS

Budget	$20,000	$10,000	$20,000	$30,000
Month	January	February	March	April
Magazine				
V			x	x
W	x		x	x
X	x	x		x
Y				x
1. Gross r.e.v.	15,500,000	6,750,000	14,200,000	18,855,000
2. Cost	$19,000	$9,000	$19,500	$28,000
3. R.e.v./$	816	750	728	673
4. Net r.e.v.	10,850,000	—	—	—
5. Frequency	1.43	—	—	—

The first indicator is *gross r.e.v.* which is the sum of the separate r.e.v.'s in the column. It is gross because intermagazine audience duplication has not been considered.

The second is the *total cost* of placing these advertisements in the particular magazines. Notice that the actual outlay each month approximates the budgeted outlay. Yet somewhat less was spent each month and by April, the total underspending had mounted to $4,500. This can be corrected in a subsequent month by spending more than that month's budget.

The third indicator, *r.e.v./$*, is obtained by dividing gross r.e.v. by cost. This figure will tend to decrease over the year, except for occasional reversals. The decrease in r.e.v./$ reflects the fact that the impact of sustained advertising, especially with a similar message, tends to diminish over time.

The fourth indicator, *net r.e.v.*, is designed to reflect *reach* during that month. For example, magazines W and X were scheduled in January. Suppose 30 per cent of the gross audience saw both magazines. Then the reach of the two magazines did not amount to 15,500,000 but rather 10,850,000 (15,500,000 × .7). Better methods are gradually being developed to handle audience duplication.

Frequency, the fifth indicator, is found by dividing the gross r.e.v. by the net r.e.v. This provides some idea of how many times the average viewer is exposed to the advertisement.

By no means do these indicators exhaust the possibilities. For example, it would be desirable to design a method of measuring the cumulated net r.e.v./$, which would take into account both duplication and replication. This and other indicators of monthly and cumulative achievement should be considered.

EPILOGUE

The last section described the procedure for selecting vehicles in a particular medium. This procedure can be applied to media other than magazines, although new problems arise. With radio and television spots, both the number of relevant media vehicles and the number of time periods (days or hours instead of months) increase considerably. Instead of a 4 by 12 matrix (4 magazines and 12 months), the media planner, or computer, may have to work with, say, a 100 by 365 scheduling matrix. Indeed it may turn out that this is not feasible and a conceptual approach different from that outlined for magazines may be needed.

If this method is used to select vehicles from two or more media, say magazines and television, then another stage of analysis is warranted. A comparison should be made of r.e.v./$ achieved with magazines versus television. If the r.e.v./$ indicator is much higher with magazines, this implies that too much of the budget was allocated to television. The budget should be reapportioned and the media planner should develop new schedules for magazines and television.

When an equilibrium has been achieved (i.e., when both magazines and television deliver a similar r.e.v./$) the two schedules should be integrated and overall indicators be prepared. That is, the five indicators at the bottom of Table 8 can now be prepared for the combined intermedia schedule as a way of evaluating total achievement.

This is still rough and not very practical. It is necessary to examine how the computer, or specially prepared tables, could be used to reduce the required work. At the same time, the model is a more realistic one than linear programing. It is in closer harmony with the intuitive ideas and procedures of media planners. It leads to a media schedule in a series of explicit steps. And consequently the final media schedule can be evaluated in terms of explicit data and assumptions, which is the aim of a model.

DOUGLAS B. BROWN*

The principle of incremental analysis as applied to media selection problems is examined by illustrating some magazine-selection problems. Although these examples are simple, the method can be extended to handle more complex problems. Incremental analysis can be applied to both print and broadcast media campaigns, but it is most suitable for scheduling print advertising.

A Practical Procedure for Media Selection

There is a growing literature dealing with mathematical methods for media selection, but so far the emphasis has been mainly on mathematical programming, in particular, linear programming and its extensions.[1] This article describes what may appear to be a fresh approach to media selection although the method has previously been applied to a number of similar problems. This method, namely incremental analysis (IA), is not faultless, but it does enable one to study media-selection models without some difficulties usually associated with mathematical programming models. In particular, using an IA approach, it is possible to explicitly account for audience duplication among media.

IA is often discussed in managerial economics textbooks, but it is not usually presented in such a way that its value for media selection is evident. Unfortunately, when it is used for media selection, a great deal of arithmetic must be performed, and extensive bookkeeping is required. However, the logic of the method is simple, and the selection procedure requires numerous repetitions of the same basic computations. IA media selection routines are, therefore, particularly suited to a properly programmed digital computer.

Although IA can be used to advantage in the selection of other types of media, for clarity our attention is on magazines. It is helpful to first define some terms concerning magazine selection. A *magazine schedule* states how many times each magazine from a specified list is to contain advertisements in the planning period. Each time a magazine is to contain an advertisement, the magazine is said to be *included in the schedule*.

When a magazine is included in the schedule, the schedule also specifies the color characteristics and the size of the advertisement. The term *advertising alternative* describes a magazine that, together with the specification of an advertisement, is under consideration for inclusion in a schedule. For example, an advertising alternative might be the insertion of a full-page, black and white ad in an issue of *Life*. An advertising alternative is said to be used each time it is included in the schedule. The scheduled insertion of nine, full-page advertisements in *Time* means that the advertising alternative of a full-page advertisement in *Time* is to be used nine times.

THE SCHEDULING PROBLEM

The determination of a list from which to select the magazines for a schedule is the media planner's art. Magazines to be included are selected partly on the basis of how well their audiences "match" the demographic description of the target audience relative to the cost of an advertisement, and partly on the basis of nonquantified but nevertheless keen intuition.[2] Of course, the total number of magazines published is so large that only a small proportion of the total can be practically considered; and after the planners have compiled a list of the ones that in their judgment might be included in the schedule, the additional benefits to be gained from investigating more alternatives are not likely to be worth the expense.

When IA is used for media selection, computer capacity limitations, operating costs, and other elements in the computing system place an upper bound on the

* Douglas B. Brown is a consultant with Arthur D. Little, Inc. The advice and criticism from W. Allen Spivey and Martin R. Warshaw, University of Michigan; Alva Schoomer, the American Stock Exchange; and Gwyn Collins, Arthur D. Little, Inc. are gratefully acknowledged.

[1] A brief bibliography of this literature is found in the References.

[2] A common index of matching is the cost of a full-page advertisement divided by the number of target-audience members the ad would reach.

Journal of Marketing Research,
Vol. IV (August 1967), 262-9

number of magazines that can be jointly studied, and it is necessary to select magazines for use in the schedule from a modest number of candidates, probably no more than 50 to 75. Thus, before using the selection algorithm, it may be necessary to eliminate some magazines from those that appear to be appropriate for the advertising message. Nevertheless, the methods to be described make it possible to study a much larger set of alternative schedules than with traditional methods.

Constraints

For any media-selection problem, there are constraints that when taken together define a large collection of feasible schedules. First, there is a budget constraint limiting the amount of money to be spent. Second, there are institutional constraints that limit the number of times it is possible to advertise using a particular advertising alternative during any campaign. For example, a full-page, four-color ad in *Fortune* may be used no more than 12 nor fewer than zero times in any one calendar year, and it must be used an integral number of times. There may also be additional budget constraints limiting the amount of money to be spent in advertising to various demographic groups or to people living in certain geographic areas, and it is possible to impose subjective constraints on the number of times various advertising alternatives may be used in combination in the same campaign. However, for the purposes of this article, we assume there are only institutional constraints and a single budget constraint. These constraints are mathematically described as follows:

(1) $\quad C_1 N_1 -- C_2 N_2 + \cdots + C_t N_t \leq M$

(Budget constraint)

$0 \leq N_1 \leq n_1$

$0 \leq N_2 \leq n_2$

$\qquad \vdots \qquad\qquad$ (Institutional constraints)

$0 \leq N_t \leq n_t,$

where:

C_i is cost of using the ith advertising alternative.

N_i is number of times the ith advertising alternative is to be used in the campaign period. The N_i's must be non-negative integers.

M is amount of advertising budget.

n_i is number of times it is possible to use the ith advertising alternative. The n_i's must be positive integers.

t is the number of advertising alternatives.

An Optimum Schedule

Any method of media selection is concerned with deriving an optimum or near optimum schedule. Intuitively, an "optimum" schedule is a feasible schedule that is as good or better than any other in terms of some

criterion, but it is useful to make this intuitive notion more explicit. Suppose we have a rule that assigns a numerical value to each feasible schedule and that this assignment is made on the basis of some criterion of schedule effectiveness. This rule is called an *objective function* provided that:

1. it assigns the same number to schedules that are equally effective in terms of the effectiveness criterion,
2. it assigns the higher number to the better schedule when one schedule is better than another in terms of this criterion.

The term *optimum schedule* refers to a feasible schedule that maximizes the numerical value of some objective function.

THE FIRST MODEL

First, we present a special case of a more general objective function to illustrate the principle of incremental analysis as simply as possible and to show that the most obvious generalization of this simple objective function is unsatisfactory. In developing this special case strong assumptions are required, but these assumptions are later relaxed and a more general objective function presented.

For every schedule. an IA objective function assigns a weighted score to each respondent in a representative sample of the target audience. The value of a respondent's score depends on which magazines he claims to have "read" in the past and on how many issues of these magazines are scheduled to carry ads. Unfortunately, the audience data needed to calculate these weighted scores are available on a continuing basis for users of only a few products.[3]

Suppose the advertiser or its agency employed a market research firm to interview 1,000 people in a probability sample of the target audience, and that the probability of including a target-audience member in the sample varied according to whether he was a light, medium, or heavy user of the product being advertised. Assume that each respondent's replies to an appropriate sequence of questions have made it possible to determine how many of the last six issues of each of 55 magazines he had read. Finally, assume that an IBM card has been prepared for each respondent, and that the number he claimed to have read of the last six issues was punched in a separate column for each magazine.

A respondent's weight for magazine i is an index of the value of his readership of this magazine when the particular ad chosen is inserted in one issue. Each respondent is assigned weights for the magazines whose issues are available for selection, expressed in some standard unit so that different respondents can be compared in a meaningful way. For the moment we defer a discussion of how these weights might be determined

---

[3] Data on the media that reach consumers of certain products can be purchased from Brand Rating Research Corporation.

and assume that each magazine a respondent "reads" is assigned the same weight, which for convenience is taken to be 1. Magazines he does not read are assigned (for him) the weight of zero. A respondent is classified as a "reader" of each magazine for which he claimed to have read four or more of the last six issues.

Let magazine i be the first magazine selected that is "read" by a given sample respondent. The respondent's weight for magazine i is the value that the selection of the first issue of this magazine contributes to his weighted score. Assume that the selection of a second magazine-issue read by a respondent makes a contribution to his weighted score which is .90 times his weight for the magazine selected.[4] Similarly, the value assigned to the selection of the third magazine-issue read by a respondent is discounted by the factor .80. This discounting of advertising exposure opportunities is based on the theory that the value of exposing a person to an additional advertisement declines as his previous exposures to the advertisement increases. Agreement is fairly general on this point, although some believe that there is an initial stage of increasing returns.[5]

A weighted score can be calculated for any schedule by summing the sample respondents' weighted-scores for that schedule. Their scores should be assigned so that it is reasonable to say that a "good" schedule is one whose weighted score is near to the score of a best schedule, and a best schedule is one whose weighted score is not exceeded by the score of any other schedule.

Calculation of a Respondent's Weighted Score

Subject to certain constraints, incremental analysis uses a heuristic selection rule to derive a "good" or a "best" schedule by selecting magazine issues one at a time until the budget is exhausted. Given the magazine issues previously selected, each selection is made so that its incremental contribution per dollar to the schedule's weighted score is at least as large as the contribution per dollar of any other available selection.

Assume that Smith, one of the sample respondents, has been classified as a reader of *Life*, *Time*, and *Newsweek*, but not *Playboy*. Suppose that the magazine schedule of one insertion each in *Life* and *Playboy* and two insertions in *Time* has been selected and that these magazine-issues were selected in the order *Life*, *Time*, *Playboy*, *Time*. The weighted score for Smith, plus the weighted scores for all other respondents, is the weighted score for this schedule.

Let the letters *WT* stand for weight and the symbols

---

[4] *Magazine-issue* refers to one issue of any magazine, while *magazine* refers to the name of a continuing series of magazine-issues such as *Life* or *Time*. For ease in exposition, we frequently refer to the selection of magazine-issues rather than to the selection of units of advertising alternatives. To make such references unambiguous, only one ad is assumed under consideration for insertion in each magazine.

[5] Empirical evidence indicates that the schedule is relatively insensitive to the choice of a sequence of discount factors provided diminishing returns are assumed.

DF_1, DF_2 and DF_3 stand for the respective discount factors for a respondent's weights for the magazines he "reads" whose issues are selected first, second, and third. Then the weighted score for Smith is calculated as:

$$(Life\ WT \times DF_1) + (Time\ WT \times DF_2) \\ + (Time\ WT \times DF_3) \\ = (1 \times 1) + (1 \times .9) + (1 \times .8) = 2.7.$$

Observe that the weighted score for Smith does not depend on the order in which the magazine-issues were selected.

Statement of Objective Function

Let DF_p be a discount factor that expresses the value of a target-audience member's readership of a pth issue containing an advertisement relative to his weight for the magazine carrying this ad. Diminishing returns are assumed so that $DF_1 > DF_2$, $DF_2 > DF_3$, and in general $DF_n > DF_{n+1}$. It is also helpful to define $DF_0 = 0$, where DF_0 is interpreted as the value of getting no issues containing the firm's ads to a target-audience member.

Second, let $r(k)$ be the number of magazine-issues included in a schedule for which the kth sample respondent has been classified as a reader. For example, suppose that respondent k^* is classified as a reader of *Life*, *Time*, and *Post*, and that he is not classified as a reader of any other magazines. Then $r(k^*) = 5$ for the schedule consisting of two issues of *Time*, three of *Life*, and two of *Newsweek*. Third, let a respondent's weight for a magazine be 1 or zero, depending on whether he is classified as a reader or a nonreader. Finally, recall that the sample size is assumed to be 1,000. The objective is to find a schedule which maximizes the function,

$$(2) \quad \begin{aligned} \sum_{k=1}^{1000} \sum_{p=0}^{r(k)} (1 \times DF_p) = \\ (DF_0 + DF_1 \cdots + DF_{r(1)}) + \\ (DF_0 + DF_1 + \cdots + DF_{r(2)}) + \\ \cdots + (DF_0 + DF_1 + \cdots DF_{r(1000)}) \end{aligned}$$

subject to constraints (1).

THE INCREMENTAL-ANALYSIS SELECTION ALGORITHM

The principle of incremental analysis is simple: using an appropriate selection rule, magazine issues are selected one at a time until the budget is gone. To specify a selection rule, it is convenient to define the marginal cost efficiency of the ith magazine (MCE_i):

$$MCE_i = \frac{\text{Amount by which the selection of an additional issue of magazine } i \text{ would increase the schedule's weighted score}}{\text{Cost per insertion in magazine } i}$$

When making the first selection, MCE, is equal to the number of sample respondents who read magazine i, divided by the cost per insertion. One issue of the magazine having the highest MCE is selected. However, to make the next selection, the MCE of each available magazine must be recalculated. Suppose, for example, that the first selection was an issue of *Life*. Assume that Smith reads *Life* and *Time* but not *Newsweek*, and that Doe reads *Newsweek* and *Time* but not *Life*. Also, as-

issue of the magazine with the highest MCE is selected. and the MCE's are recalculated. Should two or more magazines share the same maximum MCE value, a number of tie-breaking rules can be used; these include: selection of an issue of the magazine that costs the most or the least, or selection of an issue of the first magazine on the list of those tied.

The following flow chart explains the selection procedure and gives the basis for writing a computer program:

SCHEMATIC DESCRIPTION OF INCREMENTAL ANALYSIS SELECTION ALGORITHM

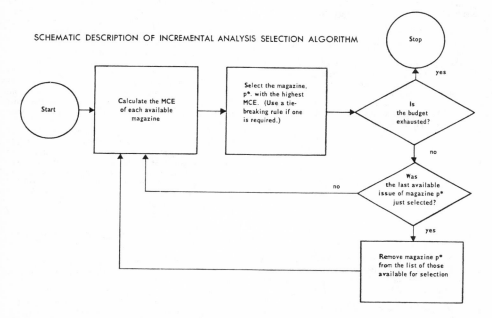

sume that $DF_2 = .90$. In calculating the MCE for *Time*, Smith's contribution to the schedule's weighted score is $1 \times DF_2 = 1 \times .9$, while Doe's contribution is $1 \times DF_1 = 1 \times 1$. Note that the contribution of Doe exceeds that of Smith because one magazine-issue that reaches Smith has already been selected. In computing the MCE for *Newsweek*, Smith makes no contribution to the schedule's weighted score, since he does not read this magazine, while Doe's contribution is $1 \times DF_1 = 1$.

In general, the MCE's must be recalculated after each selection of a magazine issue. However, a constraint limits the number of issues of a magazine that can be selected. After all available issues have been chosen, it is no longer necessary to calculate a magazine's MCE to make subsequent selections. After calculating the MCE's for all available magazines, one

Procedures for the First Model

It is interesting to note how little bookkeeping is required for the incremental analysis described. When marginal cost efficiencies are calculated, the only current information concerning a respondent that has to be stored to determine the amount by which the selection of a given magazine would contribute to his weighted score is the number of magazine-issues he reads that have so far been selected.

In practice the IBM cards for all respondents are stored as card images on magnetic tape. Each tape record contains the audience data for one respondent and the number of previously selected magazine-issues for which he is a reader. The incremental contributions of all possible next selections to the schedule's weighted score are accumulated respondent by respondent in a single pass through the data tape. Before each respondent's incremental contribution to the schedule's weighted score is determined for each possible next selection, the number of magazine-issues he reads which have thus far been selected is increased by 1 if he is a reader of the magazine selected on the previous pass through the tape. If after this updating, r magazine-issues read by a given respondent have previously been selected, the selection of a magazine he reads would contribute DF_{r+1} to the schedule's weighted score, and the selection of one he does not read would contribute nothing.

Kind of Output Information

At a minimum, the computer output should specify the magazine-issues selected, their MCE's when selected, and their order of selection. It is also helpful to present a frequency distribution of "readership" for each schedule. For example, consider a four-week campaign for which the issues of 35 popular magazines were available for selection. With the advertising budget at $100,000, the frequency distribution for one such campaign was the following:

Number of issues read (X)	Percent of respondents reading X issues of magazines
1	12.2
2	7.2
3	3.8
4	12.0
5	9.2
6	4.6
7	4.4
8	4.6
9	3.6
10 or more	7.8

The reach and frequency of a schedule can be readily estimated from the proportion of the respondents who read one or more magazine-issues and the average number of issues read by each respondent.

IA as a Heuristic-Selection Algorithm

The media selection problem is to select an optimum schedule from a large but finite set of alternative schedules. Since it is usually impractical to examine every alternative schedule, an efficient, iterative, search procedure is needed that will start with a very simple schedule and find better and better schedules in a stepwise sequence before terminating at an optimum schedule in a feasible number of steps. The incremental analysis method derives an improved schedule with each iteration, it terminates in a small number of steps, and its logic appeals to one's intuition.

Unfortunately, one cannot assert that the algorithm will always terminate at an optimum schedule except under very restrictive conditions. Nevertheless, the method should always select a good schedule—one whose weighted score is near or equal to the score of an

optimum schedule. For a small number of advertising alternatives, an IA schedule has been shown to be optimum by finding the weighted score for each feasible schedule. In applying IA to problems of a size likely to be encountered in practice, the researcher will have to judge for himself whether the method always reaches a good schedule.

The Budget Constraint

One desirable feature of incremental analysis may appear to cause difficulties. The IA selection procedure continues until the selection of some magazine-issue exhausts the budget. Depending on whether the last selection is included, there are two possible schedules —one for an advertising expenditure that is below budget and one for an expenditure that exceeds it; the best schedule for the budgeted expenditure often is not derived. However, the stated budget is not of necessity a constant; at best it is a rough estimate of the most profitable expenditure. Most firms can vary advertising spending by plus or minus five percent, and the most profitable budget cannot, in fact, be determined with greater precision than this.

Incremental analysis really completes the job of determining the best advertising expenditure. Because each advertising alternative can only be used an integral number of times, it is highly unlikely that the stated budget will be desirable from a scheduling point of view. Incremental analysis merely adjusts the budget so that good integer-valued schedules can be obtained. The basic budget level still has to be determined independent of the selection procedure.

THE ASSIGNMENT OF A RESPONDENT'S MAGAZINE WEIGHTS

In the model presented each respondent was assigned a weight for each magazine. These weights might be determined as:

(The probability of a respondent's reading the given magazine) $\times$ (The probability that he is exposed to the advertisement under consideration given that he reads an issue of the given magazine containing it) $\times$ (The effectiveness relative to one of an advertising exposure delivered by this magazine).

The probability of a respondent's reading a given magazine is estimated to be the proportion of the last six issues he claimed to have read. For example, if he claims to have read four of the last six issues of *Playboy*, his probability of reading *Playboy* is taken to be 4/6.

The probability that he is exposed to the advertisement, given that he reads an issue containing it, is estimated from his responses to questions about his thoroughness of reading and ad noting and from the size and color characteristics of the ad. An estimate of the relative effectiveness of an exposure in one magazine as compared with another is a measurement of the amount of interaction between an advertisement and a magazine. There is little empirical evidence about such interactions, and if interactions are assumed to exist, the relative effectiveness of the various advertising alternatives must be determined entirely by subjective means.

Recall that each respondent's magazine weights were assumed to be the same for magazines he reads. Such an assignment of weights appears reasonable when the following conditions hold:

1. Each respondent in the sample can be meaningfully classified as a reader or nonreader for each magazine,
2. The advertisements under consideration have the same size and color characteristics,
3. P_i, the probability that a target-audience reader of magazine i is exposed to an advertisement inserted in one issue, is the same for each magazine,
4. The exposure of a target-audience reader to advertising is thought to have the same effectiveness regardless of which magazine carries the ad.

When these conditions are not satisfied, it is probably unreasonable to assume that a respondent's magazine weights can only assume the values 1 and zero.

A Natural Extension of the Model

In order that we can examine some implications of weighting schemes, other than the one described, assume that Smith has weights for *Life* and *Time* and *Playboy* of 1.4, 1.0, and .0, respectively. The weighted score for Smith can be calculated in the same way it was for the original model if it is again assumed that the magazine-issues were selected in the order *Life, Time, Playboy, Time:*

$$(Life\ WT \times DF_1) + (Time\ WT \times DF_2)$$
$$+ (Time\ WT \times DF_3)$$
$$= (1.4 \times 1) + (1.0 \times .9) + (1.0 \times .8) = 3.10.$$

However, the weighted score for Smith now depends on the order in which the magazine-issues were selected. Consider the calculation of the weighted score for Smith when the order of selection is *Playboy, Time, Time, Life:*

$$(Time\ WT \times DF_1) + (Time\ WT \times DF_2)$$
$$+ (Life\ WT \times DF_3)$$
$$= (1.0 \times 1) + (1.0 \times .9) + (1.4 \times .8) = 3.02.$$

When Conditions 1, 2, 3, and 4 are not satisfied and unequal magazine weights are assigned one or more respondents, the method will not assign a unique value to each schedule. When more than one value can be assigned to the same schedule, no unique rank ordering of the feasible schedules is likely to exist. Thus, the most natural extension of incremental analysis to cases where unequal magazine weights are assigned is unsatisfactory.

SCHEDULE VALUATION USING A REVISED OBJECTIVE FUNCTION

The problem of a schedule's value varying with the order of magazine-issue selection can be solved if a sum of weights is discounted rather than the weights themselves. Using a revised objective function, the weighted score for Smith is calculated as:

(*DF* for three magazine-issues)

$$\times (Life\ WT + Time\ WT + Time\ WT).$$

Smith's score does not depend on the order in which the magazine-issues are selected, since the magazine weights can be added in any order. Suppose that the revised model's discount factors for one, two, and three magazine-issues are 1, .95, and .90, respectively. Then Smith's weighted score is $(.90) \times (1.4 + 1.0 + 1.0)$ or 3.06. Previously selected magazines for which Smith has zero weight are not counted in determining which discount factor to use.[6]

A Selection Procedure for the Revised Model

The selection procedure for the revised model is identical to the one described for the original model, but calculation of marginal cost efficiencies is more complicated, and more information concerning each respondent must be stored. To illustrate, it is helpful to calculate the amount by which the selection of an additional issue of *Time* would increase Smith's weighted score.

Recall that two issues of *Time*, one of *Life* and one of *Playboy* have so far been selected and that Smith's weights for *Life, Time* and *Playboy* are 1.4, 1.0, and .0, respectively. Also, assume that the discount factor for four magazine-issues is $(1 + .9 + .8 + .7)/4 = .85$. Smith's current score is given by (*DF* for three magazine-issues) $\times (Life\ WT + Time\ WT + Time\ WT) = (.90) \times (1.4 + 1 + 1) = 3.06$.

After an additional issue of *Time* has been selected, Smith's weighted score is given by (*DF* for four magazine-issues) $\times [(Life\ WT + Time\ WT + Time\ WT) + (Time\ WT)] = (.85) \times [(1.4 + 1 + 1) + (1)] = 3.74$. The incremental addition to Smith's weighted score is $(3.74 - 3.06)$ or .68. The amount by which the selection of another issue of *Time* would increase the weighted score for the schedule is calculated by adding the incremental additions to all respondents' scores.

It is necessary to store the following information about each respondent on the data tape:

1. his magazine weight for each of the magazines that can be included in the schedule. (Where more than one ad is under consideration for insertion in each magazine,

---

[6] The weighting scheme used in the objective function of the first model is a special case of the one just described. When Smith's magazine weights are all 1, his weighted score is calculated to be 2.7, using both the original and the revised objective functions.

it is necessary to store his weight for each advertising alternative.)
2. the sum of his weights for the magazines so far selected.
3. the number of magazines so far selected for which he has a non-zero magazine weight.

Weakness of the Revised Model

Unfortunately, when a respondent's magazine weights vary substantially from magazine to magazine, the selection of an additional magazine-issue can reduce his weighted score. For example, assume that Smith's weights for *Life* and *Time* are 2.0 and .1, respectively. Also assume that the discount factors for one, two, and three magazine-issues are 1.0, .95, and .90, respectively, and that one issue each of *Life* and *Time* have so far been selected. Smith's weighted score is then given by:

(*DF* for two magazine-issues)

$$\times (Life\ WT + Time\ WT)$$
$$= (.95) \times (2.0 + .1) = 1.995.$$

Suppose that another issue of *Time* is now selected. Smith's weighted score then becomes:

(*DF* for three magazine-issues)

$$\times (Life\ WT + Time\ WT + Time\ WT)$$
$$= (.90) \times (2.0 + .1 + .1) = 1.98.$$

Thus the selection of another magazine-issue reduced Smith's weighted score.

This is so because his weight for *Life* is 20 times that for *Time*. When the ratio of a respondent's maximum magazine weight to his minimum weight is less than two or three, at low levels of exposure, it is unlikely that an additional selection will reduce his weighted score, provided that a table of magazine weights similar to the one assumed is used. However, as the number of previously selected issues of magazines for which a respondent has non-zero weights increases, the chance of the next selection reducing his weighted score also increases.

THE THIRD MODEL

There are other incremental-analysis objective functions that are not subject to this weakness. For example, a frequently stated advertising objective is to maximize reach, that is to maximize the number of target-audience members who are exposed to one or more of the firm's ads. Let P_{ij} be the probability that the ith respondent is exposed to an advertisement inserted in an issue of the ith magazine.[7] Then $(1 - P_{ij})$ is the probability that respondent i is not exposed to an issue of magazine j. If we assume that the probability of a respondent's viewing an ad in one magazine is unaffected by his reading

[7] P_{ij} is the ith respondent's weight for the jth magazine provided that the relative effectiveness of an advertising exposure delivered by magazine j is taken to be 1.

an ad in other magazines, $(1 - P_{ij}) (1 - P_{ik})$ is the probability that respondent i is exposed to neither ad when one is inserted in magazine j and one in magazine k. The probability that respondent i is exposed to at least one of the two ads is therefore given by $1 - (1 - P_{ij}) (1 - P_{ik})$.

Suppose that one issue of magazine j and one issue of magazine k have so far been selected. Then it is simple to calculate the incremental addition to respondent is weighted score that results from the selection of an additional issue of magazine m:

$$[1 - (1 - P_{ij}) (1 - P_{ik}) (1 - P_{im})]$$
$$- [1 - (1 - P_{ij}) (1 - P_{ik})]$$
$$= P_{im}(1 - P_{ij}) (1 - P_{ik}).$$

Note that this is precisely the probability that respondent i is not exposed to the ads in magazines i and j and that he is exposed to the ad in magazine m. A marginal cost efficiency for magazine m can be calculated by summing $P_{im}(1 - P_{ij}) (1 - P_{ik})$ over all respondents and dividing by the cost per insertion in magazine m. The probability calculation is easily generalized so that marginal cost efficiencies can be calculated for all available magazines given that any group of magazines has previously been selected. It is, therefore, possible to derive a schedule using an incremental-analysis algorithm.

CONCLUSION

The purpose of the preceding discussion is not to recommend the use of any particular objective function in the selection of media, although those presented may be useful to some advertisers. It is to suggest what may be for some advertisers a fruitful new approach to media selection. The objective functions to which incremental analysis can be applied are no doubt numerous and, it is hoped, that the reader will find it profitable to adapt the method to a function of his own choice.

REFERENCES

1. Seymour Banks, "The Use of Incremental Analysis in the Selection of Advertising Media," *The Journal of Business of the University of Chicago*, 19 (October 1946), 232–43.
2. Frank M. Bass and Ronald T. Lonsdale, "An Exploration of Linear Programming in Media Selection," *Journal of Marketing Research*, 3 (May 1966), 179–88.
3. Douglas B. Brown and Martin R. Warshaw, "Media Selection by Linear Programming," *Journal of Marketing Research*, 2 (February 1965), 83–8.
4. Robert D. Buzzell, "Batten, Barton, Durstine, & Osborn, Incorporated; Use of Linear Programming Methods in the Selection of Advertising Media," in *Mathematical Models and Marketing Management*, Boston: Harvard University, 1964, 77–111.
5. Ralph L. Day, "Linear Programming in Media Selection," *Journal of Advertising Research*, 2 (June 1962), 40–4.
6. James F. Engel and Martin R. Warshaw, "Allocating Ad-

vertising Dollars by Linear Programming," *Journal of Advertising Research,* 4 (September 1964), 42–8.

7. Alec M. Lee and A. J. Burkart, "Some Optimization Problems in Advertising Media Planning," *Operational Research Quarterly,* 11 (September 1960), 113–22.

8. Alec M. Lee, "Decision Rules for Media Scheduling: Static Campaigns," *Operational Research Quarterly,* 13 (September 1962), 229–42.

9. Richard B. Maffei, "Planning Advertising Expenditures by Dynamic Programming Methods," *Management Technology,* 1 (December 1960), 94–100.

10. *Mathematical Methods of Media Selection, A Report of the Sixth Meeting of the ARF Operations Research Discussion Group,* New York: Advertising Research Foundation, Inc., 1961.

11. *Mathematical Programing for Better Media Selection,* Papers from region conventions, American Association of Advertising Agencies, 1961.

12. Oddvar Bie Mevik and Niels Vinding, "Two Dimensions of Media Selection, Coverage and Frequency," *Journal of Advertising Research,* 6 (March 1966), 29–34.

13. Stanley F. Stasch, "Linear Programming and Space-Time Considerations in Media Selection," *Journal of Advertising Research,* 5 (December 1965), 40–6.

14. Clark L. Wilson, "Use of Linear Programming to Optimize Media Schedules in Advertising," in Henry Gomez, ed., *Innovation—Key to Marketing Progress,* Proceedings of the 46th National Conference, American Marketing Association, 1963, 178–91.

15. Willard I. Zangwell, "Media Selection by Decision Programming," *Journal of Advertising Research,* 5 (September 1965), 30–6.

.... COMMUNICATIONS

A Practical Procedure for Media Selection: Comments

ROBERT J. SCHREIBER*

In a recent JMR article Douglas Brown presents a practical media selection method based on marginal analysis [1]. He proposes that the choice of the *next* media insertion be in the medium providing the largest increment in net effectiveness of the schedule. He points out that though the method will only produce an optimal schedule under limited conditions, it should always select a good schedule. Brown gives a clear definition of optimality, pointing out that the "term *optimal schedule* refers to a feasible schedule that maximizes the numerical value of some objective function."

Because of his definition the procedures he proposes should be carefully scrutinized. I contend that assumptions made in the development of the objective function sharply detract from the value of the procedure.

THE DISCOUNT FACTOR

Brown assumes that the second exposure to a medium carrying an ad for a campaign is worth .90 of the first,

* Robert J. Schreiber is associate director, Corporate Research, Time Inc. He is grateful to Dr. Richard Ostheimer of Time Inc., for his suggestions.

the third is worth .80 of the first, etc. He contends that empirical evidence (not cited by him) indicates that the ultimate schedule is insensitive to the sequence if there are diminishing returns. If a much sharper reduction were assumed—say, giving the second ad .1 of the first —the resulting schedule would probably use more media with fewer insertions in each. Until research is done that shows what the range of discount curves really is, it is difficult to conclude insensitivity.

A major factor omitted in this discounting is time. A second exposure six months after the first should not have the same effect as an exposure two weeks after the first because of forgetting, competitive advertising, etc. If timing is unimportant, advertisers should place all their advertising in the first quarter of the year and get it over with!

MAGAZINE WEIGHTS

Brown proposes that each respondent be assigned a weight for each magazine. The weight is the product of three factors: (1) the probability of reading the magazine, (2) the probability of seeing the ad (if the magazine has been seen), and (3) the environmental effect of the magazine. He further proposes that the first component

Journal of Marketing Research,
Vol. V (May 1968), 221–4

can be determined for a respondent: "If he claims to have read four of the last six issues of *Playboy,* his probability of reading *Playboy* is taken to be 4/6."

Even if respondents have perfect recall, the method may produce inaccurate probability estimates. Some respondents who did see four of six may have viewing probabilities quite different from .6667. For example, of 1,000 people who truly have a probability of .6667 of reading *Playboy,* the binomial theorem indicates that only 330 of them will be expected to see four out of six issues. Of the people with a probability of .8, almost a quarter of them will see four of six. Thus, how many of six issues (or any small number) are read yields a poor estimate of a respondent's probability.[1]

The second component of the weight, probability of exposure to the ad, is "estimated from his response to questions about . . . ad noting . . . ," etc. A book reviewed by Frank Orenstein in the August JMR covers the problems of that kind of data [3]. Orenstein points out that *noting scores* are related to conscious viewing and that much more is sensed than perceived.

GENERAL

The general procedure proposed by Brown is quite similar to the basic techniques of simulation. However, he treats his data in an expected value fashion and loses some of the distributional characteristics. In the follow-

---

[1] For a more complete discussion of this problem, see [2].

ing examples each of 500 people has a .5 probability of reading *Life* and a 1.0 probability of seeing the ad with a media weight of unity. By Brown's formulation, the effectiveness of four insertions in *Life* would be: $500 \times .5 \times (1 + .9 + .8 + .7) = 850$. Considering the frequency distribution of magazine readership, the binomial distribution gives:

Frequency	0	1	2	3	4
Number of people	31.25	125	187.5	125	31.25.

Then, the effectiveness would be:

$$0 + 125(1) + 187.5(1 + .9) + 125(1 + .9 + .8) \\ + 31.25(1 + .9 + .8 + .7) = 925.$$

The results are indeed different; the amount of difference greatly depends on the kind of model of the advertising process. If a probabilistic representation of readership and ad viewing is used, the problems of probability estimation and treatment of the estimates require more exploration than Brown gives them.

REFERENCES

1. Douglas B. Brown, "A Practical Method for Media Selection," *Journal of Marketing Research,* 4 (August 1967), 262–9.
2. Robert J. Schreiber, "Probability Assignments for the Simulation of Media Reach and Frequency," *Journal of Advertising Research,* (in press.)
3. Daniel Starch, *Measuring Advertising Readership and Results,* New York: McGraw-Hill Book Co., 1966.

The True Probability of Exposure

SEYMOUR BANKS*

Current media selection models use samples of a person's exposure to many media as basic inputs for calculating frequency distributions of exposure to advertising campaigns. Data come from diary reports, interviews using various aids to memory, or direct questions on frequency of reading, viewing, or listening. The merits of these techniques will not be discussed since this article concerns the use of these data not their validity (but I want only valid data).

The rarely challenged assumption that the reported

---

* Seymour Banks is vice president, Leo Burnett Company, Chicago.

frequency of a person's exposure to a medium is his latent or true frequency of exposure needs further discussion. Table 1 demonstrates the binomial distribution —each row lists the expected proportion of people who would see 0, 1, 2, 3, or 4 of 4 issues (or telecasts) of a magazine (or program) given various true probabilities of exposure. The latent probabilities are long-run averages and any reported rate of exposure is a single sample of results. Though the matching values of latent and sample probabilities receive the highest values in each row; except at the extremes of never and ever read, seen, or heard, less than half of the people with a given true (long-run) exposure probability will report the corresponding short-run frequency.

In real life, Table 1 does not exist; instead, the true probabilities must be estimated from sample frequencies. Table 2 shows such a calculation indicating conditional probabilities in the jargon of the statisticians. It is based on Table 1 by expressing each cell entry in Table 1 as a percentage of the corresponding column total. (There is also an implicit weighting based on the assumption that there are equal numbers of people with each of the five latent probabilities. These weights can be changed without interfering with the basic argument of this article.)

Brown's paper [1] assumes that the diagonal entries of Table 2 are 100 and all side-cell values are 0. Schreiber [2] warns against this assumption but does not say what the various entries are.

Basic points are:

1. It is an oversimplification to assume that true or latent probabilities of exposure for persons are identical with the expressed sample short-run proportions.

2. Treating these two sets of probabilities as identical will produce biased results except where $p = .50$. Use of sample probabilities above .5 may overestimate and use of sample proportions below .5 may underestimate the true probabilities. Where the reported exposure rate is one out of four, 41.3 percent of such reports could come from persons with latent probabilities of .5 or .75.

3. Therefore, it is necessary to build into media selection models an intervening process that will adjust these sample frequencies to more closely correspond to the true set of latent exposure probabilities.

In Table 2 identical proportions of respondents would be assigned to latent probabilities above and below that corresponding to the sample frequency only for the middle column. Moving to the left or right, unequal proportions are assigned to probabilities above and below that corresponding to the sample frequency. As-

Table 1

EXPECTED PROPORTION SEEING n OUT OF FOUR ISSUES GIVEN VARIOUS LATENT PROBABILITIES

Latent probabilities	Sample frequencies					Totals
	0	1	2	3	4	
0	1.0000	.0000	.0000	.0000	.0000	1.0000
1/4	.3164	.4219	.2109	.0469	.0039	1.0000
2/4	.0625	.2500	.3750	.2500	.0625	1.0000
3/4	.0039	.0469	.2109	.4219	.3164	1.0000
4/4	.0000	.0000	.0000	.0000	1.0000	1.0000
	1.3828	.7188	.7968	.7188	1.3828	
Expected sample frequency	.2765	.1438	.1594	.1438	.2765	1.0000

Table 2

CONDITIONAL PROPORTIONS OF RESPONDENTS WITH VARIOUS LATENT EXPOSURE RATES, GIVEN n OUT OF FOUR RECENT EXPOSURES

Latent probabilities	Sample frequencies				
	0	1	2	3	4
0	72.3	0	0	0	0
1/4	22.9	58.7	26.5	6.5	0.3
2/4	4.5	34.8	47.0	34.8	4.5
3/4	0.3	6.5	26.5	58.7	22.9
4/4	0	0	0	0	72.3
	100.0	100.0	100.0	100.0	100.0

signing all respondents with a given sample frequency to the corresponding level of true frequency will introduce bias for all situations where the sample frequency is not n out of 2n.

This dilemma cannot be avoided by assuming there will be equal numbers of people found with sample proportions on either side of .5 as shown by Table 1. Any study of actual sample proportions will show what statisticians refer to as J or reverse J distributions—most people at one extreme or another and relatively few around the middle.

Current media selection models seek to estimate exposure to a media campaign extending over a fairly long time. By simulation, each person's number of exposures is estimated by multiplying the number of opportunities for exposure through media by some estimate of his probability for seeing or hearing each medium. But assigning a sample proportion, as an estimate of a person's true or latent probability of seeing or hearing any schedule other than those for which the sample data were collected, will often generate biased values. Therefore, it will be necessary to introduce a step that adjusts these distributions of sample proportions into conditional distributions of latent probabilities analogous to those shown in Table 2.

These suggestions are easier to propose than to translate into actual results. There are at least two major difficulties: the proportions or weights applicable to each row of Table 1 are never known and there is a continuum of latent probabilities though survey procedures ask for relatively few sample frequencies. Any correction will do an injustice to the real data, but the use of the sample proportions without correction introduces bias. The reader must choose the lesser of the two evils.

REFERENCES

1. Douglas B. Brown, "A Practical Method for Media Selection," *Journal of Marketing Research*, 4 (August 1967), 262–9.
2. Robert J. Schreiber, "A Practical Procedure for Media Selection: Comments," *Journal of Marketing Research*, 5 (May, 1968), 221–2.

Reply to Schreiber and Banks

DOUGLAS B. BROWN*

I appreciate the useful comments of Robert Schreiber and Seymour Banks. This note is not intended as a rejoinder. Rather it acknowledges, once more, the limitations of incremental analysis and indicates the nature of appropriate remedies.

As will be recalled, I did not recommend any particular objective function for media selection, and I agree with Schreiber that it is usually desirable to take into account the decay of advertising effects over time. However, there are circumstances when the use of models without time discounting is appropriate. Schreiber will no doubt recall a useful distinction which Alec Lee made a few years ago [2, p. 229] between "static campaigns, i.e., those that are intended to evoke a maximum response, the time of attainment being unimportant" and "dynamic campaigns, e.g., those in which the rate of generation of response over a specified time period is paramount":

"Static advertising campaigns are not carried out to generate awareness in a certain target group. The objective is to stimulate active responses from the members of the target group . . . Impact and coverage are all that is required to define the direct effect on the target group of a campaign based upon a specific media schedule" [2, p. 233].

All the models described in "A Practical Procedure for Media Selection" were static models by Lee's definition. But the principle of incremental analysis can also be applied to scheduling dynamic campaigns although the amount of computation required to derive a schedule increases considerably.

Let me say that like Banks (and Schreiber) I want only valid data. But if faced with a problem, I make use of the data available, and even when I have the opportunity to gather my own data, practical limitations of time and money usually cause me to knowingly specify the collection of imperfect information.

The problem of specifying appropriate data to be used as a basis for media selection is particularly vexatious, because such concepts as "advertising exposures," "media weights," and the like are abstractions and inherently unmeasurable until they have been given operational definitions. The test of the usefulness of an operational definition is whether the quantity measured relates in an analytically useful way to sales or some other marketing variable of interest. In short, the only valid test of a marketing model is how well it predicts what it is supposed to predict.[1]

Unfortunately, this is a very difficult test to apply to media selection models, and as a result criticisms of a model's structure, the parameters, and the manner in which they are estimated assume increased importance. Many models have been criticized on these grounds, but have been found to be useful predictors. Hence, I find it difficult to criticize marketing models unless the assumptions or estimation procedures are clearly contrary to my experience and intuition. I am not convinced that "much more is sensed than perceived" is a valid criticism of the operational usefulness of noting scores in media selection. However, the example presented by Banks is sufficient to convince me that the method I proposed for estimating a respondent's probability of readership is erroneous.

I thank Banks for suggesting a sound alternative method, and I would like to reemphasize his point ("these weights can be changed without interfering with the basic argument of this paper") that one is free to assign any prior distribution to the probability of exposure that he chooses.

REFERENCES

1. Jerome D. Herniter and Ronald A. Howard, "Stochastic Marketing Models," in David B. Hertz and Roger T. Eddison, eds., *Progress in Operations Research*, Vol. 2, New York: John Wiley & Sons, Inc., 1964.
2. Alec M. Lee, "Decision Rules for Media Scheduling: Static Campaigns," *Operational Research Quarterly*, 13 (September 1962).

* Douglas B. Brown is consultant to Arthur D. Little, Inc.

[1] This point is developed more fully in [1, pp. 33–96].

A Probabilistic Approach to Industrial Media Selection[1]

DAVID A. AAKER

Stanford University

This disaggregative model takes into account exposure probabilities, segmentation, multiple exposures and journal effects to maximize total effective exposure for a given budget.

THIS MODEL, *Probabilistic Optimizing Model for Selecting Insertion Schedules* (POMSIS), is a disaggregative, probabilistic approach to a particular but common industrial media selection problem. Within a given budget, what journal insertion schedule will obtain the greatest impact for an advertising campaign of given length? Notice that only journal advertising is considered and that the analysis has been constrained to a limited time period.

In attempting to apply quantitative techniques to media selection, a recurring problem is how to handle multiple exposures. Most linear programming models assume that all exposures have equal impact, i.e., that ten exposures to one individual is as desirable as one exposure to each of ten people.

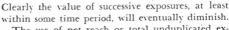

DAVID A. AAKER, now assistant professor of business administration in the University of California at Berkeley, is completing the doctoral program in business administration at Stanford University where he was a Ford Foundation Fellow. He received a B.S. from M.I.T. in 1960 and an M.S. in Operations Research from Stanford in 1967. For five years he worked in various sales management, market research, and long-range planning capacities at Texas Instruments Inc., where he also authored several instrumentation articles. He is a member of the American Marketing Association, and the ASA.

Clearly the value of successive exposures, at least within some time period, will eventually diminish.

The use of net reach or total unduplicated exposure is another approach. Progress toward identifying net reach has been made (Agostini, 1962). However, the direct use of net reach as a decision criterion assumes that a duplicated exposure has no value at all. Intuitive reasoning and empirical tests indicate that this hypothesis is a serious distortion. The *Reader's Digest*, in a recent advertisement, reports on a study conducted by Politz which indicated that the second exposure is almost as effective as the first.

Kotler (1964) suggests that the value of a journal's circulation be altered with repeated insertions in accordance with a predetermined function. The function, for example, may rise slightly with the second insertion and then fall with succeeding ones. This technique has the enticing simplicity and inherent distortions of most aggregative approaches. The function is conceived to reflect the impact of successive exposures to an individual. It will only apply to an audience, an aggregation of individuals, if the membership remains unchanged over time

[1] The author gratefully acknowledges the helpful suggestions and comments of Professors H. J. Claycamp and W. F. Massy of Stanford University and Dr. C. T. McClelland of Varian Associates.

and if all members have identical reading habits. Clearly, such assumptions are not realistic. When additional journals and other dimensions of advertising impact are introduced, an aggregative approach becomes even less appropriate.

Multiple exposures as well as other problems can be handled by integer programing or by microanalytic simulation. Both techniques allow as much realism and completeness as the data permit. However, even with modern computers, neither is a practical technique to select (as opposed to test) an optimum schedule.

POMSIS attempts a practical and realistic approach to a particular media selection problem. By disaggregating to the level of a potential exposure to individuals in a sample population, it permits the user to assign appropriate weights to successive exposures.

THE OBJECTIVE

Before describing the model in detail, the end objective should be defined carefully. While everyone would accept profit maximization as a legitimate objective of advertising, we soon find that profit maximization is not sufficiently operational and that we must turn to measures such as exposures per dollar cost as a profit surrogate. The problem is that exposures differ in value. The tenth exposure is not the same as the first. An exposure to a prime prospect is not like one to a person with no purchase potential.

To make the exposure concept more useful let us develop an artificial exposure situation to use as a standard. Further, let us label our standard as an "effective exposure" and be prepared to measure the value of other exposures against it. Consider an advertisement running in several journals. An individual will receive an "effective exposure" to the advertisement, one with a relative value of 1.0, if:

1. This exposure is the first for the particular individual.
2. The individual is a member of the customer class regarded as the most important target of the advertisement.
3. The journal involved provides the best possible environment for the advertisement.
4. The individual is actually exposed to the advertisement in that journal.

An exposure under circumstances different from our unit effective exposure will not have a value of one—it will be the product of four weights, each representing the relative value of a particular exposure as compared to the standard. Our problem can then be reformulated to one of maximizing effective exposures subject to our budget limitation. Let us examine more closely the four dimensions of the effective exposure.

Effective Exposure

The first dimension of effective exposure provides a mechanism to consider explicitly the number of times an individual is exposed to an advertisement during the time period considered. If there is one exposure it will have a relative impact of 1.0. If there are two, the second exposure might have a relative impact of 0.9 or 1.1. Similarly, the third exposure might be considered 0.5 as effective as the first.

The second dimension provides a weighting factor which is unique to the customer class or market segment to which the individual belongs. An advertisement for instrumentation, for example, may be primarily directed toward electrical engineers and instrumentation engineers. A second set of segments might include buyers, maintenance engineers and mechanical engineers. It may be of only small corporate benefit to reach chemical engineers. A weight, from 0.0 to 1.0, can be associated with a segment of the market according to the relative value of a representative individual in that segment.

The third dimension provides a weighting factor unique to the journal. It is intended to reflect the degree to which the journal enhances (or detracts from) an advertisement. One agency (Wolfe et al., 1966, pp. 84-86), in constructing such a weighting factor, found that three characteristics of the journal were enough to describe its relative impact: 1. Competitive advertising activity—an indication of the journal's acceptance as a source of information about the product. 2. The amount of editorial space devoted to subjects pertaining to the product. 3. An index of editorial quality, i.e., the editorial percentage of total pages. Other measures, such as the reproductive qualities of the journal or its positioning of advertising may be appropriate.

The fourth dimension might seem degenerate on the surface. An individual either sees the advertisement in a journal or he does not. A weighting factor of 0.0 or 1.0 seems appropriate. However, under most circumstances such a binary judgment can only be made about the past. As it is our function to make a judgment about the future we must recognize that it can only be made with uncertainty. There exists a probability (which may be difficult to determine) that an exposure will be realized. An individual may have a probability of 0.5 of reading *Electronics* and a probability of 0.4 of seeing one of its advertisements even when he does read it. The fourth dimension reflects the probability that the potential exposure will actually materialize into an actual exposure. In our example, this weighting factor would be $0.4 \times 0.5 = 0.2$.

It would be possible to include an additional dimension for the advertisement presentation. In most cases a four color, full page spread will be more effective than a half page, black and white. However, to avoid unduly complicating this discussion of POMSIS, we shall assume that only comparable presentations are being considered.

THE MODEL

The objective is to select an insertion schedule subject to budget limitations (and other constraints) that will provide the maximum number of "effective exposures" within a given time period. A heuristic is used systematically to consider insertion schedules that are possible given the constraints. The selection heuristic uses a hill-climbing technique adding (and deleting) marginal insertions until any further insertion substitutions within the constraints will only decrease the value of the insertion schedule. During the selection process each change is evaluated by determining the total effective exposures (TEE) that the resulting insertion schedule will provide.

A sample population selected from the target groups is used. In evaluating a schedule POMSIS examines every potential exposure for every individual in the sample. A potential exposure is created for each sample individual when an advertisement is inserted in a journal. Each potential exposure is rated on the four effective exposure dimensions to determine its value. When all such effective exposures are summed, the result is an indication of the effectiveness of that insertion schedule on the sample population. Using appropriate scaling factors the result is projected to the real population providing the total effective exposures generated by that insertion schedule.

Inputs to the Model

Certain information, needed to determine an insertion schedule's TEE, must be provided by the user to POMSIS. First, the user must identify the journals to be considered. A weighting factor, possibly constrained to a maximum of 1.0, must be provided for each journal. This factor contributes the journal effect for the jth journal and is termed v_j.

The population must be divided into mutually exclusive, collectively exhaustive segments. Each segment is to have an associated factor, which is termed w_k, to reflect the relative importance of an individual in the kth segment to the advertising campaign. Segmentation in industrial marketing is unique because the purchase decision is usually shared by several people. Relevant segments will normally consist of people who have a particular type of influence on the purchase decision. The size of segment k, denoted as N_k, is also needed.

From each segment a sample is required. Sampling is simplified in that a representative sample of the whole population is not necessary. The proportion of people in the sample from a certain segment need not equal the proportion of the population contained in that segment. The only requirement is that a certain minimum number (100 to 200) be obtained from each segment. Of course, the sample should be representative of the segment. Ideally, each member of the segment should have an equal chance of being selected. A customer mailing list which is considered representative of the population could be used as the source for a sample population.

For each member of the sample, individual i, we need the probability that he will be exposed to an advertisement in each journal, journal j, under consideration. This set of probabilities, which are individually termed P_{ij}, provides directly the fourth dimension of our effective exposure.

One final input requirement remains in addition to the constraint information. A judgment is required as to the relative weight of the first, second and successive exposures. Unlike a micro-analytic simulation model which can attach to each exposure a step function with a time decay, POMSIS cannot discriminate between different exposure time intervals. Thus, the time period considered by the model should be constrained to reduce the effect of different exposure time intervals. For example, the time between exposures cannot be so long that a fourth exposure might actually become another "first" exposure.

Measurement Problems

The determination of v_j, w_k, and the relative weight of successive exposures involve extremely difficult measurement problems. The determination of accurate weights would unquestionably involve research and would probably be a function of the products concerned. Further disaggregation may be appropriate as, for example, the v_j may differ for different segments. Even if no empirical data are available, an intuitive, subjective determination should provide a more realistic and useful model than ignoring or aggregating any of these dimensions. Certainly they are all considered in some manner in any final media selection decision. Since the determination of the exposure probabilities is central, a method for obtaining them will be suggested after the model is presented.

Multiple Exposure Effect

For a given insertion schedule, POMSIS determines in a probabilistic sense the number of times an individual will be exposed to the advertisement. It does not, however, know the order of the exposures. We must therefore alter our concept of the first dimension of the effective exposure. If an individual receives three exposures we can say that the average impact of each exposure is lower than if he received only one exposure. If the first exposure to an individual is considered to have a relative impact of 1.0, the second 0.9, and the third 0.5, the net effect of three exposures is to reduce the impact of each to $(1.0 + 0.9 + 0.5)/3 = 0.8$. Instead of a weight indicating the number of previous exposures, we have a weight reflecting the total number of exposures to individual i. This weight is unique to each individual and each insertion schedule. It reflects the effect of the number of times (in a probabilistic sense) the individual is exposed to an advertisement. The weight is termed the multiple exposure effect and is labeled y_1.

Since we are ultimately after total potential exposures, a legitimate question might be why not use the cumulative exposure impact for each individual? Such an approach would mean aggregating over all journals. Though we know that individual i probably will receive three exposures with a certain insertion schedule, we do not know from which journals they originated. There could be six journals in the schedule any three of which might be the source of the three exposures. If we are to retain the use of the journal factor, v_j, it is necessary to treat the multiple exposure factor, y_i, as a factor which can apply to all potential exposures. A discussion of how y_i is actually calculated will also be postponed until after the model is described.

Evaluating an Insertion Schedule

To evaluate an insertion schedule with respect to the population sample, each potential exposure created by the insertion schedule is examined. Each journal insertion in the schedule creates a potential

exposure for each individual in the sample. The effective exposure value is determined for each potential exposure. It is the product of four weights corresponding to the four dimensions of the effective exposure. In symbolic terms, the effective exposure contribution of a potential exposure is $y_i w_k v_j P_{ij}$. It reflects the multiple exposure effect, the segment effect, the journal effect, and the probability that this potential exposure will materialize.

The value of disaggregation should now be apparent. It recognizes that individuals from the same segment have different reading habits. Some read many journals and others read few. Generally, the specific journals read differ from individual to individual. It also recognizes the relevance of which journal creates the exposure. Finally, it allows the introduction of uncertainty at the level at which it occurs—an individual reading a specific journal.

To obtain the number of effective exposures that any individual i receives, we sum over all journals in the insertion schedule $\Sigma_j x_j(y_i w_k v_j P_{ij})$. The term x_j is the number of insertions in journal j. The total effective exposures received by the sample from market segment k is obtained by summing over all individuals in the sample who belong to market segment k: Σ_{iek}. Total effective exposures received by a certain market segment is obtained by including the factor N_k/n_k which explicitly scales the results to the segment size. Finally, we sum over all segments, Σ_k, to arrive at TEE, for an insertion schedule (see Figure 1).

Constraints

The basic constraint is the budget limitation. It provides that:

$$\Sigma_j c_j x_j \leq b$$

The total cost of an insertion schedule must be less than or equal to a budget, b. The term c_j is the cost of an *incremental* insertion in journal j and usually will decline as the number of insertions in journal j is increased. There are other constraints that are often desirable. Two are listed in Figure 1. The insertion constraint will prevent a schedule from including more insertions in a journal than there are issues in the time period under consideration. The minimum exposure constraint allows the targets of the campaign to be identified and their importance to be expressed quantitatively. It serves as a check on the values selected for the w_k terms. These constraints are not intended to be exhaustive. It might be desirable, for example, to require an in-

FIGURE 1

POMSIS

Select the Insertion Schedule that will maximize Total Effective Exposures:

$$TEE = \Sigma_k(N_k/n_k)\ \Sigma_{i\in k}\Sigma_j x_j(y_i w_k v_j P_{ij})$$

Subject to:

$\Sigma_j c_j x_j \leq b$ budget constraint

$x_j \leq max_j$ insertion constraint

$\Sigma_{i\in k}\Sigma_j x_j v_j p_{ij} \geq m_k$ minimum exposure constraint

where:

$k =$ index referencing the market segment
$i =$ index referencing the individual in the sample
$j =$ index referencing the journal
$N_k =$ total size of segment k
$n_k =$ sample size from segment k
$x_j =$ number of insertions in journal j
$y_i =$ weight reflecting the multiple exposure effect on individual i
$w_k =$ relative weight attached to segment k
$v_j =$ relative weight attached to journal j
$P_{ij} =$ probability that individual i is exposed to an advertisement in journal j
$c_j =$ cost of the marginal insertion in journal j (subscript denoting the insertion number suppressed)
$b =$ allowable dollar expenditures
$max_j =$ maximum number of insertions allowed in journal j
$m_k =$ minimum exposure level for segment k

sertion in a particular journal. We would then modify the insertion constraint to: $min_j \leq x_j \leq max_j$. Nearly any constraint expressable in terms such as those which have been defined could be added.

The Selection Heuristic

The selection heuristic adds insertions incrementally until the budget constraint is reached. For a given insertion schedule (initially the schedule has no insertions) the journal will be selected which will provide the most additional total effective exposures per dollar cost. The total effective exposures for the insertion schedule which consists of the original schedule plus one additional insertion is determined. The difference between the TEE so

obtained and the original TEE is the marginal contribution of that journal. Such a marginal contribution is obtained for each journal under consideration. An insertion will then be added to that journal with the highest ratio of marginal contribution to marginal insertion cost. Of course, any journal for which an addition would violate a constraint is excluded from consideration.

The new schedule has one additional insertion. The ratio of marginal contribution to marginal insertion cost is known for the journal which obtained the additional insertion. That ratio is also determined for all other journals in the new insertion schedule. For any journal r in the new schedule the ratio numerator is the difference between the new schedule TEE and the TEE of the new schedule with an insertion deleted in journal r. The ratio denominator is the cost reduction created by an insertion deletion in journal r. If the journal in the new schedule with the lowest ratio is *not the newest insertion* and if it had *not been previously removed* from the new schedule under evaluation, it is now removed. The two conditions prevent cycling. The process then repeats the previous step, selecting another journal to which to add an insertion. There is, of course, a reason for this circular step-forward, step-back, step-forward process. It may happen that the first journal selected might eventually become redundant after several other insertions are included. This is a mechanism to allow a journal once selected to be removed from the schedule.

EXAMPLE

Suppose after a few iterations, the schedule had one insertion in journal 12 and two insertions in journal 28. To find the marginal contribution for journal 24, the TEE for the schedule with one insertion in journal 12, one in journal 24, and two in journal 28 is determined. The marginal contribution is the increase in TEE over the original schedule. Dividing by the marginal insertion cost for journal 24, we have the appropriate ratio for journal 24. An insertion is made in journal 24 creating a new schedule if all other admissible journals (including journals 12 and 28) have lower ratios and no constraint is violated by such an insertion.

Before moving on, we want to evaluate the old insertions in the new schedule to see if they are still desirable. A different kind of marginal contribution is determined for journals 12 and 28. Instead of finding the TEE added by another insertion, we find the TEE lost by an insertion deletion. For journal 12 the TEE in a schedule consisting of one insertion in journal 24 and two in journal 28 is found and subtracted from the TEE in the new schedule. Dividing by the cost reduction created by the deletion of journal 12, we have the ratio of marginal contribution to marginal cost for journal 12 with respect to the new schedule. If the ratio for both journal 12 and journal 28 exceeds that of journal 24, we move on. If, however, the ratio for journal 28 is lower than that of journal 24, an insertion in journal 28 is deleted providing a similar situation was not duplicated earlier in the process. Journal 28 may be reinserted during the next cycle if it happens to qualify.

When a schedule is obtained to which no further insertions can be made without violating the insertion constraint or budget constraint, the minimum exposure constraint is checked. If it is not satisfied for every segment, the w_k for the offending segments are increased by a certain amount, perhaps 0.20. The process is then repeated from the start. The larger weighting factor attached to a segment will tend to increase the chances of those journals that have a high readership among that segment.

When insertion deletions from a new schedule are considered it may be adequate, especially when the process is not near a final schedule, to use a journal's average contribution rather than its marginal contribution. The average contribution of journal j per dollar cost is:

$$\frac{\Sigma_k(N_k/n_k) \, \Sigma_{i \in k} \, (y_i w_k v_j P_{ij})}{c_j} = p_j$$

The value of p_j is readily available and does not involve the calculation of the TEE of additional schedules.

Determining Exposure Probabilities

The model requires for each individual i in the sample the probability (P_{ij}) that he will be exposed to an advertisement in each journal under consideration. Practical considerations suggest a two step approach. For each individual in the sample we determine the probability that he will read each journal. Then we determine the conditional likelihood that any reader of each journal will be exposed to one of its advertisements.

Aided recall techniques can be used to obtain readership probabilities. Boyd et al. (forthcoming) have used such a method on a sample of professional people in the electronics industry. A questionnaire was devised which pictured the covers of over 30 technical journals. Under each picture was a choice of four boxes corresponding to:

a. Read all issues in past 12 months
b. Read 75% of issues
c. Read 50% of issues
d. Read only occasionally

The resulting frequency information obtained from members of the sample can be used as the readership probabilities. Naturally aided recall methods have problems which must be considered. The journal locations on the questionnaire should be varied to reduce positional bias. A depth interview of a subsample is desirable to detect other forms of bias such as a tendency to exaggerate readership of prestige journals. Despite the problems this does represent one method of obtaining required readership probabilities. The determination of relative journal advertisement exposure will not be discussed here. The interested reader is referred to Wolfe et al. (1966, pp. 58-63).

Determining Multiple Exposure Effect

We know the relative impact that the exposure will have as a function of the number of previous times it has been seen. Knowing the relative impact we can determine the cumulative impact and the average impact of a certain number of exposures. Table 1 summarizes with an example. Note that a somewhat artificial 1.0 is included as the average impact for zero exposures.

TABLE 1

Exposure Number	Relative Impact	Number of Exposures z_i	Cumulative Impact	Average Impact
0		0	0.0	1.0
First	1.0	1	1.0	1.0
Second	.9	2	1.9	.95
Third	.5	3	2.4	.8
Fourth	0	4	2.4	.6
Fifth	0	5	2.4	.48

Let us assume that the P_{ij}'s are independent for a given individual i. This assumption implies that the event of individual i being exposed to an advertisement in the November issue of *Industrial Research* is independent of whether he sees the advertisement in the October issue of *Iron Age*.

A new variable, z_i, is defined to be the total number of times individual i is exposed to the advertisement. Knowing the P_{ij}'s, we can determine the probability that z_i is equal to zero, one, two, three . . . for any given insertion schedule. As an example, suppose that the advertisement is to be inserted once in journal 14 and once in journal 16. Consider the individual 9 with exposure probabilities $P_{9,14} = 0.6$ and $P_{9,16} = 0.3$.

Then $P(z_9 = 0) = (1\text{-}P_{9,14})^* (1\text{-}P_{9,16}) = 0.28$ and

$P(z_9 = 1) = P_{9,14}^* (1\text{-}P_{9,16}) + (1\text{-}P_{9,14})^* P_{9,16} = 0.54$

and

$$P(z_9 = 2) = P_{9,14}^* P_{9,16} = 0.18$$

where $P(z_9 = 2)$ is the probability that individual 9 is exposed to the advertisement two times.

As Table 1 indicates the average impact of an exposure to individual i is uniquely determined if we know z_i, the number of times individual i was exposed to the message. If we knew that individual i was exposed to the advertisement three times we could say that the average impact was $2.4 \div 3$ or 0.8. Since z_i is a random variable we can make no such statement. We can, however, calculate the expected average impact for individual i (for a given insertion schedule) as follows:

$$y_i = \text{E(average impact)} = 1.0^* P(z_i = 0) + \quad (1)$$

$$1.0^* P(z_i = 1) + .95^* P(z_i = 2) + .8^* P(z_i = 3) + \ldots$$

It is now apparent why a 1.0 must be included as the average impact of zero insertions. If the $P(z_i = 0) = 0.5$ and $P(z_i = 1) = 0.5$ the appropriate expected average impact should obviously be 1.0. Only if 1.0 is included as the average impact of zero insertions will this occur. The term y_i, which is actually the expected average impact, is the final weighting factor for the multiple exposure effect. It is unique to each individual and to each insertion schedule.

The determination of the y_i's requires that each of the $P(z_i = n)$'s be calculated. Obviously, it will not always be easy to determine them directly. If we are considering 30 insertions in 20 journals, the method used in the above example will not be feasible even on a large computer. The use of an approximating device, such as the Poisson, should make the calculation quite feasible and yet provide satisfactory results.

The Poisson probability law will here take the following form:

$$P(z_i) = \frac{e^{-\mu} \mu^{z_i}}{z_i!} \quad z_i = 0,1,2,3,4 \ldots \mu = \Sigma_j x_j P_{ij} \quad (2)$$

The variable z_i can be considered to be the sum of binomial random variables, each with an expected value of P_{ij}. The expected value of z_i, $\Sigma_j x_j P_{ij}$, is then the mean of the Poisson. The variance of z_i can be shown to be $\Sigma_j x_j P_{ij}(1\text{-}P_{ij})$. If the P_{ij}'s are relatively small, the variance of z_i should be close to its mean and hence to the variance of the Poisson. (The variance of the Poisson is equal to its mean.) A severe bias in variance could be compensated by appropri-

ate alteration of the relative impact weights assigned to successive ·exposures. The Poisson has the desirable property of providing probabilities only for non-negative, integer values of the random variable.

Using the Poisson approximation the calculation problem will not be as severe as it may first appear if we assume that only the first three exposures are worthwhile. We then require only the probabilities that individual i is exposed 0,1,2,3 and over 3 times.

Examining equations (1) and (2) we can see that the expected average impact, y_i, will decrease as the $E(z_i)$, which equals $\Sigma_j x_j P_{ij}$, grows larger. This observation suggests that there might be some simple function that might give results comparable to the Poisson approximation. An example would be:

$$y_i = 1.0 \qquad \text{if } E(z_i) \text{ or } \Sigma_j x_j P_{ij} \text{ is} \leq 1.5$$

$$y_i = 5/4 - 1/6 E(z_i) \quad \text{if } E(z_i) \qquad \text{is} > 1.5$$

$$(3)$$

This function has the attraction of involving a very simple calculation. The determination of conditions under which it would be adequate can only be obtained by empirically contrasting its results with those using the more rigorous Poisson approximation.

Extending the Model

POMSIS is designed for a promotional campaign constrained to a time period for which its assumptions regarding the relative impact of successive exposures are valid. It would be desirable to extend its usefulness to the more general problem of developing insertion schedules for continuing advertising efforts. The following technique might be employed to do so:

1. Use POMSIS to determine an insertion schedule for the first four months of the year.
2. Assign the selected insertions to specific issues. Half the insertions would be expected to be assigned to the first two months and one half to the second two months.
3. Re-enter .POMSIS to determine an insertion schedule for months 3, 4, 5 and 6. Add as additional constraints the insertions already committed for months 3 and 4.
4. Continue the process until the desired time period is obtained.

This discussion was limited to the industrial context and to journal advertising. Theoretically, it is perfectly reasonable to include other media such as trade shows, direct mail, radio and television. Obviously the techniques used to determine the P_{ij}'s and other parameters will vary from medium to medium. Care will be required to make the parameter values valid between media as well as within medium. It may be helpful to apply the decompo-

52

TABLE 2

JOURNAL INPUT DATA

Journal	Probability		Cost	Journal Weight	Maximum Insertion
	p_{1j}	p_{2j}	c_j*	v_j	max_j
1	0.41	0.37	1.31	0.70	2.00
2	0.31	0.28	1.39	1.00	2.00
3	0.36	0.56	0.90	0.70	2.00
4	0.03	0.01	1.52	1.00	2.00
5	0.13	0.00	0.47	1.00	2.00
6	0.25	0.00	0.54	0.70	2.00
7	0.01	0.00	0.96	1.00	2.00
8	0.25	0.20	1.18	1.00	2.00
9	0.27	0.31	0.99	0.70	2.00
10	0.35	0.47	1.65	1.00	2.00
11	0.00	0.00	0.58	1.00	2.00
12	0.01	0.00	0.47	1.00	2.00
13	0.02	0.00	0.78	1.00	2.00
14	0.07	0.07	1.39	1.00	2.00
15	0.42	0.66	1.17	0.70	2.00
16	0.23	0.25	1.28	1.00	2.00
17	0.23	0.16	1.24	1.00	2.00
18	0.14	0.21	1.80	1.00	2.00
19	0.18	0.28	1.57	1.00	2.00
20	0.30	0.33	3.10	1.00	2.00
21	0.15	0.21	5.76	1.00	2.00
22	0.02	0.03	0.76	1.00	2.00
23	0.25	0.18	1.25	1.00	2.00
24	0.28	0.30	1.26	1.00	2.00
25	0.05	0.14	1.39	1.00	2.00
26	0.10	0.06	1.05	1.00	2.00
27	0.09	0.06	1.39	1.00	2.00
28	0.02	0.00	1.19	1.00	2.00

* In thousands of dollars. The costs of the first and second insertions are assumed to be equal.

sition concept of linear programing to reduce the problem to manageable size.

It would be interesting to use POMSIS to determine the optimum level of advertising. A natural output of the model is marginal effective exposures per marginal cost. If it were possible to convert marginal effective exposures to marginal revenue, a decision rule for obtaining the optimum advertising level would emerge. The user would simply add insertions until the ratio of marginal revenue to marginal cost reached unity.

EMPIRICAL RESULTS

A simplified version of the model was programed and a real life problem was run with it. The most significant simplification was the aggregation of the exposure probabilities into a single probability vector for each of two segments considered. As a result, an "average person" represented each segment. There is no theoretical justification for aggregation, it is purely an expedient. As a partial rationalization, we might intuitively believe that if there existed a great deal of multiple exposures in a segment to an insertion schedule it should also appear (with distortion) in the aggregated form. A sample of 75 from each segment was used to

obtain the two probability vectors. The data originated from an aided recall survey on journal readership. The conditional probability of being exposed to an advertisement given that the journal was read was assumed constant across all journals. Other simplifications have either already been mentioned or are of minor importance.

Typical of the 28 journals considered were EDN, Industrial Research, Microwaves, and Electronics. The segments were defined by job descriptors and were appropriate for a particular electronic product. Tables 2 and 3 summarize the relevant input data and the results from five of the runs. The journal weights are hypothetical. The incrementing of w_2 was necessary in Run 4a to obtain an acceptable schedule, shown as run 4b. In Table 3 the schedules are presented in the order that insertions were selected. Insertion deletions did not occur in any run shown. The average contribution of journal j per dollar cost, p_j, was used in the heuristic and is included in Table 3. Although its absolute value has no useful interpretation, it does provide an indication of the relative value of the journals in the final schedule.

Testing a normative model requires access to a controlled, real world environment or its simulation. Having neither we must be satisfied with a few

TABLE 3

SUMMARY OF RESULTS

	Run 1	Run 2	Run 3	Run 4a	Run 4b	Run 5*
Segment Weight—w_1	0.5	0.4	0.35	1.00	1.00	0.5
Segment Weight—w_2	1.0	1.0	1.0	0.40	0.90	1.0
Budget Constraint—b	8†	8	10	8	8	8
Min. Exp. Level—m_1	1.0	1.0	1.0	1.0	1.0	1.0
Min. Exp. Level—m_2	1.0	1.0	1.0	2.6	2.6	1.0

Journal Added to
Insertion Schedule
in Order of Selection

First	15	3	3	3	3	3
Second	15	3	3	3	3	3
Third	3	15	15	15	15	15
Fourth	3	15	15	15	15	15
Fifth	9	10	10	6	10	9
Sixth	9	10	10	6	10	9
Seventh	24	6	24	24	6	1
Eighth	6	—	24	24	—	6

Average Contribution
of Journal per
Dollar Cost—p_j

Journal 1	—	—	—	—	—	0.31
Journal 3	0.41	0.56	0.48	—	0.56	0.58
Journal 6	0.13	0.29	—	—	0.26	0.17
Journal 9	0.33	—	—	—	—	0.32
Journal 10	—	0.39	0.34	—	0.39	—
Journal 15	0.54	0.50	0.44	—	0.51	0.53
Journal 24	0.26	—	0.32	—	—	—

* A journal weight of 1.0 was used for all journals in Run 5.
† Thousands of Dollars.

observations. The results appear reasonable and yet not obvious, especially if the insertion order and p_j values are considered. Sensitivity analysis with the parameters indicates that none are redundant; they all affect the insertion schedule. Experience with the program on an IBM 7090 computer indicates that the model would be practical even with a sample size of several hundred and a larger schedule. Execution time for each run was under five seconds.

CONCLUSION

POMSIS is intended to help the industrial advertiser attack a common media problem. It provides a disaggregative yet practical approach. The ambition of a normative model is often to suggest concepts as well as to make available specific machinery. POMSIS is no exception. It is hoped that by focusing on disaggregative exposure probabilities, segmentation, multiple exposures, and journal effects, POMSIS can help provide the framework for better decisions.

REFERENCES

AGOSTINI, J.-M. How to Estimate Unduplicated Audience. *Journal of Advertising Research*, Vol. 2, No. 4, December 1962, pp. 11-14.

BASS, F. M. AND R. T. LONSDALE. An Exploration of Linear Programming in Media Selection. *Journal of Marketing Research*, Vol. 3, No. 2, May 1966, pp. 179-188.

BOYD, H. W., H. J. CLAYCAMP, AND C. T. McCLELLAND. "A Practical Approach to Media Selection," in progress.

BROWN, D. B. AND M. R. WARSHAW. Media Selection by Linear Programming. *Journal of Marketing Research*, Vol. 2, No. 1, February 1965, pp. 83-88.

BUZZELL, R. D. *Mathematical Models and Marketing Management*, Boston, Mass.: Division of Research, Harvard University, 1964, pp. 77-111.

DAY, R. L. Linear Programming in Media Selection. *Journal of Advertising Research*, Vol. 2, No. 2, June 1962, pp. 40-44.

KOTLER, P. "Toward an Explicit Model for Media Selection. *Journal of Advertising Research*, Vol. 4, No. 1, March 1964, pp. 34-41.

MORAN, W. T. Practical Media Models—What Must They Look Like? In *Proceedings: Eighth Annual Conference*, New York: Advertising Research Foundation, 1962, pp. 30-38.

WOLFE, H. D., J. K. BROWN, G. C. THOMPSON, AND S. H. GREENBERG. *Evaluating Media*, Business Policy Study, No. 121. New York: National Industrial Conference Board, 1966.

ZANGWILL, W. I. Media Selection by Decision Programming. *Journal of Advertising Research*, Vol. 5, No. 3, September 1965, pp. 30-36.

Despite their giant-killing reputations among politicians, the mass media are not powerful and merciless defenders or destroyers of the good society. Their influence is, in most cases, less than overwhelming, never monolithic . . . and often inconsequential.

—BERNARD C. HENNESSY

.... Computer Applications

EDITOR: *I. J. Abrams*

SUBEDITORS: *Ronald E. Frank*
Paul E. Green
Charles Kadushin
Christopher Keith
David Montgomery

DENNIS H. GENSCH*

The Ad-Me-Sim model describes a decision system for selecting the appropriate media vehicles for a given advertising message. Five sets of weekly and cumulative outputs are used as criteria for determining which vehicles are most appropriate. The model also contains a heuristic subroutine that suggests appropriate media schedules when given the advertising goals of the user.

A Computer Simulation Model for Selecting Advertising Schedules

INTRODUCTION

Selection of the best set of national magazines and national television programs to communicate a firm's advertising message to present and potential customers is a many-faceted problem. Some variables influencing the media selection process are the availability of time or space in each media vehicle, the firm's budget, whom the firm wishes to reach with a given message, the value of each repeat exposure, the environment provided by the media vehicle, the quality of the advertising copy, and the discounted cost of running a selected media package. Consequently, formulation of the media decision problem by identifying the key variables and quantifying the

relationships between these variables is not a simple task.

Several research groups have attempted to find an optimal solution to the media mix problem by using a mathematical programming technique that follows a structured set of rules (algorithms) to guarantee an optimum solution. The most commonly used of these algorithmic approaches is linear programming [8, Chapter 5; 21; 24, pp. 190–209; 10, pp. 40–4; 15; 30, pp. 78–100; 17, pp. 34–41; 12, pp. 42–8; 7, pp. 83–8; 29, pp. 40–6; 2, pp. 179–88], integer programming [31, pp. 30–6], iteration or marginal analysis [16; p. 24], and dynamic programming [20, pp. 94–100; 19, 15–23].

A general criticism of the algorithm approach is the amount and kinds of simplifications of the "real world" needed to fit the complex problem into the rigid form

---

* Dennis H. Gensch is assistant professor, Graduate School of Business, University of Pittsburgh.

Journal of Marketing Research,
Vol. VI (May 1969), 203–14

of the algorithm and to keep the size of the problem small enough to fit the memory capacities of existing computers.

For most optimizing algorithms to function under this size restraint, aggregate data must be used to estimate the reading and viewing patterns of the audience.

The aggregate data sets are treated as homogenous sets. Each individual within a homogenous data set is assumed to have the same probability of reading and viewing exposures, the same response to each commercial, and the same probability of purchase and repurchase. None of the optimizing models known to this author have attempted to document the homogeneity of sets of individuals. In fact most research on this topic indicates that the common demographic groups used in reporting advertising exposure data are not homogenous groups [24, pp. 190–209]. If the optimizing model treats groups of individuals as homogenous in the dimensions just mentioned when the aggregate sets are really not homogenous, then the model is providing results inapplicable to a real world situation.

Other types of mathematical computerized models not as rigidly constrained as optimizing models are simulation and heuristic models. The two publicized media scheduling simulation models, the Simulmatics model [3; 28; 29, pp. 40–6] and Computer Assessment of Media (CAM) model [5], both have a serious problem in obtaining real data measurements for the simulated actions of their basic cells, i.e., what combinations of magazines and television shows does an individual with given sociodemographic characteristics actually watch.

Simulation models are basically descriptive models, with the major emphasis on describing and replicating the real world. Once a model is considered to adequately describe reality, it can be made normative by the addition of heuristic rules.

The normal procedure for testing the model's descriptive adequacy is first to have the internal logic structure approved by experts in the problem area, and second to run historical data through the model and compare the historical outputs with the model's outputs.[1]

Present advertising media selection theory is vague because many of the axioms needed to construct this theory are still being identified and investigated. The advertising industry does not agree on the best way to select a media package, i.e., combination of media vehicles over a specified time period, for a given product message. Ask five different advertising agencies to select a media package for the identical product message and probably not only will there be five different media packages suggested, but also five different procedures for selecting these media packages.

---

[1] For a more complete review of advertising media selection models, see [15].

DESCRIPTION OF THE MODEL

The particular *advertising media simulation* model developed by this author will be referred to as the AD-ME-SIM model.[2] This simulation approach defines a theory of how to send a message that will reach a defined target population through the most cost-efficient advertising form, and also reach this target population the desired number of times within a given time period.

Figure 1 provides an overview of the entire model, which has three stages of input data. The first stage generates data on the population's viewing habits and will be referred to as the data generation stage.

The second stage, the individual weighting stage, identifies the target population for the advertising message. Viewing by the target population is given greater value than viewing by the non-target population. This stage gives the individual weights associated with a given message for a particular product. Therefore, if only the media package is being changed and the same kind of message is aimed at the same target population, there is no need to run the second stage more than once.

The final stage of the model, the media evaluation stage, uses the data of viewing habits and the individual weights generated in the first two stages of the model. To these data are added the media planner's evaluation of the media vehicles, the types of advertising forms available, and the value of each successive exposure to the advertising message. With this information, the various combinations of media vehicles are evaluated by organizing all the data and judgments into a logical decision system.

Data Generation Stage

The data used by other proposed simulation models to estimate the population's reading and viewing patterns have been subject to severe criticisms about cost and reliability [16, 5].

By reviewing the efforts of the Simulmatics and the CAM models, the following criteria are reached for the input on reading and viewing patterns of the population:

1. The demographic, reading, and viewing habits must all come from the same individual.
2. The data must come from real individuals, not hypothetical or imaginary individuals.
3. The sample must be large enough to be significant on a national level.
4. The cost of gathering this data must be low enough to fall within the advertising agencies' budget.

At the present some professional data gatherers make the desired information available at a cost the agencies can afford. The two main sources of data are Brand Rating Research Incorporated and W. R. Simmons Associates, who supply computer tapes providing information on 16,000 and 20,000 individuals, respectively.

---

[2] The AD-ME-SIM model, using real world data, was developed in conjunction with the J. Walter Thompson advertising agency.

Figure 1
AD-ME-SIM MODEL

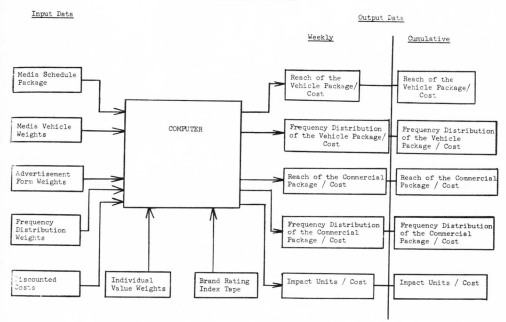

The reading and viewing preferences of each individual are listed with the individual's demographic characteristics. Because the reading and viewing preferences come from the *same individual,* it is possible to analyze accurately the duplication between various combinations of magazine and television vehicles.

The data used in developing the AD-ME-SIM model were supplied by Brand Rating Research Incorporated (BRI). They are a segment of their 1964 tape, consisting of 700 female heads of households. The original data are based on a fall "sweep" conducted in November and December, 1963. For each weekly magazine and weekly television program it is estimated, both by directly asking the individual and by such techniques as recall of articles within the magazine,[3] how many times over the last four issues or programs the individual read or viewed that particular magazine or show. For daily television programs, the individual identifies how many of the last 20 shows he has viewed. The tape gives information on about 200 television shows and 75 magazines by individual. This, for all practical purposes, includes all possible media vehicles an agency is likely to consider

in planning the television and magazine portion of a national advertising campaign.

This author feels that some attempt should be made to *predict* the population's reading and viewing preferences instead of merely running this year's media schedule against last year's data. The two months of actual data available from BRI can be used to establish basic weekly probabilities of viewing and reading for a year following the last month of actual data. The following procedure can be used to adjust the basic weekly probabilities for trend and seasonal influences and the effects of competitive viewing patterns.

The predicted probability value for each individual watching or reading a specific media vehicle in the given week is converted into a reading and viewing pattern by using a Monte Carlo system. For example, let the probability of a person watching a given show in a given week be 25 percent. Using this probability value, the computer generates a two-digit random number. If the random number is between 00 and 24, the person is said to have seen the show. If the random number is between 25 and 99, the person is said not to have seen the show.

---

[3] The exact sampling procedure is explained in detail in [5].

Figure 2

MATRICES REPRESENTING PREDICTED READING AND VIEWING PATTERNS

Individual 1

Week	Vehicle 1	2	3	....	274	275
1	0	0	2	....	0	0
2	1	0	2	....	0	0
3	0	0	3	....	0	1
4	1	0	4	....	0	0
.	.	.	.	....	.	.
.	.	.	.	....	.	.
.	.	.	.	....	.	.
.	.	.	.	....	.	.
.	.	.	.	....	.	.
.	.	.	.	....	.	.
51	0	0	5	....	0	0
52	1	0	5	....	0	0

Individual 2

Week	Vehicle 1	2	3	....	274	275
1	1	0	0	....	0	1
2	1	0	0	....	1	1
3	1	0	0	....	0	1
4	1	0	0	....	0	0
.	.	.	.	....	.	.
.	.	.	.	....	.	.
.	.	.	.	....	.	.
.	.	.	.	....	.	.
.	.	.	.	....	.	.
.	.	.	.	....	.	.
51	1	0	0	....	0	0
52	1	0	0	....	0	1

Individual 3

Week	Vehicle 1	2	3	....	274	275
1	1	0	4	....	1	0
2	1	0	5	....	1	0
3	0	0	5	....	0	0
4	1	0	4	....	0	1
.	.	.	.	....	.	.
.	.	.	.	....	.	.
.	.	.	.	....	.	.
.	.	.	.	....	.	.
.	.	.	.	....	.	.
.	.	.	.	....	.	.
51	1	0	4	....	0	1
52	1	1	5	....	0	1

The predicted reading and viewing patterns for each individual can be represented in a matrix of 52 rows and 275 columns. Each row will represent one of the 275 media vehicles (200 television shows and 75 magazines) from which media schedules can be selected, (see Figure 2).

For all television shows and magazines appearing weekly, a zero or one is placed in the matrix to show that a person either did or did not use a given media vehicle during a given week. Daily television shows have a matrix value ranging from zero to five. The zero-to-five value indicates the number of times per week the individual is estimated to view a given television show. The values for the daily shows are generated using the same Monte Carlo approach, with a discrete binomial distribution setting the ranges of the Monte Carlo numbers.

The basic probabilities obtained from the two months of BRI data are adjusted on a weekly basis to take into account the effects of trend, seasonal, and competitive influences before the Monte Carlo numbers are run through the system.

Presently the data used to estimate trend and seasonal influences come from analyzing historical data of these specific kinds of shows or magazines, i.e., estimating during what weeks and by what amount audiences of westerns or situation comedies tend to increase or decrease during the year.

Data on competitive television viewing comes primarily from syndicated information provided by TvQ. As one might guess, the more difficult prediction problems are in television, especially the new shows. Magazines have stronger trend lines and less seasonal variation that television shows. New television shows are extremely difficult to forecast, though past data can provide the forecaster with general constraints. For example, it is possible to predict that for a given target population a "good" quality western series will attract fewer viewers than a "good" quality detective series. Thus, a specific subjective judgment is necessary in new show forecasts. The quality of each new show must be judged by someone or some group.

The individual matrices are stored on a computer tape. As time passes and more current information becomes available, the computer tape should be updated. Subsequent data will reveal deviations from the initial predictions. When these deviations do not appear to be the result of chance alone, the Monte Carlo numbers should be recomputed using the more current information. The updating should be done at least monthly.

Individual Weighting Stage

The model's second stage attempts to identify the target population. Individuals the advertiser would most like his commercials to reach are given the higher individual weights. For example, a dog food manufacturer desires to weight the target population on the basis of past purchasing behavior. He assigns a weight of 10.00 to a person who owns a dog and purchases 30 cans of prepared dog food per month. He assigns a weight of 0.01 to the individual who does not own a dog and thus purchases no prepared dog food. This is the individual weight range. The entire target population is assigned weights within this range. It is then possible to compare the relative advantage of reaching an individual who purchased an average of 15 cans of dog food per month with reaching the individual who purchased 30 cans.

If more than one attribute of an individual is relevant to the weighting process, various methods for combining the importance of each attribute, such as a weighted geometric index, are available to the model user by calling the appropriate subroutine in the AD-ME-SIM computer program.

Media Evaluation Stage

Third is the decision stage of the model. At this time, the data inputs generated in the two previous stages are combined with additional judgment inputs, and the proposed media schedules are evaluated. Additional judgment inputs include: evaluation of the appropriateness of each media vehicle for the advertising message, evaluation of the relative merits of volume advertising forms (time, space, and use of color options available in presenting the advertising message), frequency distribution weights, and the discounted costs of the media vehicles selected.

The media vehicle appropriateness weight provides a means to state explicitly the commonly accepted theory that the program content, star performers, and editorial content elicit a positive or negative reaction from the audience which carries over to the audience's feeling toward the commercials presented on the show [11, 26].

To improve the accuracy of the estimated discounted cost, and at the same time save computer memory space and running time, the discounted cost for each week of the media schedule will be supplied directly by the model's user.

Evaluation Criteria Used by AD-ME-SIM Model. There are five sets of output:

1. The media schedule's vehicle reach
2. "   "   "   vehicle frequency
3. "   "   "   commercial reach

4. The media schedule's commercial frequency
5. "   "   "   impact units.

Each output is generated in static as well as cumulative form. The static output gives the values associated with the given week's media schedule. The cumulative output relates the weekly output to all past advertising undertaken in this advertising campaign.

The appendix shows the printout form of these evaluation criteria. In the 26th week of the given campaign, the vehicles used were 22 (prime time situation comedy) and 50 (daytime situation comedy); the ad forms used were 1 (60-second commercial) and 2 (30-second commercial), and the estimated discounted cost of using the specified ad forms in the indicated vehicles are stated on Page 1 of the output printout. The daytime comedy is shown five times per week, and the prime-time situation comedy is shown once per week. Page 2 prints out the five static or weekly outputs; Page 3 prints out the five cumulative outputs.

BRI estimated the number of female heads of households in the nation represented by each female head of household on the computer. In 1964, BRI estimated

Figure 3
FLOW CHART I

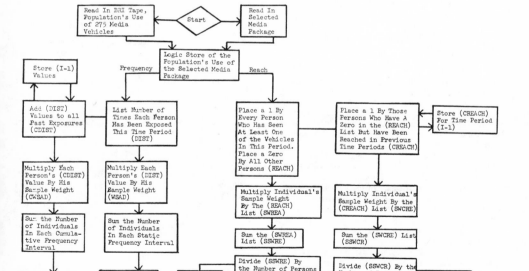

Figure 4
FLOW CHART II

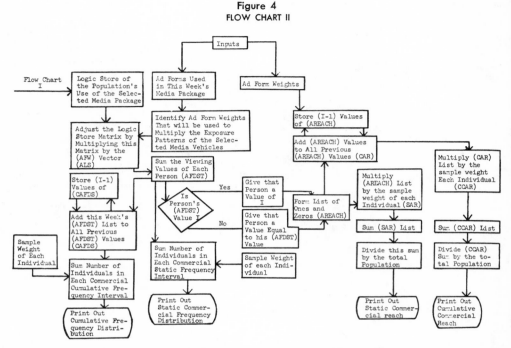

that there were 51,611,000 female heads of households in the nation. This is the number used in computing the percentage of the female heads of households reached (20,238,000 ÷ 51,611,000 = 39.11 percent) and the average number of exposures per female head of household rounded to the nearest integer (37,535,000 ÷ 51,611,000 = 1), (see Figure 3).

In the remainder of this article, each individual referred to in describing either the national population or the sample is a female head of household.

The number of individuals reached by a given set of media vehicles must be adjusted by the advertising form weights to estimate the number of individuals reached by the various commercials presented on these media vehicles. Thus the commercial reach and frequency distributions are printed out, (see Figure 4).

The last evaluation criterion is an abstract number used to represent the impact the given media schedule is estimated to have on the target population. In effect, the individual's reading and viewing exposures are adjusted to take into account the effects of the individual weights, the ad form weights, frequency weights, and the media appropriateness weights. The interaction of the basic vehicle exposure data with the judgment factors previously listed is quantified and reported in the form of abstract impact units.

The third page of the computer printout provides the values for the cumulative set of evaluation criteria. These values represent the reach, frequency, and impact attained by the entire advertising campaign over a 26-week period.

Note that the output data become "softer" as one moves down the list. The outputs shown in the appendix can be grouped under one of the five sets of evaluation criteria shown in Figure 1. With this array of outputs, an agency has several different criteria with which to evaluate a media schedule. As the agency's degree of confidence in their judgmental inputs increases, they will place more emphasis on the third, fourth, and fifth criteria.

CASE STUDY

Several products were used in testing the AD-ME-SIM model, including a nationally known soft drink, a nationally known canned dog food, and a regionally known dishwater detergent.

The judgments required by the AD-ME-SIM model must be made in relation to some given set of facts. Describing the development of an advertising campaign for canned dog food through use of the AD-ME-SIM model will increase the reader's understanding of how the model functions.

To concentrate attention on the workings of the computer model rather than delving into all of the subtleties of advertising the brand of canned dog food, a given description of the rationale for a media plan and a list of assumptions made in relation to this plan will be presented.

The following key facts summarize the marketing situation and objectives: the product is considered a mature product that has been advertised nationally for several years; the housewife is the prime purchaser of dog food; the copy will be directed at the housewife to keep her awareness and recognition of the brand name high; no new aspect of the product will be stressed in the copy; and the firm will spend $1.5 million on national television and national magazine advertising.

A committee consisting of men from both the agency and the dog food manufacturer reached the following judgments.

Individual Weights

The group decided to weight individuals by the amount of canned dog food they had purchased in the past. BRI provided this information using the following categories:

Weight	Past purchase behavior
.001	Do not use the product.
.033	Use the product less than once a month.
.066	Use the product once or twice a month.
.167	Use the product once a week.
.667	Use the product a few times a week.
1.000	Use the product daily.

Media Vehicle Appropriateness Weights

In compliance with the wishes of the BRI, the media vehicles will not be specified by name. Instead they will be identified by general classification, such as Dual Audience General "A," Newsweekly "A," or Situation Comedy "C." For magazines the committee was given the general classification and the cost of a one-page, four-color ad in that magazine. For daytime television the data consisted of the general classification, the show's audience rating, the vehicle's cost per thousand, and the cost of a 60-second commercial on the given vehicle.

A sample of the media vehicle weights is shown in Table 1.

Advertising Form Weights

To reduce the number of alternatives, the assumption was made that all commercials would represent the middle commercial on a television program. This restricted the number of commercials associated with a given television program to one. The two ad forms

Table 1
MEDIA VEHICLES, BY WEIGHT

Vehicle	Weight
Magazines	
Dual audience general A	.8
Newsweekly A	.3
Shelter A	.7
Women's service A	.6
Fashion A	.1
Miscellaneous B	.4
Daytime television programs	
Audience participation quiz A	.6
Daytime serials A	.7
Situation comedy A	.7
Five a week news A	.4
Nighttime television programs	
Situation Comedy D	.9
General drama A	.7
Audience participation quiz A	.6
Music A	.6

available for the middle commercial are the 60-second and the 30-second commercial.

Because the committee felt that there must be as much color as possible in the magazines, they ruled out the use of black and white ad forms. For magazines the two advertising forms under consideration were the full-page, four-color ad and the half-page, four-color ad.

The next step was to scale the ad form weights. The 60-second commercials were given a value of .90. This implied a judgment that 90 percent of the individuals viewing the television program would be exposed to a 60-second commercial presented in the middle of the show. The other ad forms were evaluated on the same basis. The following set of advertising form weights were obtained:

Ad form	Weight
60-second commercial	.90
30-second commercial	.67
Full-page, four-color ad	.50
Half-page, four-color ad	.30

The magazine ad forms were initially .30 and .20. These values were increased because it was estimated that the magazine would be re-read, but the television commercial would present only one opportunity for exposure.

Frequency Distribution Weights

The assumption made at the beginning of the discussion was that copy would be varied to keep the specific commercials fresh. The committee was not to be concerned with the wear-out factor of the copy. Instead they were to assign the frequency weights by determining the relative value of seeing the theme of the ad campaign for the first, tenth, etc., time within the six-month schedule.

The committee felt that *repetition* was the objective of

this campaign: constantly keep the brand name in front of the potential customer. The more frequently an individual was exposed to the ad, the better. Therefore, the set of cumulative frequency weights adopted are as follows:

Frequency interval	Frequency weight
1–10	1.00
11–20	1.05
21–30	1.10
31–40	1.15
41–50	1.20
⋮	⋮

This means that the cumulative frequency weight for each of the first ten exposures will be 1.00. The 11th to the 20th exposures will each receive a value of 1.05. This weighting system provides an increasing relative value for each additional exposure in step functions of 10 exposures each.

DEALING WITH UNCERTAINTY

The committee was uncertain about many of the exact media vehicle weights proposed. They wondered how the ranking of schedules might change if these or other factor weights were changed.

To test this, the committee proposed and ranked six alternative media schedules, each significantly different. The committee was confident that their ranking accurately represented real and absolute differences between the six schedules. The model then ranked the six schedules on the basis of vehicle exposures per dollar, commercial exposures per dollar, and impact units per dollar. The results are shown in the following tabulation:

Schedule	Ranked by committee	Vehicle exposure/ dollars	Com- mercial exposure/ dollars	Impact units/ dollars
1	1	1	1	1
2	2	2	2	3
3	3	3	4	4
4	4	4	3	2
5	5	5	5	5
6	6	6	6	6

The key factor that changed the rankings using commercial exposure per dollar and impact units per dollar was the ad form weights. In reviewing the ad form weights it was decided that these weights were rather high. Rerunning the six schedules with lower magazine ad form weights resulted in the same one-through-six ranking for all three criteria. These weights were changed from .50 and .30, to .35 and .15 respectively.

If the committee had insisted that the weights used were correct and the logical structure of the model was accurate, this would have implied that their subjective overall rating of schedules was not the logical consequence of their judgments on individual factor weights.

The committee attempted to observe the consequences of their uncertainty with respect to various factor weights. For the specific weights they designated ranges within which they were confident the particular weight would fall. The six schedules were rerun using first the maximum value of a given range and then the minimum value. Next, various combinations of maximum and minimum values for the different weights were run. Besides seeing the absolute differences in evaluating criteria, the committee was able to observe the relative difference in the ranking of the six schedules caused by changing the value weights. They were also able to observe how sensitive in both absolute and relative terms the scheduling decision is to a change in a particular weight or set of weights. For each different commercial message there will be a different mix of individual weights, ad form weights, media vehicle weights, and frequency weights. For each different mix the evaluation criteria's relative and absolute sensitivity to a given set of weights will change.

This exercise provided the committee members with some understanding of the implications of their uncertainty. The committee was able to determine how much uncertainty they were prepared to live with and when it would be worthwhile to conduct field research to narrow the range of possible weights for a specific factor.

EVALUATING PROPOSED MEDIA PACKAGES

The model now contained the experienced judgments of the advertisers indicating the relative values they placed on the factors they felt determined the effectiveness of the advertising campaign.

It was now possible to do two things. First, the advertisers could propose several alternative media schedules they considered desirable. The model evaluates and provides a relative ranking of the selected media schedules. The ranking would be multidimensional, based on the evaluation criteria discussed earlier.

A second use of the model would be to *generate* alternative media schedules by applying heuristic programming to the executive judgments placed in the model's data bank.

The advertisers initially proposed two separate schedules for evaluation. The first schedule heavily emphasized prime-time television, some daytime shows, and limited magazine advertising. The second schedule emphasized magazines, had the same number of daytime shows, and some prime-time television. Both media schedules ran for 26 weeks, and the estimated cost of each was approximately 1.5 million dollars. Using the model to evaluate the two schedules over the 26 week period, Schedule 1 was found to be superior, (see Table 2).

Sensitivity tests were run on the two schedules to determine *why* Schedule 1 was receiving better ratings. Results of a series of sensitivity tests indicated that the ad forms used were a key variable. The tests also indicated that television seemed to be generating a higher number of impact units per dollar than magazines.

With this information, the committee proposed a third schedule that emphasized the 30-second commercial over the 60-second commercial and increased the amount of television by reducing the magazine advertising. There was a substantial improvement.

Instead of proceeding further with trial and error search, the committee decided to look at some media schedules which the model could generate through use of a heuristic program.

HEURISTIC PROGRAM

The heuristic program ran each media vehicle for one month and recorded the number of impact units generated per dollar. The 275 media vehicles were ranked on the basis of impact units per dollar. The media vehicle ranked first was used as often as possible within the physical and judgmental constraints imposed. After the first ranked media vehicle had been used as often as possible, the second ranked media vehicle was used as often as possible. This process continued until the advertising budget was exhausted.

A physical constraint prevents the model from suggesting strategies that would be impossible to carry out in the real world, such as scheduling weekly ads in a monthly magazine. Besides physical constraints, some judgmental constraints are also imposed to increase the usefulness of the heuristic program. For example, one might decide to go beyond the physical constraints and further limit the number of times a given media vehicle can be used. This would provide suggested media schedules containing more diversified selection of individual media vehicles.

The first media schedule proposed by the model was run as an entity for the full campaign period. The values were recorded and stored. The heuristic program then generated a second alternative schedule by deleting the two media vehicles (with the lowest rank) in the preceding media schedule and inserting in their place the two media vehicles with the highest rank from those vehicles not already in the proposed media schedule.

This process continues to generate and evaluate media schedules until three successively generated schedules fail to improve the initial schedule. Improvement is defined as generating more impact units per dollar than the previous schedule.

The schedules are run and compared as entities because of the numerous interactions between sets of variables. In testing, it became evident that the media schedule whose individual media vehicles have the highest individual sum of values often *does not* produce the media schedule with the highest values. The sum of the parts is not always equal to the value of the whole. The heuristic program generated three schedules. Figure 5 shows the values achieved by these three schedules.

All three heuristic schedules obtained better results than the previous alternatives. The major difference be-

Table 2
COMPARISON OF SCHEDULES 1 AND 2

Criteria	Schedule 1	Schedule 2
Vehicle reach	94.83%	94.64%
Commercial reach	91.77%	91.55%
Commercial frequency distribution		
0	8.23%	8.45%
1–10	26.25	50.33
11–20	21.17	7.06
21–30	11.30	8.75
31–40	8.68	7.01
41–50	5.33	5.80
51–60	6.37	3.09
61–70	2.33	2.49
71–80	3.10	2.89
81–90	1.79	1.37
91–100	5.47	3.13
Cost per thousand impact units: $6.85		$9.85%

tween the heuristic schedules and Executive Schedule 3 was the ratio of prime-time to daytime television. The executive schedule called for two dollars' worth of prime-time television for every dollar's worth of daytime television. The heuristic programs called for roughly three dollars' worth of daytime television for every dollar spent on prime-time television. After examining the suggested heuristic programs, the committee ran several media schedules that were modifications of Heuristic Schedule 1. They eventually selected one of these modified schedules.

VALIDATION

The procedure this author will use in attempting to verify the AD-ME-SIM model is to apply internal verification to all aspects of the model and *wherever possible* to apply external verification. Where it is not possible to apply external verification, the model builder should indicate *why* it is not possible.

A committee of media experts at the J. Walter Thompson advertising agency examined the assumptions underlying the model and the logical structure of the model. It was their judgment that the assumptions and logical structure correspond to their view of reality.

It should be possible to verify externally the estimated vehicle reach and vehicle frequency distribution, the first two criteria of the AD-ME-SIM model. In the model's initial construction, a segment of the 1964 BRI tape was used. Predictions of the reading and viewing patterns of the AD-ME-SIM model could not be matched to the patterns that actually occurred in 1965 because 1965 information was not available. This author is now working with Alfred Kuehn in an attempt to refine further the prediction techniques used by the model and to validate an entire year's predicted vehicle exposures. The problem is to get individual viewing data for weeks

Figure 5

CUMULATIVE COST AS DETERMINED BY
THREE HEURISTIC SCHEDULES

Cumulative cost per
thousand impact units

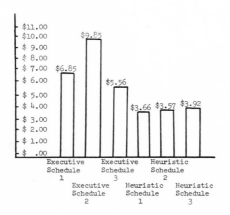

other than those in the fall and winter "sweeps" of BRI and Simmons. Prediction and validation of individual vehicle exposures will be aided immensely when BRI, Simmons, and any other professional data collectors conduct the spring and summer sweeps presently under discussion at these firms.

At present this author is not aware of obtainable data that provide an accurate measurement of the commercials actually watched and the ads actually read by the 16,000 individuals in the sample. If these data can be obtained, it should be possible to verify externally the third and fourth criteria values of the AD-ME-SIM model in much the same manner used on the first and second criteria values.

All segments of the AD-ME-SIM model have been internally validated by one group of media experts. The predicted vehicle exposure segment can and is being externally validated. The commercial exposure segment can, theoretically, be externally validated, but this is not presently being done because of a lack of real world data that measure commercial exposures. The segment of abstract impact units cannot be externally validated.

The ability to predict individual vehicle exposures within defined and narrow confidence intervals would be a contribution having considerable value to the advertising industry outside the context of the AD-ME-SIM model. Using the predicted data in context with the rest of the AD-ME-SIM model, estimates of audience duplication and repeat exposures could be made without resorting to crude formulas. The present method for estimating audience duplication is to use duplication formu-

las. It has been demonstrated that duplication formulas give very inaccurate estimates when the number of vehicles considered approaches ten, or when the media vehicles are not of the same general type, i.e., all must be women's magazines, or when other variables are changed from the case situation on which the formula is based [9, pp. 21–5; 13, pp. 21–8; 18, pp. 30–3; 22, pp. 26–9]. The AD-ME-SIM model counts the exposures for all 275 media vehicles by individual by week and thus needs no duplication formula.

Work on predicting individual exposures and then counting these exposures for a given media schedule appears to be a more rewarding course of research than deriving and attempting to keep current formulas for all combinations of 275 vehicles. The same argument applies to methods of estimating repeat exposures.

LIMITATIONS OF THE AD-ME-SIM MODEL

There is real danger that a computerized mathematical model will appear to be more powerful and capable than it really is, especially when the model is being described by its author. Past experience with quantitative models that have been oversold by their developers has already retarded the acceptance of quantitative aids in the advertising field. Therefore, let us be perfectly clear that the AD-ME-SIM model *will not guarantee* selection of the *best* media schedule.

The present state of the art does not recognize any one set of measurements, variable relationships, or evaluation criteria as correct and superior to any other sets. Lacking defined absolute standards, *no* quantitative model can truly purport to select the best *absolute* schedule.

Many readers might object to the data or judgments used in the dog food example, arguing that better data exists or that other judgment values should be used. Yet, who is to say by what method we are to know *the* best set of data and judgments to use in evaluating media schedules for dog food commercials. The AD-ME-SIM model allows each model user to use the data and judgment *he thinks* best represents reality.

At present, the AD-ME-SIM model is limited to television and magazines. Because of the relatively long lead times required by these two media in relation to the lead times required by spot television, radio, newspaper, and other forms of advertising, many advertisers make the basic television and magazine commitments and then, at a later time, fill in this basic schedule with spot TV, radio, and newspaper as they see fit. The AD-ME-SIM model is currently being expanded to include spot television.

CONCLUSION

The AD-ME-SIM model recognizes the uncertainty, because a lack of objective data and definitive theory, with which the advertising media scheduler must work. It does not purport to eliminate uncertainty by using a computerized algorithm. Empirical data gathering and testing is the way to truly reduce uncertainty.

Rather the model attempts to provide a *logical framework* through which a model user tries to work with uncertainty and to understand its implications. A series of sensitivity tests indicate in both absolute and relative terms the consequences of uncertainty on the evaluation criteria used by the media scheduler. Based on these test results, the media scheduler can decide *where* empirical research would be most beneficial in each case.

APPENDIX

PRINTOUT OF EVALUATION CRITERIA

Page 1

Media Package Selected for Week 26 Vehicle	Cost	Ad Form
22	18040	2
50	17625	1

Page 2

Results of package for week 26
Total cost = 35665
Total number of people reached = 20,238,000
  cost per thousand = 1.76 dollars
Percent of total population reached = 39.11 pct.
Total number of exposures = 37,535,000
  cost per thousand = 0.95 dollars
Average number of exposures per person = 1

Vehicle frequency distribution

Number of exposures	Frequency	Percent of population
0	31506000	60.89 pct.
1	13293000	25.69 pct.
2	2178000	4.21 pct.
3	1516000	2.93 pct.
4	1273000	2.46 pct.
5	1622000	3.13 pct.
6	356000	0.69 pct.
7	0	0.00 pct.
8	0	0.00 pct.
9	0	0.00 pct.
10	0	0.00 pct.

Ad form adjustment for number of people reached = 17924150

  cost per thousand = 1.99 dollars
Ad form percent of population reached = 34.62 pct.
Ad form adjustment for total number of exposures =3347150

  cost per thousand = 1.07 dollars
Ad form adjustment of average number of exposures
  per person = 1

Result of package for week 26

Ad form frequency distribution

Number of exposures	Frequency	Percent of population
0	32365617	62.65 pct.
1	14919697	28.88 pct.
2	1606657	3.11 pct.
3	1162373	2.25 pct.
4	609600	1.18 pct.
5	997057	1.93 pct.
6	0	0.00 pct.
7	0	0.00 pct.
8	0	0.00 pct.
9	0	0.00 pct.
10	0	0.00 pct.

Value of media package in impact units = 3759373
cost per thousand = 9.49 dollars

Page 3

The same format used for reporting the weekly results on Page 2 (above) is used again in reporting the cumulative results on Page 3. The only difference is that the cumulative frequency distribution intervals are ten-unit rather than the one-unit intervals used in the static frequency distributions. (See Table 2 for illustration of ten-unit intervals.)

REFERENCES

1. J. M. Agostini, "Analysis of Magazine Accumulative Audience," *Journal of Advertising Research*, 2 (December 1962), 24–7.
2. Frank M. Bass and Ronald T. Lonsdale, "An Exploration of Linear Programming in Media Selection," *Journal of Marketing Research*, 3 (May 1966), 179–88.
3. Alex Bernstein, "Computer Simulation of Media Exposure," *A Report of the Sixth Meeting of the ARF Operations Research Discussion Group*, New York: Advertising Research Foundation, 1961.
4. John Bower, "New Audiences of U. S. and Canadian Magazines: Seven Tests of Agostini's Formula," *Journal of Advertising Research*, 3 (March 1963), 13–20.
5. Brand Rating Research Corporation, "The Brand Rating Index Report on Consumer Preferences for Major Brands," New York: March 1964.
6. Simon R. Broadbent, "A Year's Experience of the LPE Media Model," *Proceedings*, 8th Annual Conference, New York: Advertising Research Foundation, October 2, 1962.
7. Douglas B. Brown and Martin R. Warshaw, "Media Selection by Linear Programming," *Journal of Marketing Research*, 2 (February 1965), 83–8.
8. Robert D. Buzzell, *Mathematical Models and Marketing Management*, Boston: Division of Research, Graduate School of Business Administration, Harvard University, 1964.
9. J. M. Caffyn and M. Sagovsky, "Net Audiences of British Newspapers: A Comparison of the Agostini and Sainsbury Methods," *Journal of Advertising Research*, 3 (March 1963), 21–5.
10. Ralph L. Day, "Linear Programming in Media Selection," *Journal of Advertising Research*, 2 (June 1962), 40–4.
11. *Effect of Media Context on Advertising, The*, a study conducted by *Life Magazine*, 1963, pamphlet.
12. James F. Engel and Martin R. Warshaw, "Allocating Advertising Dollars by Linear Programming," *Journal of Advertising Research*, 4 (September 1964), 42–8.
13. Fred L. Engelman, "An Empirical Formula for Audience Accumulation," *Journal of Advertising Research*, 5 (June 1965), 21–8.
14. Dennis H. Gensch, "Mathematical Computer Models Used

in Advertising Media Selection," *Journal of Marketing Research*, 5 (November 1968), 376–86.

15. L. M. Godfrey, "Media Selection by Mathematical Programming," Speech at New York Chapter, New York: The Institute of Management Sciences, October 10, 1962.

16. P. I. Jones, *The Thompson Medals and Awards for Media Research, 1965*, Kent: Tonbridge Printers, 1966.

17. Philip Kotler, "Toward an Explicit Model for Media Selection," *Journal of Advertising Research*, 4 (March 1964), 34–41.

18. Walter Kuhn, "Net Audiences of German Magazines: A New Formula," *Journal of Advertising Research*, 3 (March 1963), 30–3.

19. John D. C. Little and Leonard M. Lodish, "A Media Selection Model and its Optimization by Dynamic Programming," *Industrial Management Review*, 8 (Fall 1966), 15–23.

20. Richard B. Maffei, "Planning Advertising Expenditures by Dynamic Programming Methods," *Industrial Management Review*, 1 (December 1960), 94–100.

21. Herbert Maneloveg, "A Year of Linear Programming Media Planning for Clients," *Proceedings*, 9th Annual Conference, New York: Advertising Research Foundation, October 1963.

22. Marc Marcel, "Net Audiences of French Business Papers: Agostini's Formula Applied to Special Markets," *Journal of Advertising Research*, 3 (March 1963), 26–9.

23. William Massey, Ronald E. Frank, and Thomas M. Lodhal, "Are Purchasing Habits, Demographics, and Personality Related?", *A Report of the Ninth Meeting of the American Research Foundation Operations Research Discussion Group*, New York, 1963.

24. D. W. Miller and M. K. Starr, *Executive Decisions and Operations Research*, Englewood Cliffs, N. J.: Prentice-Hall, Inc., 1960, 190–209.

25. William T. Moran, "Practical Media Models: What Must They Look Like?", Speech at Midwest Conference, Chicago: Advertising Research Foundation, November 1962.

26. *The Rochester Study*, sponsored by *The Saturday Evening Post*, 1960, pamphlet.

27. *Simulmatics Media-Mix 1, General Description*, Simulmatics Corporation, February 1962.

28. *Simulmatics Media-Mix, Technical Description*, Simulmatics Corporation, October 1962.

29. Stanley F. Stasch, "Linear Programming and Space-Time Considerations in Media Selection," *Journal of Advertising Research*, 5 (December 1965), 40–6.

30. Clark W. Wilson, "Linear Programming Basics," *Proceedings*, 8th Annual Conference, New York: Advertising Research Foundation, October 1962, 78–100.

31. Willard I. Zangwill, "Media Selection by Decision Programming," *Journal of Advertising Research*, 5 (September 1965), 30–6.

Operations Research

January–February 1969

A MEDIA PLANNING CALCULUS

John D. C. Little

Massachusetts Institute of Technology, Cambridge, Massachusetts

and

Leonard M. Lodish

University of Pennsylvania, Philadelphia, Pennsylvania

(Received January 18, 1968)

A convenient on-line computer system selects and schedules advertising media. The system consists of a market-response model, a heuristic search routine, and a conversational input-output program. The user supplies a list of media options, a budget, and various objective and subjective data about the media options and the desired audience. The system selects a set of options and schedules them over time, seeking to maximize total market response.

The model of market response works as follows: The population is divided into market segments. People in each segment are characterized by their sales potential and media habits. Ads placed in the media options lead people to be exposed to the advertising. The pattern of exposures in each market segment is determined by media coverage and duplication data. People tend to forget exposures and so the retained exposure level decays in the absence of new advertising. The response of an individual, in terms of the fraction of sales potential realized by the advertiser, increases with exposure level but with diminishing returns. Total market response is a sum over people, market segments, and time periods. The calculation of response is based on analytic formulas that are computationally very efficient.

A maximum-seeking, heuristic calculation starts with any schedule, adds options with a high increment of response per dollar and deletes options with a low increment per dollar until no more improvement can be found for the given budget.

An on-line system, called MEDIAC, permits the use of model and heuristic at a remote console of a time-shared computer. Communication with the computer is conversational and largely self-explanatory. The system is operational. Computing costs have been a fraction of a per cent of the cost of the media scheduled. Improvements over previous schedules, as calculated by the model from the user's input data, have run from 5 per cent to over 20 per cent.

1

A N ADVERTISER buys space and time in advertising media to tell prospective customers about his product. He normally hopes that the information in his advertisements will lead people to buy his product and that they will become satisfied customers. He presumably intends the extra sales generated to yield a net profit.

The role of media in advertising, therefore, is to convey messages to prospects. Media are chosen in the course of constructing an advertising plan, the steps of which include: (1) setting the budget, (2) identifying the audience, (3) picking the advertising message, (4) preparing the copy treatment, and (5) selecting the media. The steps are not independent. Message, copy, and media all depend on the audience to be reached. Budget sets the scale of the whole operation. However, once budget and audience characteristics are set, the questions of message and copy can be fairly well separated from the question of how to expose the audience to the messages efficiently. Only the media question will be taken up here, although the other planning steps affect our formulation, because provision must be made for give and take between media selection and the rest of the plan.

The media planning problem may be stated as follows: Given a set of media options, a budget, and various data about the media and the audience to be reached, which options should be used and when should they be used in order to maximize profit or some related measure of performance? By a media option we ordinarily mean a detailed specification of the place, position, size, and other outward characteristics of an advertisement, but not the message and copy treatment. Why is the media problem challenging? Because of the multiplicity of seemingly reasonable choices usually available, because of the complexity of advertising phenomena, and because of the quantity of media decisions that must be made.

Our goal is to build a media model that will increase advertising productivity. This requires that the model lead people to make better media decisions; it requires the model to be economical to use; and it requires that the model be, in fact, used.

To establish that the model will increase productivity is difficult. Certain of the required inputs will be subjective. Many aspects of the advertising effectiveness process are poorly understood. The most satisfactory test of validity would be to predict outcomes (e.g., sales) and compare them with actual results, but the inherent variability in sales and the problem of relating sales to advertising when other marketing variables also affect response make this difficult.

Considering these obstacles, perhaps we should give up, at least until the underlying processes are better understood. Media planners obviously do not have this option. They must do something sensible with the information they have. Furthermore, they have to do this in the midst of day-to-day pressures. The important questions then are: Can we isolate the most relevant phenomena for media planning, can we put them together into a consistent structure, and can we link the media planner to the structure in a practical way? We claim the answers are yes.

Our final product will be called a media planning calculus. By a 'calculus' we mean a system of numerical procedures for transforming data and judgments into a schedule. The model supplies the structure, the user supplies the data and judgments, and the computer supplies the muscle.

What then are some of the facts and phenomena essential to media selection? The main purpose of media is to deliver messages to potential customers efficiently. Relevant to this are at least the following ideas:

1. *Market segments* for classifying customers,
2. *Sales potentials* for each segment,
3. *Exposure probabilities* for each media option in each segment,
4. *Media costs.*

Advertisers spread their campaigns over time. Why? One reason is that the effect of advertising tends to wear off. This is demonstrable; VIDALE AND WOLFE,[1] for example, display data showing the effect. Another reason is that advertising is often considered most valuable near the time of purchase, and people enter and leave the market continuously. Implicit in both these reasons is the idea that people tend to forget past exposures. In addition, both sales potential and media-exposure probability may vary with time of year. Therefore, we add the following phenomena:

5. *Forgetting* by people exposed to advertising,
6. *Seasonality* in product potential and media audience.

A recurring concern in making advertising decisions is the effect of diminishing returns. A person has only so much ability to buy a product. After some point, further advertising to him will be wasted. The phenomenon has been amply observed in practice; see, for example, BENJAMIN AND MAITLAND.[2] The diminishing returns effect is one part of the more general phenomenon of customer response. We conclude that any media selection model should consider:

7. *Individual response* to exposure, including the effect of diminishing returns.

Media planners and media data services frequently pay considerable attention to audience duplication; see, for example, METHERINGHAM.[3]

Discussion often centers around reach and frequency. The reach of a media schedule is usually defined as the fraction of people who are in the audience of at least one vehicle of the schedule. Frequency is defined as the average number of times a person is in the audience of a schedule, given that he is in the audience at least once. In terms of advertising objectives, however, more important than a person being in the audience is his actual exposure to the advertising message. We wish to consider the more basic information of how many people receive zero exposures, one exposure, two exposures, etc., and further how these are spread over time. This information is needed to assess the expected response of the various individuals in the audience and so deduce the response of the market as a whole. Therefore, we take into account:

8. The *distribution of exposures* over people and over time.

Finally, provision must be made for putting the exposures from different media options onto a common basis; i.e., it must be possible to assign relative values or weights to exposures in each option. This is always done implicitly in designing a media schedule; in a formal model it is done explicitly. We therefore add consideration of:

9. *Exposure value* for the exposures in each media option.

These, then, are minimum specifications of data and phenomena to include in a useful media model. More could be added. However, these are already more than are ordinarily used now. Most media planning is rather macroscopic, with principal attention going (perhaps quite rightly) to audience potential and simple efficiency measures like cost per thousand, sometimes with a side investigation of reach. We want to show how more phenomena can be handled with greater ease than these usually are today.

To be productive, a model must be used. To be used it should be readily available and inexpensive to operate. Modern time-shared computers with remote on-line terminals make this possible. They permit immediate access to the computer, English language communication, user-instructing programs, and low cost per use. In our system, the media planner supplies data for his own problem and he or his staff runs it. He can think about his problem at the terminal, asking questions of the model and making changes in the schedule in a problem-solving dialog.

To summarize, our goal is productivity; our approach is to set up a structure embodying the principal phenomena relevant to media selection and, through time-shared computing, make it easy and inexpensive to use. We cite the following reasons for believing that this approach will be productive. The computer is an enthusiastic clerk. Given a model, it can evaluate many more alternatives within reasonable time and cost limits than can people. A computer can handle complexity with ease, e.g., local media mixed with national media across several market segments. Changes are easy to make; therefore, there can be give and take between media selection and the rest of the advertising planning process. Sensitivity analyses can easily be made; i.e., data and assumptions can be changed to see whether they appreciably affect the outcome. This is advantageous because much advertising data is surrounded by uncertainty and controversy. The model is flexible and permits trying out a variety of assumptions. Perhaps most important, however, a model provides a unified structure for organizing the central issues of the problem. Requirements for data and judgments are defined. Criteria are chosen and consistently applied. This seems certain to bring forth better data, more careful judgments, and more relevant criteria.

The remainder of the paper is divided into the following sections: (1) literature review, (2) model, (3) optimization, (4) data considerations, (5) the on-line system, and (6) discussion. For ease of presentation the model section is further subdivided into (1) exposure concepts, (2) market response, (3) exposure arithmetic, (4) budget constraint, (5) end effects, and (6) the mathematical program.

1. LITERATURE REVIEW

THE LITERATURE on mathematical models for media selection starts about 1960, although as early as 1946 BANKS[35] developed an incremental analysis of media that contained a number of key ideas. In 1960 a simple, hypothetical media problem was formulated as a linear program by MILLER AND STARR.[4] Soon after came the major pioneering work on linear programming models done jointly by BBDO and CEIR. Descriptions of this may be found in WILSON[5] and BUZZELL.[6] The linear programming approach has been further discussed by DAY,[7] ENGEL AND WARSHAW,[8] STASCH,[9] and BASS AND LONSDALE.[10]

In all published examples of these linear programs, the objective function is linear in the number of exposures. This implies that the value of ten exposures to one person is the same as that of one exposure to each of ten people. Such an assumption does not seem reasonable, particularly at high levels of exposure, where additional exposures are ordinarily believed to have less value than previous ones. The effect of linearity on the solution is that the most efficient medium for generating exposures will usually be bought until some upper limit is reached, then the next most efficient will be bought until its limit is reached, and so on. Upper limits must be provided to prevent unreasonable schedules. However, this starts to look similar to picking a schedule without a model, except for the important point that the methods are systematic and explicit.

To get away from strict linearity, diminishing returns and other forms of market response were introduced. KOTLER,[11] for example, presents a nonlinear model. In an unpublished paper reporting on the BBDO-CEIR work, GODFREY[12] outlines a method of dealing with certain types of nonlinearities. Wilson[5] refers briefly to a method, and presumably it is the same one. More recently, BROWN AND WARSHAW[13] have published essentially the same thing. The basis of this method is a standard device for converting a nonlinear program into a linear one in the case that the objective function is separable (i.e., is the sum of functions, each of a single variable) and, for a maximization problem, concave (i.e., the functions are linear or show diminishing returns, but never increasing returns). All three of these nonlinear models have a serious drawback in that the nonlinearities of each medium are separate. Thus, a person's increase in response from seeing an ad in *Life* is the same whether he has seen zero, one, or ten ads in some other magazine. It would seem more reasonable to expect diminishing returns with total exposure.

Several further difficulties beset most of the above formulations. First, the timing of the insertions over the planning period is usually ignored, or at least set outside the model. Exceptions are Godfrey[12] and Stasch[9] who propose to allocate over time by introducing additional variables and additional constraints. Once again, however, the borderline between setting the constraints and setting the schedule tends to blur. The next difficulty is that the treatment of audience duplication is usually weak or nonexistent. Finally, a linear program permits variables to take on fractional values, whereas the number of insertions must always be an integer.

ZANGWILL[14] suggests handling the integrality problem by using integer programming, but the current state of the art in this field is not encouraging for problems of the size encountered in media selection. Furthermore, as in many of the models, Zangwill's evaluation of the effectiveness of a media choice is done almost entirely outside the model. While this may be said to offer great flexibility, much of the appeal of a model lies in having it synthesize the effectiveness of a schedule out of events that are happening at the consumer level.

Recently, CHARNES, COOPER, DeVOE, LEARNER, AND REINECKE[15] have introduced LP II, a successor to Mediametrics. Time is considered, although not forgetting. Audience duplication is brought in under the assumption of independence between media. The objective function is a weighted combination of the magnitudes of differences between target and actual values of a set of goals. The goals might include target frequencies in each market segment and more complex quantities such as 'reaching 85 per cent of the kth audience segment at time t_1.' In the examples shown, the schedule is penalized for exceeding a goal as well as for not reaching it. The choice of goals and their weights is made by the user.

Another major line of attack on media selection is microsimulation, i.e., the following of individuals through time in their media actions. An early model of this type was built by the SIMULMATICS CORPORATION.[16] The output was patterns of exposure without evaluation or optimization. MORAN[17] reports a simulation model but gives little detail. BROWN[18] and GENSCH[19] do not include time effects but do treat people individually.

The virtue of microsimulation is its potential comprehensiveness. Many phenomena can be put into the model with comparative ease. This is a mixed blessing, since the problems of model construction and testing, data gathering, and computer running time go up rapidly as detail increases. There is a danger that much of the computer time will be spent pursuing issues not really central to the decision at hand. A difficulty inherent in the simulation of individuals is that of attaining sample sizes large enough for adequate evaluation of a schedule, particularly when the schedule contains media vehicles with small audiences. Furthermore, the search for improved schedules tends to become expensive because each separate schedule evaluation may take considerable computing time. Partly for this reason, the search for improvement is frequently left outside the computer.

The discussion so far has centered on work done in the United States. Work done in England goes back in time as far or further, has generally taken different directions, and has been of excellent quality. LEE AND BURKART,[20] TAYLOR,[21] LEE,[22, 23] and ELLIS[24] have developed a series of models motivated especially by print media. Several of the models were stimulated by problems arising at British European Airways and have been applied there. These models are much more explicit in their treatment of exposure probabilities and individual response to exposure than those previously mentioned. Under certain sets of assumptions, easily applied rules for optimal media selection are worked out mathematically. In the more complicated models, which take into account market response over time, the optimization is left as an integer programming problem.

BEALE, HUGHES, AND BROADBENT[25] describe the London Press Exchange model for media schedule assessment. This is a major model brought to the point of practical application. The authors call their model a simulation, but it is perhaps fair to say that much of their computational efficiency can be traced to clever circumvention of straight simulation. The model is flexible, computable, and has been built around a considerable base of data. One notable lack is any treatment of the effect of time; there is, for example, no forgetting. The search for schedule improvement is outside the computer, although provision is made for multiple simultaneous schedule evaluations.

There are at least two reported French media models. STEINBERG, COMES, AND BARACHE[26] present a model of expected response to advertising exposures. The distribution of exposures is obtained by simulation and assumes independence of exposure opportunities. BERTIER AND DU JEU[27] develop a careful simulation of the distribution of exposures from a schedule of print media.

We relate the present work to our earlier paper.[28]   The model there incorporates nonlinear response, market segmentation, and forgetting, and is optimized by dynamic programming. However, the latter becomes computationally prohibitive with more than one or two market segments. FRANZI[29] has investigated separable programming methods for optimizing the model, but the problem of fractional solutions remains, and in the present paper we have moved away from exact optimization to heuristic methods.

A key technical innovation of the present model is a new method of calculating expected response.   Response is expanded as a power series in exposure level.   Expected response then becomes a weighted sum of the moments of the exposure-level distribution.   It is shown that the first two moments (the most important ones) require only readily available and easily manageable media coverage and duplication data.   As a result, the calculation of expected response is very efficient.   By comparison, if expected response were obtained by simulating individuals and averaging over them, the calculation might take a hundred or a thousand times as long for the same accuracy.   The speed of the basic calculation is used to gain two important advantages: First, it permits a maximum-seeking search over thousands of possible schedules and, second, it makes an on-line system feasible because answers to moderately-sized problems can be obtained in a short time.

There exists a variety of commercially secret or otherwise incompletely published work.   We are aware of some of it, but obviously cannot adequately review it.   We would be glad to have the opportunity.

2. MODEL

THE MODEL may be described briefly as follows: The population is divided into *market segments*.   People in each segment have their own *sales potential* and media habits.   A media schedule consists of *insertions* in *media options*.   An insertion brings about *exposures* to people in one or more market segments.   The exposures serve to increase the *exposure level* of individuals in the segment.   However, people are subject to *forgetting* and so the retained exposure level decays with time in the absence of new exposures. The *response* of individuals in a market segment increases with exposure level but with diminishing returns at high levels.

2.1 *Media, exposure levels, and forgetting.* To lay out the dimensions of the problem, let

M = number of media options under consideration.

T = number of time periods in the planning horizon.

S = number of market segments.

$x_{jt} = \begin{cases} 1, & \text{if an insertion is made in option } j \text{ in time period } t, \\ 0, & \text{if not.} \end{cases}$

Thus, our ultimate goal will be to set the values of the x_{jt} for $j = 1, \cdots, M$ and $t = 1, \cdots, T$.

We define several terms: A *media class* will be a general means of communication, such as television, magazines, or newspapers. A *media vehicle* will be a cohesive grouping of advertising opportunities within a class, such as a particular TV show, magazine, or newspaper. A *media option* will be a detailed, purchasable unit within a vehicle. Examples would be: a commercial minute in *Bonanza*, a 4-color full page in *Look*, and a half page in the Sunday *New York Times*. A *media insertion* will be a specific purchase of an option and includes specification of the time period of use. A collection of insertions over a planning period will be a *media schedule*.

It is assumed that a media option: (1) is available exactly once in every time period, (2) has substantial continuity of audience, and (3) has continuity in outward format. These assumptions are for conceptual convenience and are not really very restrictive. For example, if an option cannot be available in some time period, the corresponding x_{jt} can be permanently set to zero. If the media planner wishes to permit multiple insertions of the same type in one time period, multiple media options, all alike, can be created. As much detail can be included in the specification of an option as desired; for example, a geographic area can be stipulated. Several options can be grouped together and listed as one, provided that their audiences do not appreciably overlap. Ultimately the suitability of an option depends on whether the cost, exposure, and value data described below can be provided for it.

Exposure of an individual to an insertion is taken to mean that the person has perceived the presence of the ad. A number of operational measures of exposure have been developed, different measures often being appropriate for different classes of media. The particular measures to be used in a given application are selected by the media planner.

Exposure or nonexposure of an individual to an insertion is a random variable. Consider a particular person in market segment i. Let

$$z_{ijt} = \begin{cases} 1, \text{ if the person in segment } i \text{ is exposed to an insertion in media} \\ \quad \text{option } j \text{ in period } t, \\ 0, \text{ if not.} \end{cases}$$

The probability distribution of z_{ijt} is determined by media exposure probabilities and by whether or not an insertion has been made. The arithmetic of this will be taken up below. We have been tacitly assuming that the population of interest is composed of individuals. However, for certain applications, some other basic response unit may be more appropriate and, if adopted consistently, can be used without difficulty.

We next recognize that exposures in different media options should often be assigned different values or weights. One reason is format differences. A larger ad may convey more information. (A larger ad may be more likely to be noticed too, but that effect is covered under exposure probability.) Other reasons are differences in editorial climate, mood, and reader involvement. For example, some media vehicles are thought to be supportive for certain products. An important reason is differences between media classes: An exposure to a 30-second radio spot is to be rated on the same scale as an exposure to a half-page newspaper ad. At present, there is a large subjective element in such appraisals, but any final media schedule, however arrived at, implicitly includes such an evaluation.

The exposure weighting can be a bridge to other parts of the advertising plan. For example, the relative value of exposures in different media may be affected by the proposed communications task and copy opportunities. Thus, if a capacity for demonstrating the product is important, television would rate high. If accurate color reproduction is desirable, certain magazines would be good.

Exposure value may also differ somewhat from market segment to market segment. This seems particularly likely if market segments are defined by sex, education, or life style. Certain types of ads are routinely designed to appeal to special groups and may have much less effect on others. If such information is known in advance, it can be reflected in exposure value. Let

e_{ij} = exposure value (weight) for an exposure in media option j going to a person in market segment i (exposure value/exposure).

We must emphasize that exposure value is a property of the exposure itself and has nothing to do with cost, audience size, or exposure probability within the audience. For different options, exposure value answers the question: Given the choice of a person seeing an ad in *Life* or the same person seeing it in *Look*, does the advertiser have any preference and, if so, what is a numerical statement of that preference? For different market segments, the question is: Given that a man sees an ad in *Sports Illustrated* and that a woman sees it there, should a different weight be assigned to the exposure?

The units for exposure value are arbitrary except that they must later be tied to a response function. It is frequently convenient to conceive of an 'average' media-option–market-segment combination and assign it an exposure value of 1.0. Values for other options and market segments are then assigned relative to this.

Exposure is assumed to increase a desirable quantity that will be called, simply, the *exposure level* in an individual. The amount of the increase in time period t is the weighted sum of the exposures from the insertions in the period, the weights being the exposure values.

$\sum_{j-1}^{j-M} e_{ij} z_{ijt}$ = increase in exposure level of a particular individual in market segment i in time period t (exposure value/capita).

We suppose that the effect of advertising wears off because of forgetting. Specifically, it is assumed that, in the absence of new input, exposure level decreases by a constant fraction each time period. Let

y_{it} = exposure level of a particular individual in market segment i in time period t (exposure value/capita).

α = memory constant: the fraction of y_{it} retained from one time period to the next, $0 \leqq \alpha < 1$.

Then

$$y_{it} = \alpha y_{i,t-1} + \sum_{j-1}^{j-M} e_{ij} z_{ijt}. \qquad (1)$$

For empirical evidence on retention and decay, *see* ZIELSKE[30] and SIMMONS.[31] If desired, the memory constant can be permitted to depend on i and t and perhaps other factors. A typical pattern of y_{it} over time might appear as in Fig. 1.

For future reference, we note that (1) can be rewritten as

$$y_{it} = \alpha^t y_{i,0} + \sum_{s-1}^{s-t} \sum_{j-1}^{j-M} \alpha^{t-s} e_{ij} z_{ijs},$$

or, going back indefinitely, as

$$y_{it} = \sum_{s-\infty}^{s-t} \sum_{j-1}^{j-M} \alpha^{t-s} e_{ij} z_{ijs}. \qquad (2)$$

In this form, we see that the exposure level at any point in time is a weighted sum of past exposures, with ever smaller weights being attached to ever more remote exposures. If an 'average' exposure has been assigned the value 1.0, then exposure level may be described as the number of average exposures retained at a given point in time.

2.2 *Market response.* Market response is treated as follows: Each individual has a sales potential. Sales potential varies with market seg-

ment and may also be seasonal. The fraction of sales potential realized
by an advertiser in a time period depends in a nonlinear way on the person's exposure level in that time period. Exposure level varies from individual to individual within a market segment and is described by a probability distribution. Total market response is synthesized by adding up
over individuals, market segments, and time.

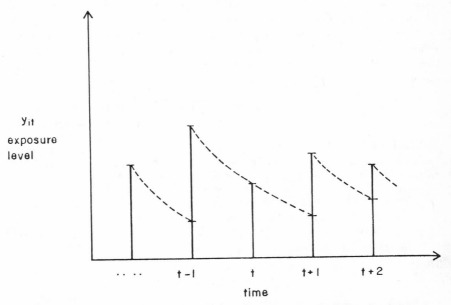

Fig. 1. Exposure level, y_{it}, over time for some indidivual. Jumps
represent new exposures for the time period. Dotted lines indicate forgetting between time periods.

Specifically, let

n_i = number of people in market segment i,

w_{it} = sales potential (weight) of a person in segment i in time period t
(potential units/capita/time period),

$r(y_{it})$ = response function: the fraction of potential realized when a person
has exposure level y_{it},

$f_{it}(\cdot)$ = probability density of y_{it}.

The response function $r(y)$ might appear as in Fig. 2. Let E denote the
taking of expected values. Then $w_{it}E\{r(y_{it})\}$ is the average realized sales
potential per person in market segment i at time t. Summing, we obtain

$$R = \sum_{i=1}^{i=S} \sum_{t=1}^{t=T} n_i w_{it} E\{r(y_{it})\} \qquad (3)$$
$$= \text{total market response (potential units)}.$$

The specific curve to be used for $r(y)$ will depend on the planner's judgment, and the empirical evidence available to him. Presumably the curve should show diminishing returns at high exposure levels. Some people feel that, at least in certain cases, the curve should show increasing returns at low levels. Others disagree; SIMON,[32] for example, argues that there is no empirical evidence to support increasing returns. A simple, versatile function with only diminishing returns is

$$r(y) = r_0 + a(1 - e^{-by}), \qquad (0 \leqq y < \infty) \quad (4)$$

where r_0, a, and b are nonnegative constants specific to the product at hand. However, our work is not restricted to this curve. Conceivably, a differ

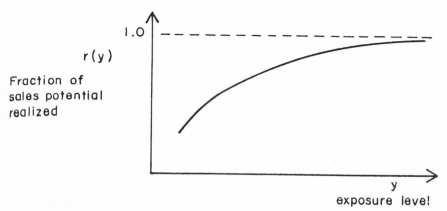

Fig. 2. Possible response curve: The average fraction of an individual's sales potential realized by the advertiser as a function of the person's exposure level.

ent function $r_{it}(y_{it})$ could be used for each i and t, but, until evidence dictates otherwise, it seems best to reflect differences between market segments and time periods simply by using sales potential as a scale factor.

The units of sales potential have not been specified. We personally tend to think of response in terms of an anticipated sales rate. Then, if sales are expressed in dollars, w_{it} has units of dollars/capita/time period and R is the expected total dollar sales to the market over the planning period. In allocating a fixed budget, however, only the shape of the response curve and the relative values of the sales potentials determine the allocation. The absolute units of the w_{it} are immaterial. Some media planners prefer to express sales potentials in arbitrary units. They feel they have a good idea of relative potentials but not of absolute potentials.

The expected response $E\{r(y_{it})\}$ for a given market segment and time period can be expressed in terms of the moments of the distribution $f_{it}(y_{it})$.

Usually only the first few moments will be needed to give a good approximation to the expected response. This will turn out to be quite convenient. For notational simplicity, we drop the subscripts i and t for the present. Let

$$\mu = E\{y\} = \text{mean of } y,$$
$$\mu_n = E\{(y-\mu)^n\} = n\text{th moment of } y \text{ about the mean}, \qquad n > 1.$$

We can expand $r(y)$ in a Taylor series about μ:

$$r(y) = r(\mu) + \sum_{k=1}^{n-1} (1/k!) r^{(k)}(\mu)(y-\mu)^k + (1/n!) r^{(n)}(y_1)(y-\mu)^n, \quad (5)$$

where $r^{(k)}(\mu)$ is the kth derivative of $r(y)$ evaluated at $y = \mu$ and y_1 is some value between y and μ. Taking expectations:

$$E\{r\} = r(\mu) + \sum_{k=2}^{n-1} (1/k!) r^{(k)}(\mu)\mu_k + (1/n!) E\{r^{(n)}(y_1)(y-\mu)^n\}. \qquad (6)$$

In practice, we would take some number of terms as our approximation and use the last term on the right to estimate the degree of approximation. Suppose, for example, we use the exponential response of (4), and retain terms through the third moment. Then (6) becomes

$$E\{r\} = r_0 + a(1 - e^{-b\mu}) + ae^{-b\mu}\{-(\tfrac{1}{2})b^2\mu_2 + (\tfrac{1}{6})b^3\mu_3\} + \epsilon_4, \qquad (7)$$

where $\epsilon_4 = -(\tfrac{1}{24})aE\{e^{-b y_1} b^4 (y-\mu)^4\}$, and $|\epsilon_4| \leq (\tfrac{1}{24})ab^4\mu_4$, since, at most, $e^{-b y_1} = 1$, and we know $(y-\mu)^4 \geq 0$.

Before leaving the response model, we observe that its conceptual generality can be broadened considerably without adding complexity. Referring back to (3), we do not have to assume that everyone in a market segment actually has the same sales potential, w_{it}, nor that everybody at exposure level y responds to the same degree, $r(y)$. The quantity w_{it} can be interpreted as the average sales potential per capita in the market segment. Similarly, $r(y)$ may be viewed as a conditional expectation, i.e., the average fraction of potential realized for a group of people having the exposure level y. Both sales potential and the fraction realized may be viewed as random variables without change in (3) if they are independent. If there is a basis for believing that sales potential and the fraction realized are not independent, then this basis can be used to subdivide the market segment into more homogeneous groups.

The empirical status of our construct of retained exposure level deserves comment. We do not conceive of exposure level as a directly observable property of an individual. Perhaps something close to it is observable and, if so, this would be very helpful. Quite likely, however, the communications process and the state of the individual involves a complex of quantities. If such is the case, they are deliberately aggregated here into a single index. Even if exposure level is not observable, the model can still, in principle, be tested empirically. Exposures are defined operationally. The sales potentials and exposure values are prespecified numbers. Therefore, if a behavioral measure of response (say, sales) is selected, it is possible to measure inputs and outputs and fit the model to data or test it against data. Essentially we would have a problem in nonlinear regression. The difficulties in doing this are substantial, and we base our claim of utility on different grounds, but the idea remains a worthwhile possibility.

To summarize up to this point, our model deals with exposures which are assigned weights, and create an exposure level, but are gradually forgotten. The exposure level determines the fraction of a person's sales potential that is realized. Averaging over people and summing over market segments and time periods gives total response. Response can conveniently be expressed in terms of the moments of the exposure-level distribution.

2.3 *Exposure arithmetic.* Our next job is to express the moments of the distribution of exposure level in terms of the media decisions, x_{jt}. The general plan is as follows: It will be shown that the mean and variance of exposure level depend only on the exposure probabilities of media singly and in pairs. Higher moments will be related to the first two. Therefore, the moments of the distribution can be calculated from exposure probability data that are not too difficult to gather and store. The exposure probabilities themselves will be developed in terms of the probability that a person is in the audience of the medium, the probability he will be exposed given that he is in the audience, and an audience seasonality factor.

Consider, for the moment, a single market segment and a single time period. We can then temporarily drop the corresponding subscripts i and t and simplify notation. Let

$$y = \text{exposure level of a particular individual,}$$
$$z_j = \begin{cases} 1, & \text{if the individual is exposed to option } j, \\ 0, & \text{if not,} \end{cases} \qquad (8)$$
$$y = \sum_{j=1}^{j=M} e_j z_j.$$

This expression appears to omit from y the carryover of exposure level from the previous time period, but carryover is a weighted sum of previous exposures, and just adds more terms to the sum. Let

$$p_j = P(z_j = 1) = P(\text{a person is exposed to option } j),$$

$$p_{jk} = P(z_j = 1, z_k = 1) = P(\text{a person is exposed to both option } j \text{ and option } k).$$

Thus p_j is a rating-points type of measure based on exposures, not just audience. The p_{jk} express the pairwise duplications. The mean of y is simply

$$E\{y\} = \sum_{j=1}^{j=M} e_j p_j. \qquad (9)$$

The second moment of y is

$$E\{y^2\} = E\{(\sum_{j=1}^{j=M} e_j z_j)^2\} = \sum_{j=1}^{j=M} \sum_{k=1}^{k=M} e_j e_k E\{z_j z_k\}$$
$$= \sum_{j=1}^{j=M} e_j^2 p_j + 2 \sum_{j=1}^{M-1} \sum_{k=j+1}^{k=M} e_j e_k p_{jk}, \tag{10}$$

or, letting $V(\cdot)$ denote variance,

$$V(y) = \sum_{j=1}^{j=M} e_j^2 p_j (1-p_j) + 2 \sum_{j=1}^{M-1} \sum_{k=j+1}^{k=M} e_j e_k (p_{jk} - p_j p_k). \tag{11}$$

Equations (9) and (11) give us $\mu = E(y)$ and $\mu_2 = V(y)$, the first two moments of y. An expression for μ_3 can also be developed and will involve three-way overlaps among media. More generally μ_n will involve n-way overlaps. High-order overlaps are expensive to collect and expensive to store in a computer. An alternative is to estimate higher moments from lower ones. For example, the first two moments can be used to determine the parameters of an analytical probability distribution such as the gamma or log normal. Then the higher moments are implied and readily deduced. So far, however, we have not found a distribution that is computationally convenient and also fits sufficiently well to live data. It appears to be fairly easy, however, to develop empirical expressions relating higher to lower moments.

Figure 3 shows plots of $\mu_n^{1/n}/\mu$ versus $\mu_2^{1/2}/\mu$ for $n=3$ and 4 based on multiple-way audience overlap data in magazines as reported by Simmons for 1966. To form a distribution of y from such data, we must specify a set of magazines, and, for each magazine, its e_j and exposure probability for readers. In Fig. 3, all e_j's and exposure probabilities have been set to one. Each plotted point comes from a distribution of y defined by a set of magazines. As may be seen, straight lines give a good fit in the range of the data. Since $\mu_n^{1/n}/\mu$ must go to zero as $\mu_2^{1/2}/\mu$ goes to zero, we have drawn a dashed line nonlinearly back to zero. Generally, it is assumed we can determine functions

$$\mu_n = \mu_n(\mu_2, \mu). \tag{12}$$

There is a useful way to increase the accuracy of the expected response calculation (6) after it has been truncated at any fixed number of moments. We observe, first, that the smaller the moments, the faster the convergence of (6), and, second, that a big contributor to the size of the moments is the block of individuals who receive no exposures (i.e., have $y=0$). Consider, therefore, the identity:

$$E\{r\} = E\{r|y=0\} P\{y=0\} + E\{r|y>0\} P\{y>0\}.$$

If we start out by calculating reach, $P\{y>0\}$, and work out the truncated

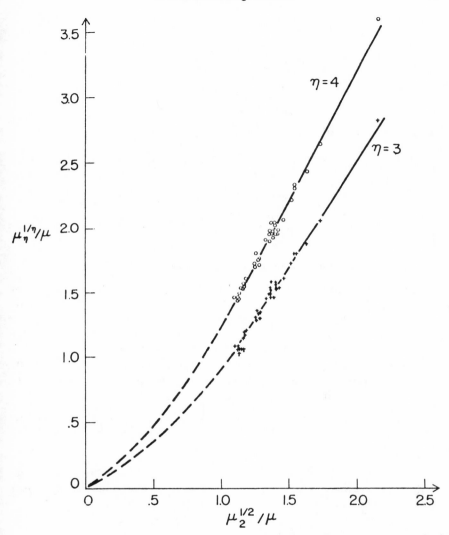

Fig. 3. Relating higher moments of the exposure level distribution
to the lower.

(6) for the population reached, i.e., $E\{r|y>0\}$, convergence will be speeded
up. Then it is straightforward to determine $E\{r|y=0\}P\{y=0\}$ and thence
$E\{r\}$.

Next we restore time-period and market-segment subscripts by the
following correspondences:

$$z_j \leftrightarrow z_{ijs},$$

$$e_j \leftrightarrow \alpha^{t-s} e_{ij},$$

$$y = \sum_{j=1}^{j=M} e_j z_j \leftrightarrow y_{it} = \sum_{s=-\infty}^{s=t} \sum_{j=1}^{j=M} \alpha^{t-s} e_{ij} z_{ijs},$$

$$p_j = P(z_j = 1) \leftrightarrow p_{j|it} = P(z_{ijt} = 1),$$

$$p_{jk} = P(z_j = 1, z_k = 1) \leftrightarrow p_{jk|its} = P(z_{ijt} = 1, z_{iks} = 1).$$

Then, using (9), (10), and (12), we obtain moments

$$\mu_{it} = E(y_{it}) = \sum_{s=-\infty}^{s=t} \sum_{j=1}^{j=M} \alpha^{t-s} e_{ij} p_{j|is}, \tag{13a}$$

$$\mu_{2it} = V(y_{it}) = \sum_{s=-\infty}^{s=t} \sum_{j=1}^{j=M} (\alpha^{t-s} e_{ij})^2 p_{j|is}$$
$$+ 2 \sum_{s=-\infty}^{t-1} \sum_{r=s+1}^{r=t} \sum_{j=1}^{j=M} \sum_{k=1}^{k=M} \alpha^{t-s} e_{ij} \alpha^{t-r} e_{ik} p_{jk|isr} \tag{13b}$$
$$+ 2 \sum_{s=-\infty}^{s=t} \sum_{j=1}^{M-1} \sum_{k=j+1}^{k=M} \alpha^{t-s} e_{ij} \alpha^{t-s} e_{ik} p_{jk|its} - \mu_{it}^2,$$

$$\mu_{nit} = \mu_n(\mu_{2it}, \mu_{it}). \tag{13c}$$

The media-exposure probabilities will be modeled further. Let

$g_{j|i} =$ *market coverage* of the media vehicle of option j in segment i, defined as the fraction of people in segment i who are in the audiences of the vehicle of option j, averaged over a year.

$s_{jt} =$ *audience seasonality*, the seasonal index for the vehicle of option j in time period t. Average value over a year is 1.0.

$h_j =$ *exposure probability for audience member*. The probability a person is exposed to an insertion in option j given that he is in the audience of the vehicle of j.

Recalling that x_{jt} is a zero-one variable indicating presence or absence of an insertion, we take

$$p_{j|it} = g_{j|i} h_j s_{jt} x_{jt}. \tag{14a}$$

This expression implicitly assumes that media-vehicle seasonality can reasonably be regarded as the same in all market segments and that h_j does not change seasonally.

Next, we want the duplication probabilities, $p_{jk|its}$. These will be modeled in two steps. First, let

$$p_{jk|its} = g_{jk|i} h_j h_k s_{jt} s_{ks} x_{jt} x_{ks}, \tag{14b}$$

where

$g_{jk|i} =$ *segment duplication:* fraction of people in segment i who are in the audience of both the vehicle of option j and the vehicle of option k averaged over a year.

Equation (14b) assumes again that the h_j are not appreciably seasonal and that the events of being exposed to option j and being exposed to option k are independent, *given* that a person is in the audience of both vehicles involved. (The events of being in the audience of one vehicle and being in the audience of another are, contrary to many media models, *not* considered independent.)

The task of developing empirical tables of $g_{jk|i}$, and storing them in a computer is formidable because of the dimensionality involved. Therefore, we have developed estimating methods based on more global data. Let

$f_{jk}=$ fraction of the total population who are in the audience of both the vehicles of j and k, averaged over a year.

$d_i=$ fraction of total population who are in segment i.

$\beta=$ an empirically determined constant.

Then we take

$$g_{jk|i}=K_{jk}(g_{j|i}g_{k|i})^{\beta}, \qquad (14c)$$

where

$$K_{jk}=f_{jk}/\sum_{i=1}^{i=S}(g_{j|i}g_{k|i})^{\beta}d_i.$$

The factor K_{jk} is a normalization constant that makes segment duplications add up to global duplication. A value of 0.65 has been developed for β by fitting to 1967 vehicle-segment data in magazines as reported by Simmons. This value and the formula (14c) have then been tested by predicting duplications in different magazines in different segments in a different year (1968). The results are shown in Fig. 4. The mean absolute percentage error is 10.7 per cent and the mean error is 1.7 per cent.

Implicitly, (14b) assumes that, aside from seasonality, the fraction of people who are in the audience both of vehicle A in January and of vehicle B in November is the same as the fraction who are in the audience of both vehicles in January (or November). This is probably a reasonably good assumption, but, in any case, we do not presently have any data one way or the other on the question.

2.4 Budget constraint. Let

$c_{jt}=$ cost of an insertion in media option j in time t (dollars/insertion).

$B=$ total budget for the planning period (dollars).

The budget constraint is

$$\sum_{j=1}^{j=M}\sum_{t=1}^{t=T}c_{jt}x_{jt}\leqq B. \qquad (15)$$

The constraint is shown as linear in the number of insertions. Published rates are considerably more complex than this, and, worse yet for planning, the prices of many purchases are negotiated. From a mathematical point of view, a difficulty with many published rates is that they are neither convex nor concave. This happens when the discount for quantity applies not only to all insertions more than a fixed amount but to all insertions.

Then the effective cost per insertion may be zero or nearly zero in some places. For example, if an advertiser has bought eight insertions and the discount break is at nine, he might be able to get the ninth free because the use of nine insertions makes him eligible for a discount on all nine. However, heuristic methods for dealing with discounts will be developed below based on successive uses of the constraint (15) with changing c_{ji}.

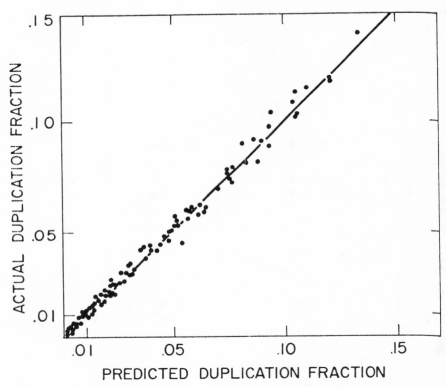

Fig. 4. Actual vs. predicted audience duplication fraction for various media pairs in various market segments.

2.5 *End effects.* The beginning and end of the planning period require special consideration. At the beginning, starting exposure levels must be specified. At the end we must find a way to evaluate advertising insertions whose effects extend beyond the planning period.

A simple and effective way to set starting exposure levels is to run the last few periods of the previous year's media schedule through the model. Ending levels for last year become starting ones for this year. Since this year's options almost always include last year's choices, the media data are readily available. If the whole previous year is run, we gain the added advantage of obtaining a comparison of the new schedule with the old under the criteria of the model.

At the other end of the planning period, we have a different problem. If we calculate response only over the planning period ($t = 1, \cdots, T$), we shall underrate the insertions during T because these also contribute to response in periods $T+1$, $T+2$, $\cdots$. Only if forgetting is very rapid or sales potential very small in periods right after T will there be no problem. A variety of approaches can be taken to correct the situation. A few extra periods can be added after T without scheduling more insertions. This solves the underrating problem but may introduce overrating as follows: The incremental response for adding an insertion in T is composed of an increment in T, another in $T+1$, another in $T+2$, etc. However, the amounts of these increments depend on the exposure levels in the time periods involved. For example, high exposure levels would mean small increments because of diminishing returns. With no new insertions after T, future exposure levels will be low and the response increments may be unnaturally large. This tends to produce an overrating of the insertions in T, although the effect can be kept under control by limiting the extra periods considered.

A better but more complicated method of handling this end effect is to add extra periods but also put a schedule of new insertions into those periods. The schedule might come from various sources, but, if we are dealing with an annual plan, the most appropriate further schedule is probably a repeat of the one the model is developing. This is a little tricky, but can be done. When an insertion is put in at t, it is also put in at $t+T$. In evaluating the incremental effect of that insertion, only its placement at t is considered. However, the incremental evaluation of an insertion at T will assume the presence of the earlier insertion at both t and $t+T$.

Notationally, the end effects will be treated as follows: Let

$E =$ the number of extra time periods added onto the end of the planning period for evaluating response.

$K+1 =$ the number of extra time periods added onto the beginning of the planning period to set starting exposure levels.

2.6 *Mathematical program.* The pieces of the model can now be pulled together and the media-selection problem presented as a mathematical program. We set up the case where the objective function involves the first n terms of the Taylor expansion (6) and end effects are treated by extending forward without new insertions. Provision is made for a set, I_1, of insertions that are required to be in the schedule and another set, I_2, required to be out.

MP. Find x_{jt} $(j=1, \cdots, M; t=1, \cdots, T)$ and maximal R subject to

$$R = \sum_{i=1}^{i=S} \sum_{t=1}^{T+E} n_i w_{it} \{ r(\mu_{it})$$
$$+ \sum_{m=2}^{m=n} (1/m!) r^{(m)}(\mu_{it}) \mu_{mit} \} \sum_{j=1}^{j=M} \sum_{t=1}^{t=T} c_j x_{jt} \leqq B,$$

$$\mu_{it} = \sum_{s=-K}^{s=t} \sum_{j=1}^{j=M} \alpha^{t-s} e_{ij} h_j g_{j|i} s_{js} x_{js},$$

$$\mu_{2it} = \sum_{s=-K}^{s=t} \sum_{j=1}^{j=M} (\alpha^{t-s} e_{ij})^2 g_{j|i} h_j s_{js} x_{js}$$
$$+ 2 \sum_{s=-K}^{t-1} \sum_{r=s+1}^{r=t} \sum_{j=1}^{j=M} \sum_{k=1}^{k=M} \alpha^{2t-r-s} e_{ij} e_{ik} g_{jk|i} h_j h_k s_{js} s_{kr} x_{js} x_{kr}$$
$$+ 2 \sum_{s=-K}^{s=t} \sum_{j=1}^{M-1} \sum_{k=j+1}^{k=M} \alpha^{2t-2s} e_{ij} e_{ik} g_{jk|i} h_j h_k s_{js} s_{ks} x_{js} x_{ks} - \mu_{it}^2,$$

$\mu_{mit} = \mu_m(\mu_{it}, \mu_{2it})$, $m = 3, \cdots, n$, $i = 1, \cdots, S$, $t = 1, \cdots, T+E$,

$x_{jt} \epsilon \{0, 1\}$ for all (j, t), $x_{jt} = 1$ for $(j, t) \epsilon I_1$, $x_{jt} = 0$ for $(j, t) \epsilon I_2$.

3. OPTIMIZATION

As a FORMAL mathematical program, MP appears to be rather intractable. It is integer and nonlinear. Practical problems are large; for example, we have already worked on problems involving twenty media options in ten time periods, or 200 zero-one variables. We have solved a deterministic version of the model in a one-market-segment problem by dynamic programming (see reference 28), but use of similar methods to solve MP does not appear reasonable.

Consequently, we have developed heuristic search methods to find schedules that are good, possibly optimal, but not necessarily guaranteed to be optimal. The basic maximum-seeking heuristic is simply that of adding to a schedule those insertions that produce a high increment of response per dollar and deleting those that produce a low decrement of response per dollar.

$HS1$: 1. Start with any schedule (e.g., an empty one).
2. For each insertion not now in the schedule, calculate the incremental response/dollar for adding that insertion. Find the insertion with the largest value and add it to the schedule.
3. Is the budget exceeded?
   No. Return to 2.
   Yes. Continue.
4. For each insertion now in the schedule, calculate the decremental response/dollar for removal. Find an insertion with the smallest value. Call it I. Is the decrement/dollar for I greater than or equal to the increment/dollar of the most recently added insertion?
   Yes. Go to 5.
   No. Delete I. Return to 3.
5. Finish.

The above search can be expected to work well when the available insertions are not too widely different in cost and their costs are relatively small compared to the total budget. Pathological cases can be constructed and further heuristics developed to counter them, but so far the simple procedure seems to be satisfactory.

Our confidence in the basic heuristic is based on several pieces of evidence. First, a deterministic problem solved exactly by dynamic programming was solved to the same solution by the heuristic. Second, the method has always given a better solution than anyone's preconceived idea of what a schedule should be. Finally there is a theoretical reason for expecting good solutions. The objective function will usually be a concave function in the decision variables. (This might not be the case if response is strongly S-shaped, but usually expected response will be well represented by a diminishing-returns curve.) Under these circumstances, a local maximum would be a global maximum if the decision variables were continuous. As it is, they are integral, but if individual insertion costs are small compared to the budget, the solution will be likely to behave as it would in the continuous case. The importance of knowing that a local maximum is likely to be a global maximum lies in the fact that our search only explores solutions (schedules) in the immediate neighborhood of the solution currently at hand, i.e., the search tests for a local maximum. Our argument suggests that, once a local maximum is found, it is unlikely that some other, quite different solution will be better.

Since media costs are discrete numbers, the cost of the final schedule will not ordinarily equal the exact budget. The search HS1 will give a schedule that slightly exceeds the budget. By dropping out the last insertion added, the schedule can be made to fall slightly below the budget.

Consider next the problem of media discounts. A useful heuristic is to introduce media at their least cost (highest discount). If they do not appear in the schedule under these conditions, they can rather safely be ignored. If they do appear, their costs can gradually be raised to whatever value actually applies. A formal procedure is as follows:

HS2: 1. Set all costs per insertion at their lowest incremental values, i.e., at the highest discount rate.

2. Solve the problem using HS1.

3. Exclude from further consideration all options not appearing in the schedule. Is the cost of each option entered at its actual average cost per insertion (including discounts) for the current schedule?

      Yes.   Go to step 5.

      No.   Continue.

4. Find the option with the largest discrepancy between the actual

average cost per insertion for the current schedule and the cost being used. For this option(s) put in the actual average cost. Return to step 2.

5. Finish.

The search is operated off-line except for Step 2. Visual inspection is often used to skip steps and save computing time. HS2 is probably not as good as IS1. The possibility of multiple local maxima seems intuitively more severe.

4. DATA CONSIDERATIONS

THE JOB OF supplying inputs is left to the user. Some people have claimed that, if they had all the needed data, the best schedule would be obvious. Experience contradicts this, but an important sidelight on the model is that users often gain valuable insights in the course of assembling the data. It is also true that gathering the inputs usually takes considerable effort. The purpose of this section is to indicate that the obstacles involved are surmountable, although we make no pretense of covering all situations.

A complete list of input requirements is given in the appendix. Certain items are straightforward. They have been developed many times before and the conceptual and measurement problems are minimal. In this category we put most market-segment data, e.g., definition, population, sales potential, and seasonality. In constructing sales potentials, it is well to remember the use to which the numbers are to be put. For example, if a branded product shows wide regional variations in level of distribution and this situation is fairly stable, a realistic sales potential for the model would be high where distribution is high, and low where distribution is low.

Media data that are reasonably straightforward include the list of media options, market-segment coverage for each vehicle, the cost per insertion, the probability of exposure to the option for a member of the audience of the vehicle, and audience duplication between pairs of vehicles. It is expected that audience duplication data may only be available for the total population, but, as previously indicated, it can usually be broken down by individual market segments through empirical estimating equations. Upper bounds on the number of insertions are generally the result of physical limitations on the number of issues, shows, etc., available in one time period. Policy restrictions may also enter. Ordinarily it seems desirable to let the model optimize freely without arbitrary constraints, but realistically these exist and, in addition, by permitting them in the model, one can test them for their effect on the solution.

Media and market-segment data are often pieced together from a variety of sources. One important source for consumer products is a national survey in which people are simultaneously interviewed as to demographic characteristics, product use, and media habits. National surveys, however, may yield rather small samples for individual market areas and for local or relatively rare, but possibly efficient, media. Sometimes a fruitful approach is to survey high-potential groups directly to uncover the media they use. Recently, a good deal of work has been done on clustering and nonmetric scaling. This may be quite helpful in defining meaningful market segments.

The more difficult inputs are the exposure values for the various media, the memory constant, and the individual response function.

The setting of the exposure values can be broken into three parts: (1) the setting of relative values among broad media classes, as TV, magazines, and newspapers; (2) an adjustment for individual vehicles or options within a media class, e.g., *Life*, *Look*, and *Newsweek*; and (3) an adjustment for market segment, e.g., men, women, and children. The latter two parts are usually handled judgmentally and often represent rather small adjustments. (Recall that exposure value has nothing to do with cost, exposure probability, or sales potential, but rather with whether it is preferred to have a person see an ad in one vehicle or another and whether it is thought that an exposure will have a greater effect on a person in one market segment or another in terms of increasing his per cent of potential realized.)

For setting relative values among media classes, an 'economic equilibrium' approach can be useful. First, a portfolio of media options is formed for each media class. The portfolio is a sample from the principal vehicles that advertisers use. Then, on the basis of some standard space unit for the class, e.g., black-and-white full pages in magazines, a cost per thousand exposures is calculated for the class. Next it is assumed that economic forces tend approximately to equalize the value obtained from different media classes when taken as a whole. Under this hypothesis, exposure value is proportional to the reciprocal of cost per thousand. Some class can be assigned the value 1.0 and then the values for other classes are calculated.

Notice that use of this method does not imply that all media classes will be equally attractive to a given advertiser. He will have his own circumstances, particularly with respect to market segmentation, sales potential, and media coverage of the segments. In addition, he may have special communications opportunities in a certain media class because of the particular needs of his product, and these may lead him to adjust the exposure value for the class.

With respect to the memory constant and individual response, a certain number of empirical studies have been published. Zielske[30] displays data on recall vs. time, as does a more recent Simmons report.[31] A BBDO booklet[33] summarizes several studies and gives a bibliography. Examples of published work displaying diminishing-returns phenomena are BENJA- MIN AND MAITLAND,[2] who measure the effect of advertising on sales, and ROHLOFF,[34] who measures pre-post brand-choice scores. These studies tend to support the basic concepts of the model and offer insight into the range of effects to be expected. When it comes to setting values for a specific application, we have generally found that media planners are able to make judgmental estimates of the needed quantities. To aid the process we have evolved a short series of questions about response. (See computer trace in Section 5.) The answers are then used to develop a response function. As with any other part of the input, if the user feels the values are known only within a range, he can make runs with different values to test the sensitivity of the results.

Some companies are fortunate enough to have performed field experi- ments that measure the effect of advertising exposures or expenditures on sales. Such measurements can be used to calibrate the model. The particular way of doing this will depend on how the experimental results are presented, but, to illustrate, suppose that the measurements indicate that a 10 per cent increase in advertising spending would result in a speci- fied sales increase and that a 10 per cent decrease in spending would pro- duce a specified sales decrease under the conditions of last year's media schedule. Then, using last year's schedule and all the model parameters except the response function, one can use the model to calculate exposure levels in each market segment and also levels 10 per cent higher and lower. Then the parameters of the response function can be determined so that the model-calculated results match the experimental values at the given points. When calibrated in this way, the model makes an allocation that is consistent with the company's best information about sales response.

5. MEDIAC: AN ON-LINE MEDIA SELECTION SYSTEM

THE MODEL and heuristics have been implemented on a time-shared com- puter. This permits a close interaction between user and model. In particular, the user obtains immediate on-line access from a remote termi- nal, English-language communication, and self-explaining operation. Working with the system on-line gives the media planner an intuitive feel for the behavior of the model and the selection process that is difficult to obtain otherwise. The model becomes not a mysterious black box, but a routine tool that acts in rather ordinary and expectable ways.

A major advantage of time-sharing is that an organization with rela- tively low total computer usage can gain access to a powerful machine without incurring the elaborate overhead in personnel, space, and cost that usually accompany big machines. The computer used for the example below is an SDS 940 at a commercial time-sharing firm.

We have called the on-line system MEDIAC. Its principal capabilities currently include: input, data storage, data alteration, schedule evaluation, schedule selection, and output. With respect to size, we have solved a problem with 24 media options, 10 time periods, and 15 market segments, and substantially larger problems are feasible.

MEDIAC presently uses an exponential response function of the form (4) with $r_0 = 0$. The a and b are fit to the answers from the response questions. Two moments are used in the Taylor series. Added accuracy is obtained by breaking off a block of population not reached, as discussed in the section on exposure arithmetic. End effects are treated by extending the planning horizon two periods and assuming that the schedule being developed will be repeated. The optimization heuristic presently adds insertions but does not delete them.

The operation of MEDIAC is best demonstrated by example. A sample problem is worked out in detail below. The problem involves four media, eight time periods, and two market segments. A summary of all input data is given in Table I. Detailed definitions of the data categories may be found in the Appendix. The data are completely hypothetical. (We had originally planned to show a problem whose output has been implemented but it would take up too much space.)

The transcript of the on-line computer session is shown in Table II. The system has a number of features not demonstrated here. For example, the data can conveniently be stored, changed, and printed out. A preliminary ranking of the media options can be made. It is based on using single insertions in isolation, and offers insight into why a schedule comes out as it does.

6. DISCUSSION

WE HAVE presented a calculus for selecting advertising media, i.e., a system of numerical procedures for transforming data and judgments into a media schedule. The goal has been to develop a tool for today, an improvement in the state of the art relative to present practice. Our calculus uses data that are available or procurable along with those judgments that seem essential to define a solution. The on line computer system is fast, easy to use, and inexpensive relative to the importance of the problem and other models of comparable scope.

There are some things the model is and some it is not. It *is* an allocation model; i.e., it takes a fixed budget and spreads it over time and market segments. It is *not*, however, a budgeting model. If market response is expressed as sales, the model appears to be capable of determining an optimal advertising budget. Such a use is unwarranted unless the model has been calibrated on sales response data. The reason is that although the allocation of a fixed budget depends on the shape of the re sponse curve, it will be fairly insensitive to modest changes and will be

TABLE I

Data for Sample Problem

PRODUCT: 'MINI-WIDGETS'

Budget: $350,000   Time periods: weeks (8)

Media options (4):	60-sec TV Program A	60-sec TV Program B	4-color page Magazine A	4-color page Magazine B
Cost/insertion	$18,000	$45,000	$26,000	$10,000
Exposure probability for audience member	0.4	0.4	0.5	0.3
Exposure value	2.0	2.5	1.5	0.75

Upper bounds: 1 insertion/period for each media option
Audience seasonality: none

Market segments (2):	Men over 20	Women over 20	Memory constant: 0.7	
Population (000)	45,000	50,000	% Potential Realized: at saturation	100
Sales potential ($/person/ week)	0.05	0.14	at 1 average exposure	50
			at 2 average exposures	70
Seasonality	none	none	at 3 average exposures	80
Initial exposure value	0	0		

Market coverage: Media vehicle duplication:

	Men	Women			TV A	TV B	Mag A	Mag B
TV A	0.01	0.12		TV A	0.030	0.020	0.030	0.020
TV B	0.25	0.18		TV B		0.110	0.070	0.020
Mag A	0.20	0.12		Mag A			0.060	0.020
Mag B	0.01	0.17		Mag B				0.080

completely insensitive to changes in scale factor. On the other hand, the optimal budget will be quite sensitive to such changes. For example, if the response function were multiplied by large constant, the allocation would not change but the optimal budget would change substantially.

We have in mind a number of extensions of MEDIAC. These include the effect of competitive advertising, the rub-off effect of other advertising by the same firm, and the possibility of certain synergistic effects. Undoubtedly, still others will be developed.

Experience with MEDIAC has been very encouraging. Several million dollars of advertising have been scheduled and implemented in the few months that the system has been operational. Although we have found

TABLE II

RUNNING THE SAMPLE PROBLEM ON-LINE AT A TELETYPE COMPUTER TERMINAL

```
 + PLEASE LOG IN: G3,A121,

   READY  11/11  20:02                     Lines marked + contain typing done by
 + -(G) (G2A011) /#INPUT/                  user. The rest was typed back by the
                                           computer (except for these explanatory
   TYPE NO. OF DOLLARS IN BUDGET,F9.       notes.)
 + 350000.,
   TYPE THE NO. OF TIME PERS,I3
 + 8,                                      User calls INPUT program to begin generat-
   TYPE NO. OF MKT SEGMENTS,I3             ing data bank. The computer asks for all
 + 2,                                      data needed. The F, I, and A letters refer
   TYPE NO. OF MEDIA,I4                    to input format.
 + 4,
    TYPE THE PERCENT OF POTENTIAL REALIZED
   AFTER COMPLETE SATURATION WITH EXPOSURES,F4
 + 100.,
   TYPE PERCENT OF POTENTIAL REALIZED
    AFTER   1AVERAGE EXPOSURES/CAPITA,F4.
 + 50.,
   TYPE PERCENT OF POTENTIAL REALIZED
    AFTER   2AVERAGE EXPOSURES/CAPITA,F4.
 + 70.,
   TYPE PERCENT OF POTENTIAL REALIZED
    AFTER   3AVERAGE EXPOSURES/CAPITA,F4.
 + 80.,
   TYPE NAME OF MKT SEG     1 A6
 + MEN...
   TYPE NO. OF PEOPLE,POTENTIAL FOR SEGMENT MEN...,2F9
 + 45000.,.05,
   TYPE NAME OF MKT SEG     2 A6
 + WOMEN.
   TYPE NO. OF PEOPLE,POTENTIAL FOR SEGMENT WOMEN.,2F9
 + 50000.,.14,
    TYPE MEMORY CONSTANT,F4.
 + .7,
   TYPE NAME OF MEDIA      1 A6
 + TVA...
   TYPE EXPOSURE VALUE,PROB. OF EXPOSURE,2F3.,OF TVA...
 + 2.0,.4,
   TYPE NAME OF MEDIA      2 A6
 + TVB...
   TYPE EXPOSURE VALUE,PROB. OF EXPOSURE,2F3.,OF TVB...
 + 2.5,.4,
   TYPE NAME OF MEDIA      3 A6
 + MAGA..
   TYPE EXPOSURE VALUE,PROB. OF EXPOSURE,2F3.,OF MAGA..
 + 1.5,.5,
   TYPE NAME OF MEDIA      4 A6
 , MAGB..
   TYPE EXPOSURE VALUE,PROB. OF EXPOSURE,2F3.,OF MAGB..
 + .75,.3,
   IF THERE IS NO MEDIA SEASONALITY,TYPE 1,OTHERWISE 2
 + 1,
   IF SEG. COVER. OF MOST MEDIA IS 0.,TYPE 1,ELSE2
 + 2,
   TYPE MKT. SEG. COVERAGE OF TVA... SEGMENTS
   MEN.WOME
   .XXX.XXX
 + .010.120
```

TABLE II—*Continued*

```
TYPE MRT. SEG. COVERAGE OF TVB... SEGMENTS
MEN.WOME
.XXX.XXX
.250.160
TYPE MRT. SEG. COVERAGE OF MAGA.. SEGMENTS
MEN.WOME
.XXX.XXX
.200.125
TYPE MRT. SEG. COVERAGE OF MAGB.. SEGMENTS
MEN.WOME
.XXX.XXX
.010.170
TYPE COST PER INSERT F6. FOR  TVA...
18000..
TYPE COST PER INSERT F6. FOR  TVB...
45000..
TYPE COST PER INSERT F6. FOR  MAGA..
26000..
TYPE COST PER INSERT F6. FOR  MAGB..
19000..
TYPE NO OF SEGS WITH SEASONAL POTENTIAL
0.
TYPE NO. OF CASES(PERIODS*MEDIA) WITH
UPPER BOUNDS NOT EQUAL TO ONE
0.
TYPEI IF DUPLS ARE AVAI, 2MEANS INDEPENDENC
1.
TYPE 1 IF DUPS ARE STORED,OTHERWISE 2
2.
TYPE DUPLICATIONS OF TVA... WITH
TVA.TVB.MAGAMAGB
.XXX.XXX.XXX.XXX
.030.020.030.020
TYPE DUPLICATIONS OF TVB... WITH
TVB.MAGAMAGB
.XXX.XXX.XXX
.110.070.020
TYPE DUPLICATIONS OF MAGA.. WITH
MAGAMAGB
.XXX.XXX
.060.020
TYPE DUPLICATIONS OF MAGB.. WITH
MAGB
.XXX
.080

*STOP*
```

The data bank for the problem is now created. It can be changed, printed out, discarded, or stored indefinitely as desired.

```
-GO (G2A011) /@MEDIAC/

TYPE 1 IF INITIAL EXPOSURES ARE ZERO,    OTHERWISE 2
1.
TYPE 1 FOR RANKING,OTHERWISE 2
2.
TYPE 1 IF SOME MEDIA HAVE ALREADY BEEN SELECTED,OTHERWISE 2
2.
```

The user calls for the MEDIAC main program which will develop a schedule from the above data.

Initial exposure zero would be appropriate for a new product.

TABLE II *Continued*

MAGA..	TIME PER	1	COST	26030.REALIZED POT.	1407.		The schedule is printed
MAGA..	TIME PER	6	COST	52000.REALIZED POT.	2529.		out as it is developed
MAGA..	TIME PER	3	COST	73000.REALIZED POT.	3767.		by the computer. MAGA is
MAGA..	TIME PER	1	COST	88000.REALIZED POT.	419.		best at first but dupli
MAGB..	TIME PER	5	COST	96000.REALIZED POT.	4571.		cation with itself and
MAGA..	TIME PER	2	COST	124000.REALIZED POT.	5712.		diminishing returns
MAGA..	TIME PER	7	COST	159000.REALIZED POT.	6567.		soon brings in other
MAGA..	TIME PER	2	COST	163000.REALIZED POT.	6939.		media which cover
MAGA..	TIME PER	4	COST	186000.REALIZED POT.	7996.		different people.
MAGB..	TIME PER	6	COST	196000.REALIZED POT.	8239.		
MAGB..	TIME PER	3	COST	206000.REALIZED POT.	6533.		
MAGA..	TIME PER	5	COST	232000.REALIZED POT.	9362.		
MAGB..	TIME PER	7	COST	242000.REALIZED POT.	9611.		
MAGB..	TIME PER	4	COST	253000.REALIZED POT.	9886.		
TV.....	TIME PER	1	COST	297000.REALIZED POT.	11399.		
TVA....	TIME PER	1	COST	315000.REALIZED POT.	11869.		
MAGB..	TIME PER	6	COST	325000.REALIZED POT.	12067.		
TVB...	TIME PER	6	COST	378000.REALIZED POT.	13073.		

MEDIAC GENERATED SCHEDULE

MEDIA	PER.	1	2	3	4	5	6	7	8		The schedule is heavy in
TVA...		X									the first period because
TVB...		X					X				initial exposure level
MAGA..		X	X	X	X	X	X	X			was zero.
MAGB..		X	X	X	X	X	X	X	X		

TYPE 1 FOR DETAILED O/P, ELSE 2
1,

SEGMENT	TIME. P	EX VAL/CP	SEG E.V.	REALIZED POTENTIAL		
MEN...	1	.43957	18431.	215.		The detailed output shows
MEN...	2	.43873	19743.	299.		level of retained exposure
MEN...	3	.45913	20661.	343.		value per capita, total re-
MEN...	4	.47342	21354.	368.		tained exposure value, and
MEN...	5	.48342	21754.	382.		total realized potential
MEN...	6	.74817	33308.	448.		for each segment in each
MEN...	7	.67814	38156.	466.		time period.
MEN...	8	.47127	21297.	401.		
MEN...	9	.32989	14845.	329.		
MEN...	10	.23092	10392.	254.		
WOMEN.	1	.40357	20179.	649.		
WOMEN.	2	.41053	20526.	862.		
WOMEN.	3	.41539	20770.	966.		
WOMEN.	4	.41880	20940.	1016.		Total time for the run in-
WOMEN.	5	.42119	21059.	1041.		cluding a data print out
WOMEN.	6	.60260	30130.	1151.		and media ranking not shown
WOMEN.	7	.54985	27492.	1204.		was less than 30 minutes
WOMEN.	8	.42307	21153.	1112.		at the terminal.
WOMEN.	9	.29615	14807.	917.		
WOMEN.	10	.20730	10365.	710.		

some people who do not want to quantify their media decisions, we have found a growing number who find the system a distinct aid. Improvements in the objective functions, as defined by the users, have ranged from about 5 per cent to 25 per cent relative to previous schedules. Some MEDIAC-computed schedules have looked much like previous ones; others have been quite different. In cases that have looked different, it has been possible to find out what data or phenomena have caused the change. So far the media planner has invariably preferred the new schedule.

How has the use of MEDIAC affected the way users think about their media planning decisions? Perhaps the most important contribution is the introduction of a relatively comprehensive problem structure. People often show a tendency to pick out one or two important issues of a problem and let these make the decision. The model leads people to look at many issues and ferret out information on all of them. The model then interrelates the information in a unified way. Usually, a relatively few numbers are in fact the key determinants of the decision, but not always are they the numbers thought in advance to be important

MEDIAC seems to move the intuitive approach of the media planner to a more productive level. More effort goes into formulating the problem than into trying to perceive the answer in one jump. Not that users automatically accept the model's answers; they test the answers against their intuition, dig into the model to find out what caused any discrepancies and, in the process, appear to be updating and enriching their intuition.

APPENDIX

MEDIAC INPUT

1. *Media characteristics:* Data needed for each media option.

    1. Name of option.

    2. Cost per insertion.

    3. Exposure probability for audience member. The probability a person is exposed to the particular ad in the vehicle given that he is in the audience of the vehicle.

    4. Upper bounds on insertions. The maximum number of times the media option can be used in each time period.

    5. Audience seasonality. The audience size for each time period for the media vehicle, expressed as an index with an average value of 1.0.

    6. Exposure value. Exposure value answers the following type of question: Given the choice of a person seeing an ad in *Life* or the same person seeing it in *Look*, does the advertiser have any preference, and, if so, what is the statement of that preference? It is usual to conceive of an average media option and assign it to a value of 1.0 and then assign values for other media options relative to it.

11. *Market characteristics:* Data needed for each market segment.

    1. Name of segment.

    2. Population.

    3. Sales potential per person in the segment. The units of sales potential are chosen by the user.

    4. Seasonality of sales potential. This is an index with a value for each time period in the advertising plan plus two time periods for ending effects. The average value over a full year is 1.00.

5. Initial average exposure value per person in the segment. As a substitute for this data, a list of the media insertions planned for two months before the computer generated schedule is to start will suffice.

III. *Media-segment data*

1. Market coverage. For each media vehicle in each segment, the fraction of the segment population who will be in the audience of the media vehicle. Essentially, this amounts to rating points in the market segment.

IV. *Media-vehicle duplications*

1. Audience duplication. For each possible pair of media vehicles the fraction of people out of the total in all segments who will be in the audience of both vehicles. Also needed is the fraction of people who will be in the audience of two appearances of the vehicle. If duplication data are not available, the system can approximate them using the assumption of independence between media.

V. *Other data needed*

1. Memory constant. The fraction of a person's exposure value that is remembered from one time period to the next.
2. The per cent of potential realized after saturation with exposures.
3. The per cent of potential realized when one, two, and three average exposures are retained by a person. (An average exposure is defined as an exposure to a media option with exposure value of 1.0.) These inputs may be viewed as expressing the expected effect of having one, two, and three exposures presented to a person in a short period of time. When combined with the saturation level, these inputs determine the diminishing returns aspect of response.
4. Number of media options, market segments, and time periods.
5. Budget.

ACKNOWLEDGMENTS

The work reported herein was supported (in part) by Project MAC, an MIT research program sponsored by the Advanced Research Projects Agency, Department of Defense, under an Office of Naval Research contract.

The authors wish to thank Fred Anderson for his help in developing the material on the higher moments shown in Fig. 3 and Charles Meyer and Fred Nagel for their help in developing duplication formulas and the data shown in Fig. 4.

REFERENCES

1. M. L. Vidale and H. B. Wolfe, "An Operations Research Study of Sales Response to Advertising," *Opns. Res.* 5, 370–381 (1957).
2. B. Benjamin and J. Maitland, "Operational Research and Advertising: Some Experiments in the Use of Analogies," *Opnal. Res. Quart.* 9, 207–217 (1958).

3. R. A. Metheringham, "Measuring the Net Cumulative Coverage of a Print Campaign," *J. Advertising Res.* 4, 23–28 (Dec. 1964).

4. D. W. Miller and M. K. Starr, *Executive Decisions and Operations Research*, Prentice Hall, Englewood Cliffs, New Jersey, 1960.

5. C. L. Wilson, "Use of Linear Programming to Optimize Media Schedules in Advertising," 178–191 in H. Gomez (ed.), *Proceedings of the Forty-Sixth National Conference of the American Marketing Association*, American Marketing Association, Chicago, 1963.

6. R. D. Buzzell, *Mathematical Models and Marketing Management*, Chapter 5, Graduate School of Business Administration, Harvard University, Boston, 1964.

7. R. L. Day, "Linear Programming in Media Selection," *J. Advertising Res.* 2, 40–44 (June 1962).

8. J. F. Engel and M. R. Warshaw, "Allocating Advertising Dollars by Linear Programming," *J. Advertising Res.* 4, 42–48 (Sept. 1964).

9. S. F. Stasch, "Linear Programming and Space-time Considerations in Media Selection," *J. Advertising Res.* 5, 40–46 (Dec. 1965).

10. F. M. Bass and R. T. Lonsdale, "An Exploration of Linear Programming in Media Selection," *J. Marketing Res.* 3, 179–188 (1966).

11. P. Kotler, "Toward an Explicit Model for Media Selection," *J. Advertising Res.* 4, 34–41 (Mar. 1964).

12. M. L. Godfrey, "Media Selection by Mathematical Programming," Talk before the Metropolitan New York Chapter of the Institute of Management Sciences, October 10, 1962.

13. D. B. Brown and M. R. Warshaw, "Media Selection by Linear Programming," *J. Marketing Res.* 2, 83–88 (1965).

14. W. I. Zangwill, "Media Selection by Decision Programming," *J. Advertising Res.* 5, 30–36 (Sept. 1965).

15. A. Charnes, W. W. Cooper, J. K. DeVoe, D. B. Learner, and W. Reinecke, "LP II: A Goal Programming Model for Media Planning," *Management Sciences Research Report No. 96*, Graduate School of Industrial Administration, Carnegie Institute of Technology, Pittsburgh, January 1967.

16. Simulmatics Corporation, "Simulmatics Media-Mix Technical Description," The Simulmatics Corporation, New York, October, 1962.

17. W. T. Moran, "Practical Media Models—What Must They Look Like," *Proc. 8th Conference of the Advertising Res. Foundation*, New York, 1962.

18. D. B. Brown, "A Practical Procedure for Media Selection," *J. Marketing Res.* 4, 262–264 (1967).

19. D. H. Gensch, "A Computer Simulation Model for Media Selection," Ph.D. Thesis, Northwestern University, 1967.

20. A. M. Lee and A. J. Burkart, "Some Optimization Problems in Advertising Media Planning," *Opnal. Res. Quart.* 11, 113–122 (1960).

21. C. J. Taylor, "Some Developments in the Theory and Application of Media Scheduling Methods," *Opnal. Res. Quart.* 14, 291–305 (1963).

22. A. M. Lee, "Decision Rules for Media Scheduling: Static Campaigns," *Opnal. Res. Quart.* 13, 229–242 (1962).

23. ———— "Decision Rules for Media Scheduling: Dynamic Campaigns," *Opnal. Res. Quart.* 14, 355–372 (1963).

24. D. M. ELLIS, "Building Up a Sequence of Optimum Media Schedules," *Opnal. Res. Quart.* 17, 413–424 (1966).

25. E. M. L. BEALE, P. A. B. HUGHES, AND S. R. BROADBENT, "A Computer Assessment of Media Schedules," *Opnal. Res. Quart.* 17, 381–412 (1966).

26. N. STEINBERG, G. COMES, AND J. BARACHE, "Un Modèle de Simulation pour Evaluer l'Efficacite d'un Plan de Supports," *The Fourth International Conference on Operational Research: Preprints of the Proceedings*, B60-66, Boston 1966.

27. P. BERTIER AND P. DUJEU, "Simulation des Comportements Aléatoires de Lecture: Le Modèle Scal," *Metra* 6, 647–659 (19567).

28. J. D. C. LITTLE AND L. M. LODISH, "A Media Selection Model and Its Optimization by Dynamic Programming," *Industrial Management Rev.* 8, 15–24 (1966).

29. G. FRANZI, "Mathematical Programming and Media Selection in Advertising," S.M. Thesis, M.I.T., Cambridge, January, 1967.

30. H. A. ZIELSKE, "The Remembering and Forgetting of Advertising," *J. Marketing* 23, 239–243 (1959).

31. W. R. SIMMONS & ASSOCIATES, "A Study of the Retention of Advertising in Five Magazines," W. R. Simmons & Associates Research, Inc., New York, 1965.

32. J. L. SIMON, "Are There Economies of Scale in Advertising? " *J. Advertising Res.* 5, 15–20 (June 1965).

33. D. B. LEARNER, "The Repetition of Advertising," Research Department, BATTEN, BARTON, DURSTINE, AND OSBORNE, New York, February 1967.

34. A. C. ROHLOFF, "Quantitative Analysis of the Effectiveness of TV Commercials," *J. Marketing Res.* 3, 239–245 (1966).

35. S. BANKS, "The Use of Incremental Analysis in the Selection of Advertising Media," *J. Business* 19, 232–243 (1946).

DAVID A. AAKER*

ADMOD is an advertising decision model which is designed to address simultaneously the budget decision, the copy decision, and the media-allocation decision. The model, which focuses upon specific consumer decisions that advertising is attempting to precipitate, is illustrated with an example.

ADMOD: An Advertising Decision Model

This article describes an Advertising Decision Model, termed ADMOD. The model is designed to make media-allocation decisions. However, its thrust differs from most other media models in two respects: (1) it includes the copy decision and the budget decision, and (2) it relies upon a different operational conception of the advertising process.

A MORE COMPREHENSIVE MODEL

There are three tactical advertising decision areas: the media budget, the budget allocation, and the copy decisions. Previous research into these decision areas has been remarkably isolated. Budget-setting models have generally used experimental design or statistical models, usually ignoring copy considerations or media placement. Media models have normally considered the budget to be fixed and similarly have ignored copy decisions, which generally involved different research traditions.

That interdependencies exist hardly needs demonstration. First, the optimal budget level will clearly depend upon the creative effort. For ineffective advertising, the optimal level may be zero. One type of copy approach will require a different level of exposure intensity than another. Second, the budget level will depend upon the type of media used and how effectively the target segments can be reached. Finally, recent research has demonstrated the interactions between copy and media scheduling. In particu-

lar, the studies by Ray and his colleagues [12, 13, 14] on repetition and Aaker and Brown [5] on vehicle source effects have shown that the assumption that these dimensions of analysis can be considered independently of copy effects is far from reasonable. Together with the classic work of Starch [18] on advertising readership, they suggest that media-allocation models should take the copy decision into account more explicitly.

There are, of course, good reasons why these interactions have been largely ignored in the past. First, the three areas are usually the responsibility of different decision makers. Firm managers set the budget, agency media specialists allocate the budget to media alternatives, and creative people make the copy decisions. There is little pressure, therefore, to integrate. Instead, a demand exists for independent efforts to aid these decision makers. Second, there have been technical and conceptual problems in the development of the machinery oriented toward media allocation and copy decisions, even when they are considered independently. Therefore, it has been productive to make advances in these areas. Indeed, it is questionable whether any real effort toward an integrative approach would be feasible without the advances that have been achieved to date in media models, copy testing, and related techniques. Finally, when media allocation or copy decisions are considered separately, the measures used need have only relative validity, since alternative choice is the goal. When budget decisions are introduced, a measure with validity in an absolute sense is necessary and new demands are imposed upon researchers.

It is now appropriate to address the budget, the media, and the copy decisions in concert. The introduction of modern information systems supported by on-line computers and model banks are effectively breaking down the isolation of the different decision makers. The media model technology is at the point

*David A. Aaker is Associate Professor of Business Administration, University of California, Berkeley. The author would like to thank the W. R. Simmons Company for making data available and Christopher Sprague and Leon Liebman of Interactive Market Systems Incorporated who provided convenient access to it. Thanks are also due to the Institute of Business and Economic Research for their research support and to Alex Chow for his able programming assistance and to the JMR reviewers for their helpful comments.

Journal of Marketing Research
Vol. XII (February 1975), 37-45

where it has achieved acceptance and demonstrated considerable validity. Progress has been made in understanding the communication process, in setting objectives, and in testing copy against these objectives. With barriers reduced, it is useful to push the field in the direction of more ambitious models.

A DIFFERENT VIEW OF THE ADVERTISING PROCESS

Most media models rely upon a model of advertising which suggests that advertising creates an advertising exposure (or some similar construct) which, in turn, creates sales. The advertising exposure level will dissipate over time but can be maintained or built up by more advertising. The heart of the model, then, is an aggregate response curve that relates exposure levels to sales (i.e., [8, 9]), or perhaps advertising expenditure levels to sales directly. ADMOD, in contrast, has a more disaggregative view of the advertising process. It focuses upon specific consumer decisions, which have long-run implications for the firm, that advertising is attempting to precipitate. For example, advertising may be directed toward inducing a consumer to try a brand for the first time, to try a brand in a new way, to change his brand attitude, or to become aware of the brand. Such consumer responses will tend to generate a future sales or profit stream to the firm which represents a certain present value. For instance, an attitude change may be linked to an increase in loyalty that will have an estimable effect upon purchases over time. A trial purchase will result in a subsequent purchase sequence which can be similarly estimated (for example, see [2]).

The concern of advertising is then upon some indicator of the probability of the consumer changing his cognitions in the desired way or taking the desired action. When the objective is to obtain new customers, an appropriate measure might be the intention to buy. Alternatively, the measure could be based upon some variable causually linked to intention to buy. For example, it may be that brand name awareness, or knowledge of a brand attribute, or familiarity with a jingle may be closely linked to intentions to make a trial purchase [6]. In any case, a construct is developed that may provide the dependent variable in studies used to estimate the various parameters in the advertising decision model. This construct will tend to be more operational than aggregate sales, partly because it will enable the researcher to exploit copy testing methodology more fully.

ADMOD

The goal of ADMOD is to select a budget level, a copy approach, and a media insertion schedule to maximize the objective function. The task of the objective function is to assign a value to a given media insertion schedule. A selection heuristic has the task of generating the various insertion schedules to be evaluated.

The Objective Function

The focus of the ADMOD objective function is not on the aggregate vehicle audience but upon sample populations selected from the various segments. In evaluating an insertion schedule, ADMOD examines its likely impact upon every individual in the sample. The impact will depend upon the net value of the decision or cognition change involved (the segment effect), the number and source of exposures to the individual created by the schedule (advertisement exposures), and the impact of the exposures upon the probability of obtaining the desired cognition change or decision (the repetition function). Using appropriate scaling factors, the result is projected to the real population, providing the total expected profit generated by that media schedule.

A sample is thus required from each segment. A representative sample of the whole population is not necessary. The proportion of people in the sample from a certain segment need not equal the proportion of the population contained in that segment. The only requirement is that a reasonable number of people from each segment—100 to 200, for example—be part of the sample. Of course, the sample should be representative of each segment. Ideally, each member of the segment should have an equal chance of being selected. When small audience media vehicles are included, it may be useful to increase the sample size somewhat. The sample size from segment s is termed n_s. The total size of segment s is termed N_s.

Before proceeding further, it is useful to define several terms. A media vehicle (indexed by j; $j = 1, ..., J$), such as *Vogue, Time,* NBC News, and Monitor Radio, provides the immediate environment for the advertisement. By specifying the vehicle, it will be assumed here that the position of the advertisement within the vehicle and the size of the advertisement is also specified. Including such factors in the model more formally would be a trivial extension. A copy alternative (indexed by c; $c = 1, ..., C$) is a creative approach. It could be the specification of refutational copy, fear appeals, the use of experimental evidence, or a particular awareness campaign. An insertion option (x_{cj}) is here defined as the insertion of a copy alternative into a vehicle. A set of insertion options is a media insertion schedule. A media insertion schedule will be constrained to have only one copy alternative; the possibility of relaxing this constraint will be considered later in the article.

The Segment Effect

The assumed objective of the advertiser is to precipitate a cognitive change or decision. The long-term value to the firm of obtaining such a result from a member of segment s is termed w_s. It will be the present value of the projected purchasing behavior pattern caused by the cognitive change or decision. Model components, such as the repetition function and vehicle source effects, are then developed using operational measures that are linked to the objective. To fix the concept, several examples will be presented.

Suppose the goal is to generate a trial purchase of a brand by segment members. In this context, w_s would be the discounted profit stream expected from a random segment member who tries the brand for the first time. The long-term value to the firm of obtaining a trial purchase will reflect the gross margin of the brand, a discount factor reflecting the cost of capital and the uncertainties of the market, the segment member's product class purchasing volume, and the degree of brand acceptance the brand is likely to obtain after the use experience [4]. An estimate of the brand acceptance can be obtained using repeat-buy statistics or by applying a formal brand choice stochastic model to a group of new triers. Parfitt and Collins [10] and Aaker [2] describe two models appropriate in this context and empirically demonstrate their validity. Aaker [3] demonstrates a method to link brand acceptance to descriptors of market segments which can be used even when a stochastic model is applied to a single data base of "new triers" of a brand. The approach could be employed to obtain w_s values for different segments.

The situation is similar when the goal is enticing a consumer to use the product in a new application or to use a product class for the first time. In that context, an important determining factor in w_s will be the consumer's acceptance of the new application after he is induced to try it. Statistics reflecting the time until the second or third use occasion or formal stochastic models of interpurchase time can be used to predict acceptance levels.

The objective could be to change a brand image. In that case, the intent could be to maintain the loyalty of existing customers and to make them less vulnerable to attacks from competing brands. With the existing image, customers may have a projected purchasing pattern that reflects a decline in purchases of the advertised brand. It may be that a new image will be associated with a more stable projection of purchasing patterns. The present value of the difference would then be w_s. Again, the best way to determine such projections is by observing the actual purchasing decisions of those who changed their perceptions of a brand. It may be that attitude theory will ultimately be helpful in providing such projections with less demanding data requirements.

Determining Exposures to the Schedule

The insertion schedule will generate exposures that will have some impact upon the objective of the advertising campaign. In this section, the exposure-generating aspect of the insertion schedule, which involves vehicle and advertisement exposure probabilities, will be developed.

Let b_{ij} be the probability that individual i will be exposed (with exposure carefully defined) to the vehicle j under consideration. It is assumed that the b_{ij} remain stable through the time period of the planned campaign. (For a discussion of this assumption, see [16].) Let h_{cj} be the conditional probability of an exposure (again, with a suitable definition) to an advertisement using copy alternative c in vehicle j, given that an exposure to vehicle j has been obtained. The latter term will depend upon the vehicle and the copy. Some vehicles have a higher advertisement exposure among their audience than others, and some creative approaches are more capable than others of attracting attention. It might be useful to condition h_{cj} upon the type of individual involved. However, the notation is already cumbersome and such extensions should be obvious. Thus, the probability that individual i reads a particular issue of *Good Housekeeping* would be b_{ij}, and the probability that an advertisement using copy approach c is exposed, given the vehicle is read, would be h_{cj}.

The product of these two terms, $b_{ij}h_{cj}$, reflect the probability that individual i will be exposed to an advertisement using copy approach c in vehicle j. Let:

$$p_{cij} = b_{ij}h_{cj},$$

where:

p_{cij} = the probability that individual i is exposed to insertion option x_{cj},

b_{ij} = the probability that individual i is exposed to vehicle j,

h_{cj} = the probability that anyone exposed to vehicle j will be exposed to insertion option x_{cj}.

Let z_i be a random variable reflecting the number of exposures received by individual i in a given insertion schedule being considered by the objective function. The value of z_i cannot be known for sure but, knowing the exposure probabilities, it is a straightforward task to obtain $f_{ci}(z_i)$, the probability distribution for z_i. The distribution can be calculated exactly by making certain independence assumptions and applying simple probability theory. For example, if there were only two insertions under consideration, insertion option x_{c5} and insertion option x_{c7}, then the probability of zero exposures would be $(1 - p_{ci5})(1 - p_{ci7})$, the probability of one exposure would be $p_{ci5}(1 - p_{ci7}) + p_{ci7}(1 - p_{ci5})$, and the probability of two exposures would be $p_{ci5}p_{ci7}$. Similar calculations can be made for schedules of any size. However, with large schedules, the calculations can become costly, and it is reasonable to consider using the raw probabilities to estimate the parameters of a probability function such as the binomial that would then become $f_{ci}(z_i)$.

The binomial distribution is attractive because it is a flexible distribution defined on positive integers and its parameters are easily estimated.[1] The use of a unimodal distribution is perfectly reasonable when only a single individual is involved, as it is in this context. In most other media models, there is the need to model the exposure probabilities across many individuals. When individuals are aggregated the resulting probability distribution is inevitably multimodal. As a result it is nearly impossible to model well with any tractable distribution. This fact motivates the use of a population sample in ADMOD.

The Repetition Function and Forgetting

ADMOD assumes that an advertising campaign of a specified duration is attempting to change cognitions or precipitate a decision. The campaign will generate a certain number of exposures for each individual i, z_i. The impact of these exposures on the probability of the desired response occurring is termed $a'_{cs}(z_i)$, the repetition function. The subscript s indicates that the repetition function will be different in general for each segment, but identical for each segment member. The subscript c reflects the fact that the repetition function will vary with the copy approach used. An awareness campaign may require only a few exposures, whereas an attitude-creation campaign may require several additional exposures to be effective. The prime superscript indicates that all exposures are associated with the maximum vehicle source effect, v_{cj}. This last assumption will shortly be relaxed.

Care must be taken to ensure that a comparable definition of exposure is used in h_{cj}, the probability of generating an advertisement exposure, and in z_i. Since the two terms appear in two different contexts, and since exposure probabilities and the repetition

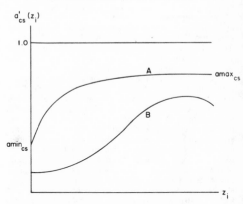

THE ADMOD REPETITION FUNCTION

functions may be estimated by separate and different techniques, it is quite possible to introduce inconsistent definitions.

One form of the repetition function is shown graphically as Curve A in the figure and algebraically as (1). It suggests that the probability of the deserved response, $a'_{cs}(z_i)$, will start at an initial level, moving geometrically to a higher level with successive exposures:

$$(1) \qquad a'_{cs}(z_i) = a\min_{cs} + a\max_{cs}(1 - \lambda_{cs}^{z_i}),$$

where:

$a\min_{cs}$ = the repetition function value in the absence of any exposures,

$a\max_{cs}$ = the limiting repetition function value as the number of exposures becomes large,

λ_{cs} = a parameter that reflects the rate at which the repetition function moves from $a\min_{cs}$ to $a\max_{cs}$.

In ADMOD there is no explicit conceptualization of forgetting. However, the development of the repetition function necessarily takes into account the length of the campaign and therefore the length of time between exposures. Curve B in the figure, for example, could reflect the fact that too few exposures will suffer from forgetting between them.

An implicit assumption in ADMOD is that the campaign is totally forgotten at its conclusion. The concept is that advertising is likely either to generate the desired change in cognitions or decision in a rather limited time period or not at all. Those that "withstand" a concentrated effort for a relatively short time will probably withstand the same campaign if

---

[1] The parameters of the binomial can be estimated from its mean and variance which are:

$$\mu = \text{mean} = \sum_j p_{cij}$$

$$\sigma^2 = \text{variance} = \sum_j p_{cij}(1 - p_{cij}).$$

The expressions are summed over all insertions in the schedule. Let π and nn be the parameters of the binomial. The estimates of these parameters, $\hat{\pi}$ and $\hat{nn}$, would be

$$\hat{nn} = \frac{\mu^2}{\mu - \sigma^2}$$

$$\hat{\pi} = \frac{\mu}{\hat{nn}}$$

The estimate of $\hat{nn}$ needs to be constrained to be less than or equal to the number of insertions in the schedule.

it is prolonged. Therefore, this forgetting assumption of the model may not be as extreme as it may first appear. It would be relatively easy to relax this assumption. It could be assumed, for example, that the average probability of a trial purchase during subsequent time periods would be fixed fractions of its value in the time period of immediate interest. The objective function would then have a value component from two or more time periods.

Another assumption of ADMOD is that the repetition function is not sensitive to when the exposures are received during the campaign period. To relax this assumption, the timing of each insertion would have to be introduced into the decision, and the repetition function would have to be conditioned on the time pattern of exposures. Such steps would, of course, add considerable detail to the model.

Clearly, the determination of the repetition function is at the heart of the model. One advantage of this formulation is that the dependent variable of the repetition function is well defined, assuming the advertising objectives are well defined. It is the probability of a cognition change or a decision, such as a decision to try a brand. A second advantage is that this type of dependent variable lends itself to laboratory study. The laboratory study, although having external validity problems, does enable the researcher to explore the repetition function in a highly controlled environment. Ray and Sawyer exposed respondents to from one to six repetitions of text advertisements in the context of a futuristic shopping system [12]. Among the measures of interest were attitude and purchase intentions. Such research can not only demonstrate useful methodology, but can also lead to repetition function norms that can help those who must estimate parameters subjectively. As Ray [11] has observed, however, repetition functions obtained in the laboratory should, as a matter of procedure, be tested and refined, first with field studies and ultimately with market tests. (See [14] for a discussion of a specific field study.)

The Vehicle Source Effect

The vehicle source effect reflects a vertical adjustment in the repetition function, the probability of precipitating the desired response as a function of exposures. The repetition function is developed under the assumption that all exposures will be associated with the optimal environment. The magazine or television programs creating the exposures are assumed to enhance the advertisement to the maximum extent possible because of their audience involvement, prestige, and other factors. All vehicle source effects are assumed to be 1.0 on a 0 to 1.0 scale. Actually, vehicle source effects will take on values between 0 and 1.0, reflecting their relative ability to enhance or detract from the impact of the advertisement exposure on the likelihood of generating the desired decision or cognitive change. The vehicle source effect for vehicles is termed v_{cj}. It is conditional on the copy approach used. Aaker and Brown [5], for example, found that the source effect of "prestige" and "expert" magazines depended upon whether an "image" or "reason why" copy was used.

In ADMOD the number of exposures an individual receives from a given insertion schedule is known probabilistically. However, it is not known exactly which insertion options in the schedule are creating the exposures. The solution is to compress the repetition function by an amount determined by the expected value of the vehicle source effect, which is simply a weighted average with those vehicles having a higher probability of creating exposures having the higher weight. The repetition function adjusted for vehicle source effects is denoted as $a_{ci}(z_i)$. Note the absence of the prime superscript and the fact that this repetition function is unique to an individual:

$$(2) \qquad a_{ci}(z_i) = a'_{cs}(z_i) \left[(\Sigma_i \, v_{cj} \, p_{cij}) \left(\frac{1}{\Sigma_j \, p_{cij}} \right) \right].$$

The effect of (2) is to reduce both $a\min_{cs}$ and $a\max_{cs}$ of (1). The researcher might believe that the vehicle source effect will not affect $a\max_{cs}$ but will affect λ_{cs}. Thus, inferior vehicle settings will tend to increase the number of exposures required until the individual reaches the $a\max_{cs}$ level. It would be a simple matter to reformulate (2) to adjust λ_{cs} (to move it toward 1.0) instead of adjusting the whole repetition function. However, this version of ADMOD uses the (2) formulation.

An Insertion Schedule's Value

The purpose of the objective function is to attach a value to a media insertion schedule. The value to the advertiser of the campaign on individual *in* segment *s* is the value of the desired result, w_s, times the probability that the advertising will stimulate that result to occur, $a_{ci}(z_i)$. If the number of exposures were known exactly, the expected value for one segment member would be $w_s \, a_{ci}(z_i)$. The problem is that the exact number of exposures that an individual will receive, given an insertion schedule, is not known. What is known is the probability distribution of the number of exposures, $f_{ci}(z_i)$. Thus, the appropriate procedure is to determine the expectation over z_i of $w_s \, a_{ci}(z_i)$, which yields the expected value from individual i:

$$w_s \sum_{z_i=0}^{\infty} a_{ci}(z_i) \, f_{ci}(z_i).$$

The total expected value received from the sample in market segment *s* is obtained by summing over all individuals in the sample who belong to that market segment: $\Sigma_{i \in s}$. The addition of the factor N_s / n_s explicitly scales the results to the segment size. Summing across segments Σ_s, and subtracting the costs of the model insertion schedule, the final objective function is obtained. It is assumed that the insertion costs for vehicle j are k_j for all vehicle j insertions—there are no media discounts. This assumption is made entirely to avoid introducing more notation. The model could handle any type of cost function.

The value of a given insertion schedule, the objective function, can thus be written:[2]

$$V = \sum_s \frac{N_s}{n_s} \sum_{i \in s} w_s \sum_{z_i=0}^{x} a_{ci}(z_i) f_{ci}(z_i) - \sum_j k_j x_{cj},$$

where:

c = index referencing the copy alternative,
i = index referencing the individual in the sample population,
j = index referencing the vehicle,
s = index referencing the market segment,
N_s = the size of segment s,
n_s = the size of the sample from segment s,
w_s = the value to the firm of the consumer action (i.e., a trial purchase) by a member of market segment s,
z_i = the number of exposures received by individual i, given the insertion schedule,
$a_{ci}(z_i)$ = the probability that the desired consumer action (i.e., a trial purchase) will occur, given the fact that z_i exposures occurred,
$f_{ci}(z_i)$ = the probability that individual i will receive exactly z_i exposures, given the insertion schedule,
k_j = the cost of an insertion in vehicle j,
x_{cj} = the insertion of copy alternative c into vehicle j ($x_{cj} = 0, 1$).

ADMOD Vs. Simulation

Because a population sample is involved, it is easy to associate the ADMOD approach with Monte Carlo simulation such as Gensch's AD-ME-SIM [7]. Actually, ADMOD provides a closed-form objective function based upon expectations as to the number of exposures and their impact upon the desired response. In a Monte Carlo simulation, a generated set of random numbers determines a specific exposure pattern for a simulated individual. Such a simulation removes inhibitions toward complexity and completeness. However, simulation requires large samples to counteract the variance introduced by the Monte Carlo approach. The larger samples and the added

---

[2]The objective function could easily be formulated to represent return on the advertising investment instead of total profit.

complexity means that a Monte Carlo simulation model is usually used only to evaluate a small number of proposed media plans. A heuristic to select among plans is usually not part of the model.

CONSTRAINTS

There is a wide variety of constraints that could be introduced. The number of insertion options considered for a given vehicle may be limited by the frequency with which the vehicle appears during the time period, for example. However, here we will formally introduce only the already mentioned constraint that only one copy alternative should be considered in any one schedule. Thus ADMOD is designed to select an insertion schedule that will maximize V, subject to the constraint that the selected schedule include only one copy alternative.

It would be possible to relax the constraint that an insertion schedule can only include one copy alternative. If it could be assumed that two copy approaches operate independently, that the two campaigns would be directed at different segments, for example, extension would not be difficult. The more interesting situation is when several copy approaches are interspersed to the same audience. Consider the possibility of using an awareness advertising campaign first, followed by a reason-why campaign. The problem is that now not only do the number of exposures need to be determined probabilistically, but also the mix between the two copy approaches. Such a technical problem can be solved relatively easily. The difficult task is to obtain the appropriate repetition function. An important function of such models as ADMOD is to identify new areas of productive research. The measurement problems associated with this discussion are undoubtedly in that category.

THE SELECTION HEURISTIC

Because of the irregular nature of the objective function, it is necessary to use a heuristic to search systematically through media insertion schedules to select one with a high value. To implement the constraint that any one schedule will include one copy alternative, the heuristic will be employed for each copy alternative. The one with the highest value will be the one selected.

The heuristic search procedure should incrementally add insertions until a stop signal is reached. It should include the capability of periodically deleting insertions that may become redundant as other insertions are added. Suitable heuristics as described in detail in [1, 9].

The Budget Level

Normally a budget constraint provides a stopping signal to the heuristic. However, in this formulation the budget level is included in the objective function. Thus, the stopping point is reached when there no longer exists any insertion option that will increase the value of the insertion schedule. Alternatively, the heuristic could require that the ratio of the value added by a marginal insertion to its marginal cost be a prespecified minimum. In any case, the budget level, the cost of that final insertion schedule, is a program output instead of an input. Its value is given by the second term in the objective function—$\Sigma_j k_j x_{cj}$. It is optimal (within the limitations of the search heuristic) in that either an increase or a decrease in the budget level would reduce the net value of the advertising campaign to the firm.

A MODEL APPLICATION

An advertising decision problem was conceptualized to illustrate the model and to provide a setting for conducting sensitivity tests. The product is a set of dishes to be sold to homemakers. Two copy approaches are considered. (For description of such advertisements, see [5].) One is an image approach ($c = 1$), and the other is a detailed, logical, reason-why approach ($c = 2$). Thirteen vehicle alternatives, shown in Table 1, were included.

The basic data were supplied by the W. R. Simmons Company. They include information on media habits and the usage levels of a wide variety of products for over 7,000 individuals. The media information was in the form of whether the respondent was exposed to zero, one, or two successive magazine issues or television programs. Thus, the b_{ij} terms become 0.0, 0.5, and 1.0. Such an approach minimizes respondent recall and interpretation difficulties. However, the use of only two issues sacrifices precision and the use of actual readership instead of a direct estimate of probabilities adds variance to the result [15].

An index of an orientation of housewives to cooking and the kitchen was developed from the product-usage variables. It was assumed that a "nonkitchen" orientation would be associated with the relatively heavy use of fast-food carry-out establishments, frozen dinners, frozen desserts, cookie mixes, instant coffee, false eyelashes, and tennis balls, and the relatively light use of such products as wine. A "kitchen segment" and a "nonkitchen segment" of 200 each were selected on the basis of this index. The total size of the segments represented by this sample was obtained, using the projective weight associated with individuals in the data base. It was 10.3 million for the kitchen segment (Segment 1) and 11.5 million for the nonkitchen segment (Segment 2).

The advertisement exposure probabilities conditional on vehicle exposure, the h_{cj} terms, were obtained using the 1973 Starch ad norms [17]. Specifically, the seen-associated score which is the percent who associated the advertiser with the advertisement was used. The relevant norms, obtained where possible for women and food products, are shown as Data Set C in Table 1.

The vehicle source effect terms were generated subjectively. A magazine image study was drawn upon (for more details see [5]), in which 30 women were asked to identify from a list of 18 women's magazines those they would regard as the most (and least) "prestigious" and the most (and least) "expert" with respect to cooking, foods, and kitchenware. The estimates are shown as Data Set A in Table 1.

The repetition function, based upon (1), has parameters that were also subjectively estimated. In doing so, the research of Ray et al. [12, 13, 14] was drawn upon. The estimates are shown in Table 2 under Run

Table 1
BASIC VEHICLE DATA

Parameter	v_{cj}				h_{cj}						k_j
Data set	A		B		C		D		E		
Copy approach (c)	1	2	1	2	1	2	1	2	1	2	
Vehicle											
1. American Home	.60	.50	.53	.65	.16	.16	.21	.21	.24	.16	14,250
2. Cosmopolitan	.46	.40	.53	.65	.24	.24	.21	.21	.36	.24	8,250
3. Family Circle	.32	.85	.53	.65	.22	.22	.21	.21	.33	.22	26,900
4. Glamour	.80	.35	.53	.65	.21	.21	.21	.21	.33	.21	7,350
5. Good Housekeeping	.62	.88	.53	.65	.26	.26	.21	.21	.39	.26	22,765
6. House & Garden	.60	.50	.53	.65	.20	.20	.21	.21	.30	.20	8,850
7. Ladies Home Journal	.68	.96	.53	.65	.26	.26	.21	.21	.39	.26	29,030
8. McCall's	.52	.74	.53	.65	.28	.28	.21	.21	.42	.28	30,750
9. Parents Magazine	.40	.65	.53	.65	.20	.20	.21	.21	.30	.20	13,565
10. Redbook	.42	.48	.53	.65	.24	.24	.21	.21	.36	.24	19,640
11. Women's Day	.48	.78	.63	.65	.21	.21	.21	.21	.31	.21	26,825
12. Good Housekeeping (1/2 page)	.46	.68	.53	.65	.15	.15	.21	.21	.23	.15	14,190
13. Ladies Home Journal (1/2 page)	.48	.66	.53	.65	.12	.12	.21	.21	.18	.12	14,350

JOURNAL OF MARKETING RESEARCH, FEBRUARY 1975

Table 2

MEDIA INSERTION SCHEDULES

Run		1		2		3		4		5	6	7	8	9	10	11	
Copy		1	2	1	2	1	2	1	2	2	2	2	2	2	2	1	2
Parameters	Segment																
v_{cj}	—	A	A	B	B	A	A	A	A	A	A	A	A	A	A	A	A
h_{cj}	—	C	C	C	C	D	D	E	E	C	C	C	C	C	C	C	C
λ	1	.55	.50	.55	.50	.55	.50	.55	.50	.40	.60	.50	.50	.50	.50	.55	.50
λ	2	.60	.55	.60	.55	.60	.55	.60	.55	.45	.65	.55	.55	.55	.55	.60	.55
amax	1	.14	.16	.14	.16	.14	.16	.14	.16	.16	.16	.16	.15	.16	.16	.14	.16
amax	2	.18	.12	.18	.12	.18	.12	.18	.12	.12	.12	.12	.15	.12	.12	.18	.12
w_s	1	7	7	7	7	7	7	7	7	7	7	6	5	6	8	10	10
w_s	2	5	5	5	5	5	5	5	5	5	5	6	7	4	6	8	8
	1																
	2			4	4			1								2	
	3												1		1		3
	4	4						5		1						7	
	5	2	4		1	4		2	4	4	4	4	4	4	4	4	6
Insertion	6																
schedule	7	2			4		1	2	4	4	2	4	4	2	4	3	4
	8				1		2	2	1	2		1	2	2		1	3
	9																
	10																
	11																
	12					1	5										
	13					4	5										
Contribution from segment: (1000's)	1	66	207	50	111	52	134	145	207	275	118	178	150	30	277	277	426
	2	92	131	61	75	76	86	185	131	175	75	157	287	35	182	153	315
Profit (1000's)		25	100	17	40	27	77	120	100	155	44	97	141	6	164	153	315
Budget (1000's)		133	238	94	146	101	143	210	238	295	149	238	296	59	295	277	426

1. The term amin was assumed to be zero. For the kitchen segment (1), amax, the asymptotic probability was assumed to be slightly higher when reason-why advertising was used (0.16) than with image advertising (0.14). For the nonkitchen segment (2), amax was assumed to be much larger for image advertising (0.18) than reason-why advertising (0.12). More than average repetition was assumed to be needed for the image advertising to the nonkitchen segment ($\lambda = 0.60$) and less than average repetition was assumed to be needed for reason-why advertising directed to the kitchen segment ($\lambda = 0.50$).

The basic w_s terms used were $7.00 for the kitchen segment and $5.00 for the nonkitchen segment. The assumption was that the kitchen segment will buy a better quality and more complete set of dishes.

Table 2 reports the results of 11 runs. In several of the runs, the results for both copy alternatives are presented. For the first run, Copy 2 provides greater profit and thus would be selected. The source of the Copy 2 profit is mainly Segment 1 because of the repetition function parameters that reflect the belief that reason-why advertising ($c = 2$) will be most effective with the kitchen segment ($s = 1$). The vehicle source effect term favored Glamour (vehicle 4) for

the image copy but gave it a low rating when reason-why copy was used. Thus, Glamour did not appear with the reason-why copy although four insertions were scheduled with the image copy.

In Run 2, the v_{cj} values are replaced by their average values (Data Set B in Table 1). As a result, Cosmopolitan, which had below-average v_{cj} values, does better. Note that the budget and profit levels are lower than in Run 1 due to the reduced v_{cj} values for Good Housekeeping and Ladies Home Journal. In Run 3, the h_{cj} terms were replaced by their average value (Data Set D in Table 1). The half-page options clearly benefitted. However, the reduced advertisement readership for Good Housekeeping, Ladies Home Journal, and McCall's (Vehicles 5, 7, and 8, respectively) caused the profit to decline from Run 1.

In Run 4, the h_{cj} terms for the image copy ($c = 1$) was increased 50% to reflect a possible hypothesis that simpler, less wordy copy will have greater exposure. The result was the only run in which Copy 1 generated larger profit than Copy 2.

Runs 5 and 6 showed the sensitivity of the budget to levels of λ. In the remaining runs, the w_s terms were altered, showing the sensitivity of the budget to the values of w_s used. Run 11, with w_s values of 10 and 8, generated a budget of more than $400,000. The average cost for the runs on a CDC6400 was $6.00. Run 11 cost $16.00.

CONCLUSIONS

The benefit of a model of this type is usually not in the machinery it makes available but, rather, in the vocabulary it creates, the structure it provides, and its suggestions for future research. Hopefully, ADMOD will contribute by providing structure and identifying productive research areas. However, the model should not be regarded as a tool of the future that is impractical given today's state of the art. It is true that measurement problems exist, particularly with respect to the determination of repetition functions. But even in this difficult area, the work of Ray and his colleagues and others have provided practical methodologies and microtheories to guide researchers.

The fact is that enormous progress has been made during the past decade in mathematical models, in computer programs, and in measurement. Further, model users are becoming more sophisticated and interdependent. It is time to consider more comprehensive decision models as viable, practical aids to decision making.

REFERENCES

1. Aaker, David A. "A Probabilistic Approach to Industrial Media Selection," *Journal of Advertising Research,* 8 (September 1968), 46-54.
2. _____. "The New-Trier Stochastic Model of Brand Choice," *Management Science,* 17 (April 1971), 435-60.
3. _____. "A Measure of Brand Acceptance," *Journal of Marketing Research,* 9 (May 1972), 160-7.
4. _____. "Toward a Normative Model of Promotional Decision Making," *Management Science,* 19 (February 1973), 593-603.
5. _____ and Philip K. Brown. "Evaluating Vehicle Source Effects," *Journal of Advertising Research,* 12 (August 1972), 11-6.
6. Claycamp, Henry J. and Lucien E. Liddy. "Prediction of New Product Performance: An Analytical Approach," *Journal of Marketing Research,* 6 (November 1969), 414-20.
7. Gensch, Dennis H. *Advertising Planning.* New York: Elsevier Scientific Publishing, 1973.
8. Little, John D. C. and Leonard M. Lodish. "A Media Selection Model and Its Optimization by Dynamic Programming," *Industrial Management Review,* 8 (Fall 1966), 15-23.
9. _____. "A Media Planning Calculus," *Operations Research,* 17 (January-February 1969), 1-35.
10. Parfitt, J. H. and B. J. K. Collins. "The Use of Consumer Panels for Brand-Share Predictions," *Journal of Marketing Research,* 5 (May 1968), 131-45.
11. Ray, Michael L. "The Present and Potential Linkages Between the Microtheoretical Notions of Behavioral Science and the Problems of Advertising: A Proposal for a Research System," paper presented at the Symposium on Behavioral and Management Science in Marketing, University of Chicago, June 1969.
12. _____ and Alan G. Sawyer. "Repetition in Media Models: A Laboratory Technique," *Journal of Marketing Research,* 8 (February 1971), 20-9.
13. _____. "Behavioral Measurement for Marketing Models," *Management Science,* Part II, 18 (December 1971), 73-89.
14. _____, and Edward C. Strong. "Frequency Effects Revisited," *Journal of Advertising Research,* 11 (February 1971), 14-20.
15. Schreiber, Robert J. "Letter to the Editor," *Management Science,* 14 (April 1968), B526-B527.
16. _____. "Instability in Media Exposure Habits," *Journal of Advertising Research,* 14 (April 1974), 13-8.
17. *Starch Adnorms, 1973.* Mamaroneck, N.Y.: Daniel Starch & Starch, 1973.
18. Starch, Daniel. *Measuring Advertising Readership and Results.* New York: McGraw-Hill, 1966.

How to Estimate Unduplicated Audiences

J.-M. Agostini
Elvinger Advertising Agency

Monsieur Agostini has developed a formula which may render unnecessary the laborious tabulation of the unduplicated audiences of combinations of three or more media vehicles. It has been successfully applied to both French and U. S. magazine data.

WHEN SEVERAL VEHICLES (magazines, newspapers, etc.) are used in an advertising campaign, it is easy to sum their audiences. But because of audience duplication, this sum A always exceeds the audience C actually reached by the combination, and it is precisely this unduplicated audience C which must be measured in order to evaluate the coverage of the campaign.

Audience analyses sometimes give data on audience duplication for vehicles taken two by two; seldom do they give data on audience duplication for a combination of three or more. But the size of the unduplicated audience of several vehicles depends not only on the number of people simultaneously covered by two, but also on the number simultaneously covered by 3, 4 . . . . n vehicles. Analyses made in the U. S. and in France have shown that readership of three or more vehicles, particularly magazines, is very common.

Therefore, when more than two vehicles are to be used, as usually happens, the unduplicated audience is rarely known. However, the press readership survey made in France by the Centre d'Etude des Supports de Publicité (CESP) in 1957 may be considered a remarkable effort in this field. Duplications were obtained for 30 magazines taken two by two—as well as for all possible combinations of 15 of the 30 magazines! Three large books were required to present the results of the 32,767 combinations possible.

These data are obviously very useful, but refer only to half the publications covered by the survey. They do not show the unduplicated audience of any magazine combination which includes a magazine not among the 15 chosen.

The purpose of this paper is to describe a shortcut method of estimating the unduplicated audience of a higher order combination of vehicles (trio, quartet, etc.) from data on the duplication of these vehicles taken two by two.

When applied to the CESP results, the proposed method leads to a satisfactory evaluation of the unduplicated audience provided by any of the 1,073,741,793 combinations possible with the 30 magazines whose paired duplications are known.

JEAN-MICHEL AGOSTINI is marketing consultant and a director of the Elvinger Advertising Agency in Paris. He received the degree of Ingénieur des Arts et Manufactures from the Ecole Centrale de Paris in 1942. After several years as a consultant in market research, he joined Elvinger in 1951 as director of research before assuming his present position. He is vice president of the Association Nationale des Practiciens en Etudes de Marché, member of the board of the Association pour le Developpement des Techniques d'Etudes de Marchés, chairman of the Collège Echanges d'Expériences of the Institut de Recherches et d'Etudes Publicitaires (IREP) and a member of the technical committee of the Centre d'Etude des Supports de Publicité (CESP). IREP and CESP perform in France many of the functions undertaken by ARF in the United States.

METHOD

Let:

a, b, c, . . . n be the vehicles of the combination, $A_a, A_b, \ldots A_n$ be their respective audiences, and A the sum of these individual audiences. Thus,

(1) $\quad A = A_a + A_b + \cdots + A_n$

Owing to duplication, the unduplicated audience C is smaller than the sum of the audiences of the vehicles, i.e.,

(2) $\quad C = zA$ where
z is a coefficient between 0 and 1.

The proposed method consists in calculating z from the square table giving the duplication of media taken two by two. This table shows the audience duplicated by two vehicles at the intersection of their row and column: D_{ab} is the number of people simultaneously covered by a and b.

	a	b	c . . . n
a	—	D_{ab}	$D_{ac} \ldots D_{an}$
b	D_{ba}	—	$D_{bc} \ldots D_{bn}$
c	D_{ca}	D_{cb}	— $\ldots D_{cn}$
.	.	.	—
.	.	.	—
.	.	.	—
n	D_{na}	D_{nb}	$D_{nc} \ldots$ —

For obvious reasons this table is symmetrical about its main diagonal, D being the half-sum of all the terms in the table.

(3) $\quad D = D_{ab} + D_{ac} + \cdots + D_{an}$
$\qquad + D_{bc} + \cdots + D_{bn}$
$\qquad \ldots$ etc.

Thus D represents the total of the two by two duplicated audiences. In the case of magazines, D represents the total of the double readerships. We have, on the other hand, the total duplicated audiences:

(1) $\quad A = A_a + A_b + \cdots + A_n$

Suppose we let

(4) $\quad x = \dfrac{D}{A}$

Now x is a factor which can be easily calculated starting from data already in our hands: the total audience of all vehicles and their two by two duplications.

We shall establish that there is a relation between x and the factor z of equation (2).

(5) $\quad z = f(x)$

We shall prove that this relation may be satisfactorily represented by a unique curve the tracing of which will be given.

Knowing x, the value of z will be found on the curve, and this equation (2) will give a fair estimate of the unduplicated audience C, which is the object of our endeavor.

THE RELATION BETWEEN x AND z

Obviously the greater the duplication between media, the less will be the unduplicated audience. The higher the value of D, the lower the value of C.

Inasmuch as $x = \dfrac{D}{A}$ and $z = \dfrac{C}{A}$, when x increases, z decreases.

When there is no duplication between media, the unduplicated audience equals the sum of the audiences. In this case, when D = 0, x = 0, and when C = A, z = 1.

Therefore when x = 0, z = 1.

Results released by the CESP enabled us to calculate the values of x and z for any combination of the 15 magazines for which the special study on unduplicated audiences was conducted.

To calculate x for a given combination, we divided the duplication between the magazines (as obtained from the two by two table) by the sum A of audiences of the magazines.

To calculate z, we divided the unduplicated audience C of the same combination (as actually observed in the special study) by the sum A of audiences of the magazines.

Theoretically we are in a position to work out 32,767 pairs of values for x and z. Actually we calculated only 98, selected at random from all combinations studied.

With x on the abscissa and z on the ordinate, we plotted 98 dots, the setting out of which clearly shows that the relation between x and z can be accurately depicted by a continuous curve (see Figure 1).

Such a curve was traced through the 98 dots. The accuracy of the graphic tool thus obtained was very satisfactory. The difference between the value of z read from the curve and the true value was in 90 per cent of the cases less than .01 and never more than .02.

We then tried to translate this curve into an equation. The tracing of the curve looks like an equilateral hyperbola asymptotic to the x axis. Obviously when vehicles are added to a combination, the sum A may increase indefinitely while C must necessarily tend toward a limit, i.e., z must tend

FIGURE 1

OBSERVED RELATIONSHIP BETWEEN UNDUPLICATED (z) AND PAIR-WISE DUPLICATED (x) COEFFICIENTS OF THE TOTAL AUDIENCE

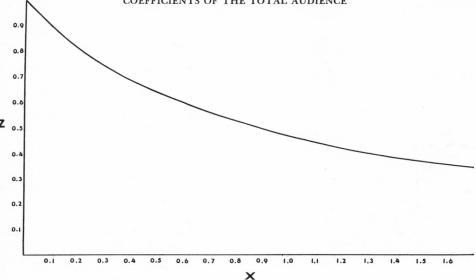

toward zero. The curve $z = f(x)$ must therefore have the x axis as its asymptote.

Accordingly we tried an equation of this form:

$$(6) \quad z = \frac{1}{Kx + 1}$$

We found that when $K = 1.125$, equation (6) represented perfectly the section of the curve traced on the chart up to $x = 1.7$, the highest value of x observed in magazine combinations used to obtain the curve.

PRACTICAL EXAMPLE

Let us, for example, take four magazines, the unduplicated audience of which has been calculated in the CESP special study. This will enable us to judge the accuracy of the proposed graphic method.

Suppose we have to estimate the unduplicated audience of the following four magazines, knowing the individual audience of each:

	Readers (in 000's)
Selection	4,741
Jours de France	1,573
La Vie Catholique	2,447
Nous Deux	4,143

ADVERTISING RESEARCH

We also know their two by two duplications:

	S	JF	VC	ND
Selection	—	638	663	697
Jours de France		—	275	186
La Vie Catholique			—	283
Nous Deux				—

We calculate

$A = 4,741 + 1,573 + 2,447 + 4,143 = 12,904$

$D = 638 + 663 + 697 + 275 + 186 + 283$
$= 2,742$

hence $x = \dfrac{D}{A} = 0.21$

On the curve we read the z value for $x = .21$, namely,

$z = .805$

hence $C = zA = .805 \, (12,904) = 10,400$

The true value of C given by the CESP special study was 10,468.

OTHER APPLICATIONS

The curve $z = f(x)$ on which the method is based was derived empirically from data on 15 French magazines. We have found that estimates obtained from the curve closely match the results actually

13

obtained in the CESP special study. But this is no proof that the curve is valid for other media than those which served to build it. We therefore decided to test the proposed method beyond those 15 magazines.

The CESP survey tabulated the unduplicated audience of a few groups of media other than the 15 chosen magazines. When the two by two duplications are given as well, it is possible to apply our method and compare the estimate obtained with the actual result. We conducted three tests with:

a. five women's magazines (of which only one was part of the 15);

b. five general magazines (of which none was part of the 15);

c. eleven Paris dailies.

In the three cases, the proposed method has led us to a fairly close estimate of the unduplicated audience:

	Estimated Audience	Actual Audience	Difference
a.	5,700,000	5,837,000	2.3%
b.	6,200,000	6,210,000	0.2%
c.	6,000,000	6,160,000	2.6%

All media previously mentioned are French publications the audiences of which were measured by this same CESP survey. It seemed advisable to test the proposed method with U. S. magazines. This we were able to do thanks to the 1954 *Life* report, *A Study of Duplication*. In this study, audience duplications of five U. S. magazines (*Life, Saturday Evening Post, Look, Ladies' Home Journal, This Week*) were analyzed.

Specifically, unduplicated audiences were given for all combinations of three, four and five magazines. In each case these audiences were analyzed according to sex and income. We thus have a total of 96 results regarding unduplicated audiences—16

combinations for each of six groups (one over-all, two sexes and three income levels). The same audiences were evaluated by applying our method with the same constant, K = 1.125. Results:

In 82 cases, the difference between the actual audience and the estimated audience was less than one per cent.

In ten cases, this difference lay between one and two per cent.

In four cases, this difference exceeded two per cent (maximum 2.7 per cent).

It appears that the proposed method has a wide field of application.

CONCLUSIONS

If it is true that the only information required to estimate an unduplicated audience is the total audience and two by two vehicle duplications, then great economy of effort is possible. Instead of undertaking the fantastic amount of tabulation required to calculate the unduplicated audiences of all possible combinations of a restricted number of vehicles, it is preferable to set up, for all vehicles, a series of square tables of their two by two duplications, each table containing these duplications within one stratum. It should be noted that to evaluate the unduplicated audience of a combination of vehicles within a stratum (e.g., an age group), one must know the duplications *within this stratum*. Knowledge of duplications for the whole sample is not sufficient.

We feel that an analysis of the two by two duplications by strata for any individual audience analysis is much more efficient than a repetition of such voluminous work as the CESP special study. We must not forget, however, that if this tremendous enterprise had not been undertaken, we would not have found a method to save us from doing it in the future.

General observations drawn from particulars are the jewels of knowledge, comprehending great store in a little room.

—JOHN LOCKE

Measuring the Net Cumulative Coverage of a Print Campaign

RICHARD A. METHERINGHAM

Foote, Cone & Belding Ltd.

The author shows one way to estimate the net cumulative coverage and frequency distribution of a print schedule from the duplicated audiences of pairs of publications and pairs of issues.

DESPITE AN ABUNDANCE of information little dreamed of a decade ago, the media planner still lacks some of the basic tools he needs. This is particularly true in the case of audience duplication. When a schedule encompasses both print and broadcast media, assessing the number of different people reached is largely a matter of guesswork. Generally, the net coverage of print and broadcast are estimated separately. But when it comes to marrying these two parts together, the amount of duplication is either guessed at or ignored.

Moreover, print coverage, based on average-issue readership, ignores the effect of repeat reading of different issues of the same publication. As early as 1953, Alfred Politz demonstrated that this cumulative readership is far from negligible: whereas an average issue of *Life* was read by 22.1 per cent of individuals, this figure increased to 50.6 per cent over six issues. It would not be rash to say that most net coverage estimates bear little resemblance to fact. (Note: the word "readership," used here in the European sense, means roughly the same thing as "audience" in the U.S.)

Besides knowing how many different people are reached, it is equally important to know the frequency distribution of the advertising exposures, since some frequency patterns should be better than others in view of the advertising strategy.

Nuttall (1962) recently focused attention on some of these problems and suggested techniques for solving them. The present paper shows how to estimate the net coverage and frequency distribution of a print schedule, making allowance for the cumulative effect of more than one insertion in any publication. The only data required are those on the

RICHARD A. METHERING-
HAM is a director in charge of marketing, research, and media at Foote, Cone & Belding Ltd., London. Previously he was a director in charge of marketing and research at Lambe & Robinson, Ltd., which has since become Benton & Bowles, Ltd. He received a B.S. in mathematics from London University. He is a member of the Institute of Practitioners in Advertising and the British Market Research Society.

duplication of publications/issues in pairs.

At present not even these minimum data are at hand. Pairwise duplication between national newspapers and magazines has long been a feature of readership surveys, but we still lack the corresponding within-publication data. Getting these data presents no insuperable research problem, and the benefits to the media planner would be out of all proportion to the additional costs.

In theory the method about to be explained could be applied to broadcast as well as print media. Practical difficulties make this impossible, at least at present in Britain. But the method still should add precision in one area of media planning.

METHOD

Net Coverage: Single Insertions

First let us take the relatively simple case of estimating the net coverage of a schedule consisting of a single insertion in a number of publications. Here we can ignore duplication between different issues of the same publication and can determine net coverage by sorting punched cards. Since card sorting is lengthy and expensive, various alternatives have been tried in the past, some laborious and most not very accurate. The best one appears to be Agostini's (1961) method. Based on a study of French magazines, he devised an empirical formula which related net coverage to the sum of the pairwise duplications, which are usually tabulated in readership surveys. The formula appears to give close estimates for a number of American as well as French magazines.

But the formula does not give reliable results for British publications. In extensive tests, we found estimates which were in error by as much as 17 percentage points, which is clearly unacceptable. When we tried to make Agostini's equation work by determining a separate constant for each readership survey, the "constant" turned out to be very variable even within the same survey. This was most disappointing in view of the method's simplicity.

Still, one feels instinctively that Agostini is right. Common sense tells us that there should be a relationship between the total coverage and the coverage taken in pairs. Thus we shall seek a formula which depends only on the coverage of individual publications and on the coverage of pairs.

Let p_i be the "cover" or the proportion of the relevant population reading the ith publication, where $i = 1, 2, \ldots n$ publications. Similarly, $q_i = 1 - p_i$, is the noncover of the ith publication.

Let the noncover of any two publications (i.e., the proportion reading neither) be q_{ij}. The sum of all such pairs will be indicated by $\sum q_{ij}$. Similarly, $\sum q_{ijk}$ is the sum of noncover of any three publications.

Now $\sum q_i$ will consist of n terms, $\sum q_{ij}$ will consist of $\binom{n}{2}$ terms, and in general $\sum q_{ij} \ldots$, where there are r subscripts, will consist of $\binom{n}{r}$ terms (i.e., the number of combinations of n things taken r at a time).

Consider the sequence whose general term is

$$k_r = \frac{\sum q_{ij} \cdots \text{(to r subscripts)}}{\binom{n}{r}} \qquad (1)$$

The first term of this sequence, $k_1 = \frac{\sum q_i}{n}$ is the average noncover of the n publications. The second term, $k_2 = \frac{\sum q_{ij}}{\binom{n}{2}}$ is the average noncover of any two of the n publications, and so on for the remaining terms. The last term is $k_n = q_{123 \ldots n}$, there being no summation sign since this term occurs only once.

Then, $1 - k_n = 1 - q_{123 \ldots n}$ will be the net cover of the n publications. (Net cover is the British expression for net audience or reach.)

The values of k_1 and k_2 are known from the data. If we can find a formula which links all the n terms of the sequence, we can calculate k_n, the last and required term. As shown later, the general term k_r (where r can take any value from 1 to n), should be closely approximated by the formula:

$$k_r = \frac{s(s+1)(s+2) \cdots (s+r-1)}{t(t+1)(t+2) \cdots (t+r-1)} \cdots \cdots \qquad (2)$$

s and t may have positive or negative values, but s must be greater than n. If not, at some point between the first and the nth terms the sequence becomes negative or zero. We could show that for the class of data under consideration, s is always greater than n, so there is no restriction in practice on the values of s and t.

The values of s and t are determined by the relations

$$k_1 = s/t$$

$$k_2 = \frac{s(s+1)}{t(t+1)}$$

from which we get

$$s = \frac{k_1^2 - k_1 k_2}{k_2 - k_1^2}$$

and $t = \frac{s}{k_1}$

24

The required last term of the sequence is then given by

$$k_n = \frac{s(s+1)(s+2)\ldots(s+n-1)}{t(t+1)(t+2)\ldots(t+n-1)}$$

Table 1 shows how each term as calculated by formula (2) compares with an actual card sort. The five newspapers used were *The People, Sunday Express, News of the World, Daily Mirror,* and *Daily Express.*

TABLE 1

NONCOVERAGE OF FIVE BRITISH NEWSPAPERS

Number of Newspapers	k_r	Actual Noncoverage	Estimated Noncoverage
One	k_1	.587	.587
Two	k_2	.358	.358
Three	k_3	.224	.226
Four	k_4	.144	.147
All five	k_5	.097	.098

The net coverage is $1 - k_5 = 0.903$ (estimated: 0.902). The approximation will not always be this close, but we found close agreement in a large number of trials, comprising combinations of widely differing media.

In estimating net coverage, we are interested only in the last term k_n, and the intermediate terms would not be calculated. They are presented in Table 1 to show that all terms, not merely the last, give good approximations.

Table 2 compares the actual with estimated coverage, expressed as percentages, of schedules

TABLE 2

COMBINATIONS OF NINE BRITISH NEWSPAPERS

Net Coverage

Combination	Actual %	Estimated %	Difference
ABCD	87.5	86.7	+0.8
BDFG	75.1	76.0	−0.9
AFGI	74.5	73.7	+0.8
ABFH	78.0	78.9	−0.9
CEFG	58.5	58.2	+0.3
ABHI	82.0	82.0	0.0
ABCDE	88.3	87.4	+0.9
ABGHI	82.8	82.7	+0.1
BEGHI	79.1	78.5	+0.6
DEFHI	87.6	86.8	+0.8
ACDHI	90.3	90.2	−0.1
BCDHI	88.3	88.9	−0.6
BCDEFGHI	92.6	92.3	+0.3
ACDEFGHI	93.2	92.6	+0.6
ABDEFGHI	91.7	91.3	+0.4
ABCEFGHI	91.9	91.2	+0.7
ABCDFGHI	93.5	93.5	0.0
ABCDEGHI	92.4	92.3	+0.1
ABCDEFGHI	94.0	94.1	−0.1

A	The People	F	Daily Mail
B	Sunday Pictorial	G	Daily Sketch
C	Sunday Express	H	Daily Mirror
D	News of the World	I	Daily Express
E	Daily Herald		

based on combinations of nine newspapers. Alternative methods of estimating the net coverage, including Agostini's, do not give very good results for this set of examples.

These results demonstrate the accuracy which can be expected, and also illustrate that, unlike most approximate methods, the error does not increase with the number of publications in combination. In fact, the error tends to be smaller, the larger the schedule. The average error for four-paper combinations was 0.74 per cent; for five-paper combinations it was 0.50 per cent; and for eight-paper combinations 0.42 per cent.

The calculations can be made quickly, either with a slide rule, desk calculator, or a table of logarithms. The equation for k_n lends itself admirably to calculation by the slide rule, because of the alternate multiplications and divisions. If a slide rule such as the Otis-King is used, which is equivalent to a much longer desk model, the results will be accurate to the third decimal place.

If $k_1{}^2$ is equal to k_2, then the values of s and t become infinite. In this case, the duplication is normal (i.e., chance), and k_n is simply $k_1{}^n$.

Net Coverage: Multiple Insertions

Let us turn now to the estimation of the net coverage of a series of insertions in a number of publications. We now must take account not only of the duplication among publications, but also among the various issues of each.

This presents no difficulty if the basic formula (2) for k_r approximates to the cumulative audience over a number of issues of the same publication. In other words, if the same formula approximates equally well, whether the duplication is between or within media, then in order to calculate the net coverage of the schedule we have only to restate the problem in the following terms:

Required is the net coverage of the nine publications $A_1, B_2, B_4, C_1, C_4, C_6, D_1, D_3, D_5$, where the subscripts refer to the week of insertion. The data given will be:

1. The readership (p) of an average issue of each of A, B, C, and D. Note that $p_{B_2} = p_{B_4}$, and similarly for C and D. That is, we assume readership is the same for any issue of a publication.

2. The net coverage of each of the 36 pairs of issues, such as A_1B_2, A_1B_4, and so on. Note that $p_{A_1B_2} = p_{A_1B_4}$; $p_{A_1C_1} = p_{A_1C_4} = p_{A_1C_6}$; and so on.

In fact there will only be six different pairs *between* publications: AB, AC, AD, BC, BD, CD.

Within publications, there will be just three different combinations, $p_{B_2B_4}$, $p_{C_1C_4}$, and $p_{D_1D_3}$, since duplication within a publication is fairly constant and we can assume that $p_{C_1C_6} = p_{C_1C_4} = p_{C_4C_6}$ and $p_{D_1D_3} = p_{D_1D_5} = p_{D_3D_5}$. The calculation then proceeds exactly as for nine publications.

All this assumes that our formula will apply to duplication within, as well as between publications. Hyett (1958) showed that the cumulative noncover of n issues of a publication is closely approximated by the nth moment about the origin of the Beta variate.

Hyett assumes a personal probability (q) of not reading any issue of the publication, and further assumes that these probabilities are distributed over the population in accordance with the Beta variate, defined by

$$\phi(q) = \frac{q^{l-1}(1-q)^{m-1}}{B(l, m)}$$

$$o < q < 1.$$

On these assumptions, the cumulative noncover, q_n, is given by

$$q_n = \int_o^1 \phi(q) q^n dq$$

The integral converges if $l > o$, $m > o$; q_n is thus the nth moment about the origin of $\phi(q)$, and is equal to

$$\frac{l(l+1)\ldots(l+n-1)}{(l+m)(l+m+1)\ldots(l+m+n-1)}$$

The values of the parameters l and m are determined by the known values of q_1 and q_2, where q_1 is the noncover of any issue, and q_2 the noncover of any two issues.

Hyett's formula has been tested against U.S. data provided by Politz and British data derived from the Attwood panel. The fit has been good in all cases examined so far.

Now, our sequence (1), viz.

$$\frac{\Sigma q_i}{n}, \frac{\Sigma q_{ij}}{\binom{n}{2}}, \ldots q_{123\ldots n}$$

in the case of n issues of the same publication reduces to the sequence, $q_1, q_2 \ldots q_n$ in Hyett's notation, it being assumed that the readership of any issue is constant, as also is the readership of any two, any three, and so on.

Moreover, our formula (2) on k_r is identical with Hyett's writing $s = l$ and $t = l + m$.

For the case of duplication within media, then, our formula has been tried and tested.

The genesis of the basic formula is now clear. Since cumulative readership over n issues of a single publication is only a special instance of duplication among n publications, be they the same or different, it seemed likely that Hyett's formula would apply, mutatis mutandis, to the general case.

There is, however, an important difference between the two formulas. In Hyett's formula, the parameters must be positive, otherwise the integral does not converge. This is always the case when the duplication is within a publication. But on duplication between publications, our parameters s and t frequently assume negative values. Therefore, we must entirely separate our formula from the Beta variate and any suppositions about a probability distribution. It is an empirical formula, whose parameters can be either both positive or both negative. In the special case of within-publication duplication it coincides with Hyett's formula.

TABLE 3
HYPOTHETICAL PUBLICATION SCHEDULE

	Insertions		
Week	A	B	C
1		X	X
2			X
3	X		
4		X	X

Housewives reading		Net coverage of pairs		Cumulative coverage (any 2 issues)	
A	10%	AB	28%	B	36%
B	20	AC	37	C	51
C	30	BC	44		

In calculating net coverage, the procedure may be clearer if we use a numerical example. Table 3 presents a hypothetical three-publication schedule, with two insertions in one publication and three in another, and gives readership data.

The steps in the calculation are then as follows:

1. $\Sigma q_1 = .90 + 2(.80) + 3(.70)$
   $= 4.60$

2. $\Sigma q_{ij} = 2(.72) + 3(.63) + .64 + 6(.56) + 3(.49)$
   $= 8.80$

   corresponding to the combinations:

   $A_3B_1, A_3B_4, A_3C_1, A_3C_2, A_3C_4, B_1B_4, B_1C_1, B_1C_2, B_1C_4, B_2C_1, B_2C_2, B_2C_4, C_1C_2, C_1C_4, C_2C_4.$

3. $\Sigma q_{1/n} = 4.60/6 = .767$
   $\Sigma q_{ij} / \binom{n}{2} = 8.80/15 = .587$

4. $s = \frac{.767^2 - (.767)(.587)}{.587 - (.767)^2} = -138$
   $t = \frac{-138}{.767} = -180$

5. $q_{123456} = \frac{(138)(137)(136)(135)(134)(133)}{(180)(179)(178)(177)(176)(175)} = 0.198$

6. Net coverage $= 1 - .198 = .802$ (80.2 per cent)

We can check the accuracy of the result in this case, because the values for the net coverage in pairs (Table 3), while hypothetical, were deliberately chosen so that the duplication is normal (i.e., chance duplication). This being so, the net coverage of the whole schedule is simply $1 - (.90)(.80)^2 (.70)^3 = .802$. This agrees exactly with the estimated coverage.

Note that the net coverage as usually computed, ignoring within-publication effects, would have been $1 - (.90)(.80)(.70) = .496$, or 49.6 per cent, as compared with the true value of 80.2 per cent.

Frequency Distribution

Before discussing how to estimate the frequency distribution, let me digress briefly on Waring's theorem. With this powerful theorem, first enunciated in 1792, we can calculate the proportion reading, 1) just t out of n publications, and 2) at least t out of n publications, given the proportions reading respectively any one, any two, . . . n.

As before, let p_i be the proportion reading the ith publication, P_{ij} the proportion reading both i and j, and so on. We are no longer speaking of net coverage; it is now a question of *both* as distinct from *either or*. There is, of course, a connection between the two. In the case of two publications, if we let $[p_{12}]$ indicate net coverage, and p_{12} the proportion reading both 1 and 2, then

$$[p_{12}] = p_1 + p_2 - p_{12}$$

and in the general case

$$\Sigma [p_{ij}] = (n - 1) \Sigma p_i - \Sigma p_{ij}.$$

Waring's theorem states that the proportion reading exactly t out of n publications is given by

$$\sum_{r=t}^{r=n} (-1)^{r-1} \binom{r}{t} \Sigma p_r \ldots \quad (3)$$

and at least t out of n by:

$$\sum_{r=t}^{r=n} (-1)^{r-t} \binom{r-1}{t-1} \Sigma p_r \ldots \quad (4)$$

where r denotes the number of subscripts in Σp. For example, in our notation, if r is one, the term is Σp_1; if r is two, Σp_{ij}, and so on.

As an example, in the case in which n is four, the proportion reading just two out of four will be:

$$_2) \Sigma p_{ij} - \binom{3}{2} \Sigma p_{ijk} + \binom{4}{2} p_{1234}$$

We can now estimate the frequency distribution, provided we are given the values of Σp_{ij} . . . etc. These can be obtained in exactly the same way as the q's, and the same basic formula (2) for k_r

applies. That is, given the first two terms in the sequence $\dfrac{\Sigma p_i}{n}, \dfrac{\Sigma p_{ij}}{\binom{2}{}}$ . . . we can calculate all the subsequent terms by formula (2).

Thus, from the original data of Table 3, we have

$$\Sigma p_i = 1.400 \quad \frac{\Sigma p_i}{n} = .233$$

$$\Sigma p_{ij} = 0.800 \quad \frac{\Sigma p_{ij}}{\binom{2}{}} = .053$$

in which we derive,

$$\begin{aligned} \Sigma p_{ij} &= (n - 1) \Sigma p_i - \Sigma [p_{ij}] \\ &= 5(1.40) - [2(.28) + 3(.37) + (.36) \\ &\quad + 6(.44) + 3(.51)] \\ &= 7.00 - 6.20 = 0.80 \end{aligned}$$

whence

$$s = \frac{(.233)^2 - (.233)(.053)}{.053 - (.233)^2} = -42$$

and

$$t = \frac{-42}{.233} = -180$$

Applying formula (2), we get the successive terms of the sequence as shown in col. 1 in Table 4. Col. 2 gives the number of terms involved, and col. 3 (col. 1 multiplied by col. 2) shows the values of Σp_i, Σp_{ij} etc. The proportion reading just one publication therefore is $1.400 - 2(.8000) + 3(.2400) - 4(.0397) + 5(.0034) - 6(.0001) = .3776$. Similarly for 2, 3, 4, 5 and 6. These results are shown in Table 5.

TABLE 4
EQUATION VALUES—HYPOTHETICAL SCHEDULE

(1) $\Sigma p_r \Big/ \binom{n}{r}$	(2) No. of terms	(3) Σp_r
.23333	6	1.4000
.05333	15	.8000
.01200	20	.2400
.00265	15	.0397
.00057	6	.0034
.00012	1	.0001

TABLE 5
FREQUENCY DISTRIBUTION—HYPOTHETICAL SCHEDULE

Number of publications read	Actual (predetermined) %	Estimated %	Standard calculation* %
0	19.8	19.8	50.4
1	37.5	37.8	5.6
2	28.7	28.6	12.6
3	11.2	11.2	23.0
4	2.3	2.3	2.4
5	0.5	0.3	5.4
6	—	—	0.6
	100.0	100.0	100.0

* Ignores within-publication duplication.

Since it is, in fact, chance duplication, the actual frequencies will be the coefficients of t^r in the expansion of $(.90 + .10t)(.80 + .20t)^2(.70 + .30t)^3$, where $r = 0, 1, 2 \ldots 6$, and these are shown in the "actual" column of Table 5.

The agreement between actual and estimated frequencies in Table 5 is very good. Moreover, you can see the great difference between these two frequencies and the third column, or standard calculation, which is based on the assumption that the same people read B in week 1 as in week 4, and similarly for C. While this difference would be much less with the nonchance duplication one normally finds, any distribution which ignores duplication within media is quite unrealistic.

In practice, the entire distribution is rarely needed. We usually are more concerned with estimating only a few groups, such as the proportion of persons reading less than three, three or more but less than five, etc. In this event, formula (4) avoids the necessity of calculating individual frequencies.

Using an indirect and simulated approach we have demonstrated that our basic formula is applicable both to within-publication and between-publication duplication when tested against observed data. Thus, there is a strong a priori argument in favor of the method's validity. We have further shown that in the special case of chance duplication, the method provides very good approximations of the net coverage and frequency distribution. Final confirmation must await more experimental data.

Television and Radio Applications

In the case of print readership, which has been our only concern so far, research shows that the proportion reading any issue is about constant over a short period. Research also shows that the proportion reading any two issues is constant. This is less likely to be true for radio and television. Competing programmes may depress or inflate the size of an audience on any one occasion.

If the audience of any two of a series of broadcasts of the same programme remains constant, or approximately so, then the formula should apply. To see whether enough constancy exists, we compared actual cumulative audiences for several radio and television programmes (Politz, 1953) with estimates using the basic formula. Table 6 shows the approximations are very close in the case of radio, and, although not so close for television, of sufficient accuracy for predictive purposes. If we had the

data, we would very likely find that the formula also applies to between-programme duplication.

TABLE 6
CUMULATIVE RADIO AND TV AUDIENCES (%)

	Jack Benny (Radio)		Amos 'n' Andy (Radio)	
	Actual	Estimated	Actual	Estimated
1.	15.0	15.0	14.1	14.1
2.	24.0	24.0	22.4	22.4
3.	30.3	30.2	27.9	28.1
4.	35.1	34.9	32.1	32.2

	Charlie McCarthy (Radio)	
	Actual	Estimated
1.	10.5	10.5
2.	17.0	17.0
3.	21.5	21.7
4.	25.0	25.2

	Red Skelton (TV)		Colgate Comedy Hour (TV)	
	Actual	Estimated	Actual	Estimated
1.	19.4	19.4	23.6	23.6
2.	29.2	29.2	33.7	33.7
3.	35.2	35.4	39.2	39.8
4.	39.2	40.0	42.6	44.0

	Your Show of Shows (TV)		Texaco Star Theatre (TV)	
	Actual	Estimated	Actual	Estimated
1.	23.1	23.1	18.7	18.7
2.	33.2	33.2	28.3	28.3
3.	38.8	39.3	34.2	34.5
4.	42.3	43.0	38.0	38.9

Leaving aside the question of the validity and accuracy of the formula as applied to broadcast, there remains the problem of the many additional observations needed when each new vehicle is added to the comparison. For a schedule comprising n different programmes and publications, $\frac{n}{2}(n+1)$ observations would be needed. In Britain, typical schedules embrace at least 20 national newspapers and magazines, and perhaps 700 different television time slots during the year. Over a quarter of a million observations would be required.

The bulk of the data required to apply the method to a print campaign has already been published. All we need now are data on the duplication between two issues of each major newspaper and magazine. If these data were available, the media planner could at once make realistic estimates of coverage and frequency. At present such estimates are far from realistic.

REFERENCES
AGOSTINI, J.-M. How to Estimate Unduplicated Audiences. *Journal of Advertising Research*, Vol. 1, No. 3, March 1961, pp. 11-14.
HYETT, G. P. Paper read to the Statistics Seminar, London School of Economics, February 1958.
NUTTALL, C. G. F. *The Measurement of Press Readership.* London: London Press Exchange, 1962.
POLITZ, ALFRED, RESEARCH, INC. *A Study of Four Media— Their Accumulative and Repeat Audiences.* New York: Time, Inc., 1953.

Net Audiences of U.S. and Canadian Magazines: Seven Tests of Agostini's Formula[1]

JOHN BOWER

Wheaton Glass Company

In 1961 a new estimation procedure promised to end laborious tabulations of unduplicated audiences. Bower finds it works—up to a point.

THE PROBLEM of estimating a net audience—that number of persons reached one or more times by a combination of magazines or newspapers—has been recognized for many years. Any practical estimation technique must be accurate within acceptable limits and less costly than a tabulation by hand or machine.

One method meets these criteria and is probably the best known attempt to estimate net or unduplicated audience: the Agostini technique. It requires a knowledge only of individual vehicle audiences and their duplications in pairs, the smallest combination. More complicated techniques would be less desirable even if they were as accurate. Furthermore, Agostini's work is an original hypothesis that deserves to be thoroughly tested before other methods are proposed.

What follows is an analysis of the Agostini technique applied to magazine readership studies, with suggestions for improving it when it errs.

To test Agostini's method, gross audience and pairwise duplications must be known for each vehicle combination. The actual unduplicated audience must also have been tabulated in order to check the estimate. Few readership studies contain this information. Some studies require extensive tabulations just to obtain pairwise duplications. One large body of such tabulations is a press readership survey made in France by the Centre d'Etude des Supports de Publicité (CESP) in 1957,

JOHN BOWER received a B.S. in economics in 1960 and an M.B.A. in marketing in 1962 from the Wharton School of Finance and Commerce, University of Pennsylvania. As a graduate student he worked with Behavior Systems, a university-affiliated research and consulting organization owned by Professor Wroe Alderson and directed by Dr. Kenneth Middleton. His work there included studies for a national drug firm on medical advertising. He is a management trainee at the Wheaton Glass Company, Millville, N. J.

[1] This paper was prepared by Dr. Rita Senf from a thesis presented by Mr. Bower to the Wharton School of the University of Pennsylvania in partial fulfillment of the requirements for the M.B.A. degree. Besides Dr. Senf, Mr. Bower also wishes to thank Professor Wroe Alderson, Dr. Edward Brink, Dr. Kenneth Middleton, Dr. Charles K. Ramond, Mr. William Korbel, and Miss Joan Hatcher for their guidance.

in which the net audiences of 32,767 combinations of 15 magazines were actually counted. Unfortunately, these tabulations were not accessible in time to be considered in this study.

Several surveys have investigated duplications of media other than magazines. Newspapers and TV have recently been studied in some detail. In order to have reasonably similar data, however, we decided to limit our analysis to national magazines studied in published readership surveys.

This report is based on seven readership reports by national magazines in the U.S. and Canada. Six published studies show the net audiences—actually tabulated—of 605 vehicle combinations. Net audiences of another 35 combinations were made available by Behavior Systems, Inc. These 640 cases probably constitute the great majority of all U.S. and Canadian magazine combinations whose net audiences have been tabulated.

These seven surveys, though internally consistent, are not strictly comparable. They cover 22 years during which considerable improvement was made in question design, sampling technique, and tabulation practice. The definition of a reader ranges from a person who claims to have "seen" the magazine to one who says he has read at least so many pages or articles. The 35 combinations provided by Behavior Systems couple specialized medical journals with general medical publications. The survey of Canadian publications involved bilingual readership in the Province of Quebec. For these reasons each survey must be reported separately, and our conclusion cannot be a blanket acceptance or rejection of the Agostini method.

The Agostini Technique

Agostini's technique was presented in his article, "How to Estimate Unduplicated Audiences," in the March 1961 issue of this *Journal*. A summary of the main features follows.

The vehicles of a combination are designated as a, b, c, . . . n, and the respective audiences of the vehicles as A_a, A_b, . . . A_n. The sum of the audiences of the vehicles is A. Because of duplication, the unduplicated audience C is almost always smaller than the gross audience A; therefore $C = zA$, where z is a coefficient between 0 and 1.

The Agostini method estimates z from another variable, x. A matrix is set up showing the duplicated audience of all possible pairs of vehicles in the combination being considered. This matrix is symmetrical about its main diagonal; D is the sum of the pairwise duplications to one side of the diagonal. The variable x is defined as D/A. When values of D and A are given in a readership study, x can easily be determined.

Agostini suggested that z can be satisfactorily estimated from x: "Obviously, the greater the duplication between media, the less will be the unduplicated audience. The higher the value of D, the lower the value of C. Inasmuch as $x = D/A$ and $z = C/A$, when x increases, z decreases. When there is no duplication between media, the unduplicated audience equals the sum of the audiences. In this case, when $D = 0$, $x = 0$, and when $C = A$, $z = 1$" (Agostini, 1961, p. 12).

The basis of the Agostini technique is the observed relationship between the variables x and z. Of the 32,767 combinations in the CESP study, Agostini chose 98 at random. From the observed A, D, and C values he calculated and plotted the corresponding x and z values. The resulting curve resembled an equilateral hyperbola asymptotic to the x axis. Thus with the addition of vehicles to a combination, A may increase without limit, while C must decrease, i.e., z must approach zero as a limit. An equation of the form $z = 1/(Kx + 1)$ was fitted to the data, with a resulting constant K of 1.125. This equation appears to fit the plotted values very closely, as shown in Figure 1.

Agostini made several tests of the accuracy of the formula when applied to both French and American readership studies. For the *Life* report, *A Study of Four Media*, he found that 85 per cent of the cases he tested had less than 1.0 per cent error, and that the maximum error was 2.7 per cent.

The Agostini method is not the only way to estimate unduplicated audiences, but it is probably the least complicated. It is based on the assumption of random readership among homogeneous groups of vehicles. It was constructed and tested on such combinations, i.e., vehicles appealing to the same audience, such as general circulation magazines, or daily newspapers. There is thus some reason to believe that the technique may not be as accurate when applied to combinations of nonhomogeneous vehicles.

Another possible source of inaccuracy is the relation between the number of vehicles in the combination and the error of estimate. The larger the number of vehicles, the more tenuous becomes any relationship between duplications and net audience.

14

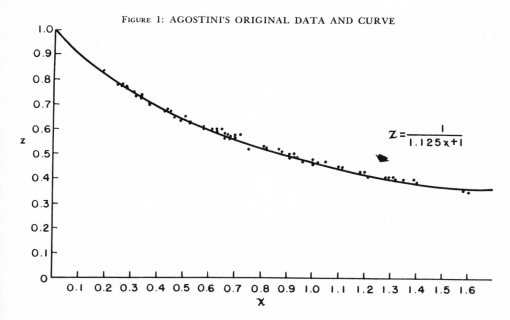

FIGURE 1: AGOSTINI'S ORIGINAL DATA AND CURVE

$$Z = \frac{1}{1.125x+1}$$

The Seven Surveys

The 640 cases having the necessary data to test the Agostini technique were obtained from the following studies, listed in chronological order:

A. Life 1939: Data were published by Time, Inc. in "Life's Continuing Study of Magazine Audiences, Report No. 2," May 1939. Covered *Collier's, Liberty, Life,* and *Saturday Evening Post.*

B. CARF: "Audience Study of 11 Magazines in Canada" was conducted in 1949 by the Advertising Research Foundation on behalf of the Canadian Advertising Research Foundation. Covered four French magazines (*La Revue Moderne, La Revue Populaire, Le Samedi, Selection du Reader's Digest*); and seven English magazines, including two women's (*Canadian Home Journal, Chatelaine*) and five general (*Maclean's, National Home Monthly, New Liberty,* and the Canadian editions of *Time* and *Reader's Digest*). Provided two sets of data—B1, ten combinations of English magazines, and B2, ten combinations involving both English and French magazines.

C. Look 1952: "National Study of Magazine Audiences, 1952" was conducted by Crossley, Inc. for Look Magazine. Covered nine magazines, including five weeklies (*Collier's, Life, Look, Saturday Evening Post, Better Homes and Gardens*) and four monthlies (*Good Housekeeping, Ladies' Home Journal, McCall's, Woman's Home Companion*).

D. Life 1953: "A Study of Four Media: Their Accumulative and Repeat Audiences" was conducted for Life Magazine by Alfred Politz Research, Inc., published by Time, Inc. Covered *Life, Saturday Evening Post, Look, Ladies' Home Journal,* and *This Week.*

E. Look 1955: "The Audiences of Nine Magazines: Their Size and Characteristics" was a national study conducted by Alfred Politz Research, Inc. for Look Magazine. Covered the same magazines as Study C.

F. Four Medical: "The Audience of 4 Medical Magazines" was done for Medical Economics by Alfred Politz Media

Studies in 1959. Covered *Medical Economics, Journal of the American Medical Association, Modern Medicine,* and *MD Medical Newsmagazine.*

G. Behavior Systems: Unpublished data covered seven general medical and seven specialized medical journals.

METHOD

The necessary computations from the published raw data were done by computer. The gross audience A was found by working backwards from the sample percentages used to project the studies to the total population. Matrices showing duplicated audiences of all pairs were prepared and used to calculate D. The tabulated net audience C was given in the original publications.

For each combination the following six calculations were made:

1. $x = D_p/A$; the sum of pairwise duplications expressed as a percentage of the sum of the audiences.
2. $z_a = C_a/A$; the actual unduplicated audience expressed as a percentage of the sum of the audiences—the actual or tabulated figure which Agostini's formula seeks to estimate.
3. $z_e = 1/(1.125x + 1)$; the estimate of z calculated by Agostini's formula.
4. $C_e = z_eA$; the estimate of unduplicated audience calculated by multiplying the sum of the audiences, A, by z_e.
5. $(C_e - C_a)/C_a$; the error of Agostini's estimate, with the difference expressed as a percentage, positive or negative, of C_a.
6. Relative standard deviation of the pairwise duplication; D_p is divided by the number of D_p's, giving a mean D_p. This figure is subtracted from each individual D_p and

each difference or d is squared. The d^2's are summed and divided by the number of D_p's. The square root of the result divided by the mean D_p yields the relative standard deviation of pairwise duplication.

The first analysis evaluated the error of estimate resulting from application of Agostini's formula. Each readership study was considered separately; the per cent average (arithmetic) error was calculated for each study, plus a weighted average for all 640 cases. Table 1 presents the results. The actual z values, as calculated by computer, are shown in Figures 2 through 6, with Agostini's curve superimposed in each graph for comparison.

TABLE 1
PER CENT AVERAGE ERROR FOR THE VARIOUS STUDIES

Study	N	Average Error
A. Life 1939	5	1.7%
B. CARF		
1. English	10	1.9
2. English and French	10	5.2
C. Look 1952	210	2.3
D. Life 1953	80*	9.8
E. Look 1955	285	1.1
F. Four Medical	5	15.0
G. Behavior Systems	35	6.8
Overall Weighted Average	640	3.1

* Editor's note: This figure differs from Agostini's report in the original article. There were 96 possible combinations (six sets of 16); Bower evidently omitted the set of 16 combinations for the total.

Within the individual studies error was inspected to see if it varied with changes in group size or group composition. Table 2 shows results for various group sizes. From these limited data, error appears to increase with group size.

TABLE 2
RELATION BETWEEN AVERAGE ERROR AND GROUP SIZE

Study	Combinations	Average Error
Look 1952	Trios	1.9%
	Quartets	2.5
Look 1955	Trios	1.1
	Quartets	1.4
Four Medical	Trios	13.3
	Quartets	17.5
Behavior Systems	Trios	3.3
	Quartets	5.7
	Quintets	5.9
	Sextets	9.9
	Septets	13.3

In the CARF study (Table 1) error was somewhat higher for combinations of English and French magazines than for English magazines alone, suggesting that error estimates vary with the heterogeneity of the combinations. The extraordinarily high error for the Four Medical study (Table 1) was later discovered to be due to a basic computational error; however, before that discovery, one

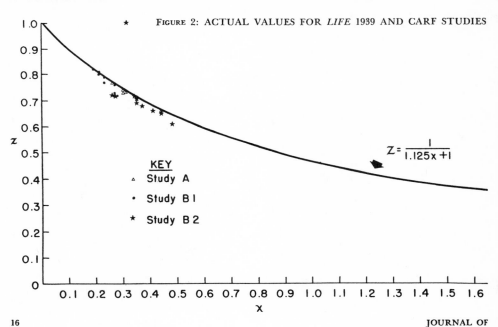

FIGURE 2: ACTUAL VALUES FOR *LIFE* 1939 AND CARF STUDIES

$$Z = \frac{1}{1.125x + 1}$$

KEY

△ Study A

• Study B 1

★ Study B 2

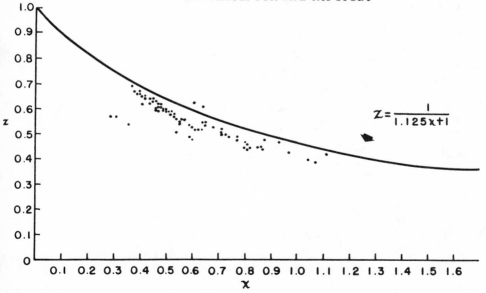

FIGURE 3: ACTUAL VALUES FOR *LOOK* 1952 STUDY

$$Z = \frac{1}{1.125x + 1}$$

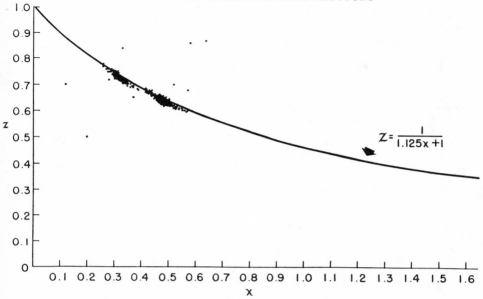

FIGURE 4: ACTUAL VALUES FOR *LIFE* 1953 STUDY

$$Z = \frac{1}{1.125x + 1}$$

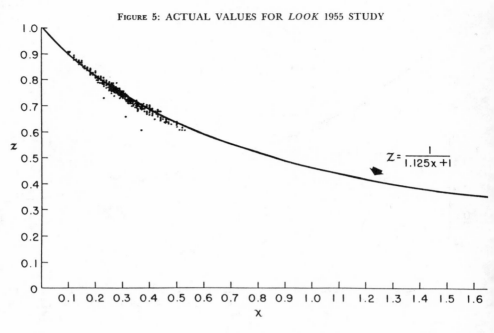

FIGURE 5: ACTUAL VALUES FOR *LOOK* 1955 STUDY

$$Z = \frac{1}{1.125x + 1}$$

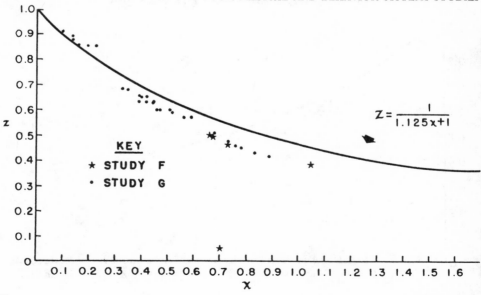

FIGURE 6: ACTUAL VALUES FOR THE FOUR MEDICAL AND BEHAVIOR SYSTEMS STUDIES

KEY

★ STUDY F

• STUDY G

$$Z = \frac{1}{1.125x + 1}$$

FIGURE 7

SCHEMATIC REPRESENTATION OF THE RELATION BETWEEN
ACTUAL VALUES AND ESTIMATES BY AGOSTINI'S FORMULA

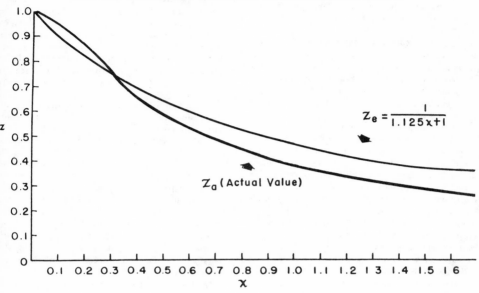

$$Z_e = \frac{1}{1.125x + 1}$$

Z_a (Actual Value)

possible explanation was entertained that this large error might be due to nonhomogeneous group composition.

An experiment was designed to test this hypothesis, using the Behavior Systems data. From the seven general and seven specialized medical journals, seven combinations for each of five group sizes (3, 4, 5, 6, and 7) were chosen; thus there were seven sets of calculations for each group size. One set consisted of combinations containing only general medical journals, one of all specialized journals, and the remaining five were varying combinations of general and specialty journals arranged so that error could be noted as group composition varied. Average error was computed for these combinations. The results were: for the combinations containing all general journals, 8.2 per cent; for the mixed combinations, 4.3, 7.0, 8.3, 5.6, and 8.0 per cent; and for all specialty journals, 6.5 per cent. Thus there was no apparent systematic relationship between size of error and group composition.

A further attempt was made to analyze the error inherent in the Agostini formula by calculating the Pearson product-moment correlation between error and the relative standard deviation of pairwise duplication. Using a random sample of 100 cases, the coefficient of correlation, r, was .61, establishing a positive relationship with near certainty. The coefficient of determination, r^2, was .37, indicating that a little over a third of the variation in the estimating error can be attributed to variation in the relative standard deviation of pairwise duplication.

Of the 640 cases, only ten per cent showed a negative error; these were concentrated mainly at x values below .30, with none above x values of .70. This finding suggests that the actual functional relationship between x and z must cross the curve found by Agostini. Twenty cases selected at random led to the relationship schematized in Figure 7. It would seem that in general the Agostini formula leads to z estimates higher than the actual values, and that the constant of 1.125 is too small, resulting in chronic overestimates.

CONCLUSIONS

The Agostini technique appears to be generally applicable to magazine readership studies of the kinds considered in this report and provides estimates within acceptable limits of error. The weighted average error for the 640 cases was 3.1 per cent. The general applicability of the technique is established by the fact that the Behavior Systems study and the bilingual portion of the CARF study showed average error of 6.8 and 5.2 per cent, respectively. Both these studies involved heterogeneous combinations of vehicles and had heterogeneous groups of respondents.

The Agostini technique may not be acceptable as stated for estimating the unduplicated audience of combinations involving more than five or six vehicles. Most readership studies do not calculate net audience data for combinations exceeding five vehicles; but the indication is that error does increase with group size, since in every case considered here the estimating error was higher for quartets than for trios. For the Behavior Systems data, error increased from 3.3 per cent for trios to 13.3 per cent for septets. Thus pairwise duplication appears to become less and less accurate for predicting net audience as group size increases. Unfortunately, too few cases of higher-order combinations were available to test this hypothesis thoroughly.

The Agostini technique must be based on the assumption of random readership among vehicles. This statement is supported by the positive correlation between estimating error and pairwise duplication, and by the larger, although still tolerable, error in the studies containing heterogeneous combinations, namely, the CARF, Four Medical, and Behavior Systems studies. Homogeneous vehicles are by definition similar in nature and presumably in the audience that reads them. We had thought that error was a function of the relative proportion of general and specialty vehicles in a combination, but this assumption was not supported when tested by varying the group composition. At the time this latter test was made, we did not take into consideration that the test involved a homogeneous audience. The fact is that readers are grouped by the vehicles they read; vehicles are not grouped by the audiences they reach. Homogeneous vehicles, then, have relatively similar and high probabilities of multiple readership, since they appeal to similar readers. Vehicles can be arranged in groups that reach the same basic audience. Within these groups of homogeneous vehicles the probabilities are random as to number of magazines read and as to duplication. But the probabilities between *different* groups of homogeneous vehicles cannot be random. For example, consider a homogeneous group of vehicles such as women's magazines, or general business magazines. Probabilities within each of these groups would be random, and within each group readership could be quite closely estimated; but the number of readers of magazines of *both* types could not be accurately estimated.

It was not possible to test this hypothesis directly, since the available readership studies dealt with fairly homogeneous groups of vehicles, usually general readership, national circulation, magazines. However, some indirect evidence can be cited. It was observed that variance in pairwise duplication increased with group size, probably because the number of pairs increases more than arithmetically as group size increases. With these increases, the homogeneity of the group is lessened. This limits the effectiveness of estimations based on pairs, as shown by the correlation where 37 per cent of the estimation error was a result of variance among the pairs, and by the increase of error with increased group size.

Agostini's formula does not always give an accurate representation of the functional relation between x and z. As was seen in the plotted figures, the formula results in overestimates, suggesting that the constant 1.125 is too small. Since 90 per cent of the cases tested showed a positive error, use of this constant *cannot* yield the lowest possible average error. It is conceivable that a constant could be found such as to yield both positive and negative errors, with an average error close to zero, and still varying within tolerable limits.

A correction factor could be constructed to compensate for the lack of estimating accuracy found in larger vehicle combinations. It is felt that this error is inherent in the use of pairs as a basis for estimating higher-order combinations and should not be confused with error resulting from the poor fit of a formula to an observed function. This error appears to increase in some explainable way with group size. Not enough cases of large size were available to try to determine such a correction factor, but it should be relatively easy to derive a straight percentage correction for each group size from the large number of large combinations in the CESP study.

Net Audiences of British Newspapers: A Comparison of the Agostini and Sainsbury Methods

J. M. Caffyn and M. Sagovsky

The London Press Exchange Limited

A technique originated 25 years ago gives accurate estimates when duplicated audience is high.

In March 1961 this *Journal* published J.-M. Agostini's fascinating paper, "How to Estimate Unduplicated Audiences," which reported a formula for estimating the net coverage of three or more publications without actually tabulating it. The formula had been arrived at empirically after the study of survey data on 15 out of 30 French magazines, and was found to apply also to the results of a 1953 *Life* study covering five American magazines.

Agostini's formula naturally aroused considerable interest in the United Kingdom, but it was found that in the media circumstances operating here the formula had certain limitations. Other ways of tackling the problem, used at the London Press Exchange, may be of interest.

To begin with, general magazines are much less important as an advertising medium in the United Kingdom than in either France or the U.S.A. Characteristics associated with general magazines in those two countries are found here in our mass-circulation national dailies, e.g., national cover with generally normal duplication.

JOHN CAFFYN is director of the Communications Research Division of The London Press Exchange Ltd. He studied mathematics and English at Trinity College, Cambridge. He has been in advertising for 11 years, and joined LPE Television Ltd. before commercial TV began in the U. K. He headed the LPE team which investigated new ways of measuring the audiences to TV commercials; the results of this survey were published in August 1962. He plans the agency's media and advertising research projects, devises techniques of use in planning appropriations, and advises on media strategy.

MARIANNA SAGOVSKY works in the Communications Research Division of The London Press Exchange Ltd. She studied mathematics at Trinity College, Dublin, and began her career in the LPE's marketing department. For the last three years she has worked on long-term projects, including research into the audience of press advertisements and linear programing in media selection. Born in London of White Russian parents, Miss Sagovsky is bilingual in English and Russian.

Again, Agostini's formula did not concern itself with the problem of "mixed" press vehicles, which in this country is more often before us than not. The formula had been developed from publications within one medium, no allowance being made for the effect of adding, say, one daily paper to a schedule containing only magazines. The high degree of duplication arising from this sort of mixed schedule may tend to invalidate the Agostini estimates.

Finally, the Agostini formula requires a knowledge of duplications. The IPA National Readership Surveys published in the United Kingdom give a general picture of duplication for men, women, and housewives. They do not give duplications by class, age, or region.

Against these problems, methods of estimating net cover developed by E. J. Sainsbury at the London Press Exchange (and used there for some 25 years) combine simplicity with flexibility and on the whole produce estimates of great accuracy. It is possible, moreover, to get a reasonable estimate of net cover by demographic breakdowns within which the IPA does not supply duplication data.

Press media in the United Kingdom fall into two categories:

1. General cases for which Agostini's formula may be satisfactory due to low or normal duplication: national dailies, some Sundays, some general weeklies, and general monthlies.

2. General cases for which Agostini's formula is likely to be less satisfactory due to high duplication: some Sundays, some general weeklies, women's weeklies, women's monthlies, and all mixed schedules.

Sainsbury's Methods

The two Sainsbury methods—Normal and Modified—have a common basis, the Modified being an extension of the Normal. The concept used is that of non-cover. For two publications, A and B, we get a diagram like that shown in Figure 1.

For three publications, A, B, and C, we get a diagram like that shown in Figure 2.

To obtain the net audience of two publications by the Sainsbury Normal Method, multiply the non-cover of A by the non-cover of B to obtain the non-cover of both publications, and then subtract this from 100 per cent. Similarly for three publications, multiply the non-cover figures for A, B, and C together to obtain the net non-cover figure for ABC, and then subtract from 100 per cent.

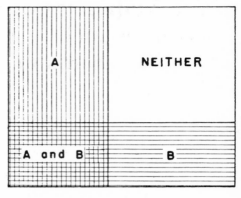

FIGURE 1

NON-COVER FOR READERS OF TWO PUBLICATIONS

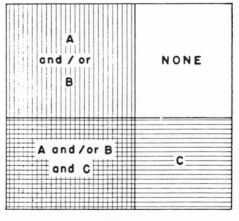

FIGURE 2

NON-COVER FOR READERS OF THREE PUBLICATIONS

For example, suppose that A is read by 40 per cent of the universe and B by 30 per cent. Then the per cent non-cover is 60 for A and 70 for B. The net non-cover of A and B is 60 x 70 or 42 per cent, so the net cover is 58 per cent.

Similarly for three publications, if the per cent cover is 40 for A, 30 for B, and 20 for C, we multiply the corresponding non-cover percentages. Then the net non-cover of A, B, and C is 60 x 70 x 80 or 33.6 per cent, and the net cover is 66.4 per cent.

The Sainsbury Normal Method can, of course, be

extended to any number of publications. It is the only way of estimating the net cover for breakdowns in which the degree of duplication is not known (either of total readership, or of subgroups such as class, age, and region).

Where the duplication in pairs is known, the process is adjusted and becomes the Sainsbury Modified Method. In our example for three publications, supposing we know, in addition to the figures already given, the per cent net cover of the publications in pairs: AB 57, AC 50, and BC 45.

We will adjust B and C to base A (choosing the publication with the highest individual cover as the base). That is, we need to know what figure together with 40 per cent will, on the basis of normal duplication, give us the net cover with B of 57 per cent and with C of 50 per cent. We find in the case of B that non-cover AB divided by non-cover A is 43/60 or 71.7 per cent; and in the case of C, non-cover AC divided by non-cover A is 50/60 or 83.3 per cent. This modifies the per cent cover figure for B from 30 to 28.3 and for C from 20 to 16.7.

Multiplying our new non-cover figures of 60.0, 71.7, and 83.3, we get 35.8 per cent, which gives us a net cover for the three publications of 64.2 per cent, as compared with the Sainsbury Normal estimate of 66.4 per cent.

Some Examples

The following examples are based on a complete card sorting analysis of all combinations of six national newspapers. Given the data of Table 1 for readership by all adults aged 35 or over, what is the unduplicated audience of the combination *Daily Herald* (2), *Daily Mirror* (3), and *Daily Sketch* (6)?

TABLE 1
COVERAGE BY INDIVIDUAL PAPERS AND
PAIRS OF PAPERS

Individual Papers	Number of Cards	% Cover
1. Daily Express	2033	34.1
2. Daily Herald	830	13.9
3. Daily Mirror	2097	35.2
4. News of the World	2754	46.2
5. Daily Mail	1214	20.4
6. Daily Sketch	606	10.2
Pairs of Papers		
2, 3	2575	43.2
2, 4	3015	50.6
2, 6	1324	22.2
3, 4	3563	59.7
3, 6	2365	39.7
4, 6	2987	50.1
Base	5964	100.0

First applying Agostini's Method, the reader can verify that the sum of the audiences, A, is 3,533, D is 802, and C is 2,814, or 47.2 per cent.

With the Sainsbury Normal Method, we multiply the non-cover of 2, 3, and 6 (86.1, 64.8, and 89.8) and get 50.1 per cent; therefore the cover is 49.9 per cent.

To apply the Sainsbury Modified Method, we note that in this combination paper 3 has the highest individual cover and is therefore taken as base. Papers 2 and 6 are adjusted to base 3, for which non-cover is 64.8 per cent. For paper 2, non-cover 2,3 divided by non-cover 3 is 87.7 per cent. For paper 6, non-cover 3,6 divided by non-cover 3 is 93.1 per cent. Multiplying 87.7, 64.8, and 93.1 gives 52.9 per cent non-cover, or 47.1 per cent cover for the 2,3,6 combination.

To summarize the results, compared with the true cover as tabulated of 47.3 per cent, the Agostini Method gives 47.2 per cent, the Sainsbury Normal 49.9 per cent, and the Sainsbury Modified 47.1 per cent.

Now to the above three national dailies let us add a national Sunday paper, *News of the World* (4). Given the data in Table 1, how many persons are reached by one or more of these four papers?

With the Agostini Method A is 6,287, D is 3,032, and C is 4,076, or 68.3 per cent.

For the Sainsbury Normal Method we multiply 86.1, 64.8, 53.8, and 89.8, obtaining 27.0 per cent; thus the cover is 73.0 per cent.

Next applying the Sainsbury Modified Method, papers 2, 3, and 6 must be adjusted to base 4, except that since paper 6 has a higher duplication with 3 than with 4, it is adjusted to 3 rather than to 4. The results of the adjustments are as follows:

	Adjusted to		
	4	3	2
Paper			
3	74.9		
2	91.8	87.7	
6	92.8	93.1	90.4

For the calculation we use the highest non-cover figure in each row. On longer schedules all combinations must be considered in this form, but no paper is adjusted to one lower in coverage than itself.

Multiplying the modified figures for papers 2, 3, 4, and 6 of 91.8, 74.9, 53.8, and 93.1 gives 34.4 per cent non-cover. Thus for the combination the cover is 65.6 per cent.

To summarize the results for the combination 2,3,4,6, compared with the true cover of 64.9 per cent, the Agostini Method gave 68.3, Sainsbury Normal 73.0, and Sainsbury Modified 65.6 per cent.

Comparison of Methods

For all the combinations of the six papers, Table 2 presents the differences between the true cover and the estimates by the three methods. Inspection of Table 2 shows that the Sainsbury Modified Method will almost always underestimate slightly, while Agostini's Method will usually overestimate on a mixed schedule and underestimate on an unmixed one.

For the 42 combinations, the most nearly correct estimate, including ties when they occur, is as follows: Agostini 14, Sainsbury Modified 21, Sainsbury Normal 10. In practice, of course, at the London Press Exchange we would use the Sainsbury Modified Method for publications of this kind. The most nearly correct figures then become: Agostini 15, Sainsbury Modified 28.

Figure 3 shows, in vertical pairs, for the corresponding x values, the actual z values and the estimates of z by the Sainsbury Modified Method, with Agostini's hyperbola superimposed for comparison.

A schedule consisting entirely of national papers —especially if they are all national daily papers— offers the kind of context where Agostini's formula is most likely to be satisfactory. A clue to the potential weakness of the formula when used in the United Kingdom can be seen in Table 2: for not one of all the possible combinations that included the Sunday paper (4) did it give the most nearly correct estimate.

TABLE 2

COMPARISON OF TRUE COVER WITH THE THREE ESTIMATES

Combination of Papers	True Net Cover %	Agostini %	Sainsbury Modified %	Sainsbury Normal %	Combination of Papers	True Net Cover %	Agostini %	Sainsbury Modified %	Sainsbury Normal %
Trios					**Quartets**				
123	65.6	0	—1.7	—2.4	1234*	76.6	+5.2	—1.1	+3.6
124*	67.8	+2.1	—0.6	+1.6	1235	76.7	—0.7	—4.9	—6.0
125	58.1	—0.6	—1.9	—3.3	1236	68.7	—0.6	—2.4	—1.8
126	50.6	—0.6	—0.7	—1.5	1245*	76.0	+2.8	—2.0	—0.3
134*	73.9	+4.7	—0.5	+3.1	1246*	70.3	+2.4	—0.8	+2.2
135	70.4	0	—2.6	—4.4	1256	63.3	—1.3	—2.9	—3.9
136	62.2	+0.1	—0.6	—0.6	1345*	81.4	+5.3	—2.5	+0.3
145*	72.7	+2.0	—1.0	—1.0	1346*	75.5	+4.7	—0.3	+3.9
146*	67.0	+1.7	—0.1	+1.2	1356	73.3	—0.4	—3.2	—3.8
156	54.4	—0.3	—0.6	—1.6	1456*	74.9	+2.4	—1.2	—0.3
234*	62.8	+3.5	+0.3	+7.2	2345*	72.0	+3.9	—1.3	+4.1
235	57.4	—0.4	—1.1	—1.8	2346*	64.9	+3.4	+0.7	+8.1
236	47.3	—0.1	—0.2	+2.6	2356	60.9	—0.9	—1.5	—0.8
245*	61.2	+1.1	—0.4	+1.9	2456*	64.1	+1.2	—0.4	+2.7
246*	54.1	+0.7	+0.1	+4.3	3456*	71.1	+3.3	—0.7	+4.0
256	39.2	—0.7	—0.5	—0.7	**Quintets**				
345*	69.2	+3.4	—1.0	+3.0	12345*	83.9	+5.6	—3.3	+0.3
346*	61.9	+2.9	+0.7	+6.8	12346*	78.2	+5.0	—1.0	+4.1
356	53.9	—0.3	—0.3	—0.3	12356	79.4	—1.3	—5.6	—5.7
456*	60.5	+0.5	—0.1	+0.9	12456*	78.1	+3.0	—2.2	+0.1
					13456*	82.7	+5.2	—2.4	+0.8
					23456*	73.8	+3.7	—1.1	+4.7
					Sextet				
					123456*	85.2	+5.4	—3.3	+0.6

* Combination contains the national Sunday paper.

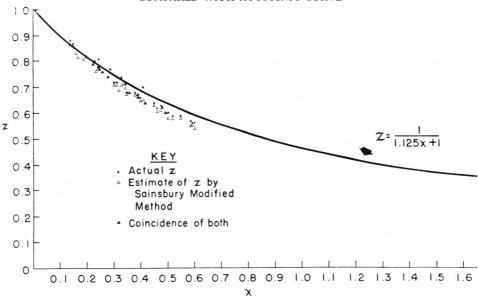

FIGURE 3

ACTUAL VALUES AND SAINSBURY MODIFIED ESTIMATES,
COMPARED WITH AGOSTINI'S CURVE

$$Z = \frac{1}{1.125x + 1}$$

KEY

. Actual z

△ Estimate of z by
Sainsbury Modified
Method

▲ Coincidence of both

A less satisfactory result from this formula occurred in estimating the net cover of A, B, and C1 adults (the three highest social grades) achieved by a combination of four national Sunday papers (*News of the World, People, Sunday Pictorial, Sunday Express*) and the weekly *Radio Times*. For the combination of the four Sunday papers the true cover was 75.0 per cent; the estimates were: Agostini 77.7, Sainsbury Normal 77.6, and Sainsbury Modified 75.0 per cent. For the same papers plus *Radio Times* the true cover was 92.8 per cent, and the estimates were: Agostini 102.5, Sainsbury Normal 92.5, and Sainsbury Modified 90.6 per cent.

Postscript

If we consider all combinations of three or more papers of the six papers in the examples, and list the value of Agostini's x (= D/A) against the size of the error in Agostini's estimates of cover, there seems to be an obvious relationship.

In order to minimize the error, it would seem that Agostini's factor, Kx + 1, would have to increase as the size of x increases; within the structure of the formula, this implies a changing value for K. It would also appear from this particular analysis that the value for K would have to change slightly according to the number of papers being considered.

Although this may seem a paradox, all exact science is dominated by the idea of approximation.
—BERTRAND RUSSELL

Net Audiences of German Magazines: A New Formula[1]

WALTHER KUHN

DIVO Institute

Herr Kuhn finds that the equation one should
use to estimate the net audience of a combination
of vehicles depends on the number of vehicles.

LARGE READERSHIP STUDIES generally report the audiences of single vehicles, along with tables of the duplicated audiences of all possible pairs. Not usually shown are the net audiences of combinations of two or more magazines.

To report the audiences of all combinations of all magazines in large studies will not be possible in the foreseeable future, even with the help of electronic data processing systems. From the 44 magazines in the German readership study of 1961 there are 17.6 billion combinations! To list them all, even in print small enough to get 300 combinations

on a page, would require some 58 million volumes of a thousand pages each. The most thorough attempt at such tabulation, to our knowledge, is the listing of all combinations of 15 magazines (from a total of 30) in three large volumes reporting the readership study done in France by SEMA under the auspices of the CESP in 1957. In Germany complete duplication analyses have been carried out with up to ten magazines.

Following a paper read by J.-M. Agostini to the ESOMAR Congress at The Hague (1960), we attempted to apply to German data the mathematical procedure presented there and used in the CESP study. Our observations are based on data from the quantitative German readership study carried out in 1961 by the DIVO Institute under the auspices of the Arbeitsgemeinschaft Leseranalyse e.V., Essen-Heidhausen, referred to here as LA 61. The results of the study are based on a random sample of that part of the population of the Federal Republic of West Germany aged 16-70. The sample included

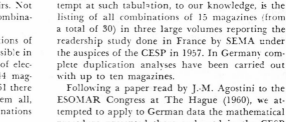

WALTHER KUHN directs the statistical section of DIVO, Institut fur Wirtschaftsforschung, Sozialforschung, und Angewandte Mathematik in Frankfurt-am-Main. He received his statistical and mathematical education at the universities of Heidelberg, Cologne, and Mainz, and later worked with several governmental and municipal statistical organizations. In 1957 he joined the DIVO Institute, a member of the METRA group, where his duties include the planning and organization of market and audience research and the evaluation of surveys. He belongs to the Deutsche Statistische Gesellschaft.

[1] Originally published in German as "Die Nettoreichweitenbestimmung einer Kombination von Zeitschriften: Eine Näherungslösung," *Metra*, Vol. 1, No. 2, 1962, pp. 155-164. Translated by Thomas K. Crowl.

13,972 cases. We found in our studies, as did Agostini in the CESP study, regular relationships. These relationships, however, exhibited a different form. In particular, they depended on the number of magazines in the combination.

As Agostini has shown and using his notation, the coefficient z can be expressed as a function of x in the form of a curve—more explicitly, by a formula corresponding to the type of curve chosen. One can therefore write $z = f(x)$ and, after obtaining the value of x, determine z as a function of x; then the size of C (the unduplicated audience of the combination) can be determined with sufficient exactness.

The relation between x and z is obviously inverse: as x grows larger, z must get smaller. Of the various curves which could express this relationship, Agostini chose the hyperbola; he gives the explicit equation as $z = 1/(Kx + 1)$, where K as determined empirically is 1.125. Agreement between the values obtained by this formula and by actual count in the CESP study was exceptionally close.

Our application of Agostini's original formula to the LA 61 data led to discrepancies of up to five per cent. In an attempt to reduce these errors, we calculated the hyperbolic equation of best fit for these LA 61 data; this gave a K value of 1.162, or four hundredths more than Agostini's K of 1.125. Even with this improved K value there were still discrepancies of up to two per cent. This relatively poor agreement and, more importantly, the fact that our K value differed from Agostini's, caused us to proceed along the following lines.

The duplication tables of the DIVO Institute contained a total of 700 combinations which could be used for our purposes. From all possible combinations, we selected 35 each from those containing three through eight magazines, all seven combinations of nine magazines, and the single combination of ten. A graph of each type of combination, with x the abscissa and z the ordinate, resulted in a continuous curve of the form $z = e^{-K_n x}$.

The coefficients K_n were obtained empirically from the shape of the curve and gave the values in Table 1. The sequence of the K values suggests a general formula. For the examined cases, K_3 to K_{10}, a recursive formula was devised:

$$K_n = K_{n-1} - \cfrac{1}{n - \left(\cfrac{n-a}{2}\right)^2}$$

where $n > 3$, $K_3 = 1$, and $a = 2$ when n is even and 3 when n is odd. As Table 1 shows, values for

K_n from the formula agree extremely well with the values obtained empirically. Figure 1 shows the curves corresponding to the values of K_n obtained by the recursive formula.

TABLE 1
COMPARISON OF K VALUES
DETERMINED EMPIRICALLY AND BY FORMULA

Number of Magazines in the Combination	Obtained Values of K_n:	
	Empirically	By Formula
3	1	1
4	.893	.889
5	.831	.826
6	.769	.763
7	.715	.723
8	.683	.683
9	.663	.655
10	.627	.627

EXAMPLES

We want to give several examples that test the formula and the exactness of our reasoning. Suppose the unduplicated audience of a combination of five magazines is requested. We have the following audience figures from the tables of LA 61: *Hör Zu* 4,058; *Quick* 3,231; *Revue* 2,501; *Neue Illustrierte* 2,041; and *Constanze* 2,220. The sum of the audiences, A, equals 14,051. We also have the duplicated audience figures for combinations of two magazines from LA 61:

	Quick	Revue	Neue Ill.	Constanze
Hör Zu	1136	935	752	817
Quick		1690	1417	1317
Revue			1247	1087
Neue Illustrierte				1016

Adding all figures in the above table, D is 11,414, the sum of the duplicated audiences for all pairs of magazines.

Remember that $x = D/A$, in this case .812. For an x value of .812 we read from the curve the corresponding z value of .51. Therefore the unduplicated audience C of the combination is zA or 7,166. By actual count the unduplicated audience was 7,351. In percentages based on a sample of 13,972 cases, one gets 51.3 by the formula and 52.5 by actual count. This agreement is very satisfactory.

Let us take a quartet as a further example. The audience values obtained from LA 61 are as follows: *Stern* 3,702, *Quick* 3,231, *Spiegel* 1,354, and *Das Beste aus Reader's Digest* 1,132. The sum A is 9,419. The duplicated audiences of pairs of magazines are:

	Quick	Spiegel	Das Beste
Stern	2221	948	444
Quick		841	388
Spiegel			289

FIGURE 1

FAMILY OF CURVES FOR VALUES OF n FROM 3 TO 10,
COMPARED WITH AGOSTINI'S CURVE

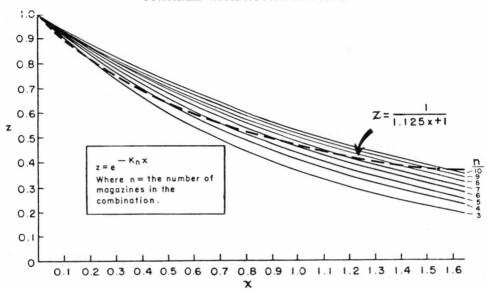

The sum D is 5,131 and x is .545. The corresponding z value on the curve is .61, and C is 5,746. By actual count the unduplicated audience of the quartet was 5,484. In percentages the results are: by formula 41.1, by count 39.3.

We have purposely shown here those examples in which the *largest* errors occurred in order to make clear the applicability of the procedure which has been developed. In none of the 180 selected combinations was the error more than 1.8 per cent. In 130 combinations it was less than 1.0 per cent.

We are aware of the inadequacies of the demonstrated procedure and concede that complete multiple-duplication tables cannot be substituted for by the procedure described above. Indeed, even to calculate the table might be as expensive as the actual count itself. But in all cases where a decision among a few combinations must be reached rapidly, their unduplicated audiences can be estimated with sufficient accuracy for comparison with one another.

The procedure, incidentally, is in no way restricted to combinations of single magazines but is also valid for combinations of categories of magazines. The unduplicated audience of the combination of all weekly picture magazines, all radio-television magazines, and all film magazines was 70.0 per cent from the curve (with n = 3) and 68.3 per cent by actual count. For the combination of all weekly picture magazines, all Sunday magazines of topical interest, all weekly entertainment magazines, and all monthly magazines, the unduplicated audience was 58.0 per cent from the curve (with n = 4) and 58.6 per cent by actual tabulation.

SUMMARY

To determine the unduplicated audience of a combination of more than two magazines, it is necessary to know only the audiences of the individual magazines in the combination and the duplicated audiences of all possible pairs. Agostini described the functional relationships existing between these quantities by a simple hyperbolic function which was independent of the number of magazines in the combination. An investigation of German data, however, revealed a different exponential function of the form e^{-Kx}, where the coefficient K depends on the number of magazines in the combination.

The DIVO Institute, having material on combinations of up to ten magazines at its disposal, was able to determine the explicit functions empirically and to find in the exponent of the functions a simple recursive formula for the K coefficients. There was satisfactory agreement between the audience figures obtained from the new mathematical procedure and from an actual count; the largest errors were about 1.8 per cent.

We agree with Agostini that this procedure can also be applied unchanged to duplication analyses within segments of the sample, both for combinations of single magazines and for combinations of categories of magazines. For example, dupli-

cation data of persons aged 16-40, or of housewives, or of persons in a specific income class, should follow the same laws. Unfortunately we in Germany had no data which would permit us to check this claim. Another inadequacy is that we have not been able to examine the validity of the recursive formula for K_n when n is larger than ten. Moreover, it appears that through an appropriate consideration of exclusive readership of the magazines in the combination, the procedure can be improved still further.

Despite these imperfections, we are convinced that a simple and rational instrument, with whose help recurring problems can be solved satisfactorily, has been placed at the disposal of the media analyst.

REFERENCE

AGOSTINI, J.-M. A Short-Cut Method for Estimating the Unduplicated Audience of a Combination of Media. In *ESOMAR Congress Papers*, The Hague, September 1960. Revised and published as "How to Estimate Unduplicated Audiences" in the March 1961 issue of this *Journal*.

The mathematician may be compared to a designer of garments, who is utterly oblivious of the creatures whom his garments may fit. To be sure, his art originated in the necessity for clothing such creatures, but this was long ago; to this day a shape will occasionally appear which will fit into the garment as if the garment had been made for it. Then there is no end of surprise and delight.
—TOBIAS DANTZIG

Net Audiences of French Business Papers: Agostini's Formula Applied to Special Markets[1]

MARCEL MARC

R. L. Dupuy

Monsieur Marc extends his colleague's method to
the specialized audiences of French business papers.

CAN THE METHODS used to calculate the net audiences of mass magazines also be used for trade magazines? By calculation methods I refer particularly to Agostini's famous formula, which has proven to be so accurate and easy to use in French media research.

As soon as one studies the readership of the specialized press, he is surprised by the number of publications read regularly by those interested in particular fields. It is not unusual to find a majority of persons in a certain profession reading three or four different magazines in that field. Such reading is not a diversion but a necessity.

MARCEL MARC is media director of the R. L. Dupuy advertising agency in Paris. During World War II he was an infantry officer in the French army and then a prisoner of war for five years. For ten years after the war he directed a group of technical publications. He has been president of the Syndicat des Chefs de Publicité de la Presse de Paris, and general secretary of the Fédération Francaise de la Publicité. He is vice chairman of the Institut de Recherches et d'Etudes Publicitaires, and lectures at the Ecole Supérieure de Publicité and at the Centre de Recherches des Chefs d'Entreprises.

The duplication of readership between these magazines is therefore particularly high, and it would be risky to apply unthinkingly mathematical formulas so valuable in other circumstances. Today Agostini's formula is well known, appreciated, and applied. But can it be verified other than in the context of French national magazines? Remember that it was found empirically, not derived mathematically from basic premises.

Table 1 shows data obtained by the R. L. Dupuy agency in a recent survey of French furniture manufacturers, each of whom was asked about his readership of five furniture magazines. For the sake of discretion we have replaced the names of these magazines with letters of the alphabet.

As has been demonstrated elsewhere (Marc, 1960), the actual net audience (C) of five magazines may be tabulated as follows:

The sum of the audiences (A)
— the sum of the duplications (D)
+ the sum of the triplications
— the sum of the quadruplications
+ the quintuplication
= Net unduplicated audience (C).

[1] Adapted from *Etude de la Couverture Réalisée par Plusieurs Revues Techniques sur une Clientèle Spécialisée*, published in November 1962 as Study No. 6 Bis by the Institut de Recherches et d'Etudes Publicitaires (IREP) in Paris. Translated by Charles K. Ramond.

TABLE 1

TABULATED AUDIENCES AND OVERLAPS OF FIVE FURNITURE MAGAZINES

Singles		Duplications		Triplications		Quadruplications		Quintuplication	
a	225	ab	183	abc	154	abcd	62	abcde	40
b	285	ac	181	abd	75	abce	97		
c	300	ad	84	abe	103	abde	45		
d	153	ae	120	acd	67	acde	41		
e	183	bc	228	ace	113	bcde	55		
		bd	117	ade	46				
		be	144	bcd	93				
		cd	115	bce	132				
		ce	164	bde	63				
		de	74	cde	62				
	1146*		1410*		908		300		40

* The sum of the individual audiences, 1146, is Agostini's A. The sum of the duplications, 1410, is Agostini's D.

Substituting the actual values from Table 1, we have C = 1146 — 1410 + 908 — 300 + 40 = 384. In similar fashion we tabulated the exact audience of each combination of these five magazines. There are 26 such combinations: ten pairs, ten trios, five quartets, and one quintet.

Then for each combination we calculated x and z as defined by Agostini: x is the sum of the duplications (D) divided by the sum of the audiences of all magazines (A); z is the unduplicated audience of the combination (C), also divided by the sum of the audiences of all magazines (A). Agostini

found that a plot of x against z gave a regular hyperbola. When we made the same plot for our 26 combinations of furniture magazines, we found these 26 points fell on a hyperbola like that of Agostini but not coincident with it. Figure 1 shows that the curve for our furniture magazines falls below Agostini's curve for general magazines, and differs only in its value of the coefficient K. In the hyperbola z = 1/(Kx + 1), the value of K required for our data is 1.6 rather than the 1.125 found by Agostini.

We may hypothesize that in different contexts

FIGURE 1

UNDUPLICATED AUDIENCE OF FURNITURE MAGAZINES:
ACTUAL VALUES, AGOSTINI'S CURVE, AND NEW HYPERBOLA

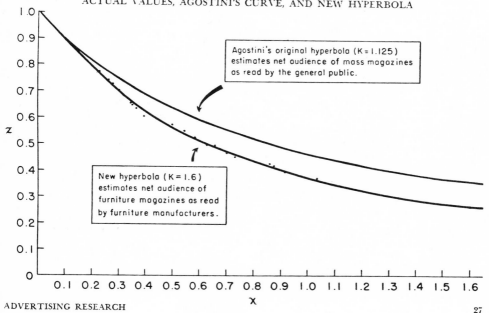

Agostini's original hyperbola (K = 1.125) estimates net audience of mass magazines as read by the general public.

New hyperbola (K = 1.6) estimates net audience of furniture magazines as read by furniture manufacturers.

FIGURE 2

NUMBERS OF MAGAZINES READ BY:

THE FRENCH PUBLIC (K = 1.125)

FRENCH FURNITURE MANUFACTURERS
(K = 1.6)

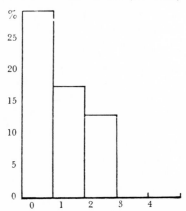

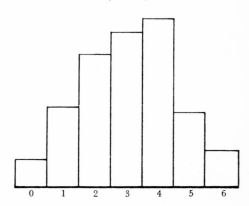

of readership we will find various hyperbolas to represent the relationship between unduplicated audience and pairwise duplications, and that these hyperbolas will differ only in their respective values of K. It is impossible to verify this hypothesis in this study. But if we adopt it provisionally, then we must find a way of calculating the constant K that can be used or applied in all contexts of readership.

There is a mathematical link between x and z shown in the equations which define them.

$$x = \frac{\Sigma \text{ duplications}}{\Sigma \text{ audiences}}, \text{ and } z =$$

$$\frac{\Sigma \text{ audiences} - \Sigma \text{ duplications} + \Sigma \text{ triplications, etc.}}{\Sigma \text{ audiences}}$$

Note the common elements in these equations: the sum of the audiences and the sum of the duplications. Those elements which occur only in the equation for z are the sum of the triplications, the quadruplications, and so on. Insofar as z is related mathematically to x, it is necessary that the higher-order elements not be independent of the two common elements, but be determined by them. The mathematical link between duplications and higher-order multiplications of readership should vary with K. Thus K reflects the way the population is distributed by number of magazines read.

This frequency distribution by number of magazines read is nothing more than a quantitative

definition of what we have been calling up to now "the context of readership." Figure 2 gives an illustration of how this distribution differs with different values of K.

If we ignore nonreaders (readers of no magazines), then the rest of the population makes up the net audience of all magazines. To get the *total* audience of all magazines, we would simply add the readers of one magazine, the readers of two, of three, and so on. We can then calculate K for that particular point at which:

$$x = \frac{\text{Sum of the duplications between all magazines}}{\text{Sum of the audiences of all magazines}}$$

$$\text{and } z = \frac{\text{The net audience of all magazines}}{\text{The sum of the audiences of all magazines}}.$$

This we have undertaken elsewhere (Marc, 1962b). There we have shown that K is the quotient of four finite series composed only of the numbers of persons who read various numbers of magazines. The formula is: K =

$$\frac{(L_2 + 2L_3 \ldots + [n-1]L_n)(L_1 + 2L_2 + \ldots n L_n)}{(L_1 + L_2 \ldots + L_n)(L_2 + 3L_3 + 6L_4 \ldots + {}_nC_2 L_n)}$$

where L_1 stands for readers of just one magazine, L_2 for readers of just two, etc., and ${}_nC_2$ stands for the number of possible combinations of n things taken two at a time, in this case the number of possible pairs of n magazines.

Having expressed K in terms of the context of

readership, it remains only to check our two hypotheses. Expressed formally these are:

1. that z remains a hyperbolic function of x in the different contexts of readership, that is, in those populations that are differently distributed according to the numbers of magazines read. In other words, the hyperbola $z = 1/(Kx + 1)$ varies in different populations only in the value of K.

2. that the calculated value of K which considers all magazines studied and all of the population studied is not fortuitous. It remains applicable to that limited number of magazines; for them, K is constant.

We tested these hypotheses in four different readership surveys: furniture magazines as read by furniture manufacturers, business magazines as read by businessmen, mass magazines as read by businessmen, and laundry and dry cleaning magazines as read by operators of these services. These were among several studies undertaken by R. L. Dupuy on the readers of the specialized press. We tabulated in each study the actual net audience of five magazines by the method described above. Table 2 shows that our *estimate* of the net audience, made by applying the two hypotheses above, gave virtually the same results.

TABLE 2

ESTIMATED AND ACTUAL NET AUDIENCES
OF FOUR QUINTETS

Type of Magazine	Est.	Actual	Base	K
Furniture	385	384	400	1.607
Businessmen	633	632	695	1.436
General	535	536	695	1.318
Laundry	156	151	166	1.510

To illustrate the stability of the coefficient K within a given survey, we plot in Figure 3 data from the study of furniture magazines. Each cross stands for one of the 26 combinations of two, three, four, or five magazines. The ordinate represents the tabu-

FIGURE 3

DATA SHOWING K IS CONSTANT IN FURNITURE
MAGAZINE STUDY

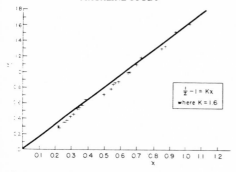

$$\frac{1}{z} - 1 = Kx$$
where K = 1.6

lated value of $(1/z) - 1$, while the abscissa is Agostini's x. It can be shown that

$$K = \frac{\frac{1}{z} - 1}{x}$$

hence if K is indeed a constant, a plot of the above numerator against the denominator should be a straight line. Figure 3 shows that the 26 points do coincide rather well with a straight line. The slope of this particular line is the value of the coefficient K, 1.6.

CONCLUSION

Chance alone cannot account for results as consistent as the tests shown here. It now seems possible to calculate accurately the net audience of a combination of trade journals without tabulation. It is sufficient to know the audience of all magazines, their duplications in pairs, and the general distribution of the population according to the number of magazines read.

This kind of information is obtained by survey more easily than by tabulating audiences of all combinations, especially when they are as numerous as the 32,767 published by the CESP in its first survey! The calculations are easy and quick, witness the four tests shown here. Moreover, the method is well known, being that of Agostini, which we have extended here only by varying the value of the coefficient K.

This extension generalizes the application of Agostini's method to trade journals and to the readership of general magazines by specific clienteles such as businessmen. It is obvious that businessmen do not read magazines in the same way as does the general public. Nor is it certain that Germans, Englishmen, Italians, and Americans read combinations of magazines as do the French. Teenagers and oldsters, rich people and poor people, farmers and urbanites—no subgroup necessarily reads magazines as does the average person. But by varying the coefficient K in Agostini's hyperbola, it should be possible to estimate the net audience reached by any vehicle combination within each group.

REFERENCES

MARC. MARCEL. Comment Evoluent Couverture et Répétition dans une Action Publicitaire Utilisant les Périodiques Nationaux. Paris: Institut de Recherches et d'Etudes Publicitaires, March 1960.

MARC. MARCEL. L'Action Conjugée des Supports de Press. Vendre, No. 384, February 1962.

MARC. MARCEL. Étude de la Couverture Réalisée par Plusieurs Revues Techniques sur une Clientéle Spécialisée. Paris: Institut de Recherches et d'Etudes Publicitaires, November 1962.

Measuring the Cumulative Net Coverage
of Any Combination of Media

PIERRE HOFMANS*

➤ Despite computers and simulation methods, "naive" media calculation methods which give immediate information still have a place. The proposed method measures, with great accuracy, the total number of readers, viewers,
or listeners of a combination of media and issues. It can be used on a total population figure or on any desired
category of readers, on absolute or percentage figures. It requires just paper and pencil, or, for more speed,
a desk calculator.

DEFINITIONS

Net coverage (C_n) of a combination of n papers is the
number of readers of at least one of these papers. Thus
net coverage counts the number of different *readers*
exposed to the n papers without consideration of readership of two or more (duplication, triplication). In
contrast, *gross coverage* is simply the *sum of the* n
audiences, $\sum_n A$; thus equating one person reading two
papers with two people each reading one.

Cumulative audience (A_n) of a paper (or a radio or
TV program, or movie) is the number of different
readers reached after n issues of the paper. One
may anticipate this number to be higher than that
of a single issue, because it would be exceptional
that readers of a second, third, or n^{th} issue be *all*
the same as those of the first issue. Like net coverage,
cumulative audience is a count of different *readers*,
while *gross audience* is the *sum* of the various *issue
audiences*.

Cumulative net coverage (C_c) of a combination of
papers, each appearing more than once, is the total
number of readers of this combination of papers and
issues. It takes into account:

1. duplication, triplication, etc. between papers and
2. increase in audience after two, three, or n issues.

This cumulative net coverage of a media, expressed
either in absolute figures or in percentage of total, is
the most complete measure of an important part of the
advertising effort: the total number of people exposed to
at least one message.

CALCULATION OF NET COVERAGE

At the Esomar Congress of 1960, J. M. Agostini [1]
reported on a method of calculating net coverage. This
shortcut method makes use of data on the audience of
each paper and the duplication by a pair of audiences,

* Pierre Hofmans is a director at Masius-Claeys, S.A., Brussels,
a wholly owned branch of Masius International. He is in charge of
Petfoods, a subsidiary of Mars, Inc.

usually provided by most media studies. When considering a combination of n papers, call $\sum_n A$ the sum of
their (n) audiences, and $\sum D$ the sum of the $[n(n -
1)]/2$ duplications. The net coverage C_n is then given by
the formula:

$$(1) \qquad C_n = \frac{(\sum_n A)^2}{\sum_n A + K \sum D},$$

in which K is, as in Agostini's method, a constant equal
to 1.125.

Many advertising people have used this formula.
Each time a verification was possible, the calculated
value of C_n was sufficiently close to the value of C_n as
measured by the study. Possibly this high precision
results because Formula (1), though having been empirically constructed, is close to the exact formula:

$$(2) \quad C_n = \sum_n A - \sum D + \sum T - \sum Q + ...,$$

where

$\sum_n A$ is the sum of the audiences,
$\sum_n D$ is the sum of the duplications,
$\sum T$ is the sum of the triplications,
$\sum Q$ is the sum of the quadruplications, etc.

Formula (1) can be modified as:

$$(3) \qquad C_n = \frac{\sum_n A}{1 + K \dfrac{\sum D}{\sum_n A}},$$

or

$$(4) \quad C_n = \sum_n A - K \sum D + \frac{(K \sum D)^2}{\sum_n A} - \frac{(K \sum D)^3}{(\sum_n A)^2} + \cdots$$

Formulas (2) and (4) are similar in form.

269

Table 1
VALUES OF A AND KD FOR THE 1964 POLITZ MAGAZINE STUDY [7]
(Figures in thousands)

Magazine[a]	Magazine[a]										
	1	2	3	4	5	6	7	8	9	10	11
1	18,770	5,892	7,101	6,660	6,754	6,828	8,815	9,524	3,622	7,202	4,895
2		14,270	6,544	6,166	5,756	6,175	7,947	8,151	2,757	4,748	6,647
3			14,750	7,429	6,548	7,095	8,803	8,640	3,661	5,740	5,266
4				14,890	6,336	6,437	9,627	8,677	3,591	6,575	4,701
5					30,500	16,261	8,766	16,356	3,162	11,247	4,767
6						28,760	9,446	13,733	3,720	10,089	4,939
7							21,430	12,109	5,391	7,317	6,145
8								36,320	4,600	12,927	6,739
9									9,470	3,065	2,583
10										22,880	4,234
11											12,380

[a] 1 = *Better Homes & Gardens*. 2 = *Family Circle*. 3 = *Good Housekeeping*. 4 = *Ladies Home Journal*. 5 = *Life*. 6 = *Look*. 7 = *McCall's*. 8 = *Reader's Digest*. 9 = *Redbook*. 10 = *Saturday Evening Post*. 11 = *Woman's Day*.

If only two papers are considered, Formulas (1) and (2) become:

$$(5) \qquad C_2 = \frac{A_1 + A_2}{1 + K \dfrac{D 2}{A_1 + A_2}},$$

$$(6) \qquad C_2 = A_1 - A_2 - D 2.$$

Combining Formulas (5) and (6) gives, for K, a value

$$(7) \qquad K = \frac{\sum_2 A}{C_2},$$

which is not a constant, but a variable depending on the pair of papers considered. Therefore, K will vary for different pairs of papers. For convenience, the different values of

$$(8) \qquad KD = \frac{\sum_2 A (\sum_2 A - C_2)}{C_2},$$

are calculated for the last Politz Study (Table 1). Only figures contained in this table are needed to calculate all 2,036 possible coverage combinations of the eleven magazines of the study. Highly satisfactory precision, within one percent, is obtained, as shown in two examples that follow.

The formula in which the different values of A and of KD must be introduced is slightly different from Formula (1). Instead of adding the $[n(n-1)] 2$ different values of D and multiplying the sum by $K (= 1.125)$ to obtain KD, the $[n(n-1)] 2$ different values of KD are added to obtain $\sum KD$. The correct formula is obtained by calculating the net coverage:

$$(9) \qquad C_n = \frac{(\sum A)^2}{\sum_n A - \sum KD}.$$

First example: To calculate the net coverage of the combination *Life* + *Look* + *Mc Call's* + *Reader's Digest* + *Saturday Evening Post*, the 10 appropriate values of KD must first be selected, then added. A value for $\sum KD$ of 118,251 is obtained. Since the value of $\sum A$ is 139,890, the net coverage is:

$$C = \frac{139,890)^2}{139,890 + 118,251} = 75,808.$$

The study gives a value of 74,630 (thousand adult readers). The difference, 1,178, represents less than one percent of the total population of 120,36 0 adult people.

Second example: The combination of all eleven magazines gives a net coverage of 83,180,000, with a sampling tolerance of 2,680,000 adult readers (2 2 percent). Formula (9), with $A = 224,420$ and $KD = 388,906$, gives a result of 82,117,000, a difference of 0.9 percent, easily within the admitted tolerance.

The hypothesis that replacing a rigid constant with an adapted variable might provide more accurate results was verified using all available figures for United States, French and Belgian combinations of magazines (Table 2).

This greater precision, leads to the belief that K, far from being a constant valid for all pairs of papers, is a variable which depends on each pair of papers considered. Moreover, one can see that K also varies with the number of papers introduced in the combination. For instance, if the five magazines covered by the 1956 Politz Study are considered:

1. Ten pairs of magazines give ten different values of K_2, with an average value of 1.251.
2. Ten groups of three magazines give ten different values of K_3, with an average value of 1.254.
3. Five groups of four magazines give five different values of K_4, with an average value of 1.262.

4. The group of five magazines has a value of K_5 of 1.271.

The variation is small enough to be neglected. In fact, all the figures of Table 2 for Formula (9) are calculated on the base of K_2 with satisfactory results. But the tendency for K to increase with the number of issues will have to be remembered when cumulative audiences are studied.

CALCULATION OF THE CUMULATIVE AUDIENCE

The similarity between reading 2, 3, ... , n different papers and reading 2, 3, ... , n different issues of the same paper suggests use of Formula (9), after making the necessary substitutions, to calculate the cumulative audience.

Net coverage	Cumulative audience
n = number of papers	n = number of issues
$\sum_n A$ = sum of audiences, all different	nA_1 = sum of audiences, all the same
$D = \sum_2 A - C$, duplication between papers	$d = 2A_1 - A_2$ duplication between issues of a paper
(8) $KD = \dfrac{\sum_2 A \times D}{\sum_2 A - D}$	(10) $kd = \dfrac{2A_1 \times d}{2A_1 - d}$
$[n(n-1)]/2$ = number of KD's. Since all values of KD are different, the sum of all different values of KD are calculated.	$[n(n-1)]/2$ = number of kd's Since all values of kd are the same, the common value of kd is multiplied by $[n(n-1)]/2$.
(9) $C = \dfrac{\left(\sum_n A\right)^2}{\sum_n A + \sum_n KD}$	(11) $A_n = \dfrac{(nA_1)^2}{nA_1 + \dfrac{n(n-1)}{2} kd}$

Since Formula (9) allows calculation of the net coverage of any combination of papers when the individual audiences and the pairwise coverage of these papers is known, similarly, Formula (11) might allow calculation of the cumulative audience of any number of issues if the average audience and the cumulative audience after two issues are known. However, when Formula (11) is compared with results of different studies, one sees that, from the third issue on, the successive values obtained for A_n are below the measured values, and that the divergence increases as n gets larger.

It can be concluded from this that one of the values introduced in Formula (11) varies with the number of issues. It cannot be the audience A_1 (calculated in all studies as an average value valid issue after issue); and as shown below, it cannot be the duplication d.

Constancy of d, *Duplication of Cumulative Audience*

If it is admitted that the average audience A_1 remains constant, then,

$$A_1 = A_1,$$
$$A_2 = 2A_1 - d_2,$$
$$A_3 = 3A_1 - 3d_3 + t_3,$$
$$A_4 = 4A_1 - 6d_4 + 4t_4 - q_4,$$
$$A_5 = \text{etc.}$$

In these relations, d_2, d_3, d_4, . . . , are the different values of the duplication; t_3, t_4, ... , are the different values of the triplication; q_4, . . . , are the different values of the quadruplication, etc.

If it is admitted that the duplication remains constant, then $2A_1 - A_2 = d_2 = d_3 = d_4 = \ldots$. Thus,

$$A_3 = 3A_1 - 3(2A_1 - A_2) + t_3,$$

and

$$3A_1 - 3A_2 + A_3 = t_3 = t_4 = \ldots .$$

Similarly,

$$A_4 = 4A_1 - 6(2A_1 - A_2) + 4(3A_1 - 3A_2 + A_3) - q_4,$$

and

$$4A_1 - 6A_2 + 4A_3 - A_4 = q_4 = \ldots .$$

One could continue similarly and obtain a formula for the number of ultra-loyal readers of n issues on n:

$$nA_1 - \frac{n(n-1)}{2!} A_2 + \frac{n(n-1)(n-2)}{3!} A_3$$
$$- \cdots \pm nA_{n-1} \pm A_n .$$

This formula can be verified using the 1959 Politz Study [6], up to $n = 3$. In this case the formula is

$$t = 3A_1 - 3A_2 + A_3 .$$

For instance, *Life* 1959 with $A_1 = 15,320$, $A_2 = 20,930$. $A_3 = 24,290$ has a triplication of 7,450. The formula gives 7,460 (thousand readers).

Variation of k *with issues*

Since audience A_1 and duplication d remain constant, the value which in Formula (11) varies with n can only be k.

It has been shown that the value of K in Formula (9) varies with the number of papers introduced in the combination. In the same way, the value of k in Formula (11) varies with the number of issues. The variation of K could be neglected, but it is necessary to take the variation of k into account and to introduce in Formula (11) the proper values of k_3, k_4, . . . , k_n instead of the value

$$k_2 = \frac{2A_1}{A_2} .$$

How does k_n vary?

Table 2

NET COVERAGE ESTIMATES FROM FORMULAS (1) AND (9)

Combination	Net coverage from study	Formula (1)		Formula (9)	
		Number	Pct. diff.	Number	Pct. diff.
Life + Post + Look + LHJ + This Week. Total population: 119,600,000 readers [8].	58,650	59,220	+0.57	58,715	+0.05
Life + Post + Look + LHJ + Reader's Digest. Total population: 49,140,000 households [9].	31,850	33,788	+4	32,103	+0.5
Sélection du *Reader's Digest + Jours de France + La Vie Catholique + Nous Deux*. Total population: 28,818,000 readers [5].	10,468	10,414	−0.19	10,483	+0.05
Femmes d'Aujourd'hui + Rijk der Vrouw + Libelle + Rosita + Bonnes Soirées. Total population: 3,190,000 women readers [2].	1,343	1,300	−1.35	1,332	−0.35
Paris-Match + Marie Claire + Télé 7-Jours. Total population: 31,663,000 readers [4].	13,199	13,329	+0.4	13,169	−0.1
Life + Look + McCall's + Reader's Digest + Post. Total population: 120,360,000 adult readers [10].	74,630	78,473	+3	75,808	+1
Life + Look + McCall's + Reader's Digest + Post + Better Homes & Gardens + Family Circle Good Housekeeping + LHJ + Redbook + Woman's Day. Total population: 120,360,000 adult readers [10].	83,180	84,780	+1.3	82,117	+0.9

From Formula (11),

$$(12) \qquad k_n = \frac{2A_1}{d(n - 1)} \cdot \frac{nA_1 - A_n}{A_n}.$$

If we call

$$x = \frac{A_n}{nA_1 - A_n},$$

$$k_n = \frac{2A_1}{d(n - 1)} \cdot \frac{1}{x}.$$

VALUES OF $x = \dfrac{A_n}{nA_1 - A_n}$ IN FUNCTION OF $n - 1$

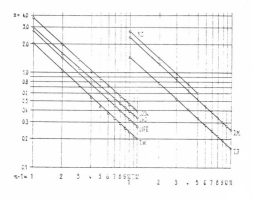

The values of x as a function of $(n - 1)$ can be calculated. For example, these values were calculated for four out of five papers studied by Politz in 1953 [7], and for the three papers studied by SOFRES in 1964 [4], and were put on a log-log graph (Figure).

When all the successive points of each paper are joined, a line which can be considered approximately straight is drawn. Since this line is negative, the relation between x and $(n - 1)$ will be of the form:

$$\log x = b - a \log (n - 1),$$

or

$$\log \frac{A_n}{nA_1 - A_n} = b - a \log (n - 1).$$

When $n = 2$

$$\log \frac{A_2}{2A_1 - A_2} = b.$$

Thus,

$$\log \frac{A_n}{nA_1 - A_n} = \log \frac{A_2}{2A_1 - A_2} - a \log (n - 1 .$$

or

$$(13) \qquad \frac{nA_1 - A_n}{A_n} = \frac{2A_1 - A_2}{A_2} \cdot (n - 1)^a.$$

But

$$(12) \qquad k_n = \frac{2A_1}{d(n - 1)} \cdot \frac{nA_1 - A_n}{A_n}.$$

Table 3
CUMULATIVE AUDIENCE BY FORMULA (14)

Magazine	Coverage		Cumulative audience from study		Formula (14)		a
			Number	Sampling error (pct.)	Number	Pct. diff.	
Life [7]	Total Pop.: 42.440,000	A_1	11,880	4.2			0.9395
		A_6	22,470	4.8	22,508	0.1	
		A_{13}	25,640	4.6	26,028	0.9	
	Age 40–49 Pop.: 11.080,000	A_1	3,300	5.6			id
		A_6	6,400	6.2	6,352	0.4	
		A_{13}	7,350	5.8	7,370	0.2	
	Education:finish high school Pop.: 7.410,000	A_1	2,870	6.9			id.
		A_6	5,050	6.4	5,137	1.2	
		A_{13}	5,590	5.8	5,870	3.8	
	Do not have TV Pop.: 31.300,000	A_1	7,550	4.3			id.
		A_6	15,030	5.2	15,006	0.1	
		A_{13}	17,380	5.1	17,538	0.5	
Life [8]	Total Pop.: 119.600,000	A_1	26,450	1.4			0.9333
		A_6	60,500	2.3	60,287	0.2	
		A_{13}	73,050	3.0	73,225	0.1	
Post [8]	Total	A_1	14,050	1.1			0.9176
		A_6	35,400	2.1	34,975	0.4	
		A_{13}	45,650	2.6	44,040	1.3	
Look [8]	Total	A_1	18,050	1.2			0.9337
		A_6	50,000	2.5	49,480	0.4	
		A_{13}	66,350	3.3	63,553	2.3	
LHJ [8]	Total	A_1	11,500	1.0			0.9081
		A_6	28,600	2.0	28,305	0.2	
		A_{13}	37,650	2.6	35,736	1.6	
This Week [8]	Total	A_1	23,000	1.5			0.9686
		A_6	42,250	2.4	41,820	0.4	
		A_{13}	49,750	2.9	46,921	2.4	
Life [9]	Total Pop.: 49.140,000	A_1	15,320	1.0			0.9401
		A_6	29,710	1.4	29,593	0.2	
		A_{13}	34,440	N.A.	34,357	0.2	
Post [9]	Total	A_1	9,530	0.9			0.9042
		A_6	20,680	1.4	20,511	0.3	
		A_{13}	25,400	N.A.	25,054	0.7	
Look [9]	Total	A_1	11,690	1.0			0.9344
		A_6	25,900	1.5	25,773	0.3	
		A_{13}	31,350	N.A.	31,008	0.7	
RD [9]	Total	A_1	17,680	1.3			0.9390
		A_6	30,580	1.5	30,441	0.3	
		A_{13}	34,840	N.A.	34,540	0.6	
LHJ [9]	Total	A_1	9,550	1.1			0.9346
		A_6	19,830	1.5	19,724	0.2	
		A_{13}	23,600	N.A.	23,349	0.5	
Paris Match [4]	Total Pop.: 31.663,000	A_1	8,026	N.A.			0.9164
		A_6	16,838	N.A.	16,954	0.4	
		A_{12}	19,243	N.A.	20,103	2.7	
Télé 7 Jours [4]	Total	A_1	5,379	N.A.			0.9155
		A_6	8,096	N.A.	8,103	0.0	
		A_{12}	8,857	N.A.	9,040	0.6	
Marie Claire [4]	Total	A_1	4,282	N.A.			0.9110
		A_6	9,746	N.A.	9,922	0.6	
		A_{12}	N.A.				
Femmes d'Aujourd'hui [4]	Total Pop.: 16.500,000	A_1	3,040	N.A.			0.8648
		A_6	5,790	N.A.	5,783	0.1	
		A_{12}	6,910	N.A.	6,938	0.2	

Table 4
VALUES OF THE CONSTANT 'a' IN POLITZ STUDIES

Magazine	1952 [4]	1953 [5]	1959 [6]	Weighted average 1953/59
Life	0.9346	0.9333	0.9401	0.9362
Saturday Evening Post		0.9170	0.9042	0.9110
Look		0.9337	0.9344	0.9340
Ladies Home Journal		0.9081	0.9346	0.9217
Reader's Digest			0.9390	0.9390
Weighted average		0.9399	0.9333	0.9366

Hence:

$$k_2 = \frac{2A_1}{d} \cdot \frac{2A_1 - A_2}{A_2},$$

and, thus

$$\frac{nA_1 - A_n}{A_n} = \frac{k_n \cdot d(n-1)}{2A_1},$$

$$\frac{2A_1 - A_2}{A_2} = \frac{k_2 \cdot d}{2A_1}.$$

By introducing these values in (13)

$$k_n (n-1) \frac{d}{2A_1} = k_2 (n-1)^a \frac{d}{2A_1},$$

or

$$k_n (n-1) = k_2 (n-1)^a.$$

The Final Formula

Formula (11) becomes finally,

$$(14) \qquad A_n = \frac{(nA_1)^2}{nA_1 + \dfrac{n(n-1)^a}{2} \cdot kd}.$$

This formula can be used to calculate the cumulative audience of any paper, any radio or TV program, or any movie. To use this formula, it is necessary and sufficient to know the value of A_1 and two different values of A_n, say A_n and A_m (with $m > n$).

The value of kd can be extracted from Formula (14), since:

$$(15) \qquad kd = \frac{2nA_1 (nA_1 - A_n)}{nA_n (n-1)^a}.$$

In the particular case of $n = 2$, (15) becomes:

$$(16) \qquad kd = \frac{2A_2 (2A_1 - A_2)}{A_2},$$

which is, in fact, identical to Formula (10).

The value of a can be extracted from (13) by the following process:

$$(n-1)^a = \frac{nA_1 - A_n}{A_n} \cdot \frac{A_2}{2A_1 - A_2},$$

$$(m-1)^a = \frac{mA_1 - A_m}{A_m} \cdot \frac{A_2}{2A_1 - A_2},$$

$$(17) \qquad a = \frac{\log \dfrac{A_n (mA_1 - A_m)}{A_m (nA_1 - A_n)}}{\log \dfrac{m-1}{n-1}}.$$

In the particular case of $n = 2$ and $m = 3$, (17) becomes

$$(18) \qquad a = \frac{\log \dfrac{(3A_1 - A_3)A_2}{(2A_1 - A_2)A_3}}{\log 2}.$$

In the examples given in Table 3, calculation of A_n is based on a value of a with $m = 4$ and $n = 2$. Results are completely satisfactory; differences with the "official" results are never higher than 2.4 percent even within the socioeconomic groups (Table 3). Once again these differences are always smaller than the sampling errors.

Stability of the Main Parameters. Table 3 shows that satisfactory results are obtained by using a common value of a for calculating the cumulative audience in total *and within socioeconomic groups.* This leads to the belief that the value of a is a constant proper to the magazine, independent of the considered universe, and perhaps independent of the different studies [1] (Table 4).[1]

The Politz Studies gave an opportunity to check the constancy of the duplication coefficient, another main parameter defined by J. Durand [3, p. 11] as

$$(19) \qquad \lambda = \frac{\log A_1 A_2}{\log D},$$

in which A_1 and A_2 are the audiences of the two magazines considered, and D is the duplication. These values must be introduced in (19) in the form of probabilities. In the case of the cumulative audience, $A_2 = A_1$, and the formula becomes:

$$(20) \qquad \lambda = \frac{2 \log A_1}{\log d}.$$

Table 5 shows the values of this duplication coefficient. If the stability of this value is admitted, the average value could then be used as the value which would have been obtained in 1964; if the last Politz Study had measured the cumulative audience. By introducing the

---

[1] This is in line with the conclusions of J. Durand, of Research Dept. of Publicis-Paris [3, p. 9] that some parameters in relation to the duplication are independent of the date of the study, the socioeconomic group, etc.

Table 5

VALUES OF THE DUPLICATION COEFFICIENT λ IN POLITZ STUDIES

Magazine	[7] 1952	[8] 1953	[9] 1959	Average 1953/59	d (est.)	kd (est.)
Life	1.49	1.42	1.43	1.42	17,360	24,266
Saturday Evening Post		1.50	1.51	1.51	14,320	20,842
Look		1.37	1.42	1.39	15,350	20,937
Reader's Digest				1.49	24,130	36,133
McCalls (est.)				1.47	11,490	15,698

average value of λ and the 1964 value of A_1 in the formula:

$$(21) \qquad \log d = \frac{1}{\lambda} 2 \log A_1,$$

one obtains the 1964 theoretical value for d, and thus for kd for the magazine considered (Table 5). With these values of kd and the values of the constant a (Table 4), it is possible to estimate the cumulative audience of the five magazines for which the last Politz Study provides exposure information (except for McCall's, for which there is no element to calculate the duplication coefficient; however, since the values of this coefficient for the different magazines are close, to McCall's may be attributed the average of λ, 1.47.)

The combination of issue audience, issue exposures and cumulative audience estimates is of interest because it leads to estimates of average numbers of issues read and average number of issue exposures per reader of n issues of a magazine.

For example, an average issue of Reader's Digest has an audience of 36,320,000 readers. This audience generates 5.2 issue exposures per reader or a total of 188,490,000 issue exposures. Six issues of Reader's Digest yield the following estimates:

a) Gross audience of 217,920,000 (6 × 36,320,000).
b) Total Issue Exposure of 1,130,940,000 (6 × 188,490,000).
c) Cumulative audience of 66,950,000 readers (as estimated by Formula 14).

Thus: Average Number of Issues Read Reader = a/c = 3.3.
Avg. Number of Issue Exposures Reader = b/c = 17.9.

CALCULATION OF CUMULATIVE NET COVERAGE

The similarity between Formulas (9) and (14) suggests combining them to obtain a general formula for the calculation of the cumulative net coverage of a series of media, each appearing more than once:

$$(22) \qquad C_c = \frac{(\sum A)^2}{\sum A + \sum KD + \sum kd}.$$

To use this formula, it is necessary to know exactly what the different symbols represent.

The sum of audiences $\sum A$ is the sum of all values nA_1. Suppose there are three papers, with respective audience and number of issues:

1. 30 × 3.
2. 20 × 2.
3. 10 × 8.

The gross sum of audience is then:

$$\sum A = (3 \times 20) + (2 \times 20) + (8 \times 10) = 210.$$

The sum of the different values of KD must also take the schedule frequency into account; each value of KD must be multiplied by the product of the two numbers of issues. In fact, if Paper a appears three times and Paper b twice, the duplication occurs six times:

Each value of kd must be multiplied, as in (14), by $[n(n-1)]/2$, where n is the number of issues of the paper considered. The several products must be totaled.

Table 6 checks (22) on the French magazines studied by SOFRES [4]. The following are the steps in the calculation of the cumulative net coverage of the combination. 3 Paris Match + 2 Marie Claire + 3 Télé 7 Jours:

1. $\sum A = (3 \times 8,026) + (2 \times 4,282) + (3 \times 5,370)$
= 48.779.

2. $\sum KD = (6 \times 2,736) + (9 \times 2,234) + (6 \times 1,098)$
= 43.110.

3. $\sum kd = \dfrac{3 \times 2^{0.9164} \times 6.760}{2} + 3141$
$+ \dfrac{3 \times 2^{0.9155} \times 7.354}{2} = 43,080.$

4. $C_c = \dfrac{(48,779)^2}{48,779 + 43.110 + 43,080} = 17,629.$

Table 6
PARAMETERS OF 3 FRENCH MAGAZINES [8]

a	kd	Magazine	A and KD		
			PM	MC	T7
0.9164	6.760	Paris Match	8,026	2,736	2,234
0.9110	3.141	Marie Claire		4,282	1,098
0.9155	7.354	Télé 7 Jours			5,379

Note: All readers. Total population: 31,663,000.

This answer differs from the figure given by the study (17,952) by 1.05 percent of the total population (31,663,000). Similarly, the combination 6 PM + 3 MC + 6 $T7$ gives 19,933 (difference: 2.8 percent); the combination 12 PM + 6 MC + 12 $T7$ gives 21,935 (difference: 1.9 percent).

The precision of Formula (22) thus seems sufficient. The calculation could be simplified by using, for all papers of a study, a common average value for the constant a. Then, one might calculate once all the different values of $[n(n - 1)a]$ 2. Table 4 gives the average value of a for the two Politz Studies of 1953 and 1959, and the average value of 0.9366 which could be used for the 1964 study.

If all papers are introduced in (22) with the same number of issues, the calculation becomes much more simple and rapid. Here are the steps in calculating the combination of six issues of the five magazines of the

Table 8
MONTHLY NET COVERAGE CALCULATION OF THE PARAMETERS

Parameter	W (Weeklies)	F (Fortnightlies)	M (Monthlies)	
A	$4 A_w$	$- 2 A_f$	$+ A_m$	
KD	$16 KD_w$	$- 8 KD_{wf}$	$+ 4 KD_{wm}$	(W)
		$- 4 KD_f$	$+ 2 KD_{fm}$	(F)
			$+ KD_m$	(M)
kd	$2 \times 3^a \times kd_v$	$- kd_f$		

Politz Study of 1959 (parameters are shown in Table 7; $a = 0.9333$).

1. $\sum A = 6 \times (15,320 + 9,530 + 11,690 + 17.680 + 9,550) = 382,620.$

2. $\sum KD = 6 \times 6 \times (5,600 + 7,846 + 10,300 + 5.509 + 4,496 + 6,597 + 4,392 + 7.150 + 4,378 + 6.634) = 2,264,472.$

3. $\sum kd = \dfrac{6 \times 5^{0.9333}}{2} \times (14,214 + 7,950 + 8.946 + 19,383 + 8,084) = 13,476 \times 58.577$
$= 789,384.$

Table 7
CUMULATIVE NET COVERAGE FOR 1959 POLITZ STUDY [6]

	kd	Magazine	A and KD				
			Life	Post	Look	RD	LHJ
a. Parameters	14,214	Life	15,320	5,600	7,846	10,300	5,509
	7,950	Post		9,530	4,496	6,597	4,392
	8,946	Look			11,690	7,150	4,378
	19,383	RD				17,680	6,634
	8,084	LHJ					9,550
				Formula	Study	Difference	
b. Four issues of three magazines		Life + Post + Look		35,211	35,070	0.3%	
		Life + Post + RD		37,993	37,600	0.8	
		Life + Post + LHJ		34,159	34,460	0.6	
		Life + Look + RD		38,936	38,110	1.7	
		Life + Look + LHJ		35,397	35,120	0.6	
$C_4 = \dfrac{(4.4)^2}{4.4 + 16KD - 5.576kd}$		Life + RD + LHJ		38,031	37,500	1.1	
		Post + Look + RD		37,261	36,760	1.0	
		Post + Look + LHJ		31,917	32,780	0.9	
		Post + RD + LHJ		34,511	34,880	0.8	
		Look + RD + LHJ		37,326	36,600	0.7	
c. Three issues of four magazines		Life + Post + Look + RD		37,353	37,920	1.2	
		Life + Post + Look + LHJ		35,371	35,400	0.0	
$C_3 = \dfrac{(3.4)^2}{3.4 + 9KD - 2.864kd}$		Life + Post + RD + LHJ		37,574	37,310	0.5	
		Life + Look + RD + LHJ		38,706	37,860	1.7	
		Post + Look + RD + LHJ		36,727	36,510	0.4	

Note: All households. Total population: 49,140,000.

Table 9
CALCULATION OF MONTHLY NET COVERAGE AND ISSUE EXPOSURE [10]

	Variable	W $(Life + Post)$	F $(Look)$	M $(RD + McC)$	
1.	$A =$	$4 \times (30,500 + 22,880)$	$+2 \times (28,760)$	$+36,320 + 21,430$	
2.	$KD =$	$16 \times (11,247)$	$+8 \times (16,261 + 10,089)$	$+4 \times (16,356 + 8,766 + 7,317 + 12,927)$	(W)
				$+2 \times (13,733 + 9,446)$	(F)
				$+12,109$	(M)
3.	$a =$	0.9246			
4.	$kd =$	$5.522 \times (24,266 + 20,842)$	$+10,089$		
5.	$C_n =$	$\dfrac{(328,790)^2}{328,790 + 630,683 + 270,023} = 87,920$			
6.	Total issue exp. $=$	$4 \times (45,070 + 42,170)$	$+2 \times (45,350)$	$+188,490 + 70,260$	
7.	Issue exp. per reader $=$	$\dfrac{698,410}{87,920} = 7.9$			

Note: All adults. Total population: 120,360,000. Values of A and KD: see Table 1. Value of kd: see Table 5. Value of $'a'$: see Table 4, weighted average for *Life + Post*.

$$4. \quad C_c = \frac{(382.620)^2}{3.436.476} = 42.601,000 \text{ households.}$$

The difference between this figure and the one given by the study (41,740) is 1.75 percent, one of the highest differences ever found with this formula (see other checks in Table 7).

Monthly Net Coverage

It is unusual for a media plan to attribute the same schedule frequency to all papers. But it is appropriate to consider, as maximum coverage of an advertising campaign, the monthly figure, i.e., in the case of a weekly paper the coverage figure obtained by four issues, *even if the schedule plans more than four issues for the campaign*. Voluntary restriction in coverage, accepted by most advertisers, is justified by two facts: 1. As revealed by all studies on audience accumulation, a paper accumulates audience more and more slowly as the number of issues increases. That is, after four issues, a paper has already acquired the bulk of its ultimate audience accumulation. 2. Though it is agreed that coverage means "readers of *at least one* issue," it is also true that readers of one or two issues in twelve have no chance to be exposed to a sufficient number of advertising messages. They cannot be considered reached by the campaign, but only by one advertisement.

Admitting the monthly coverage as maximum coverage

figure is, in fact, a step in the right direction for considering a selective audience—in this case a selective audience of readers meeting the criterion of sufficiently frequent exposure.

Calculation of the monthly net coverage of a series of papers must take into account the edition frequency of each paper. Table 8 shows how, and Table 9 shows, as an example, the steps in the calculation of the monthly net coverage of the five "APX" magazines of the 1964 Politz study. This calculation is based on the assumptions previously set forth on ways these magazines accumulate, and the result (71.0 percent of all adult readers) cannot be verified.

The per reader monthly exposure (7.9) is markedly higher than that of a simple, noncumulative combination of the five papers (5.2).

REFERENCES

1. J. M. Agostini. *A Short-cut Method for Estimating the Unduplicated Audience of a Combination of Media*, The Hague: ESOMAR Congress. September 11–16, 1960.
2. *Belgium Media Study*. Brussels: Centre d'Etude Belge des Supports de Publicité, 1960.
3. Jacques Durand, *L'Analyse Statistique de la Duplication*. Paris: Institut de Recherches et d'Etudes Publicitaires (IREP). Study No. 11, November 1964.
4. *Etude des 3 Supports*, Paris: Société Française d'Enquêtes par Sondage (SOFRES), 1965.
5. *France Media Study*, Paris: Centre d'Etude des Supports de Publicité. 1959.
6. Pierre Hofmans. *Une Méthode Pratique pour calculer la Couver-*

ture Nette Cumulée d'une Série de Supports. Paris: IREP, Study No. 12, June 1965.

7. Alfred Politz Research, Inc., A Study of Four Media—A Study of Duplication, New York: Time, Inc., 1953.

8. ———, A Study of the Household Accumulative Audience of Life, New York: Time, Inc., 1952.

9. ———, Life Study of Consumer Expenditures. New York: Time, Inc., 1959.

10. ———, Main Report: 1964 Politz Magazine Study, New York: Alfred Politz Media Studies, 1965.

11. Synergie-Roc, Femmes d'Aujourd'hui, Paris: Régies d'Aujourd' hui, 1964.

ROBERT S. HEADEN, JAY E. KLOMPMAKER, and JESSE E. TEEL, JR.*

A probabilistic model is developed that relates advertising schedule variables
to the attendant audience exposure pattern. Results of a large-sample test
of the model are presented, as well as an example of a practical application.

Predicting Audience Exposure to Spot TV Advertising Schedules

INTRODUCTION

Media analysts translating an advertising budget into a specific media plan typically must choose from a very large number of both between-media and within-medium combinations of alternative media vehicles. Each specific combination chosen will yield a unique audience exposure pattern (i.e., the number of people, households, women, and other possible demographic groupings that are exposed to 1, 2, ..., m of the vehicles selected). Thus to evaluate the plans, the media buyer must answer two essential questions about each: (1) what proportion of the total potential audience will be exposed to the advertisements in the schedule, and (2) how often will each exposed audience member see an advertisement in the schedule?

Early media research focused on the first question and concerned measures variously called "unduplicated audience," "accumulated audience," "net coverage," and "reach"—depending upon the particular medium being discussed, the time period in which the media schedule was to be run, and the country where the research was being done. Herein, the term "reach" is considered synonymous with all the other terms and thus is a summary measure of an audience exposure pattern.

If discussion is restricted to broadcast media, where audience exposure to individual media vehicles typically is expressed in terms of ratings or rating points (the percentage of a given audience exposed), the total audience of a schedule as measured by gross rating points (GRPs) divided by the reach of the schedule equals average frequency of exposure, as expressed in the following definitional relation: GRP = (reach) (average frequency). Average frequency is the average number of times the typical audience member is exposed to the vehicles that comprise the schedule and is another summary measure of the audience exposure pattern.

Recent research interest in media exposure has focused on measuring the complete frequency distribution of exposure (i.e., the percentage of the audience exposed 1, 2, ..., m times to a schedule) and not merely reach and average frequency. Research has indicated an optimal range of number of exposures for most advertised products [7, 9–11, 16] although the precise upper and lower limits of this range have not been firmly established. Suppose the media analyst knew that three exposures were required before satisfactory levels of awareness, recall, brand comprehension, or some other communication measure would be obtained. He then would need an estimate of the proportion of the audience expected to attain or exceed this level of exposure, rather than just the summary measures of reach and average frequency, to choose effectively between alternative advertising plans.

There are comprehensive models of the advertising process that attempt to schedule advertising so as to optimize a criterion such as sales per advertising dollar—MEDIAC [12]—or the present value of consumers' cognitive changes or actions—ADMOD [1]. The accuracy of the final solution determined by these models can be affected greatly by the accuracy of the internal algorithm that estimates audience exposure for the schedules under consideration. Thus, researchers modeling the complete advertising process also need a method for accurately predicting the audience exposure pattern that will be generated by a given advertising schedule.

*Robert S. Headen is Associate Professor of Business Administration and Jay E. Klompmaker is Assistant Professor of Business Administration at the University of North Carolina and Jesse E. Teel, Jr., is Assistant Professor of Marketing at the University of Alabama.

1

Journal of Marketing Research
Vol. XIV (February 1977), 1–9

Table 1
DIMENSIONS OF THE SAMPLE DATA

A. *Gross rating points*

GRP range of schedules	No. of schedules	%
1–100	318	13.1
101–200	617	25.5
201–300	588	24.3
301–400	465	19.2
401–500	252	10.4
>500	184	7.6
	2424	100.1

B. *Schedule intensity*

No. of commercials in schedule	No. of schedules	%
1–10	424	17.5
11–20	825	34.0
21–30	522	21.5
31–40	331	13.7
41–50	183	7.5
51–60	81	3.3
>60	58	2.4
	2424	99.9

C. *Average spot rating of schedules*

Range	2.0–37.8
Mean	12.1
Standard deviation	5.2

D. *Daypart distribution of schedules*
1. *Pure dayparts*

	No. of schedules	%
Day	214	8.8
Early fringe	347	14.3
Prime	127	5.2
Late fringe	145	6.0

2. *Combination dayparts*

	No. of schedules	%
2—dayparts	1049	43.3
3—dayparts	359	14.8
4—dayparts	183	7.6
	2424	100.0

E. *Size of markets*

No. of stations in market	No. of schedules	%
1	316	13.0
2	295	12.2
3	601	24.8
4	552	22.8
5	--	--
6	660	27.2
	2424	100.0

F. *Number of stations used in schedule*

No. of stations used	No. of Schedules	%
1	607	25.0
2	965	39.8
3	310	12.8
4	542	22.4
	2424	100.0

This report presents large-sample results on the distributional form appropriate for modeling audience exposure distributions for local or spot television markets. Spot television is a particularly suitable area for study because of the paucity of published research on estimating audience exposure for this medium. In fact, there has been little audience exposure research in the entire broadcast media field. The objective of this research was to develop a method of predicting audience exposure patterns for spot TV advertising schedules.

THE DATA

The data consisted of 2424 tabulated exposure distributions resulting from simulated media schedules run in a cross-section of local TV markets in the United States. The tabulations were made by a major research agency from diary data on household TV viewing habits and were based on schedules of one-week duration. The sample was widely stratified so that a variety of conditions and situations normally encountered in practice could be evaluated. The schedules varied in terms of: (1) the intensity of the schedule as measured by the gross rating point (GRP) level, number of commercials, and average spot rating; (2) daypart distribution,[1] including pure dayparts as well as combined dayparts; and (3) station coverage in terms of the number of stations used of the number available in the market. These dimensions of the data base are shown in Table 1. Clearly, the range of GRP and the number of commercials cover all levels likely to be found in practice. About 35% of the sample consisted of schedules solely within one daypart and the rest of the schedules combined dayparts. All schedules in the data were local rather than network and covered small as well as large TV markets, from markets with only one station to markets with six stations.

DEVELOPMENT OF THE MODEL

Theoretical Formulation of the Model

Prior research has shown that the beta-binomial distribution models the audience exposure process very closely [8]. The formulation of the beta-binomial model of audience exposure used in this study is as follows.

Let n = number of spots in the schedule.

r = number of spots in the schedule seen by a household, $0 \le r \le n$.

---

[1] Daypart divides the TV advertising day into four time segments (Eastern Standard Time):
1. Day—from sign-on to approximately 5:30 p.m.
2. Early fringe—from 5:30–8:00 p.m.
3. Prime—8:00–11:00 p.m.
4. Late fringe—11:00 p.m. until sign-off.

Pure daypart schedules contained only spots scheduled within one daypart such as prime. Combined daypart schedules contained some spots within one daypart category and the rest in one or more of the other daypart categories. For example, a schedule with spots in day and spots in early fringe is a combined daypart schedule and is designated as day-early fringe.

p = probability of exposure to a spot in the schedule for a given household.

$f_b(r|n, p)$ = the binomial density function for r = 0, 1, 2, ..., n given parameters n and p.

The binomial distribution determines the probability that a given household will be exposed exactly one time, two times, ..., n times to the schedule. But the potential audience is composed of many households, so the parameter p varies from household to household over the heterogeneous population and becomes a random variable, p^*, that is assumed to be independent over households. This random variable follows a beta distribution with parameters a and b, and density function $f_\beta(p^*|a, b)$. The proportion of the audience that will be exposed exactly one time, two times, ..., n times is determined by compounding the beta distribution with the binomial and expanding the resulting beta-binomial. The beta-binomial distribution is characterized by three parameters—a, b, and n—and a density function given by:

$$f_{BBD}(r) = \int_0^1 f_b(r|n, p^*) f_\beta(p^*|a, b)\, dp^*.$$

Assumptions and Interpretation of the Model

At the micro level, the probability of exposure to the schedule for the ith household, p_i, is the average probability of exposure to the specific set of spots contained in the schedule, and can be specified in terms of the household's probability of exposure to each of the n spots as follows.

Let p_{ij} = the ith household's probability of exposure to spot j, $1 \le j \le n$

then $p_i = \left(\sum_{j=1}^n p_{ij} \right) / n$.

Thus, p_i is household i's probability of exposure to a "composite" or "average" spot and may not necessarily equal household i's actual probability of exposure to any particular spot in the schedule. The binomial distribution with parameters n and p_i is used to estimate the probability that household i will be exposed r times to the "composite" spot, $0 \le r \le n$. P_i is *assumed to be constant* over the n trials, and n is interpreted as n *repeated, independent* trials of the "composite" spot.

At the macro or population level, the set $\{p_i\}$ is assumed to be independent over households and *beta distributed* and thus the random variable p^* is defined.

Estimation of the Model

Because n, the number of spots in the schedule, is known, one only needs to estimate the values of a and b to predict the beta-binomial audience exposure distribution associated with any advertising schedule. In addition, it is known that the mean of the distribution equals GRP which is also known for any schedule. Consequently, an estimate of the variance of the BBD would permit determination of the parameters a and b by simultaneous solution of the moment equations.

On the basis of this reasoning, the research began with a study of the regression estimators of the variance, $V(r)$, of the beta-binomial distribution. The variance was calculated from the moment formulas by use of parameter estimates derived from empirically fitting the beta-binomial to observed exposure distributions. Because prior empirical evidence indicated that the relationship between the characteristics of an advertising schedule and the resultant audience exposure pattern is nonlinear [15, 18], the following model was used in the regression analysis.

(1) $$V(r) = A x_1^{B_1} x_2^{B_2} x_3^{B_3} x_4^{B_4} \epsilon$$

where:

$V(r)$ = variance of the fitted BBD.
x_1 = number of spots in the schedule.
x_2 = number of TV stations used.
x_3 = number of TV stations available.
x_4 = average spot rating for the schedule.
ϵ = disturbance term.

If one takes natural logarithms, this equation is transformed into an equation that can be estimated by ordinary least squares regression.

An additional dimension of the effect of spot TV advertising schedules upon audience exposure patterns is the qualitative factor, daypart. This division of the TV day reflects the fact that audience viewing habits differ from one daypart category to another. Consequently, the regression relationship between the variance of the audience exposure distribution and the parameters of the associated advertising schedule should vary across dayparts. This proposition was formulated as an hypothesis and tested by the procedure developed by Chow [5].

Table 2 presents the results of the test for equality of the regression relationship in the different daypart categories. As anticipated, there were significant differences in the regression coefficients across the daypart variable. Thus it was not feasible to represent the relationship between the variance of the BBD and

Table 2

TEST OF EQUALITY OF REGRESSION ACROSS DAYPART VARIABLE

Source of residual error	Sums of squares	Degrees of freedom	F statistic	P less than
Across dayparts	10.460	12		.001
			23.841	
Within dayparts	30.179	813		

Table 3
RESULTS OF THE REGRESSION ANALYSIS

		Beta coefficients, variable			Degrees of freedom	F ratio	R^2	Daypart category
	$Log\ x_1$	$Log\ x_2$	$Log\ x_3$	$Log\ x_4$				
Equation 1	.911	-.156	.176	.253		1200.0	.979	day
t ratios	(59.8)	(-8.3)	(7.6)	(11.2)	102			
Equation 2	.973	-.329	.140	.338		1488.0	.973	early fringe
t ratios	(72.9)	(-19.1)	(6.1)	(14.9)	165			
Equation 3	.790	-.245	.042	.448		1120.0	.987	prime
t ratios	(51.4)	(-11.0)	(1.25)ᵃ	(12.5)	58			
Equation 4	.896	-.396	.172	.390		344.6	.952	late fringe
t ratios	(30.8)	(-11.0)	(4.3)	(12.1)	69			
Equation 5	1.05	-.295	.215	.389		737.9	.970	day and early
t ratios	(45.6)	(-11.5)	(7.2)	(13.0)	91			fringe
Equation 6	1.151	-.264	.021	.396		779.2	.974	day and prime
t ratios	(53.7)	(-11.4)	(0.7)ᵃ	(13.4)	83			
Equation 7	.946	-.302	.220	.198		803.8	.973	day and late
t ratios	(52.9)	(-13.2)	(9.5)	(11.0)	89			fringe
Equation 8	1.145	-.368	.099	.390		671.1	.947	early fringe
t ratios	(44.1)	(-14.1)	(3.2)	(10.1)	150			and prime
Equation 9	.979	-.351	.153	.297		682.3	.969	prime and
t ratios	(48.2)	(-14.3)	(6.1)	(15.1)	86			late fringe
Equation 10	1.054	-.409	.215	.362		652.1	.966	day, early fringe,
t ratios	(40.8)	(-16.5)	(7.7)	(16.6)	91			and late fringe
Equation 11	1.039	-.436	.190	.226		491.8	.962	early fringe, prime,
t ratios	(39.8)	(-15.1)	(6.2)	(9.0)	78			and late fringe
Equation 12	1.120	-.227	.121	.421		879.2	.978	day, early fringe,
t ratios	(40.5)	(-11.5)	(5.6)	(10.1)	147			prime, and late fringe

Each equation was of the form:

$$Log\ V(r) = Log\ A + \sum_{i=1}^{4} \beta_i\ Log\ x_i + Log\ \epsilon.$$

ᵃNot significant.

the characteristics of the advertising schedule with a pooled regression model. Consequently, separate regression equations were estimated for each of the 12 possible daypart combinations contained in the data.

Table 3 presents the results of the regression analysis and shows the standardized coefficients, t-ratios, and coefficients of multiple determination for each of the 12 regression equations. The overall F-test was clearly significant in each case. The coefficient of multiple determination, R^2, was very high for each equation and almost all individual t ratios were significant. These 12 equations were developed from a total of 1209 randomly chosen audience exposure distributions, or approximately one-half of the available data.

SPLIT SAMPLE TEST OF THE MODEL

That portion of the sample data not used in fitting the regression equations was used to test the predictive ability of the model. This sample consisted of 1215 observed exposure distributions. To facilitate the test, the 12 separate regression equations were combined into one equivalent equation by representing dayparts by dummy variables that adjusted both the intercept term and the real variable slope coefficients in the equation.

The test procedure consisted of: (1) using the regression equation to predict the variance of the exposure distribution, (2) solving for the parameters of the distribution using the first two moments, and (3) using these values as the values of the parameters of a specific BBD that then generated the exposure distribution for the given schedule.

Estimating the variance of the BBD and deriving the parameters introduced the possibility of cumulative errors in the predicted distribution. Therefore, the final step was to measure the closeness of fit between the predicted and the observed audience exposure distributions on two criteria.

First, predicted reach was compared with observed reach to determine the amount of error in this important measure of schedule coverage. Although media planners now desire more than just an estimate of reach

Table 4
DIFFERENCE BETWEEN PREDICTED REACH AND OBSERVED REACH

Absolute mean error	.032	Standard deviation	.026
Mean error	0.000	Standard deviation	.041

Table 5
CLOSENESS OF FIT BETWEEN PREDICTED AND OBSERVED DISTRIBUTIONS AS MEASURED BY KOLMOGOROV-SMIRNOV ONE-SAMPLE D-STATISTIC

Absolute difference (D-value)	No. of schedules	%	Cumulative %
.01	10	0.8	0.8
.02	74	6.1	6.9
.03	145	11.9	18.8
.04	209	17.2	36.0
.05	212	17.5	53.5
.06	167	13.7	67.2
.07	136	11.2	78.4
.08	110	9.1	87.5
.09	65	5.3	92.8
.10	38	3.2	96.0
.11	22	1.8	97.8
.12	13	1.0	98.8
.13	4	0.4	99.2
.14	4	0.3	99.5
.15	3	0.3	99.8
.16	3	0.2	100.0
Total	1215	100.0	

Mean absolute difference = .052; standard deviation = .025.

from a predictive tool, they still want an accurate estimate of reach. Second, the closeness of fit between the predicted and observed distributions was evaluated on the basis of the Kolmogorov-Smirnov one-sample D-statistic. The D-statistic measures the greatest absolute deviation between the cumulative theoretical and the cumulative observed distributions. It is the maximum error in the estimation of the proportion of the audience exposed any specified number of times or more to a particular schedule. Because the media analyst frequently plans advertising with a goal of a minimum number of exposures for a certain percentage of the target audience, the D-statistic provides a confidence bound on the plan for attaining that goal.

Table 4 shows the comparison between predicted and observed audience reach. As indicated, there is a mean error of 0.000 and a mean absolute error of .032 with 48.1% of the errors representing underestimates and 51.9% overestimates. In view of the sampling errors inherent in current media estimates, predicted reach is well within an acceptable accuracy range.

Table 5 contains an analysis of the fit between the predicted and observed distributions as measured by the Kolmogorov-Smirnov D-statistic. In 96% of the cases, the maximum absolute error over the range of possible frequencies was .10, and 87% of the predicted distributions were within .08.

Table 6 is an analysis of the prediction errors for the frequency classes 0 through 8. It indicates that the model has a systematic tendency to overestimate frequency class 1 and to underestimate frequency classes 2 through 6. However, the average error and standard deviation of the errors for each frequency class are relatively small.

Table 7 shows results obtained from cross-tabulating prediction error signs for adjacent frequency classes. The purpose of this analysis was to determine whether the beta-binomial audience exposure model produced a systematic error pattern. That is, the research question was whether the model followed an overprediction of one frequency class with an underprediction of the succeeding frequency class. The schedules were split into those containing an even number of spots and those containing an odd number of spots because an earlier method of estimating advertising audience exposure patterns resulted in systematic error patterns of opposite signs for these two types of schedules [17]. The beta-binomial model showed a slight tendency toward a systematic error pattern for frequency classes 0, 1, and 2 but the direction of the errors did not differ for schedules with odd and even numbers of spots.

The number of spots per schedule, n, was correlated with the Kolmogorov-Smirnov measure of goodness of fit, D, to determine whether advertising intensity accounted for most of the lack of fit shown by the model. The results were an R of .2164 and an R^2 of .0468 which indicate that D varies with n but n

Table 6
ANALYSIS OF ESTIMATION ERRORS FOR EIGHT FREQUENCY CLASSES

Frequency of exposure	Average estimation error	Standard deviation of errors	Percentage of underestimates	Percentage with no error	Percentage of overestimates
0	0.000	0.041	48.1	0.0	51.9
1	0.024	0.035	23.2	0.0	76.8
2	-0.008	0.027	58.9	0.1	41.0
3	-0.012	0.022	70.1	0.4	29.5
4	-0.010	0.018	68.2	1.6	30.2
5	-0.005	0.015	58.2	3.4	38.4
6	-0.004	0.015	53.1	5.5	41.4
7	-0.0002	0.012	44.6	8.3	47.1
8	0.000	0.018	37.6	12.2	50.2

Table 7

CROSS-TABULATION OF ESTIMATION ERRORS BETWEEN ADJACENT FREQUENCY CLASSES

Frequency classes	First class underestimated and second overestimated	First class overestimated and second underestimated	Both first and second class overestimated	Both first and second class underestimated	Both first and second class estimated correctly	Total observations
		Schedules with even number of spots				
0 and 1	262	127	181	33	0	603
1 and 2	48	259	183	112	1	603
2 and 3	105	158	76	259	5	603
3 and 4	116	97	82	300	8	603
4 and 5	141	78	102	255	27	603
5 and 6	117	105	132	215	34	603
6 and 7	131	73	191	149	59	603
7 and 8	126	86	137	180	74	603
		Schedules with odd number of spots				
0 and 1	273	107	213	19	0	612
1 and 2	33	254	232	93	0	612
2 and 3	92	175	90	255	0	612
3 and 4	100	102	73	326	11	612
4 and 5	137	81	90	290	14	612
5 and 6	123	82	135	240	32	612
6 and 7	127	86	163	195	41	612
7 and 8	123	85	178	152	74	612

does not explain a disproportionate amount of the variance in D.

On the whole, and particularly in view of the large size of the sample and varied nature of the data, the results contained in Tables 4–7 indicate that the model has little systematic error, is a suitable tool for practical applications, and supports the strong regression relationship presented in Table 3.

EXAMPLE OF MODEL USE

Given the characteristics of a proposed spot TV schedule in terms of the number of commercials to be used, the GRP level, the number of stations used, the number of stations available in the local market, and the particular dayparts in which spots are to be placed, the model will estimate the complete audience exposure distribution for the schedule. Obviously, a large number of alternative schedules and advertising budgets can be evaluated quickly and at small cost. The analyst can then evaluate marginal tradeoffs, such as the effect of shifts in the dayparts used.

For a specific example, suppose that a media analyst believes that a threshold level of exposure for his product is two and that exposure beyond the level of four is probably unnecessary. Thus, he is interested in maximizing the proportion of the target audience within the range of two to four. Further, suppose that he is evaluating two proposed spot TV schedules. Schedule 1 has 185 GRPs spread over 10 spots and will run on one of the three available stations in prime time. Schedule 2 has 180 GRPs spread over 10 spots and will run on all three of the available stations in prime time. The analyst knows that schedule 2 will generate greater reach than schedule 1, but he is unsure

of the exposure pattern that may result in the critical range of two to four exposures. Table 8 gives the exposure distributions predicted by the model. Not only does schedule 2 have a higher reach, but also the proportion of the audience exposed two to four times is 42% compared with only 30% for schedule 1. Thus, schedule 2 is more effective at generating exposures in the critical range even though the GRP level and, consequently, the cost is essentially the same for both schedules.

Researchers familiar with the work of Agostini [2, 3] and Metheringham [14] may wonder how the beta-binomial audience exposure model handles the problem of duplicated audience among the different commercials in the schedule, because the major thrust of these earlier works was measurement of audience duplication. An attractive feature of this model in relation to the earlier approaches is that it does not require estimates of the audience shared by all possible pairs of vehicles in the schedule. These data generally are not available for spot TV because of the large number of spot markets and the multiplicity of times available for spot commercials. In fact, the BBD does not directly measure audience duplication between vehicles in the schedule. However, the model does not ignore the distinction between within-channel and across-channel audience duplication or the difference between audience duplication within a daypart and that across dayparts. The estimates of the beta-binomial parameters are derived from the regression equation for the distribution's variance. Differences in audience duplication patterns across and within dayparts are incorporated in the model by use of a separate regression equation for each daypart category. The model distinguishes between within- and across-channel audience duplication by employing the number of stations used in the schedule and the total number of stations available in the market as independent variables in the regression equations. Additionally, the beta distribution internally accounts for audience duplication between spots in the schedule. Because the beta distribution models the probability of exposure to the advertising schedule over the audience, it includes information on both individuals who are heavy viewers and individuals who are light viewers of the programs included in the given schedule. Figure 1 shows the graphs of the beta distributions associated with schedules 1 and 2 and provides more information

on this aspect of the model. The beta distribution of schedule 2 indicates a close grouping of probabilities of exposure among audience members whereas that of schedule 1 is reasonably dispersed. Channel loyalty immediately comes to mind as a natural explanation for the dispersion of the beta distribution of schedule 1. This possibility can be analyzed further by comparing schedule reach predicted by the BBD with actual reach, and also with an estimate of reach predicted by one of the earlier techniques. Although lack of pairwise duplication data precludes use of either the Agostini or the Metheringham method, reach can be estimated by the Sainsbury "normal" technique which assumes that probability of exposure to one spot in

Table 8
DISTRIBUTION OF AUDIENCE EXPOSURES

Schedule 1

GRP = 185   Spots = 10   Stations used = 1
Available stations = 3   Daypart = Prime

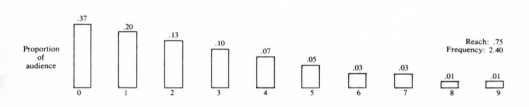

NUMBER OF TIMES EXPOSED

Schedule 2

GRP = 180   Spots = 10   Stations used = 3
Available stations = 3   Daypart = Prime

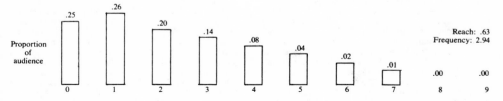

NUMBER OF TIMES EXPOSED

FIGURE 1

PROBABILITY OF EXPOSURE TO THE SCHEDULE

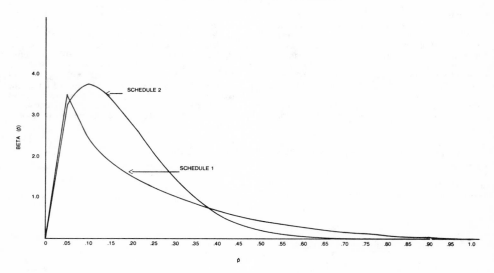

the schedule is independent of probability of exposure to any other spot in the schedule [4]. The BBD reach predictions were .630 and .750, respectively, whereas the actual figures were .60 and .76. In comparison, Sainsbury estimates were .871 and .869 for schedules 1 and 2. Although the Sainsbury method overestimated in both cases, schedule 1 estimates contained the greatest error. This result is not surprising as other researchers have found audience duplication probabilities to be reasonably independent across channels, but not within a channel as a result of channel loyalty [6].

Limitations of the Model

The beta-binomial assumes that a household's probability of exposure to any spot in the schedule is equal to the household's average probability of exposure to the set of spots contained in the schedule and that trials or showings of the composite spot are independent. Although the beta-binomial model closely fit a large number of observed spot TV exposure distributions, there are advertising schedules that seriously violate these basic assumptions—e.g., advertising schedules containing a subgroup of spots scheduled on the same program. Almost all audience members exposed to one spot in this subgroup also would be exposed to the other spots in the subgroup. Thus, if there were three spots in the subgroup, the

segment of the audience viewing the program carrying these spots would all be exposed three or more times in violation of the assumptions of the model. The practical result is that the exposure distribution would be multimodal and could not be modeled by a beta-binomial as the BBD is normally a unimodal and at best a bimodal distribution. Hence, the model should be used with caution in the evaluation of advertising schedules likely to result in a multimodal exposure distribution.

CONCLUSIONS

As with all attempts to explain and predict actual marketing phenomena, the spot TV audience exposure model herein developed has limitations. For example, the model has not been verified for target audiences that may comprise demographic groups other than household units. Also, only one-week schedules are considered. However, the empirical evidence based on a large split-sample test clearly establishes the model as an accurate predictor of audience exposure patterns for one-week advertising schedules run in local or spot TV markets, an area of research notable for a paucity of published results.

All models of the advertising process that attempt to be comprehensive and to measure the impact of advertising schedules with respect to any criterion of effectiveness must, as part of their formulation, measure the relationship between schedule characteristics and resulting audience exposure patterns. In fact, it was noted recently that the assumptions about media audience duplication patterns and subsequent estimates of exposure have a marked effect upon the solution obtained by an optimizing media model [13, 19]. Consequently the beta-binomial audience exposure model may be very useful to researchers studying other aspects of the advertising process. For example, researchers studying communication effects such as recall, comprehension, and preference must first measure exposure. Also, as indicated for the example given, advertising efficiency studies can be facilitated greatly by the procedures developed here. A researcher or practitioner wondering whether a change in the daypart distribution of commercials is a better tradeoff than adding another channel or station to the schedule can quickly analyze the effects of both actions.

Finally, the results of this research indicate an approach or theoretical framework for studying audience exposure distributions for all types of broadcast media. The logic employed in constructing the theoretical model should apply equally well to network TV and to spot and network radio. Studying the effects of advertising schedules upon audience exposure patterns within the framework of a theoretical model should advance understanding of the underlying process that generates audience exposure.

REFERENCES

1. Aaker, David A. "Admod: An Advertising Decision Model," *Journal of Marketing Research*, 12 (February 1975), 37-45.
2. Agostini, J. M. "Analysis of Magazine Accumulative Audience." *Journal of Advertising Research*, 2 (December 1962), 24-7.
3. ———. "How to Estimate Unduplicated Audiences," *Journal of Advertising Research*, 1 (March 1961), 11-4.
4. Caffyn, J. M. and M. Sagovsky. "Net Audiences of British Newspapers: A Comparison of the Agostini and Sainsbury Methods," *Journal of Advertising Research*, 3 (March 1963), 21-4.
5. Chow, G. C. "Tests of Equality Between Sets of Coefficients in Two Linear Regressions," *Econometrika*, 28 (July 1960), 591-605.
6. Goodhardt, G. J. and Ehrenberg, A. S. C. "Duplication of Television Viewing Between and Within Channels," *Journal of Marketing Research*, 6 (May 1969), 169-78.
7. Grass, Robert C. and Wallace H. Wallace. "Satiation Effects of TV Commercials," *Journal of Advertising Research*, 9 (September 1969), 3-8.
8. Headen, Robert S., Jay E. Klompmaker, and Jesse E. Teel, Jr. "An Empirical Examination of Spot TV Audience Exposure Patterns," *Journal of Advertising Research*, 16 (December 1976).
9. Krugman, Herbert E. "Processes Underlying Exposure to Advertising," *American Psychologist*, 23 (April 1968), 245-53.
10. ———. "What Makes Advertising Effective?" *Harvard Business Review*, 53 (March-April 1975), 96-103.
11. ———. "Why Three Exposures May Be Enough," *Journal of Advertising Research*, 12 (December 1972), 11-4.
12. Little, J. D. C. and L. M. Lodish. "A Media Planning Calculus," *Operations Research*, 17 (January 1969), 1-35.
13. Lodish, L. M. "A Note on Modeling the Relationship of Diminishing Returns to Media Overlap for the Media Planning Problem," *Management Science*, 22 (September 1975), 111-5.
14. Metheringham, Richard A. "Measuring the Net Cumulative Coverage of a Print Campaign," *Journal of Advertising Research*, 4 (December 1964), 23-8.
15. Radio Advertising Bureau, Inc. "Major Discoveries About Radio Reach and Frequency Revisited." New York: Radio Advertising Bureau, Inc. (undated).
16. Ray, Michael L. and Alan G. Sawyer. "Repetition in Media Models: A Laboratory Technique," *Journal of Marketing Research*, 8 (February 1971), 20-9.
17. Schreiber, Robert J. "The Metheringham Method for Media Mix: An Evaluation," *Journal of Advertising Research*, 9 (June 1969), 54-6.
18. Young, Lawrence F. "Estimating Radio Reach," *Journal of Advertising Research*, 12 (October 1972), 37-41.
19. Zufryden, Fred S. "Examining the Pattern of Response Behavior in a Media Model," *Management Science*, 22 (September 1975), 116-24.

MANAGEMENT SCIENCE
Vol. 27, No. 6, June 1981
Printed in U.S.A.

A NONSTATIONARY MODEL OF BINARY CHOICE APPLIED TO MEDIA EXPOSURE*

DARIUS J. SABAVALA† AND DONALD G. MORRISON‡

In the field of media research, the beta binomial has performed very well for estimating the distribution of the frequency of exposures to a media vehicle. However, long-term projections have shown consistent biases. The *beta binomial geometric* model, an extension of the well-known beta binomial model, which incorporates non-stationarity of individuals' exposure probabilities, is able to account for these errors. In addition this *beta binomial geometric* framework provides insights into the sensitivity of various media statistics to non-stationarity. This model is a particular operationalization of Howard's general Dynamic Inference Model [5]. The paper focuses on applications to some television viewing and magazine readership data. The properties of the model, estimation of the parameters and statistical tests are also presented. Finally, some future research possibilities are discussed.
(MARKETING; MARKETING—ADVERTISING/PROMOTION; PROBABILITY—APPLICATIONS)

1. Introduction

Stochastic models have been widely applied in studying marketing phenomena. These models, which usually specify the micro-level (individual) process and then aggregate up to the macro-level (aggregate) process, fall into the general class of probability mixture models. While the models have increased in complexity and richness, one particular aspect has been relatively neglected. We refer to the ways in which the process changes over time or the non-stationary, dynamic nature of the process. This paper makes a modest effort in incorporating this non-stationary component and focuses on an application that is especially appropriate. Simple stationary models *appear* to describe the phenomenon of exposure of audiences to advertising media very well. However, if in fact the process is not stationary, projections from the model can be quite misleading.

The problem of estimating audience exposure to media is an important one, both for the marketing manager, who must spend the advertising budget effectively and efficiently, and for the seller of media space and time, whose rates and profits depend upon the audience. The quantities that are usually monitored are reach and frequency. The *reach* is the proportion (or number) of a given population exposed at least once to one or more issues of one or more media. The *frequency* distribution of exposures describes the proportion (or number) of a given population who have been exposed to exactly zero, one, two, etc. of one or more issues of one or more media.

Stochastic models, in particular the beta binomial, have been extensively applied to the media exposure problem. This model was first proposed in the media exposure context by Hyett [6]. Since that time, additional models based on the beta binomial have been developed; for example, see Greene and Stock [2]. Chandon [1] provides a

*Accepted by Donald R. Lehmann, former Departmental Editor; received April 22, 1980. This paper has been with the authors 6 weeks for 2 revisions.
†Cornell University.
‡Columbia University.

637

thorough review of the literature. The beta binomial model is a binary outcome, zero order, stationary and heterogenous model that has been widely used to describe various phenomena. In concept, the beta binomial is the aggregate distribution resulting from a binomial process at the individual level and assuming that the binomial probability varies over the population according to a beta distribution.

While the beta binomial model *fits* the observed data extremely well, long-run *projections* beyond the observed data show a *consistent* bias. Reach is underestimated and the high frequencies are overestimated. Using an example provided by Schreiber [10], for a weekly magazine and a sample of 4000 adult women, the fit of the beta binomial to four issue data is very good. However, when this information is used to project forward for another four issues we find:

# Issues Read	Fit to 4 issue data		Projection to 8 issues	
	Actual	Estimated	Actual	Estimated
0	2616	2614	2140	2431
1	300	327	383	264
2	264	232	274	165
3	240	245	202	136
4	580	582	292	125
5			128	123
6			116	131
7			110	167
8			355	458
Total	4000	4000	4000	4000

The reach, which is the complement of the proportion reading 0 issues, is underestimated, and the proportion reading 7 or 8 issues is overestimated.[1]

Schreiber [10] has proposed an *ad hoc* explanation for this phenomenon. He argues that the stationarity assumption of the beta binomial may not be valid, that is, individual exposure probabilities may be changing. Past studies [2], [10] have empirically shown that the beta distribution which captures individual heterogeneity, is fairly stable over time, for a given media vehicle. Then, if individual probabilities change, they must do so in such a way that the aggregate distribution remains the same. This implies that some of the near-zero probabilities must increase. Therefore, the actual reach will be greater than predicted by a stationary model. Conversely, some of the near-one probabilities must decrease and the actual frequencies of high exposure must be less than predicted by a stationary model.

The stationarity assumption of the beta binomial has received some attention in the literature. Chandon [1], in an effort similar to Schreiber's, has also investigated the effect on reach and frequency predictions of assuming that individual's probabilities are stationary, when, in fact, they are changing. Sabavala and Morrison [7] describe a test of stationarity for the beta binomial based on a two-period transition matrix.

The model presented in this paper is a non-stationary extension of the beta binomial. A renewal process for individual probabilities is specified. An individual

---

[1] These and other data are analyzed further in §3 below.

keeps a probability value for a geometrically distributed period of time. At the time of renewal, an independent draw is made from the same beta distribution. If we assume that the beta distribution of p values remains unchanged over time and the geometric parameter is the same for all individuals then we have a *beta binomial geometric* process, characterized by the two beta parameters and the one geometric parameter. This model is a special case of Howard's Dynamic Inference Model [5], a nonstationary parametric process where the parameters are renewed in some given manner.[2]

There are three important reasons for applying this nonstationary model to the media exposure problem. The first is that shifting individual probabilities can explain the empirically established bias in projections using a stationary model. Second, the model proposed is a more general version of the beta binomial and therefore, statistical tests may be used to compare the models with respect to how they fit observed data. Finally, and most important, although the robust beta binomial fits observed data very well, *if the underlying process is truly nonstationary, then projections will be misleading and the parameter estimates will be incorrect*.

The next section discusses the media exposure problem in the context of the beta binomial geometric model. A conceptual description of the beta binomial geometric is included and the assumptions are discussed. The third section presents some empirical results for television viewing and magazine readership. The fourth section concludes by evaluating the performance and potential of the beta binomial geometric for media exposure estimation and by suggesting some directions for further research.

2.   Estimating Media Exposure Using the Beta Binomial Geometric Model

2.1   *The Problem*

The problem facing the decision-maker is how to evaluate alternative media vehicles. While the ultimate criterion is the sales generated by an exposure to the advertisement, this paper focuses on the exposure to the vehicle.[3] For a given target population, the problem often involves determining an appropriate tradeoff between the number of individuals who are exposed (at least once) and the number of repeat exposures. This choice depends upon the advertiser's objectives, the nature and newness of the product or service being advertised, and the amount and complexity of the information being communicated.

The objective is to estimate the frequency distribution of the number of exposures, k, out of a set of r opportunities. These r opportunities may be issues of a magazine or telecasts of a television program. In addition to the distribution of k, which provides reach and frequency, measures of loyalty are often useful in the media context. These are derived below in the beta binomial geometric framework.

---

[2] An alternative approach to the problem of nonstationarity is to allow the model parameters to be time dependent or functions of exogenous factors; see Heckman and Willis [4] for a study of labor force participation and Headen, Klompmaker and Teel [3] for audience estimation for advertising schedules.

[3] The exposure event is defined as being exposed (at least once) at a given opportunity. Therefore, for print vehicles, an individual exposed to two issues of a magazine counts as two exposures, but an individual exposed twice to the same issue counts only once. For this reason, media researchers also seek to learn something about the nature of the exposure, by focusing on the ads themselves and the editorial content, as well as the pattern of readership.

2.2 *The Model*

In this section, we present a conceptual description of the beta binomial geometric model. (Appendix A provides the derivation of the beta binomial geometric probability distribution and its properties. Parameter estimation and some tests are given in Appendix B.) The following assumptions characterize the process by which consumers are exposed to media vehicles:

(i) For each individual, exposure on a given exposure opportunity is Bernoulli, p.

(ii) Individuals' exposure probabilities, p, are distributed over the population according to a beta (m, n) distribution.

$$f_\beta(p; m, n) = \frac{\Gamma(m + n)}{\Gamma(m)\Gamma(n)} p^{m-1}(1 - p)^{n-1} \quad \text{for } 0 < p < 1 \quad \text{and} \quad m, n > 0. \quad (1)$$

(iii) Individuals retain a specific p value for a geometrically distributed (with parameter ρ) number of trials, t. That is,

$$P(t; \rho) = \rho(1 - \rho)^{t-1} \quad \text{for } t = 1, 2, \ldots, \quad \text{and} \quad 0 < \rho < 1. \quad (2)$$

(iv) Individuals' exposure probabilities, p, are renewed from the beta (m, n) distribution, (1). Renewed p values are independent of previous p values.

(v) The geometric parameter ρ is the same for all individuals.

(vi) The beta (m, n) distribution does not change over exposure opportunities.

The resulting process is termed the beta binomial geometric and in the following discussion will be referred to as BBG (m, n, ρ).

These assumptions imply that at each choice occasion, individuals have a constant probability (ρ) of making a renewal. While individuals may have different p-values, the propensity to change (ρ) is assumed to be constant over the population. Heterogeneity of individuals' probabilities is allowed for by use of a beta distribution. The beta, which has been widely used in probability mixture models, is flexible and, mathematically, quite tractable. It is the natural conjugate of the Bernoulli, where p is unknown, and is useful in the usual prior-posterior analysis. Finally, we should emphasize that the process is assumed stable with respect to the population distribution of p-values over time.

An appropriate question is whether the assumptions are plausible in the media exposure context. As mentioned above, the beta is a very flexible distribution and a good choice for capturing the heterogeneity. Past media studies [2], [10] have supported a stable distribution of p-values over time. The binomial assumption (i.e., zero-order, constant p, independent trials) at the individual level has also received some support [2], especially in stable, repetitious situations.[4] The assumption of independence in the renewal process implies that an individual may have very different p-values over time. While this may appear to be difficult to justify, it should be noted that exposure to media is dependent on several random factors that influence the lifestyle and daily routine of individuals.

Let the sequence of outcomes on r exposure opportunities be observed as X for a

---

[4]It is possible to incorporate a higher-order effect and non-stationarity. The resulting model can be very complex. An appealing model that extends the beta binomial geometric in this fashion is currently being researched; see Schmittlein and Morrison [9]. Our purpose in this paper is to evaluate the application potential of a simple nonstationary process.

given individual. Each element of $\mathbf{X}$, X_i [for $i = r, (r - 1), \ldots, 2, 1$], is a binary $(0/1)$ variable with a '1' denoting exposure to the media vehicle. The time index is arranged so that $i = 1$ is most recent. The probability of $\mathbf{X}$ under the BBG (m, n, ρ) process, denoted as $P[\mathbf{X}; m, n, \rho, r]$, must be found by a series of substitutions; see Appendix A.1. There are 2^r possible outcome sequences that can be observed and the distribution over these 2^r possibilities is the BBG distribution.

Let k be the number of successes in $\mathbf{X}$. The distribution of k, the frequency of exposures, may be found from $P[\mathbf{X}; m, n, \rho, r]$. The expected value of k is:

$$E(k) = rm/(m + n). \tag{3}$$

This is the same as that for the beta binomial since the p values are all being renewed from the same distribution. The variance of k is found to be:

$$\text{Var}(k) = \frac{rmn(1 + m + n) + 2mn\sum_{i=1}^{i=r-1}(r - i)(1 - \rho)^i}{(1 + m + n)(m + n)^2} \tag{4}$$

The variance of k does depend on ρ, and decreases as ρ increases from 0 to 1.

When $\rho = 0$, no renewal takes place and the BBG process reduces to a beta binomial. That is, individual processes are stationary, Bernoulli and heterogeneity is captured by a beta (m, n) distribution.

When $\rho = 1$, individuals' p-values are renewed at each occasion and the BBG $(m, n, 1)$ process is equivalent to a homogeneous binomial, where any individual has an expected p-value of $[m/(m + n)]$. Since individuals are not distinguishable, individual heterogeneity is not accounted for.

As ρ varies from 0 to 1, we move from a completely stationary and heterogeneous process to a completely nonstationary and homogeneous process. These different properties, stationarity and homogeneity, are confounded. If individuals keep their p-values throughout the period of interest, then each individual is distinct and characterized by a particular p-value. However, as individuals renew their probabilities, the ability to distinguish individuals, on the basis of their p-values, decreases. While this would be true for any stochastic renewal scheme, the condition is exacerbated by independent renewals.

Data requirements for the beta binomial geometric model are greater than for the beta binomial. For the simple beta binomial model the probability of an observed sequence of outcomes depends only on the number of 'successes' (or binary outcomes of interest) and the total number of trials. However, if individual probabilities can change, then the order in which the outcomes occur affects the probability of the particular sequence. Therefore, in order to be able to estimate the beta binomial geometric parameters, it is not sufficient to know merely the distribution of number of exposures. The complete distribution of ordered outcome sequences, which may be obtained from panel data, is required. Appendix B.1 describes maximum likelihood estimation when such panel data are available. It may also be possible to construct outcomes sequences from a survey using recall, although the accuracy may decline considerably.

However, panel or panel-type data are not always available. With this motivation, an alternative estimation method is derived in Appendix B.2. This method uses, as input, frequency data measured at two points in time for the same sample of individuals. The application to magazine readership data reported below demonstrates the feasibility of this approach.

2.3 *Media Measures*

The reach achieved in r trials for the beta binomial geometric is:

$$R_r = 1 - P[\mathbf{O}; m, n, \rho, r], \tag{5}$$

where $\mathbf{O}$ is an observed outcome vector of r failures and P $[\mathbf{O}; m, n, \rho, r]$ may be computed as shown in Appendix A.3. Reach is an appropriate criterion for comparing media vehicles if maximum penetration of the advertising is desired. It should be noted that being exposed to the vehicle does not imply that the individual has been exposed to the advertisement. In addition, it may be that a minimum number of exposures to the message is required. In this case it is necessary to compare media vehicles on the basis of the probability of being exposed at least the minimum number of times. For the probability of k exposures we need to sum P $[\mathbf{X}; m, n, \rho, r]$ over all $\mathbf{X}$ containing k 1's.

Another concept of interest is that of audience loyalty. Loyalty is the tendency for individuals to be exposed to a media vehicle consistently over several opportunities. Two media vehicles may have the same total number of exposures but different degrees of repeat exposures. This notion of loyalty is directly related to the frequency of exposures. Further, the media vehicle exhibiting greater loyalty is expected to be less vulnerable to competitive efforts.

A traditional measure of loyalty is the repeat probability or the conditional probability of being exposed on any occasion given an exposure on some other (usually the previous) occasion. In unpublished magazine audience research, W. Simmons has used this quantity which he termed the Loyalty Rate (LR). Let X_i and X_j be the binary outcomes on the ith and jth choice occasions respectively. Then,

$$\text{LR}_{ij} = P[X_i = 1 \mid X_j = 1]. \tag{6}$$

According to our time scale, $j > i$. The Turnover Rate (TR) is the complement of LR and may be interpreted as the switching probability between occasions j and i:

$$\text{TR}_{ij} = 1 - \text{LR}_{ij}. \tag{7}$$

In addition, a Polarization Index (PI) has been proposed in [8]. This index, which reflects the degree of polarization of preference exhibited by the distribution of p-values, is the correlation between X_i and X_j:

$$\text{PI}_{ij} = \frac{E[X_i X_j] - E[X_i]E[X_j]}{\sqrt{\text{Var}[X_i]\text{Var}[X_j]}}. \tag{8}$$

PI has been presented in [8] as measuring a dimension (almost) independent of the mean exposure rate and thereby providing additional information on the vehicle. It is recognized that other measures of loyalty and polarization do exist. No single index can serve all purposes as a situation can always be constructed that would diminish the value of a particular index.

In Appendix A.3 these quantities are derived for a BBG (m, n, ρ) given r exposure opportunities. The resulting expressions are:

$$LR_{ij} = \frac{m(1 + m + n) + n(1 - \rho)^{j-i}}{(1 + m + n)(m + n)}, \tag{9}$$

$$TR_{ij} = \frac{n[(1 + m + n) - (1 - \rho)^{j-i}]}{(1 + m + n)(m + n)}, \tag{10}$$

$$PI_{ij} = \frac{(1 - \rho)^{j-i}}{(1 + m + n)}. \tag{11}$$

When $\rho = 0$, these quantities refer to the beta binomial and due to the independence and stationarity assumptions do not depend on i and j:

$$LR^{bb} = (1 + m)/(1 + m + n),$$

$$PI^{bb} = 1/(1 + m + n).$$

When $\rho = 1$, the situation is equivalent to a homogeneous binomial where, due to the homogeneity and stationarity assumptions, the repeat probability is the expected value of the probability and the correlation between X_i and X_j is zero:

$$LR^{b} = m/(m + n),$$

$$PI^{b} = 0.$$

3. Empirical Results

Two sets of data are analyzed to illustrate the application of the BBG model to the media exposure problem. The first consists of television viewing panel data, where the distribution of 0/1 outcome sequences is known. The second data set consists of frequency data measured at different times on the same sample. The parameter estimation methods and tests that are used are presented in Appendix B.

3.1 Application to Panel Data

The data consist of viewing behavior for 556 households (with 603 television sets) for three time slots over five days. The data were obtained from diaries maintained by assigned household members. There were four daily programs (or channels) on in each time slot giving twelve cases for analysis, with five telecasts for each. The programs will nominally be referred to by the corresponding time slot and channel.

A preliminary test was conducted for each program to see whether the mean number of viewers was constant over the five telecasts. This is a necessary condition in our model, since the aggregate distribution is stable over time. Chi-square tests for homogeneity of the share distributions over the five telecasts showed that the observed data did not differ significantly from those expected assuming constant means.

Maximum likelihood estimates of the parameters for BBG and BB (ρ constrained to 0) models were determined (see Appendix B.1) and are shown in Table 1. Goodness-of-fit results for each model are also shown. The fits are good in many cases, but due to the limited data and small sample size, the results must be cautiously interpreted.

TABLE 1

T.V. Panel Data—Parameter Estimates and Test Results for Data Set 1

	BBG Parameters			Beta Binomial Parameters		BBG Fit[1] p^4	BB Fit[2] p^4	Likelihood Ratio Test[3] $-2\log\lambda$	p^4
	m	n	ρ	m	n				
Time Period 1									
Channel 1	0.029	0.405	0.077	0.045	0.614	a	a	7.76	d
Channel 2	0.085	0.597	0.012	0.090	0.634	c	b	0.40	a
Channel 3	0.055	0.783	0.022	0.060	0.849	c	b	0.34	a
Channel 4	0.069	1.085	0.049	0.083	1.287	c	b	1.20	a
Time Period 2									
Channel 1	0.038	0.579	0.073	0.054	0.805	a	a	4.95	c
Channel 2	0.106	0.685	0.000	0.106	0.685	a	a	0.00	a
Channel 3	0.067	1.211	0.092	0.090	1.588	d	c	0.00	a
Channel 4	0.137	1.127	0.000	0.137	1.127	a	a	0.00	a
Time Period 3									
Channel 1	0.073	0.856	0.111	0.115	1.337	a	a	8.09	d
Channel 2	0.124	1.407	0.104	0.177	2.004	c	c	3.98	c
Channel 3	0.112	1.290	0.192	0.215	2.480	b	a	10.08	d
Channel 4	0.057	1.165	0.085	0.078	1.569	a	a	2.38	a

1. Chi-square goodness-of-fit test on distribution of k, dof = 1.
2. Chi-square goodness-of-fit test on distribution of k, dof = 2.
3. Test statistic ($-2\log\lambda$) is distributed chi-square, dof = 1.
4. p-level: a: $p > 0.10$
   b: $0.10 > p > 0.05$
   c: $0.05 > p > 0.01$
   d: $0.01 > p$

Estimated ρ values range from 0.00 (for time period 2, channels 2 and 4) to 0.19 (for time period 3, channel 3). The m and n estimates are such that the corresponding beta distributions are either U- or reverse-J-shaped, which is consistent with shapes most frequently encountered in practice.

Table 1 also includes results of a likelihood ratio test of the null BB hypothesis against the alternate BBG. In effect, this test examines whether a model with $\rho > 0$ is preferred to one with $\rho = 0$. In five of the twelve cases the BBG is preferred over the BB and Channel 1 exhibits a significant ρ value, that is greater than 0, in all three time slots.

The Average Rating (which is the proportion of all television sets tuned to a program), Polarization Index and Loyalty Rate are shown in Table 2 for the twelve programs. PI and LR have been computed for the BB model as well as for the BBG, in the latter case for 1 and 4 occasions apart (1,2 and 1,5). For now, let us refer to the indices for the BBG, assumed to be the true model. To choose a program in time period 3 so as to get the largest audience possible for one telecast, pick either channel 1, 2 or 3. However, if over several telecasts maximum penetration is desired, then we should pick channel 3 which has the lowest correlation (PI) between different telecasts. Suppose that a concept to be communicated requires repeated exposures. From time period 2, pick either channel 1 or 2 which have the largest PI values. To make a further

TABLE 2
T.V. Panel Data—Indices for Data Set 1

	Average Rating* (%)	BBG MODEL				BB MODEL	
		$PI_{1.2}$	$PI_{1.5}$	$LR_{1.2}$	$LR_{1.5}$	PI	LR
Time Period 1							
Channel 1	6.8	0.644	0.506	0.667	0.539	0.603	0.630
Channel 2	12.4	0.587	0.567	0.639	0.621	0.580	0.632
Channel 3	6.6	0.532	0.498	0.563	0.531	0.524	0.555
Channel 4	6.0	0.442	0.380	0.475	0.417	0.422	0.457
Time Period 2							
Channel 1	6.3	0.573	0.457	0.600	0.490	0.538	0.567
Channel 2	13.3	0.558	0.558	0.618	0.618	0.558	0.618
Channel 3	5.4	0.399	0.298	0.430	0.335	0.373	0.407
Channel 4	10.9	0.442	0.442	0.502	0.502	0.442	0.502
Time Period 3							
Channel 1	7.9	0.461	0.324	0.503	0.377	0.408	0.455
Channel 2	8.1	0.354	0.255	0.406	0.315	0.314	0.370
Channel 3	8.0	0.336	0.177	0.389	0.243	0.271	0.329
Channel 4	4.7	0.412	0.315	0.439	0.347	0.378	0.407

*The Average Rating is the proportion of all television sets tuned to a station in a given time slot.

distinction, suppose it is preferable that these exposures be received 4 telecasts apart. Then, $PI_{1.5}$ shows that channel 2 should be preferred over channel 1. With the beta binomial, we cannot distinguish such differences.

The limited data base did not allow any predictive tests. When periods 1–4 were used to predict period 5, there was no real difference between the BB and BBG predictions. With low values of ρ, one period is too short a time for the effects of non-stationarity to be felt. However, overall, the results do suggest that the BBG model may be a better representation of the true process than the BB model and support the need for greater availability of panel-type data.

3.2 Application to Frequency Data

Panel-type data for media exposure are often not available. However, frequency data on the same individuals at two different points in time are collected. For example, individuals may be asked: "Of the last ____ issues of ____, how many did you read?" at two points in time. The issue periods referred to need not be adjacent, but must not be overlapping.

The second data set consists of magazine readership of 4000 adult women measured at two points in time.[5] For each of one monthly and two weekly magazines, the respondents were asked, "Of the last 4 issues of ____, how many did you read?" in

[5]These data have been analyzed by Schreiber [10].

TABLE 3

(A) *Observed and Estimated Beta Binomial Frequency Distributions for Data Set 2*

Issues Read		0	1	2	3	4
Magazine 1 (Monthly):						
December 1964	Observed	2187	297	373	156	987
	Expected	2190	320	241	279	970
May 1965	Observed	2166	324	297	160	1053
	Expected	2172	299	226	266	1037
Magazine 2 (Weekly):						
December 1964	Observed	2616	300	264	240	580
	Expected	2614	327	232	245	582
May 1965	Observed	2612	334	277	213	564
	Expected	2613	339	240	250	557
Magazine 3 (Weekly):						
December 1964	Observed	2932	243	177	144	504
	Expected	2933	231	162	176	497
May 1965	Observed	2886	297	104	257	456
	Expected	2886	268	186	195	465

(B) *Beta Binomial Parameter Estimates and Fit Statistics for Data Set 2*

		Magazine 1		Magazine 2		Magazine 3	
		Dec. '64	May '65	Dec. '64	May '65	Dec. '64	May '65
Parameters:	m	0.1178	0.1101	0.1039	0.1088	0.0644	0.0770
	n	0.2237	0.1992	0.3275	0.3493	0.2709	0.3225
$\chi^2$2(d.o.f.)		128.48	66.90	6.75	7.02	7.93	59.18

December 1964 and again in May 1965. Therefore, for the monthly magazine we know the exposure frequency for September–December 1964 and February–May 1965.

Table 3 shows the observed and fitted (beta-binomial) frequency distributions in each of the issue periods. It is clear that the aggregate distributions have remained quite stable from December 1964 through May 1965. The distributions fit quite well for the weekly magazines but poorly for the mid-frequency range of the monthly magazine.

Using the estimation method described in Appendix B.2, for each of the three magazines, the parameter values of m, n and ρ corresponding to the minimum mean-square error were chosen.[6] Although two of the three ρ values (0.104, 0.023, 0.027) are quite small, the improvement in prediction of period 2 frequencies given period 1 data is impressive, compared with the stationary beta-binomial. This is clearly seen for magazine 2 in Table 4. Also, note that between the two measured periods for

[6]Three criteria, mean square error, mean absolute deviation and chi-square, were in close agreement in indicating the best ρ value. Further, the criteria as functions of ρ were smooth and quite peaked around the best value of ρ. The resulting estimates were:

	Magazine 1	Magazine 2	Magazine 3
m:	0.040	0.091	0.053
n:	0.075	0.286	0.223
ρ:	0.104	0.023	0.027

magazine 2, 32.7% of the sample are expected to have shifted probabilities, given by $[1 - (1 - 0.023)^{17}]$. The mean absolute errors in estimating the conditional frequencies for the three magazines are 55.7, 50.7 and 49.7 for the BB and correspondingly 19.2, 14.7, and 17.4 for the BBG.

With respect to the stationary beta binomial, too few individuals retain their previous frequencies (the diagonal elements of the transition matrix), while too many seem to be making large changes in the number of issues read (from 0 to 4 and from 4 to 0). The BBG model corrects for quite a large part of the errors. The pattern of BB errors is in agreement with a previous study using television data [7].

Table 5 gives projected and actual frequency distributions over eight issues, based on four-issue data. In each case, the BBG predicts much better than the BB, and dramatically better for magazine 2. The mean absolute errors in estimating the frequency distribution are 105.1, 103.6 and 105.0 for the BB and correspondingly 42.8, 29.0 and 35.3 for the BBG. The mean absolute percentage errors are 25.0, 30.2 and 34.7 for the BB and correspondingly 17.2, 10.3 and 16.2 for the BBG.

In summary, the results have demonstrated the usefulness of the BBG over the BB for making conditional predictions of magazine readership and for projecting the frequency distribution of exposures. While some of the discrepancies of actual and expected values were quite large, the point to be stressed is the substantial effect of ρ in improving the fit. The feasibility of deriving parameter estimates, using the method in Appendix B.2, from two-period frequency data is also worth noting.[7]

TABLE 4
Observed and Expected Conditional Transition Frequencies for Data Set 2

Magazine 2 (Weekly)
Observed:

	0	1	2	3	4	Total
0:	2140	199	120	55	102	2616
1:	184	43	37	19	17	300
2:	111	38	32	45	38	264
3:	72	34	46	36	52	240
4:	105	20	42	58	355	580

Errors—BB or BBG ($\rho = 0$):

	0	1	2	3	4
0:	− 291	61	84	46	100
1:	57	− 45	− 15	− 6	9
2:	70	− 27	− 38	− 12	7
3:	63	7	− 3	− 36	− 31
4:	103	12	14	− 26	− 103

Errors—BBG ($\rho = 0.023$):

	0	1	2	3	4
0:	− 25	31	36	− 12	− 30
1:	30	− 17	0	− 4	− 8
2:	17	− 8	− 14	5	0
3:	6	9	11	− 12	− 14
4:	− 26	− 7	8	− 8	33

[7] There are two points to note about the estimation procedure. First, for large values of ρ (given), m and n tend to 0 and the maximum likelihood method may have difficulty in converging. Second, as the number of opportunities for change increases, the proportion of individuals who shift approaches 1 and the period 1 frequencies become independent of period 2 frequencies.

TABLE 5

Observed and Expected* Frequencies of Exposure For Data Set 2

A. Magazine 1 (Monthly)

Frequency	Observed	BB Expected ($\rho = 0$)	BBG Expected ($\rho = 0.104$)
0	1710	2009	1753
1	306	253	287
2	313	177	285
3	168	157	202
4	382	144	296
5	159	131	185
6	133	126	195
7	120	164	147
8	709	839	649

B. Magazine 2 (Weekly)

Frequency	Observed	BB Expected ($\rho = 0$)	BBG Expected ($\rho = 0.023$)
0	2140	2431	2165
1	383	264	322
2	274	165	239
3	202	136	217
4	292	125	357
5	128	123	127
6	116	131	120
7	110	167	132
8	355	458	322

C. Magazine 3 (Weekly)

Frequency	Observed	BB Expected ($\rho = 0$)	BBG Expected ($\rho = 0.027$)
0	2495	2800	2529
1	336	204	268
2	164	124	187
3	196	97	162
4	247	84	344
5	118	80	83
6	70	84	75
7	97	115	84
8	277	413	268

*Number of issues read out of 8, given the information on the number of issues read out of the first 4.

4. Conclusions

The media exposure problem has been addressed by use of the beta binomial geometric model. This model explicitly incorporates a nonstationary mechanism in the context of binary choice, which accounts for the consistent bias found in long-term projections of reach and frequency of media exposure. In addition, the beta binomial geometric framework provides insight into the performance of the widely used beta binomial model and the sensitivity of various media statistics under conditions of non–stationarity. The size of the ρ parameter indicates the degree of non-stationarity. For advertisers, the forecasts of reach and frequency are better, even for small values of ρ. For the managers of the media vehicles, the size of ρ indicates the degree of audience stability. For example, television networks might take this factor into account while scheduling programs.

The empirical results demonstrate the feasibility and desirability of using the BBG model for estimation of media exposure. In the case of the television viewing panel data, the BBG performed significantly better than the beta binomial in only 5 of 12 cases. However, the implications of ignoring the non-stationarity argue for its use *in general*. Since the beta binomial is a special case of the BBG, this would be a more conservative approach although the data requirements and estimation are more complicated. The application to the two-period frequency data on magazine readership was encouraging for two reasons. Conditional predictions were much better for the BBG than the beta binomial. Also, the estimation procedure that was devised worked quite efficiently for the three magazines.

To summarize, the beta binomial geometric is a simple model which can yield considerable insight into individuals' non-stationarity of media exposure. The model accounts for the consistent empirical bias of the beta binomial and provides better estimates of the degree of audience turnover and polarization.

There are several opportunities for further research. First, any one of the model components may be extended. For example, Schmittlein and Morrison [9] allow for higher order (short-run) effects instead of the zero-order assumption made in this paper. This could also be done within a multinomial context. Second, while individuals may renew their probabilities, the renewed probabilities are independent of their previous values. It may be more appropriate to incorporate some dependence of the renewed individual probability on the previous value. In cases where loyalty and commitment to a vehicle are high, this dependence will be positive, while in cases where individuals seek variety, a negative correlation would be expected. Third, the media application has been restricted to the problem of audience accumulation for a single media vehicle. Most advertisers would like to address the question of duplication across multiple media vehicles as well. Finally, ρ need not remain stationary but could reflect the degree of disequilibrium in the system, part of which may be in the manager's control.

Our approach is one of the simplest for incorporating nonstationarity. The enhanced data requirements and computational problems indicate that more complex models will present great challenges. While other basic approaches to the problem of non-stationarity are possible, this stochastic approach seems fruitful for many settings in the social sciences where the number of casual factors is large and the relationships too complex to model explicitly.

Appendix A: The Beta Binomial Geometric Model

A.1   Derivation of the BBG Probability Distribution

Assume:

1. Each individual's outcome (0/1) is generated by a Bernoulli process, p.

2. At any given choice occasion, p is distributed beta (m, n) across individuals.

$$f_\beta(p; m, n) = \frac{\Gamma(m+n)}{\Gamma(m)\Gamma(n)} p^{m-1}(1-p)^{n-1} \quad \text{for } 0 < p < 1 \quad \text{and} \quad m, n > 0. \quad (A.1)$$

3. Individuals retain a particular p value for a geometrically distributed number of trials, at which time the p value is renewed. The geometric (ρ) distribution of the number of trials between renewals is

$$P(t; \rho) = \rho(1-\rho)^{t-1}, \quad \text{for } t = 1, 2, 3 \ldots \quad \text{and} \quad 0 < \rho < 1. \quad (A.2)$$

4. At each renewal, individuals obtain a new p value, independent of the previous p value, from a beta (m, n) distribution.

5. Each individual has the same geometric renewal parameter, ρ.

Assumptions 1–5 define a beta binomial geometric process, BBG (m, n, ρ).

X denotes the sequence of outcomes on r trials for a given individual. Each element of X, X_i [for $i = r, (r-1), \ldots, 2, 1$], is a binary $(0/1)$ variable. The time index is arranged so that $i = 1$ is the most recent. We would like to find the probability of X under the BBG (m, n, ρ) process, denoted as $P[X; m, n, \rho, r]$. There are 2^r possible outcome sequences for a given BBG probability distribution.

For r trials there are $(r-1)$ opportunities for renewal. This is because for the first trial it does not matter whether p has just been changed or has remained the same. Since either a change occurs or it does not, there are 2^{r-1} possible change sequences. Let there be l renewals of p in the r trials and let c be the vector of change points, c_j, for $j = 1, 2, \ldots, l$, with j specified so that c_1 is the most recent change. Note that l can be no more than $(r-1)$ and no less than 0. For a given change sequence, we can find the probability of c in terms of ρ,

$$P[c; \rho, r] = \rho^l(1-\rho)^{r-1-l}. \quad (A.3)$$

For l renewals, there are $(l+1)$ segments within each of which the process parameters remain constant. These segments are defined on the time scale as:

$$[r, (c_l + 1)], [c_l, (c_{l-1} + 1)], \ldots, [c_2, (c_1 + 1)], [c_1, 1].$$

Note that segment $[a, b]$ covers the periods from $i = a$ through $i = b$. Also, if $l = 0$ then the segment with no renewal covers the entire period $[r, 1]$.

For example, let $r = 5$, $l = 2$, $c = [2, 4]$. This means that there were two renewals of p in 5 choice occasions, at $i = 4$ and at $i = 2$. At $i = 5$, p_1 (say) is in effect. Then, a change occurs and p_2 is drawn and remains in effect for $i = 4, 3$. At $i = 2$, p_3 is drawn and remains in effect for $i = 2, 1$. The segments with constant p are $[5, 5]$, $[4, 3]$, $[2, 1]$.

For any segment $[a, b]$, let $x(a, b)$ represent the observed outcome sequence, i.e. $x(a, b)$ is a partition of X, and let $k(a, b)$ represent the number of successes. Let $P_x[a, b]$ be the probability of having observed $x(a, b)$. Since the segments have been defined as having constant p, then $P_x[a, b]$ is the simple beta binomial probability:

$$P_x[a, b] = \frac{B[m + k(a, b), n + a - b + 1 - k(a, b)]}{B(m, n)}, \quad (A.4)$$

where $B(m, n) = \Gamma(m)\Gamma(n)/\Gamma(m+n)$.

Given that renewal process outcomes are independent,

$$P[\mathbf{X}|\mathbf{c}; m,n,r] = P_x[r,(c_l+1)] \times P_x[c_l,(c_{l-1}+1)]$$
$$\times \ldots \times P_x[c_2,(c_1+1)] \times P_x[c_1,1]. \qquad (A.5)$$

Using equations (A.3) and (A.4) we can find:

$$P[\mathbf{X}; m,n,\rho,r] = \sum_s P[\mathbf{X}|\mathbf{c}_s; m,n,r] \times P[\mathbf{c}_s; \rho,r],$$

$$\text{for } m,n > 0, 0 \leq \rho \leq 1, r \geq 2, \qquad (A.6)$$

where the summation is carried out over all possible change sequences indexed by $s = 1, 2, \ldots, 2^{r-1}$. When $r = 1$, no changes can take place and $P[\mathbf{X}; m,n,\rho,1]$ is identical to the beta binomial.

A.2   Properties of the BBG Model

(i) Define k as the number of successes in $\mathbf{X}$. The probability distribution of k may be found using (A.6). Then, the expected value of k is:

$$E(k) = rm/(m+n). \qquad (A.7)$$

This is the same as that for the beta binomial since the p values are all being renewed from the same distribution. The variance of k is:

$$\text{Var}(k) = \frac{rmn(1+m+n) + 2mn\sum_{i=1}^{i=r-1}(r-i)(1-\rho)^i}{(1+m+n)(m+n)^2}. \qquad (A.8)$$

The variance of k does depend on ρ. As ρ approaches 1, the variance approaches a minimum value $[rmn/(m+n)^2]$. As ρ approaches 0, the variance reaches its maximum value corresponding to the variance of k in a BB model.

(ii) When $\rho = 0$, no renewal takes place and the BBG process reduces to the BB. When $\rho = 1$, individuals' p-values are renewed at each occasion and the BBG $(m,n,1)$ process is equivalent to a homogeneous binomial, where any individual has an expected p-value of $[m/(m+n)]$.

(iii) Consider the conditional probability of a success on the next outcome $(i = 0)$ given that we have observed $\mathbf{X}$, that is, $P(X_0 = 1 | \mathbf{X}; m,n,\rho,r)$. In order to evaluate this probability, use:

$$P[X_0|\mathbf{X}; m,n,\rho,r] = \sum_s P[X_0|\mathbf{c}_s, \mathbf{X}; m,n,\rho,r] \times P[\mathbf{c}_s|\mathbf{X}; m,n,\rho,r], \qquad (A.9)$$

where the summation is carried out over all possible change sequences. The first term within the summation on the right-hand side of (A.9) is the probability of a success given $\mathbf{X}$ and $\mathbf{c}$. Due to the independent renewals, only the most recent segment of no change is relevant to X_0. If no change occurs at $i = 0$ then $[c_1, 1]$ is the relevant history, if a change occurs at $i = 0$ then no history is relevant. These events occur with probabilities $(1 - \rho)$ and ρ respectively. Therefore:

$$P[X_0|\mathbf{c}, \mathbf{X}; m,n,p,r] = \{(1-\rho) \times P[X_0|c_1, x(c_1,1); m,n,\rho,r]\}$$
$$+ \{\rho \times P[X_0|c_0 = 0; m,n,\rho,r]\},$$

where $c_0 = 0$ indicates that a renewal takes place at $i = 0$. Making use of the conjugate property of the beta binomial,

$$P[X_0 | c, X; m, n, \rho, r] = (1 - \rho) \left[\frac{m + k(c_1, 1)}{m + n + c_1} \right] + \rho \left[\frac{m}{m + n} \right]. \qquad (A.10)$$

The second term within the summation on the right-hand side of (A.9) is the probability of the change vector c, given X. By Bayes' Theorem,

$$P[c | X; m, n, \rho, r] = \frac{P[X | c; m, n, \rho, r] \times P[c; \rho, r]}{P[X; m, n, \rho, r]}. \qquad (A.11)$$

The right-hand side may be found from equations (A.5), (A.3) and (A.6). Finally, $P[X_0 | X; m, n, \rho, r]$ may be found from equations (A.9), (A.10) and (A.11).

(iv) The BBG probabilities depend upon the order of the outcomes, X_i. In fact, different BBG processes can yield the same distribution of k. For example, it may be shown that the distributions of k for two parameterizations, BBG (0.25, 0.75, 0.80) and BBG (1.50, 4.50, 0.50), for $r = 4$, are very similar. The effect of larger ρ values is to make the distribution more concentrated around the mean. The U-shaped beta (0.25, 0.75) combined with a large ρ value (0.8) to become *equivalent* to a uni-modal beta (1.5, 4.5) with a smaller value of ρ (0.5). In general, given a distribution of the frequency of exposures from some BBG process it is possible to find a large (perhaps infinite) number of different BBG models that would fit these data perfectly.

(v) If only frequency data are available and are assumed to come from a true BBG process, then m and n may be estimated for a given value of ρ. If we constrain $\rho = 0$, then we are in effect assuming stationarity and we can examine the performance of the BB when the true process is BBG. We have seen above in (iv) that the BBG with ρ constrained to zero will be able to *fit* the distribution well. However, use of the constrained model for *predictions* can be very misleading. Suppose that the constrained model (BB) is fit to data for T outcomes. The following conclusions may be drawn:

(a) For a given ρ, $P(O)$, where O is an observed outcome vector of no successes, will be fit very well at $r = T$, but will be underestimated for $r < T$ and overestimated at $r > T$.

(b) As ρ varies from 0 to 1, the error in estimation of $P(O)$ for $r \neq T$ is zero at $\rho = 0$, increases to a maximum for some intermediate values of ρ and decreases to zero at $\rho = 1$.

(c) The probability of exposure on the next trial for an individual, conditional on k exposures over the r trials is $P(1 | k)$. For a given ρ and r, $P(1 | k)$ is underestimated for k below $E(k)$ and overestimated for k above $E(k)$.

A.3   Derivation of Media Statistics

The measures of Reach (R), Loyalty Rate (LR) and Polarization Index (PI) are relevant for the media exposure application of the BBG.

The reach achieved in r trials is defined as

$$R_r = 1 - P(O; m, n, \rho, r), \qquad (A.12)$$

where O is an outcome vector of r zeros and $P(O; m, n, \rho, r)$ may be computed using (A.6).

The Loyalty Rate is defined as the conditional exposure probability

$$LR_{ij} = P[X_i = 1 | X_j = 1] \qquad (A.13)$$

where X_i and X_j are binary outcomes on the ith and jth trials; note that in our scale $j > i$.

The Polarization Index is defined as the correlation

$$PI_{ij} = \frac{E[X_iX_j] - E[X_i]E[X_j]}{\sqrt{\mathrm{Var}[X_i]\mathrm{Var}[X_j]}} . \qquad (A.14)$$

Note that

$$E[X_i] = E[X_j] = m/(m+n), \qquad (A.15)$$

and

$$\mathrm{Var}[X_i] = \mathrm{Var}[X_j] = mn/(m+n)^2. \qquad (A.16)$$

LR_{ij} and PI_{ij} are derived as shown below. Central to the determination of LR_{ij} and PI_{ij} is the joint probability of $X_i = 1$ and $X_j = 1$. This quantity depends on whether there was a renewal between periods j and i. Let Δ_{ij} denote the event that at least one change occurred during $[i, j]$ and $\overline{\Delta}_{ij}$ the event that no change occurred. Then:

$$P[\overline{\Delta}_{ij}] = (1 - \rho)^{j-i} \qquad (A.17)$$

$$P[\Delta_{ij}] = 1 - (1 - \rho)^{j-i}. \qquad (A.18)$$

We can write:

$$P[X_i = 1 \quad \text{and} \quad X_j = 1] = P[X_i = 1 \quad \text{and} \quad X_j = 1 | \Delta_{ij}]P[\Delta_{ij}]$$
$$+ P[X_i = 1 \quad \text{and} \quad X_j = 1 | \overline{\Delta}_{ij}]P[\overline{\Delta}_{ij}]. \qquad (A.19)$$

If Δ_{ij} occurred, then $P[X_i = 1]$ and $P[X_j = 1]$ are given only by the prior distribution with an expected value of $m/(m+n)$. If $\overline{\Delta}_{ij}$ occurred, then X_j affects $P[X_i = 1]$ and may be found by the conjugate property of the beta binomial. Using this information and equations (A.17), (A.18),

$$P[X_i = 1 \quad \text{and} \quad X_j = 1] = \frac{m^2(1 + m + n) + mn(1 - \rho)^{j-i}}{(m+n)^2(1 + m + n)} . \qquad (A.20)$$

The Loyalty Rate may be found using equations (A.13), (A.15) and (A.20) as follows:

$$LR_{ij} = \frac{m(1 + m + n) + n(1 - \rho)^{j-i}}{(1 + m + n)(m + n)} . \qquad (A.21)$$

The Polarization Index may be found using equations (A.14), (A.15), (A.16) and (A.20) as:

$$PI_{ij} = \frac{(1 - \rho)^{j-i}}{(1 + m + n)} . \qquad (A.22)$$

Appendix B: Parameter Estimation and Tests for the BBG Model

B.1   Estimation of BBG parameters Using Panel Data

Maximum likelihood estimates may be obtained by numerical methods as analytical results cannot easily be derived for the complicated likelihood function. The method requires panel data. Let the different outcome sequences be denoted by $\mathbf{X}_i$ for $i = 1, 2, \ldots, 2^r$. Let

$$P_i = P[\mathbf{X}_i; m, n, \rho, r], \quad \text{for } i = 1, 2, \ldots, 2^r, \tag{B.1}$$

be the beta binomial geometric probability. If the observed frequencies of $\mathbf{X}_i$ are 0_i then the likelihood of having observed the sample is given by

$$L(m, n, \rho) = \prod_{i=1}^{i=2^r} (P_i)^{0_i}. \tag{B.2}$$

Instead of maximizing $L(m, n, \rho)$ it is easier to maximize L_0, the logarithmic transform of L, with respect to m, n and ρ.

$$L_0(m, n, \rho) = \sum_{i=1}^{i=2^r} 0_i \log P_i. \tag{B.3}$$

The estimates m^*, n^* and ρ^* are defined by:

$$L_0^* = L_0(m^*, n^*, \rho^*) > L_0(m, n, \rho), \quad \text{for } m, n > 0, 0 \leqslant \rho \leqslant 1. \tag{B.4}$$

B.2   Estimation of BBG Parameters Using Two Period Frequency Data

Suppose we have observed the number of outcomes of interest for a sample of individuals during two non-overlapping periods. Then, if a BBG process is in effect, we can predict the frequency in the second period conditional upon the frequency in the first period. We must take into account any shifting in probabilities that takes place between the two periods—this will depend upon the number of opportunities for renewal and the value of the geometric parameter. One approach would be to find the BBG parameters using a numerical search maximum likelihood (see Appendix B.1) method over the joint two-period frequency distribution. An alternative approach that is computationally more viable is presented below.

Define the following:

$k_1, k_2,$ = Frequency of outcomes of interest in periods 1, 2 respectively.

r_1, r_2 = Number of choice occasions in periods, 1, 2 respectively.

m, n, ρ = "True" BBG parameters.

$\quad t$ = Number of opportunities for renewal *between* the r_1 and r_2 choice occasions.

$\quad O_{ij}$ = Observed frequency transition matrix; $i = 0, 1, \ldots, r_1$ and $j = 0, 1, \ldots, r_2$.

$\quad N_i = \sum_{j=0}^{r_2} O_{ij}; i = 0, 1, \ldots, r_1$.

$P_{\text{BBG}}(k)$ = Beta binomial geometric probability (with parameters m, n, ρ) of the frequency of outcomes of interest; $k = 0, 1, \ldots, r$.

$P_{\text{BBG}}(k)$ may be found from equations (A.4), (A.1) and (A.2). The conditional probability of k_2 in r_2, given k_1 in r_1, can be found as:

$$P(k_2 \text{ in } r_2 | k_1 \text{ in } r_1) = P(\text{Renewal in } t)P_{\text{BBG}}(k_1 \text{ in } r_1)P_{\text{BBG}}(k_2 \text{ in } r_2)$$

$$+ P(\text{No renewal in } t)P_{\text{BBG}}(k_2 \text{ in } r_2 | k_1 \text{ in } r_1)$$

$$= \left[1 - (1 - \rho)' \right] P_{\text{BBG}}(k_1 \text{ in } r_1)P_{\text{BBG}}(k_2 \text{ in } r_2)$$

$$+ (1 - \rho)' P_{\text{BBG}} \left[(k_1 + k_2)\text{in}(r_1 + r_2) | k_1 \text{ in } r_1 \right]. \quad \text{(B.5)}$$

The expected frequencies are:

$$E_{ij} = N_i P(j \text{ in } r_2 | i \text{ in } r_1). \quad \text{(B.6)}$$

Three goodness-of-fit statistics that may be computed are:

$$x^2 = \sum_i \sum_j \frac{(O_{ij} - E_{ij})^2}{E_{ij}}. \quad \text{(B.7)}$$

$$MSE = \sum_i \sum_j (O_{ij} - E_{ij})^2 / \left[(r_1 + 1)(r_2 + 1) \right]. \quad \text{(B.8)}$$

$$MAD = \sum_i \sum_j |O_{ij} - E_{ij}| / \left[(r_1 + 1)(r_2 + 1) \right]. \quad \text{(B.9)}$$

The estimation procedure is:

Step 1: Choose a value for $\hat{\rho}$.

Step 2: Given this value of $\hat{\rho}$, obtain maximum likelihood estimates of $\hat{m}$ and $\hat{n}$ using period 1 data, $\{N_i\}$.

Step 3: Compute $\{E_{ij}\}$ using (B.5) and (B.6).

Step 4: For these values of E_{ij} compute x^2, MSE and MAD using equations (B.7), (B.8) and (B.9).

Step 5: Repeat steps 1–4 for a coarse grid on $\hat{\rho}$.

Step 6: Choose the $\hat{\rho}$ value corresponding to the lowest values of the goodness-of-fit measures and repeat steps 1–4 for a finer grid around this best value of $\hat{\rho}$. Repeat until the desired precision on $\hat{\rho}$ is obtained.

The fit criteria are usually in close agreement with each other and are "well behaved" (i.e., smooth and unimodal) over different values of $\hat{\rho}$.

B.3 Testing the BBG Model

Three tests of the beta binomial geometric are discussed below, and may be used to evaluate the importance of incorporating nonstationarity.

The objective is to determine whether the proposed BBG is significantly better than an alternative model, the BB. The logic of applying these tests is as follows. The chi-square goodness-of-fit test will establish whether the models fit the distribution of outcome sequences adequately. The fit of the BBG will be at least as good as the BB. However, the criterion of parsimony would dictate that we use the BB model (i.e., BBG with $\rho = 0$) unless the additional parameter and complexity are warranted. Since we derive maximum likelihood estimators, we may address this question with the likelihood ratio test.

In addition, managerial use of the model requires some predictive validation. This may be done by predicting the probability of exposure conditional upon the frequency of successes (or sequence of outcomes observed) and by making reach and frequency projections.

Chi-square Goodness-of-fit test. The goodness-of-fit of the BBG model to the observed distribution of the outcome sequences may be tested by the usual chi-square statistic. Let $\mathbf{X}_i$ for $i = 1, 2, \ldots, 2^r$, represent the possible outcome sequences over r opportunities. Let the observed frequency of $\mathbf{X}_i$ in a sample of N individuals be O_i. Then, we can evaluate the BBG probabilities for a given m, n and ρ and the expected frequency of $\mathbf{X}_i$ may be found as:

$$E_i = N \times P[\mathbf{X}_i; m, n, \rho, r].$$

Under the null hypothesis that the observed data are from a BBG (m, n, ρ, r) process, the statistic

$$\chi^2 = \sum_{i=1}^{i=2^r} (E_i - O_i)^2 / E_i,$$

will have a chi-square distribution with $2^r - 4$ degrees of freedom. There are 2^r cells but one degree of freedom is lost due to matching the total number of individuals and three additional degrees of freedom are lost in estimating m, n and ρ.

Likelihood Ratio Test. Since the BB is a constrained form of the BBG model, a likelihood ratio test may be used to compare the null BB against the alternate BBG:

$$H_0: \text{BBG}(m', n', 0), \qquad H_A: \text{BBG}(m^*, n^*, \rho^*).$$

The BBG $(m', n', 0)$ model is the BB. The maximum likelihood estimates are m', n' for the H_0 model and m^*, n^*, ρ^* for the H_A model. Under H_0, for large samples, the test statistic $[-2 \log_e(\lambda)]$ is distributed chi-square with 1 degree of freedom where λ is the likelihood ratio given by:

$$\lambda = \frac{L'}{L^*} = \frac{\text{likelihood value for BBG } (m', n', 0)}{\text{likelihood value for BBG } (m^*, n^*, \rho^*)}.$$

The number of degrees of freedom is equal to 1, which is the difference of the number of H_A parameters (3) and the number of H_0 parameters (2).

Predictive tests of media exposure. One test of the BBG model would be to examine its performance in making conditional predictions. That is, estimating the probabilities of exposure conditional upon the past frequency of exposures, i.e., $P(1 \mid k)$, or conditional upon the past sequence of outcomes, i.e., $P(X_0 \mid \mathbf{X})$. This performance may be compared with that based on the BB. The BBG model may also be tested on its ability to make accurate long-run projections of the frequency distribution of exposures. For example, based on four telecasts of a television program, the expected frequencies using the BBG model for 8, 12, 16, 20 telecasts may be computed and compared with the observed frequencies. The long-term panel data that would be required for such predictive tests are available for television, being collected by Nielsen, Inc. and other television rating services. For print media, panel data have typically not been collected in the U.S. but are being collected in Europe and Britain.[8]

[8] The authors would like to thank Seymour Banks (Leo Burnett, USA), Jerome Green (Marketmath, Inc.) and Robert Schreiber (Sports Illustrated) for collectively resurrecting some of the data that are used, and William Trigeiro (Ph.D. student, Cornell University) for his programming assistance.

References

1. CHANDON, J., *A Comparative Study of Media Exposure Models*, Ph.D. Dissertation, Northwestern University, 1976.
2. GREENE, J. D. AND STOCK, J. S., *Advertising Reach and Frequency in Magazines*, Reader's Digest Association, Inc., 1971.
3. HEADEN, R. S., KLOMPMAKER, J. E. AND TEEL, J. E., JR., "Predicting Audience Exposure to Spot T.V. Advertising," *J. Marketing Res.*, Vol. 14, No. 1 (1977), pp. 1–9.
4. HECKMAN, J. J. AND WILLIS, R. J., "A Beta-Logistical Model for the Analysis of Sequential Labor Force Participation by Married Women," presented at the Third World Congress of the Econometric Society, 1975.
5. HOWARD, R. A., "Dynamic Inference," *Operations Res.*, Vol. 13, No. 2 (1965), pp. 712–733.
6. HYETT, G. P., *The Measurement of Readership*, London School of Economics Paper, 1958.
7. SABAVALA, D. J. AND MORRISON, D. G., "A Stationarity Test for the Beta Binomial Model," *J. Business Res.* (to appear).
8. ———— AND ————, "Television Show Loyalty: A Beta Binomial Model Using Recall Data," *J. Advertising Res.*, Vol. 17, No. 6 (1977), pp. 35–43.
9. SCHMITTLEIN, D. C. AND MORRISON, D. G., "A Non-Stationary Markovian Binary Choice Model," Working Paper, Columbia University, 1978.
10. SCHREIBER, R. J., "Instability in Media Exposure Habits," *J. Advertising Res.*, Vol. 14, No. 2 (1974), pp. 13–17.

An empirical test of the...

Performance of Four Exposure Distribution Models

John D. Leckenby and Shizue Kishi

Usage of exposure distribution models is now an important element in media planning. Although many proprietary models are available, the usefulness of such models rests on the accuracy of the methods utilized to estimate the actual underlying observed exposure distributions. Unfortunately, observed distributions are generally unknown in day-to-day practice. Therefore, it may be questioned whether one model performs adequately for various types of schedules and for various types of population groups. Media schedules used in a variety of marketing situations differ by their levels of gross audience and duplications as well as by number of vehicles and number of insertions. If such schedule properties can provide useful information about the performance of various exposure distribution models, it may be possible to select the most appropriate model to evaluate the effectiveness of alternative media schedules.

A key problem in identifying salient schedule properties as indicators of model performance lies in the develop-

ment of appropriate definitions of estimation error. This study defines and examines error factors in four multivehicle, multi-insertion exposure distribution models on 45 magazine schedules. Among these four models, the Kwerel-Geometric Distribution model (KGD) and the Hofmans-Geometric Distribution model (HGD) are newly developed by the authors. The methods utilized in the KGD and HGD models are shown in Appendix A. The other two models are the Metheringham Beta Binomial Distribution model (BBD) and the Compound Dirichlet Multinomial Distribution model (DMD). The estimation methods employed for the BBD and the DMD will be described subsequently.

The purposes of this report are: (1) to compare two models (HGD and KGD) which have never before been tested on a large number of schedules with two models (BBD and DMD) which have been tested previously; and (2) to determine whether or not structural properties of media schedules can explain the levels of error inherent in these models;

this determination serves as a basis for providing media researchers with guidance in choosing the appropriate exposure distribution model in view of the characteristics of the schedules at hand.

Some limited information currently is available regarding the performance of exposure distribution models. The Metheringham method and the regression approach taken by Headen et al. (1976, 1977, 1979) are two methods of applying the beta–binomial distribution that are representative of approaches commonly used to estimate exposure distributions. Errors in these two methods have been studied on the following criteria: (1) the sum of the absolute differences at each exposure level and its ratio to the unduplicated reach (Liebman and Lee, 1974); (2) peak patterns (Liebman and Lee, 1974; Chandon, 1976); (3) the number of over- and under-estimations (Schreiber, 1969; Chandon, 1976); (4) the number of times the reach estimate is within the 95 percent confidence interval of the survey data (Liebman and Lee, 1974; Chandon,

35

1976); and (5) maximum cumulative differences and the proportion of the audience misclassified (Headen et al., 1966, 1977, 1979).

The Metheringham method has been known to overestimate reach and odd-numbered frequencies and underestimate even-numbered frequencies (Schreiber, 1969; Chandon, 1976). The results of performance tests with 57 print schedules showed that the Metheringham method does not produce secondary peaks (Liebman and Lee, 1974; Chandon, 1976); it is also reported that the Metheringham method produces a smooth frequency distribution with a mode very close to zero (Schreiber, 1969). The beta–binomial distribution has been found superior to the negative binomial distribution with lower chi-square and Kolmogorov-Smirnov D statistics in predicting exposure distributions to spot TV schedules (Headen et al., 1976). The same distribution has been found to perform as well in network TV schedules as in spot TV schedules (Headen et al., 1979). In the study of spot TV schedules, in contrast to the results for print schedules, the BBD was found to have a tendency to underesti-mate the proportion of the audience exposed two to six times out of a total of eight exposures while it overestimated the proportion exposed one time (Headen et al., 1977). Headen et al. (1976) showed the BBD performed poorly in schedules with intense GRPs where all available stations in a market were utilized.

The Compound Dirichlet Multinomial Distribution model (DMD), which is an extended application of the beta–binomial distribution, was found superior to the Metheringham BBD regarding the number of peak concordances and the number of correct shapes reproduced in the test of the same 57 print schedules used by Liebman and Lee (Chandon, 1976). The same study also reported that the DMD had an opposite systematic bias to that of the BBD, with a tendency to underestimate odd-numbered frequencies.

Although many proprietary models are available for the estimation of reach and exposure distributions, only limited information is available about their performance under a variety of circumstances. It is unlikely that any one model will provide a high level of accuracy under all media schedule conditions. Therefore, it is important to develop a set of factors, as attempted in this study, which help to specify the schedule conditions under which particular models perform satisfactorily. Clearly, this study cannot examine the proprietary models in any detailed manner; however, two well-known models, the BBD and DMD, as well as two lesser known models, the HGD and KGD, can be examined. It should be pointed out that all of these models are easily utilized in practice and are mathematically tractable; the authors have programmed each of these in both BASIC and FORTRAN in interactive as well as in batch mode of usage.

ters of the BBD are estimated from the average single-issue audience and the average net audience of pairs. While the BBD parameters are calculated for the entire schedule by averaging the probabilities of exposure across vehicles in the Metheringham BBD, the BBD parameters are estimated separately for each vehicle in the DMD to obtain the Dirichlet Multinomial parameter. The exposure distribution is fitted to the compound multinomial distribution, as discussed by Mosimann (1962), by enumerating all possible combinations of obtaining exactly i number of exposures in the schedule. The exact estimation methods for the BBD and the DMD used in this study are described in detail in Leckenby (1981).

The Kwerel-Geometric Distribution model (KGD) is an extension of Kwerel's macro-specification, single-insertion model (Kwerel, 1964, 1968, 1969) into the multi-vehicle, multi-insertion case. As shown in Appendix A, the KGD formula used to estimate the exposure distribution is based upon the Inclusion/Exclusion Principle (Riorden, 1958; Takács, 1967; Brualdi, 1977) where the

Methodology

Models. The Metheringham method (Metheringham, 1964) has been shown to be equivalent to the beta–binomial distribution (BBD), where the parame-

John D. Leckenby is associate professor in the Department of Advertising, University of Illinois at Urbana-Champaign.

Shizue Kishi is a research assistant and doctoral student in the Department of Advertising, University of Illinois at Urbana-Champaign.

sums of i-duplications (higher-order duplications) beyond two are estimated, based on the two known quantities, sum of duplications and number of insertions. Hofmans-Geometric Distribution model (HGD) has been developed by the authors by combining Hofmans' reach formula (Hofmans, 1966) with the geometric distribution. Hofmans' reach formula is a modification of Agostini's formula, where duplication coefficients are introduced in place of Agostini's constant "K" (Agostini, 1961) to reflect differing degrees of duplications among different pairs of insertions.

Data. Forty-five magazine schedules, from among 47 different magazine vehicles, were selected to generate observed frequency distributions for the total adult population (base = 130,326,000). Data were taken from the 1972 *W.R. Simmons Study of Selective Markets and the Media Reaching Them.* The 47 magazines were selected from various magazine groups such as business and finance, general appeal, news, men's, women's, sports, and special appeal, including weeklies, biweeklies, and monthlies. The test schedules varied by average-issue audience, size of vehicles (in terms of three categories: small, medium, and large audience) and degree of within-duplications and of between-duplications. Among the 45 test schedules, 34 consisted of four vehicles and 11 consisted of three vehicles. The number of insertions in each vehicle was limited to two, since observed data were available only for one and two insertions. Table 1 shows two observed distributions representative of the 45 schedules used in the analysis.

Definitions of "Error" in the Exposure Distribution. Four different definitions of error were used in this study based upon the absolute differences between the observed and the estimated frequencies. In addition, the number of over- and under-estimations by ±5 percent of the observed frequencies was also studied. Error was defined as indicated below:

Sum of errors across exposure levels (E_i):

$$E_i = \Sigma \left| o_{ij} - e_{ij} \right| (j = 1, \ldots, n) \quad (1)$$

where: o_{ij} = observed frequency at exposure level j of schedule i

e_{ij} = estimated frequency at exposure level j of schedule i,

Percentage error in exposure distribution (PE_i):

$$PE_i = (\Sigma \left| o_{ij} - e_{ij} \right|) / \Sigma o_{ij} \quad (2)$$

where: Σo_{ij} = observed reach of schedule i,

Average percentage error (APE):

$$APE = (\Sigma PE_i) / K \quad (3)$$

where: K = total number of schedules,

Average percentage error at each exposure level j (APE_j):

$$APE_j = \Sigma (\left| o_{ij} - e_{ij} \right| / o_{ij}) / K. \quad (4)$$

Testing Procedure. The main interest of this study was to identify error factors among the observable schedule properties which might contribute to increased or decreased estimation errors in each model. This purpose called for statistical methods other than nonparametric tests of goodness of fit such as chi-square or Kolmogorov-Smirnov tests. The first part of the error analysis was conducted using step-wise regression analysis with the sum of errors across exposure levels (E_i) as the dependent variable (see equation 5 below). The second part of the error analysis concentrated on clarifying the magnitude of estimation errors associated with the levels of error factors. One-way analysis of variance was conducted for this purpose, where the percentage error in exposure distribution (PE_i) was used

Table 1
Examples of Observed and Estimated Exposure Distributions

Schedule A: Large Gross Audience • High Duplication
Parade-Family Circle-Life-Fortune

Number of Exposures	('000) Observed	BBD	DMD	HGD	KGD
0	52,683	48,283	51,764	51,973	55,987
1	25,868	36,654	22,601	30,845	21,377
2	30,359	22,876	39,372	21,495	26,689
3	10,905	12,604	5,882	15,957	17,220
4	7,731	6,146	9,006	7,404	6,944
5	1,898	2,593	296	2,199	1,792
6	810	901	1,315	408	289
7	71	232	2	43	27
8	2	34	83	2	1
% Error		29.22	27.40	26.59	21.45

Schedule B: Medium Gross Audience • Low Duplication
Life-National Observer-Dun's Review-Psychology Today

Number of Exposures	('000) Observed	BBD	DMD	HGD	KGD
0	80,231	77,965	80,189	80,763	76,500
1	28,542	35,303	27,531	28,023	39,537
2	18,794	12,331	20,923	17,635	8,950
3	1,856	3,617	683	3,449	4,102
4	742	894	959	421	1,175
5	135	181	2	33	215
6	26	28	36	2	25
7	0	3	0	0	2
8	0	0	0	0	0
% Error		30.70	10.37	8.80	48.19

as the dependent variable via the arc sine transformation. Percentage error was transformed in the following manner:

$$\text{Sin}^{-1}(PE_j) = 2 \cdot \text{Tan}^{-1}\left(\frac{(PE_j)}{1 + \sqrt{1 - (PE_j)^2}}\right)$$

The arc sine transformation is a standard method of introducing variance stabilization for proportional data (Dixon and Massey, 1969). The same error factors as used in the step-wise regression were treated as categorical variables. Each error factor (except the number of vehicles and the vehicle size) was split into three groups of equal size. The level definitions are given for each factor in Table 6. The number of vehicles had two categories (3 and 4 vehicles) and the combination of vehicle size had four categories as described in Appendix B.

The *accuracy* of estimation was studied using three different measures: (1) average percentage error (APE); (2) average percentage error at each exposure level (APE_j); and (3) the number of over- and under-estimations at each exposure level. While the first two, APE and APE_j, serve as summary measures of errors defined in absolute numbers, the third measure was constructed as an indicator of both magnitude and direction of errors. This test was selected over chi-square or Kolmogorov-Smirnov tests, since the latter two do not indicate the *direction* of errors nor indicate specific error patterns at each exposure level, although they do indicate the overall goodness of fit.

Error Factors. Since all of the 45 test schedules had the same population base,

only schedule properties were considered in defining error factors. Nine schedule properties were hypothesized as error factors, i.e., the factors which could affect the magnitude of estimation errors. (The definitions of these factors are given in Appendix B.) Then, the errors in the exposure distributions were estimated by the following regression equation:

$$E_j = a + \Sigma\ b_k\ x_k + e\ (k = 1, \ldots, 12) \quad (5)$$

where: x_1 = gross audience
x_2 = sum of between-duplications
x_3 = sum of within-duplications
x_4 = number of vehicles
x_5 = combination of large, medium, and small vehicles
x_6 = combination of large and medium vehicles
x_7 = combination of large and small vehicles
x_8 = combination of medium and small vehicles
x_9 = sum of between-duplications/gross audience
x_{10} = sum of within-duplications/gross audience
x_{11} = sum of duplications
x_{12} = sum of duplications/gross audience

The number of vehicles and the combination of vehicle size were treated as dummy variables. Since four different combinations of vehicle size were used as dummy variables (x_5 to x_4), a total of 12 predictors was used. For the number of

vehicles (x_4), four vehicles were assigned 1 and three vehicles were assigned 0.

Results

Performance of Four Models. Table 2 contains the average percentage error across 45 test schedules (APE) and the average error at each exposure level (APE_j).

With regard to the average error

Table 3
Number of Over/Under Estimations ±5 percent

Number of Exposures		BBD	DMD	HGD	KGD
1	over	45	5	22	19
	under	0	29	9	22
	within ±5%	0	11	14	4
2	over	0	45	0	6
	under	45	0	41	33
	within	0	0	4	6
3	over	40	0	44	44
	under	1	45	0	1
	within	4	0	1	0
4	over	3	38	11	9
	under	39	3	28	28
	within	3	4	6	8
5	over	40	0	27	24
	under	4	45	16	18
	within	1	0	2	3
6	over	23	40	0	4
	under	13	5	44	39
	within	9	0	1	2
7	over	29	0	2	3
	under	5	30	29	29
	within	0	4	3	2
8	over	17	19	0	0
	under	12	12	28	29
	within	5	3	6	5
total number of within ±5%		22	22	37	30

Note: Exposures 1 to 6 have a total of 45 schedules and exposures 7 and 8 have 34.

Table 2
Average Percentage Error

At Each Exposure Level

Model	APE_1	APE_2	APE_3	APE_4	APE_5	APE_6	APE_7	APE_8	Average % of 45 Schedules APE
BBD	39.19	27.33	29.51	20.39	108.93	154.26	329.08	214.33	31.29
DMD	12.19	31.98	61.09	20.40	90.66	186.66	86.46	544.30	22.23
HGD	18.67	23.62	64.44	21.59	47.27	62.95	58.61	76.96	25.71
KGD	24.26	22.40	74.23	20.81	49.19	78.56	71.84	80.57	30.87

across 45 schedules, the DMD had the smallest error (22.23 percent), HGD had the second smallest error (25.71 percent), and the BBD and KGD had 31.29 percent and 30.87 percent, respectively. The average percentage error at each exposure level (APE_j) tends to increase toward the end of the distribution, especially in the BBD and DMD, due, in part, to the smaller base size at these levels.

The accuracy of model estimation was also tested by comparing the number of over- and under-estimations by ±5 percent of the observed frequencies at exposures one to eight. As is shown in Table 3, the BBD and DMD have relatively clear-cut error patterns: The BBD tends to overestimate at the odd-numbered exposures for the first five exposures, while the DMD tends to underestimate at the odd-numbered exposures and overestimate at the even-numbered exposures. The HGD and KGD have relatively similar patterns to that of the BBD, with a tendency toward underestimation at the even-numbered exposure levels.

While the DMD had the smallest average percentage error (APE), HGD and KGD outperformed the DMD with respect to the total number of estimations within the ±5 percent range: HGD had a total of 37 close estimations, KGD had a total of 30, and both the BBD and DMD had 22. Based upon the total number of close estimations, HGD was superior to the DMD and the other two models.

Error Factors in the Four Models. Table 4 contains the standardized regression coefficients of error factors (equation 5) and the significance levels of F ratios to test Multiple R. Generally, more than 90 percent of the variance in the errors was explained by the 12 predictors constructed from the test schedule properties. *Gross audience* was the most important error factor for the BBD, DMD, and KGD. In these three models, the size of estimation error increases as the size of gross audience becomes large. In the BBD, the error also increases as the ratio of the sum of within-duplications to gross audience becomes large; the error increases as a

Table 4
Multiple Regression:
Errors in Exposure Distribution

	Standardized Regression Coefficients			
	BBD	DMD	HGD	KGD
Gross Audience	.675[a]	1.003[a]		.708[a]
Σ Bet. Dup.				
Σ Wt. Dup.			.986[a]	
n. of vehicles	.180[a]			
L-M-S	.085	−.116[a]	−.063[c]	
L-M	.156[c]	−.057 (p−.072)		.223[d]
L-S		−.117[a]	−.087[a]	
M-S				
Σ Bet. Dup./A				
Σ Wt. Dup./A	.660[a]			
Σ Dup.	−.632[a]			
Σ Dup./A				
R^2	.909	.969	.978	.654
F	63.150[a]	317.523[a]	610.169[a]	39.630[a]

a = p ≤ .001, b = p ≤ .005, c = p ≤ .01, d = p ≤ .05

larger proportion of the target audience is exposed to the same vehicles more than once, where the size of the gross audience is held constant. In the HGD, the estimation error increases as the size of total within-duplications increases.

The size of vehicles (small, medium, or large audience) in the media schedules also explained, in part, the error in estimation. In the BBD and KGD, the error tends to increase when only large- and medium-size vehicles (L-M) are used in a schedule. On the other hand, the combination of all different sizes (L-M-S) and that of large and small vehicles (L-S) contribute to a decrease in the estimation error in the DMD and HGD.

Table 5 shows F ratios and results of Duncan Multiple-Range Tests of group means (Duncan, 1955). This analysis was particularly informative regarding the error patterns in the DMD and HGD. In the DMD and HGD, the error tends to become larger as the size of five factors (gross audience, sum of between-dupli-

cations, its ratio to gross audience, sum of within-duplications, and sum of duplications) becomes larger. In these two models, the error becomes larger particularly when the sum of between-duplications or its ratio to gross audience is larger. The HGD had slightly smaller estimation errors than those of the DMD when these factors were medium to small in magnitude. In contrast to the DMD and HGD, the magnitude of estimation error did not always increase with the level of error factors in the BBD and KGD. In the BBD, the greatest error was observed for schedules with a small ratio of sum of between-duplications to gross audience (mean = .38). The KGD had its largest estimation error when large- and medium-size vehicles were used in a schedule (mean = .41).

Discussion

Hofmans-Geometric Distribution model (HGD) was found to perform bet-

Table 5
One-way Analysis of Variance:
F Ratios
(Cell Means)

	BBD	DMD	HGD	KGD
Gross	.018	5.683[c]	14.253[a]	1.167
Audience	(.32)(.32)(.32)	(.32)(.28)(.23)	(.35)(.23)(.20)	(.36)(.33)(.27)
	H M L	H *M* *L*	H *M* *L*	M L H
Σ Bet. Dup.	.807	13.227[a]	24.47[a]	1.605
	(.34)(.32)(.30)	(.34)(.28)(.21)	(.36)(.24)(.18)	(.36)(.34)(.26)
	M L H	*H M L*	H *M* *L*	H L M
Σ Wt. Dup.	.468	4.200[d]	13.548[a]	1.205
	(.34)(.32)(.31)	(.32)(.26)(.24)	(.35)(.23)(.21)	(.36)(.33)(.27)
	M H L	M *M* *L*	H *M* *L*	M L H
Σ Bet. Dup./A	6.624[b]	11.389[a]	29.585[a]	1.424
	(.38)(.30)(.28)	(.34)(.27)(.22)	(.36)(.24)(.18)	(.37)(.31)(.28)
	L *H* *M*	*H M L*	*H M L*	H L M
Σ Wt. Dup./A	4.108[d]	3.093	12.144[a]	.303
	(.35)(.34)(.27)	(.31)(.28)(.24)	(.34)(.24)(.20)	(.34)(.31)(.30
	H M L	H M L	H *M* *L*	L M H
E Dup.	.035	8.822[a]	17.116[a]	1.078
	(.33)(.32)(.32)	(.32)(.29)(.21)	(.35)(.25)(.19)	(.35)(.33)(.27)
	L M H	*H M L*	*H M L*	M L H
Number of	.874	.036	.800	3.036
Vehicles	(.33)(.30)	(.28)(.27)	(.27)(.24)	(.39)(.30)
	4 3	4 3	4 3	3 4
Vehicle Size	.342	2.125	6.324[a]	1.867
	LMS (.35)	LM (.32)	LM (.36)	LM (.41)
	LM (.32)	Same (.29)	Same (.27)	LS/MS (.33)
	Same (.31)	LMS (.24)	LMS (.25)	Same (.31)
	LS/MS (.31)	LS/MS (.24)	LS/MS (.18)	LS/MS (.23)

$a = p \leq .001$, $b = \leq .005$, $c = \leq .01$, $d = \leq$ .05

Note: 1. Numbers in the parentheses are transformed cell means of high (H), medium (M), and low (L) groups.
2. The groups not in italics indicate no significant differences (H M L). (H *M L*) indicates H is significantly different from M and L, but no significant difference between M and L. (*H M L*) indicates all groups are significantly different at the less than .05 level in Duncan Multiple-Range Test.
3. In Hofmans-Geometric, LM (vehicle size) was significantly different from the other three groups, and there was also a significant difference between Same and LS/MS.
4. For ΣDup./A, the same schedules were categorized as those in Σ Bet. Dup./A.

ter than the BBD, DMD, and KGD on the criterion of the number of close estimations across exposure levels. Each model's systematic biases toward over- and under-estimations were identified in the performance tests. For the Metheringham BBD, the same error pattern was observed as reported by Schreiber

(1969): The BBD had a tendency to overestimate odd-numbered frequencies.

The DMD has been reported to be superior to the BBD regarding peak concordances and the reproduction of shapes (Chandon, 1976). Although peak concordance was not included in our definitions of error, an additional analy-

sis showed that the BBD had a peak at one exposure (zero exposure excluded) 45 times out of the 45 test schedules. The DMD, on the other hand, produced peaks at exposure levels 2, 4, 6 and 8. Since peaks occurred at exposure levels 1, 2, or 4 in the observed frequency distributions, the DMD accentuates the shape with additional peaks.

The geometric distribution was applied, for the first time in this study, to generate exposure distributions using the extended Kwerel's reach formula and Hofmans' reach formula. The accuracy of exposure distribution estimates depends partly upon the reach estimate in the KGD and HGD (Appendix A). In another study conducted by the authors, using the same 45 schedules of this study, Kwerel's extended reach formula had more underestimations than Hofmans'. Hofmans' formula had an average estimation error of 3.05 percent, while Kwerel's had 6.03 percent (Kishi and Leckenby, 1981). This relative accuracy of Hofmans' reach formula may be considered a reason for the better performance of the HGD over KGD in the current study.

Among those schedule properties identified as error factors, the number of insertions was fixed at two and the number of vehicles was either three or four. For further generalization of the findings of this study, more variations in these two factors need to be introduced, although limtied data presently are available for more than two insertions. In the analysis of error factors, two different definitions of error were used (E_i in the step-wise regression and PE_i in the one-way ANOVA). It may be more appropriate to use the same definitions in these analyses, possibly the percentage error (transformed), especially when using schedules of different size.

Conclusion

Some suggestions for selecting exposure distribution models in media decision-making are provided, in Table 6, as a summary of this study. The specification of schedule conditions is provided

Table 6
Summary of Findings and Recommendations

Structure of Media Schedules	*Recommended Models*
Gross Audience	
High (above 95%)	(1) Kwerel-G
Medium (48-95%)	(1) Hofmans-G (2) DMD
Low (below 48%)	(1) Hofmans-G (2) DMD
Sum of Between-Duplication	
High (above 52%)	All models have large errors
Medium (12-52%)	(1) Hofmans-G (2) Kwerel-G
Low (below 12%)	(1) Hofmans-G (2) DMD
Sum of Within-Duplication	
High (above 31%)	(1) Kwerel-G
Medium (15-31%)	(1) Hofmans-G (2) DMD
Low (below 15%)	(1) Hofmans-G (2) DMD
Sum of Between-Duplication/A	
High (above .53)	(1) BBD
Medium (.34-.53)	(1) Hofmans-G (2) any other models
Low (below .34)	(1) Hofmans-G (2) DMD
Sum of Within-Duplication/A	
High (above .33)	All models have large errors
Medium (.18-.33)	(1) Hofmans-G (2) DMD (3) Kwerel-G
Low (below .18)	(1) Hofmans-G (2) DMD (3) BBD
Sum of Duplication (Between + Within)	
High (above 83%)	(1) Kwerel-G
Medium (26-83%)	(1) Hofmans-G (2) DMD
Low (below 26%)	(1) Hofmans-G (2) DMD
Vehicle Size	
Large-Medium-Small	Any models except BBD
Large-Medium	All models have large errors
Large-Small	(1) Hofmans-G (2) DMD
Medium-Small	(1) Hofmans-G (2) DMD
Same Size	(1) Hofmans-G (2) DMD

Note: 1. For sum of Duplication/Gross Audience, the same models are recommended as in the Sum of Between-Duplication/Gross Audience with the following three categories: High = above .85, Medium = .64–.85, Low = below .64. The number of vehicles is not included in this list.

2. Numbers in the parentheses were derived from the 3- to 4-vehicle schedules used in this study. All percentage figures are proportions to the population (130,326,000).

on the left side of Table 6; on the right side of this table the recommended models are indicated from most preferred (1) to least preferred (3) for the conditions on the left-hand side. For example, if the schedule at hand was characterized by medium gross audience (48 to 95 percent of the population), low sum of duplication (within plus between equaling about 26 percent or less of the population), and vehicles all about the same audience size, the most desirable model of those examined in this study would be Hofmans-G model (HGD).

This study found the following error patterns in the four models:

(1) For large gross-audience sched-

ules, all models except the KGD have relatively large estimation errors.

(2) For schedules with large between-duplications, the percentage error is relatively large in all models.

(3) The HGD and DMD perform better with small rather than large schedules: These two models have substantially less error under small gross audience, within-duplication, and sum of duplication characteristics.

(4) On the contrary, the KGD has slightly less error with large gross audience, within-duplication, and sum-of-duplication schedule characteristics.

(5) Although the BBD has relatively greater error than the other models, the size of estimation error is relatively stable across different levels of error factors.

This study attempted to empirically explain the performance of four exposure distribution models. To proceed with future research on model performance and error factors, a sample of media schedules which is large in comparison to that utilized in the present study and representative of actual schedules will need to be developed. Also, it may be desirable to develop and test a larger set of models, some of which may have been tested only on print or broadcast schedules on the same set of observed schedules, to improve our knowledge of the performance of exposure distribution models generally.

References

Agostini, J.M., How to Estimate Unduplicated Audience, *Journal of Advertising Research* 1, 3 (1961): 11-14.

Brualdi, Richard A. *Introduction to Combinatorics*. New York, North Holland: 1977.

Chandon, Jean-Louis Jose. *A Comparative Study of Media Exposure Models*. Doctoral Dissertation, Northwestern University, 1976.

Chaundy, Theodore. *The Differential Calculus.* Oxford University Press, 1935.

Dixon, Wilfrid J. and Massey, Frank J. *Introduction to Statistical Analysis,* New York, McGraw-Hill: 1969.

Duncan, David B., Multiple Range and Multiple F-Tests. *Biometrics* 2 (1955): 1-42.

Headen, Robert S., Klompmaker, Jay E. and Teel, Jesse E. TV Audience Exposure. *Journal of Advertising Research* 16, 6 (1976): 49-52.

_____. Predicting Audience Exposure to Spot TV Advertising Schedules. *Journal of Marketing Research* 16 (1977): 1-9.

_____. Predicting Network TV Viewing Pattern, *Journal of Advertising Research* 19, 4 (1979): 49-54.

Hofmans, Pierre. Measuring the Net Cumulative Coverage of Any Combination of Media. *Journal of Marketing Research* 3 (1966): 269-278.

Kishi, Shizue and Leckenby, John D.

Error Factors in Exposure Distribution Models. In *Proceedings of American Academy of Advertising.* Gainesville, Florida, 1981.

Kwerel, Seymour M. *Estimating the Unduplicated Audience of a Combination of Media Vehicles: Integrated Theory and Estimation Methods.* Doctoral Dissertation, Columbia University, 1964.

_____. Information Retrieval for Media Planning. *Management Science* 15, 4 (1968): 137-160.

_____. Estimating Unduplicated Audience and Exposure Distribution. *Journal of Advertising Research* 9, 2 (1969): 46-53.

Leckenby, John D. Exposure Distribution Models: Some Estimation Methods in Application. Paper presented at the American Academy of Advertising Convention, April, 1981.

Liebman, Leon and Lee, Edward. Reach and Frequency Estimating Services. *Journal of Advertising Research* 14, 4 (1974): 23-25.

Metheringham, Richard A. Measuring the Net Cumulative Coverage of a Print Campaign. *Journal of Advertising Research* 4, 4 (1964): 23-28.

Mosimann, James E. On the Compound Multinomial Distribution, the Multivariate β-Distribution, and Correlations among Proportions *Biometrika* 49 (1962): 65-82.

Riorden, John. *An Introduction to Combinatorial Analysis,* New York, John Wiley: 1958.

Schreiber, Robert J. The Metheringham Method for Media Mix: An Evaluation. *Journal of Advertising Research* 9, 2 (1969): 54-56.

Smith, William B. *Infinitesimal Analysis.* New York: MacMillan, 1898.

Takács, Lajos. On the Method of Inclusion and Exclusion. *Journal of the American Statistical Association,* 62, 317 (1967): 102-113.

Waring, E. *On the Principles of Translating Algebraic Quantities into Probable Relations and Annuities, etc.* Cambridge: 1792.

Appendix A
Kwerel-Geometric Distribution Model

The exposure distribution is estimated based upon the unduplicated reach (R), gross audience (A), and sum of duplication (D). In this extended multi-insertion model, the last term, sum of duplication, is modified so that it includes both sum of between-duplication and sum of within-duplication. The unduplicated reach is estimated by averaging the upper bound (B_U) and the lower bound (B_L) of reach. Formula 1A for the unduplicated reach is derived by averaging the upper bound and the lower bound of the average frequency, where the upper bound of average frequency is obtained by dividing gross audience by the lower bound of reach and the lower bound of the average frequency is obtained by dividing gross audience by the upper bound of reach. Since average frequency is gross audience divided by unduplicated reach (A/R), formula 1A is obtained by solving the following equation for the unduplicated reach (R):

$$\frac{A}{R} = (\frac{A}{B_L} + \frac{A}{B_U}) / 2 \text{ or } R = 2(B_U)B_L) / (B_U + B_L).$$

The unduplicated reach is defined then as:
$$R = 2(B_U)(B_L) / (B_U + B_L) \hspace{3cm} \text{(1A)}$$
$$\text{where: } B_U = A - \frac{2}{N} D$$
$$B_L = (h + 1)\overline{A} - \frac{h(h + 1)}{2} (\overline{D})$$

h = minimum number from (N-1) and K where N is the total number of insertions and K is the largest integer contained in the quantity $\overline{A}/\overline{D}$.

$\overline{D} = \dfrac{2D}{N(N-1)}$: average duplication

$\overline{A} = A/N$: average of vehicle audiences

For the definitions of gross audience (A) and sum of duplications (D), see equations 1B and 6B in Appendix B.

The exposure distribution is generated using the following formulas for the geometric probability distribution:

Probability of one exposure

$$P_1 = A - \frac{2}{N-1} D\{1 + (1 - \hat{K}) + (1 - \hat{K})^2 + \ldots + (1 - \hat{K})^{N-2}\} \tag{2A}$$

Probability of "i" number of exposures

$$P_i = \binom{N}{i}\hat{K}^{i-2}(1 - \hat{K})^{N-i}(\overline{D}) \; (i = 2, \ldots, N) \tag{3A}$$

where: $\hat{K} = 1 - (1 - \hat{K})$ and $(1 - \hat{K})$ is the positive root of the following equation of $(N-2)$th degree.

A positive root $(1 - \hat{K})$ always exists and has a value between 0 and 1. This root is obtained by using an iterative method such as Newton's method (Smith, 1898; Chaundy, 1935):

$$A - R - \frac{2D}{N(N-1)} \{ \sum_{i=1}^{N-1} (N-1)(1-K)^{i-1} \} = 0. \tag{4A}$$

Though it has not been indicated previously by Kwerel or others, formulas 2A and 3A are derived from the Inclusion/Exclusion Principle, where the unduplicated reach (R) is defined as follows:

$$R = S_1 - S_2 + S_3 - S_4 \ldots + (-1)^{N+1}S_N \tag{5A}$$

where: S_i = sum of i-duplications.

Then, the probability of i exposures (P_i) is defined using Waring's theorem (Waring, 1792):

$$P^i = S_i - \binom{i+1}{i}S_{i+1} + \binom{i+2}{i}S_{i+2} \cdots + (-1)^{N+1}S_N. \tag{6A}$$

The formulas 2A and 3A are also written in a similar form to Waring's theorem defined in 6A. For example, the probability of one exposure for N = 4 is written as follows using equations 6A and 2A, respectively:

$$P_1 = S_1 - 2S_2 + 3S_3 - 4S_4 \tag{6A'}$$
$$P_1 = S - 2S_2 + 2\hat{K}S_2 - \frac{2}{3}\hat{K}^2S_2. \tag{2A'}$$

Hofmans-Geometric Distribution Model

This exposure distribution is obtained using the same method (geometric distribution) as was used in the Kwerel-Geometric method except that Hofmans' reach formula is used to calculate R. The unduplicated reach (R) is obtained by the following formula:

$$R = \frac{A^2}{A + KD + kd} \tag{7A}$$

where: $KD = \Sigma\Sigma \; n_i n_j K_{ij} d_{ij}$: total between duplications

$K_{ij} = (A_i + A_j) / (A_i + A_j - d_{ij})$

$kd = \dfrac{\Sigma n_i(n_i - 1)^a}{2}(k_i d_i)$: sum of within duplications

$$a = \frac{\log\left[\dfrac{A_n(mA_1 - A_m)}{(A_m(nA_1 - A_n)}\right]}{\log\left[\dfrac{m-1}{n-1}\right](m>n)}$$

A_m = coverage of m insertions in a given vehicle
A_n = coverage of n insertions in a given vehicle.

APPENDIX B

Definitions of Error Factors

1. Gross audience $= \Sigma\, n_i A_i = A$ (1B)

    where: n_i = number of insertions in vehicle i

             A_i = single-issue audience of vehicle i

2. Sum of between-duplications $= \Sigma\, n_i\, n_j\, d_{ij}$ (2B)

    where: d_{ij} = pair-wise duplication between vehicles i and j

3. Sum of within-duplications $= \Sigma\, \binom{n_i}{2}\, d_i$ (3B)

    where: d_i = duplication within vehicle i

          $\binom{n_i}{2}$ = number of combinations of taking 2 out of n_i

4. Ratio of sum of between-duplications to gross audience

    $= (\Sigma\, n_i\, n_j\, d_{ij})\, /A$ (4B)

5. Ratio of sum of within-duplications to gross audience

    $= (\Sigma\, \binom{n_i}{2}\, d_i)\, /A$ (5B)

6. Sum of duplications $= \Sigma\, n_i\, n_j\, d_{ij} + \Sigma\, \binom{n_i}{2}\, d_i$ (6B)

7. Ratio of sum of duplications to gross audience

    $= (\Sigma\, n_i\, n_j\, d_{ij} + \Sigma\, \binom{n_i}{2}\, d_i)\, /A$ (7B)

8. Number of vehicles

    4 vehicles in 34 schedules

    3 vehicles in 11 schedules

9. Combination of vehicle size in a schedule

    L-M-S in 8 schedules

    L-M in 8 schedules

    L-S or M-S in 10 schedules

    same size in 19 schedules

    where: L = large audience size (15.35 + percent of population)

            M = medium audience size (15.34-3.84 percent)

            S = small audience size (under 3.83 percent)

IN MEMORIAM
Josef M. Sansone

The Advertising Research Foundation is grieved to announce the death of our devoted and able colleague, Josef M. Sansone, at age 66. He died March 30, 1982 of a heart attack.

He had been with the Advertising Research Foundation since 1972 in charge of advertising operations. He had much to do with the success of this Journal.

For 22 years he was with BBDO as research manager, then as associate research director. Among his responsibilities was the BBDO national panel and the Syracuse, N.Y. panel, the latter a pet project of Bruce Barton and Alex Osborne. It brought Syracuse the cognomen, "Test City, U.S.A."

From 1945 to 1950 he was with Young & Rubicam.

Mr. Sansone received a B.A. from Columbia Teachers College in 1939 and an M.A. from Columbia University in 1950.

Titles in This Series

10.
C. Samuel Craig and Brian Sternthal, editors. Repetition Effects Over the Years: An Anthology of Classic Articles. 1985

11.
John K. Crippen. Successful Direct-Mail Methods. 1936

12.
Ernest Dichter. The Strategy of Desire. 1960

13.
Ben Duffy. Advertising Media and Markets. 1939

14.
Warren Benson Dygert. Radio as an Advertising Medium. 1939

15.
Francis Reed Eldridge. Advertising and Selling Abroad. 1930

16.
J. George Frederick, editor. Masters of Advertising Copy: Principles and Practice of Copy Writing According to its Leading Practitioners. 1925

17.
George French. Advertising: The Social and Economic Problem. 1915

18.
Max A. Geller. Advertising at the Crossroads: Federal Regulation vs. Voluntary Controls. 1952

19.
Avijit Ghosh and C. Samuel Craig. The Relationship of Advertising Expenditures to Sales: An Anthology of Classic Articles. 1985

20.
Albert E. Haase. The Advertising Appropriation, How to Determine It and How to Administer It. 1931

21.
S. Roland Hall. The Advertising Handbook, 1921

22.
S. Roland Hall. Retail Advertising and Selling. 1924

23.
Harry Levi Hollingworth. Advertising and Selling: Principles of Appeal and Response. 1913

24.
Floyd Y. Keeler and Albert E. Haase. The Advertising Agency, Procedure and Practice. 1927

25.
H. J. Kenner. The Fight for Truth in Advertising. 1936

26.
Otto Kleppner. Advertising Procedure. 1925

27.
Harden Bryant Leachman. The Early Advertising Scene. 1949

28.
E. St. Elmo Lewis. Financial Advertising, for Commercial and Savings Banks, Trust, Title Insurance, and Safe Deposit Companies, Investment Houses. 1908

29.
R. Bigelow Lockwood. Industrial Advertising Copy. 1929

30.
D. B. Lucas and C. E. Benson. Psychology for Advertisers. 1930

31.
Darrell B. Lucas and Steuart H. Britt. Measuring Advertising Effectiveness. 1963

32.
Papers of the American Association of Advertising Agencies. 1927

33.
Printer's Ink. Fifty Years 1888–1938. 1938

34.
Jason Rogers. Building Newspaper Advertising. 1919

35.
George Presbury Rowell. Forty Years an Advertising Agent, 1865–1905. 1906

36.
Walter Dill Scott. The Theory of Advertising: A Simple Exposition of the Principles of Psychology in Their Relation to Successful Advertising. 1903

37.
Daniel Starch. Principles of Advertising. 1923

38.
Harry Tipper, George Burton Hotchkiss, Harry L. Hollingworth, and Frank Alvah Parsons. Advertising, Its Principles and Practices. 1915

39.
Roland S. Vaile. Economics of Advertising. 1927

40.
Helen Woodward. Through Many Windows. 1926